150 Years of History

1857 - 2007

St. Cloud First United Methodist Church

By

Annette DeCourcy Towler

Gertrude Gove

Nancy Gundersen

Janet Gray

Lois Barron

2009
Published by
First United Methodist Church
302 5th Ave So
St. Cloud, Minnesota 56301

Library of Congress Cataloging-in-Publication Data [pending]

Towler, Annette DeCourcy, editor/writer, Nancy Gundersen, writer/editor, Gertrude Gove, writer
150 years of history 1857 – 2007, St. Cloud First United Methodist : citing History, membership lists, ministers appointed
1st ed. p. cm.
ISBN: 0-61529055-8 (alk. paper)
1. Church – History 2. History – Church

© 2009
Annette DeCourcy Towler, Gertrude Gove,
Nancy Gundersen, Janet Gray, Lois Barron

ALL RIGHTS RESERVED

No part of this book may be reproduced,
in any form or by any means including
electronic and Internet reproduction
without permission of the copyright
holder, except for brief passages that may
be quoted by a reviewer.

Published by
St. Cloud First United Methodist Church
302 5th Ave. South
St. Cloud, Minnesota, 56301

Printed in the United States of America

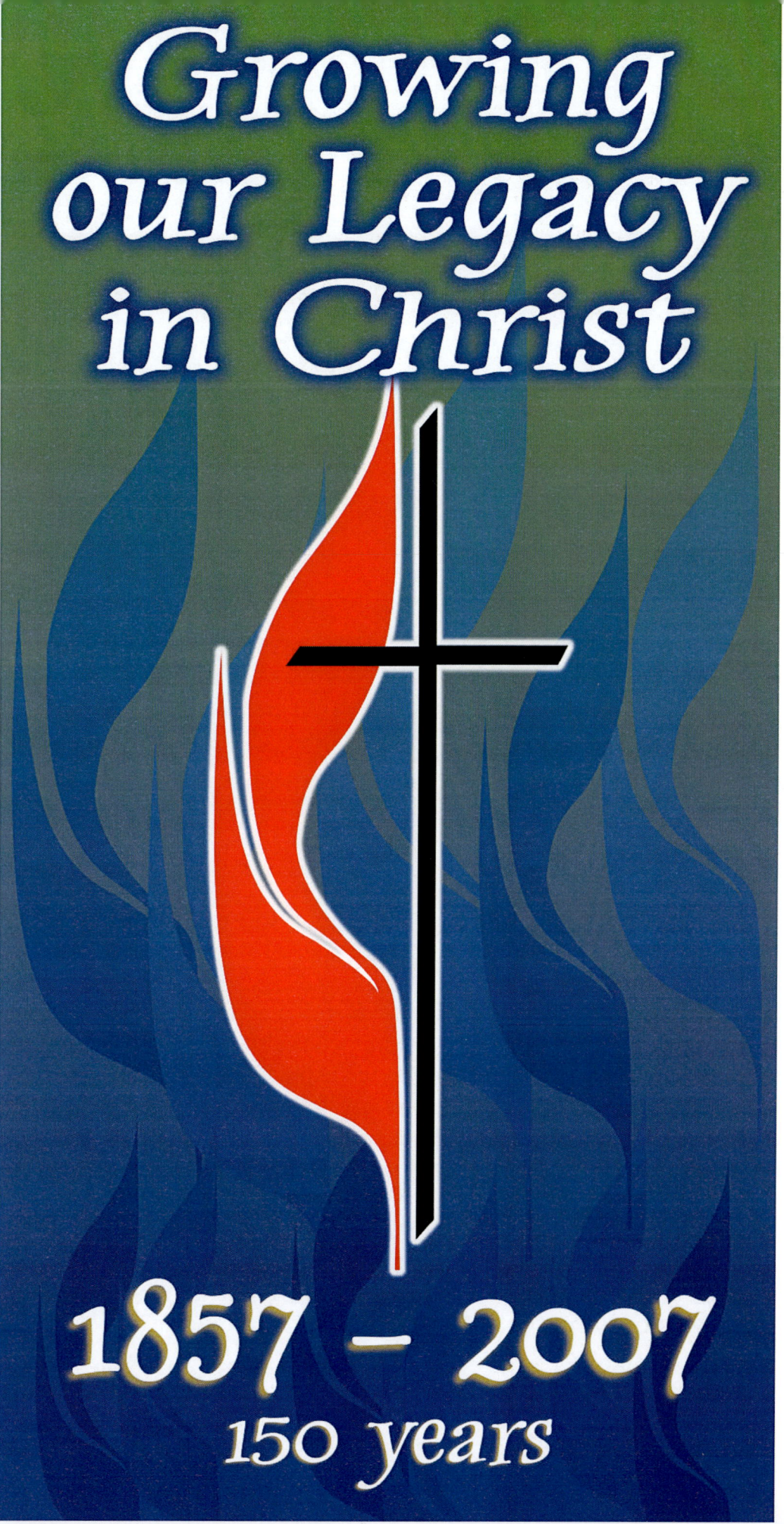

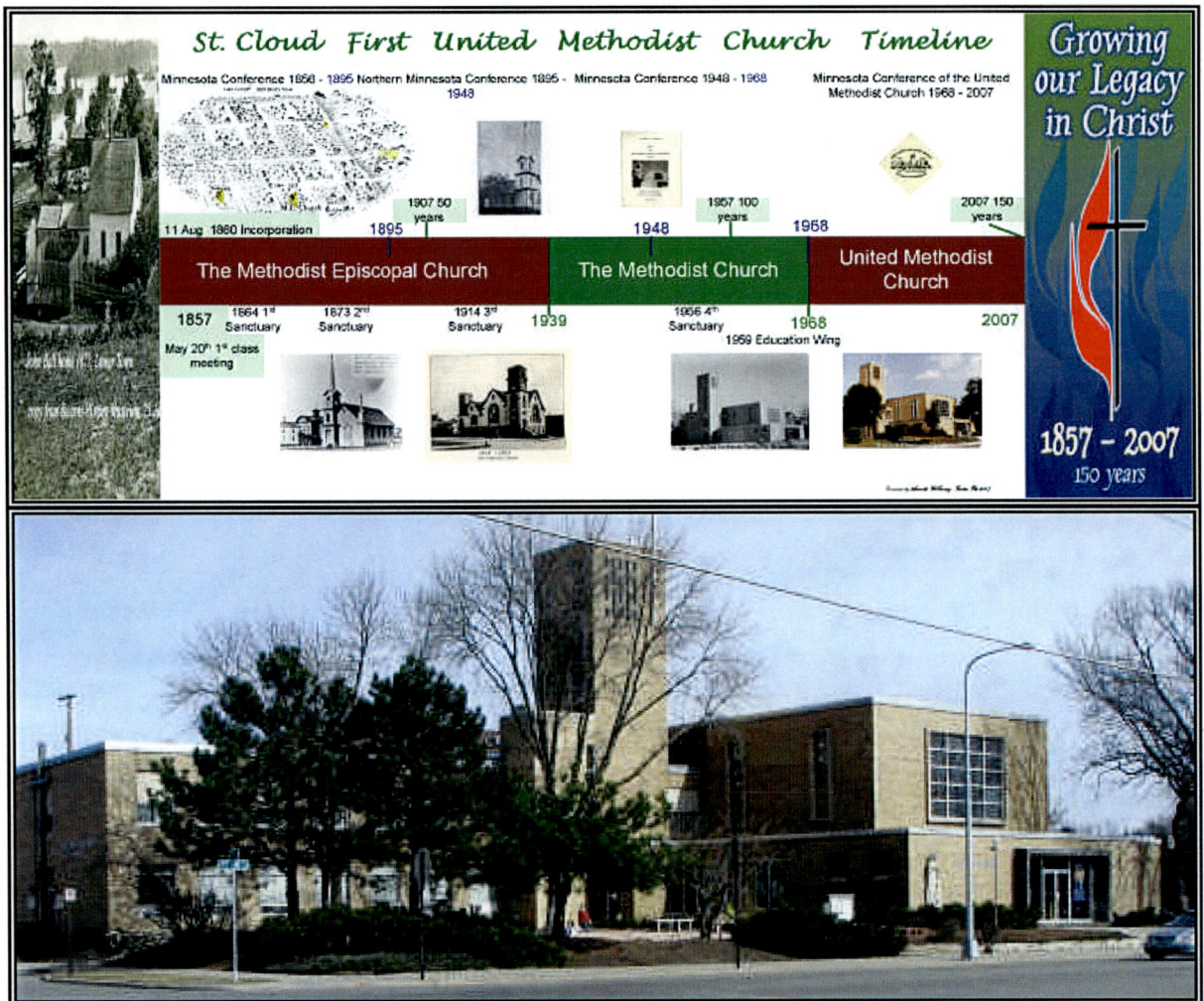

Greetings from Revd William F. Meier, Pastor
150th Anniversary Book

In the book titled *Godric*, a work of literary art centered loosely on St. Godric of 12th Century England, we find him landing on the shore of the holy island of Farne in the North Sea. He is greeted by the legendary St. Cuthbert, or rather a vision of him, since he died there some four hundred years before. Cuthbert says to Godric that he was expected there long before he arrived. Godric was puzzled by this greeting saying, "I came here as a stranger, and I came by chance." To explain this enigmatic phrase Cuthbert says, "When a man leaves home, he leaves behind some scrap of his heart. Is it not so, Godric?" He then thinks of his beloved father that he was missing back home and nodded in agreement. Then St. Cuthbert adds, "It's the same with a place a man is going to. Only then he sends a scrap of his heart ahead."

We live in the present of course, but in much of our mind's time we are scanning the past and pondering the future. From this pivot of time we see some wondrous things in our church's life. The pioneering spirit of our spiritual ancestors lies clearly in our hearts - scraps of their hearts live deeply within ours. In the pages of this history we find those scraps…courageous, generous, faith-filled, deeply caring, hard-working, joyful, forward thinking and community justice shaping people upon whose shoulders we stand. We read here of the hope, healing, and wholeness found at First Church. Scraps of our hearts are left behind in the "home" that is our past. This is why we so enjoy these old photographs and stories - they connect us deeply with our hearts and the memories that we hold dear. Those who study how memory is stored in our brains' cells tell us that we remember things that help us make meaning. The meaning we find here at First Church will bind many memories or "scraps" for years to come.

Standing at this pivot point in our history, I am sincerely honored to serve this congregation; the reputation and ministry of those who have served here before me, both clergy and lay people, truly lead me to a sense of humility. I am sustained by what they have sent on ahead.

The pivot of the present moment gives us hope. We continue to offer a vital ministry that is needed in this region, and let us not forget that we are sending scraps of our hearts on ahead of us into the future. And we take our spiritual strength and DNA into that future. May those who gather a book (or other media) for our 200th Anniversary find us faithful to the spiritual heritage we've been given, and may we supply them with scraps that inspire them to faithfulness, acts of love, and great joy!

In Christ,

Rev. William F. Meier

Rev. William F. Meier

MISSION STATEMENT

The mission of First United Methodist Church is to create and build Christian community through inviting, forming, and sending faithful, active disciples of Jesus Christ.

CORE VALUES

We value... the building of an inclusive faith community where people's lives are enhanced by healing, reconciliation, justice and joy.

We value... theological diversity as reflected in the United Methodist heritage and within the bounds of revealed scripture, tradition, experience, and reason.

We value...faith formation in people of all ages and faith development and challenge throughout a person's lifetime.

We value... worship reflecting God's grace and initiative through strong preaching and visual; messages by using the creative arts and an ardent music ministry.

We value... working with other faith communities and agencies whenever and wherever there are issues and needs which invite a common endeavor.

We value... the biblical call to social justice in the lives of all people through awareness and action.

We value... the unique and diverse gifts of each person in this faith community and the need for this giftedness to be used in God's redemptive work in the world.

We value... the encouragement and fostering of the giving of ourselves and our resources toward benevolent stewardship, toward mission, and intentional outreach.

VISION STATEMENT

First United Methodist Church celebrates God's transforming love as seen in Jesus Christ as we worship, learn, build spirit-filled community and reach out to our world. We seek to be a people of hope, promise, healing, justice and joy. We seek to share the gospel of Jesus Christ with those who do not belong to a faith community. We celebrate diversity, and welcome persons from all walks of life. We also strive to nurture, name, and call out the giftedness of each person for the work of redemptive love in all God's creation.

FOUR VISION PRIORITIES (Developed 2005-2006)

Spirituality: Nourish individuals in Biblical faith and Christian spirituality in a way that strengthens and transforms personal lives and this faith community.

Welcoming Community: Be an open, inviting and welcoming community practicing Christ like hospitality that leads to vibrant growth and connects people in meaningful Christian relationships.

Children and Families: Engage parents, children and youth to nurture them in a growing faith by means of our intentional focus, vital programming, and expanded resources.

Social Justice: Live out the Biblical message of justice, peace and love in the St. Cloud region; and the world through hope-filled actions of advocacy, networking, and hands-on service with the poor and marginalized.

DEDICATION

*To all past and current members of this Church,
who have kept
"Growing our Legacy in Christ"
for 150 years.*

Especially to

[signature: Geo. P. Crosby]

[signature: Gertrude B. Gove]

[signature: Earle Thompson]

[signature: Helen Cater Bensen]

[signature: Everett Rasmussen]

[signature: Dorothy M. Strueve]

[signature: Beulah Rose Hutchens]

*And all unnamed Church Historians
who have kept our Legacy alive
and safe for future generations.*

ACKNOWLEDGMENTS

Annette DeCourcy Towler

First United Methodist Church was very fortunate to have Gertrude Gove as the church historian for many years. She wrote and published a number of books for St. Cloud, Minnesota, and this church, making the gathering of history much easier for this 150th Anniversary project.

The following books have been written for Minnesota Methodists. Dr. Chauncey Hobart's *History of Minnesota Methodism, 1887*; Charles Nelson Pace, *Our Fathers Built, 1956*; and Bishop T. Otto Nall, *Minnesota Methodism: Forever Beginning, 1969*.

Miss Gove quoted frequently from both Dr. Hobart's book and *History of Stearns County, Minnesota,* which are two volumes written by William Bell Mitchell. Mitchell was the nephew of Jane Grey Swisshelm, editor of the *St. Cloud Visiter/Visitor* (renamed the *Democrat*). Mitchell was also an editor of the *St. Cloud Times*. Mitchell's history used information from their newspapers archives.

In 1982, Everett Rasmussen compiled a brief, updated church history for the 125th Anniversary celebration. Parts of that found their way into the newest history.

The Stearns County History Museum's reference library and staff members John Decker and Bob Lommell were also good resources. Their combined knowledge of the early history of St. Cloud helped give depth to information on the early years, especially for Lower Town, Everett School and the St. Cloud Seminary.

Many pictures which are used in this book are in First Church's archives. They include Earle Thompson's slides, scrapbooks and pictures, Dan Schneider-Bryan and Jim Towler's current photos. Other photo sources were the Stearns History Museum and Harold Zosel's postcard collection. The Minnesota United Methodist Conference Archives, Minneapolis; Kathy Spencer Johnson, archivist, provided both pictures and additional articles.

Beulah Rose Hutchens, a long-time member of First United Methodist Church, has been Church Historian for over 20 years. She is now a retired school teacher, and has accumulated much knowledge and history of this church. Beulah Rose has been responsible for displays in the hall display case, and has kept the memorial books up-to-date. She has also created many scrapbooks for our archives of newspaper articles and pictures. Her input has been invaluable.

This book was requested by the 150th Anniversary Committee, which asked that it include Miss Gove's earlier histories on the first hundred years. Nancy Gundersen wrote the story of the most recent fifty years. The book publishing team, led by Annette DeCourcy Towler, included Nancy Gundersen, Lois Barron and Janet Gray. They did editing and photo selections. Indexing was done by Annette DeCourcy Towler, with considerable help from Cheryl Towler Krichbaum and Lois Barron. Other added history includes the list of our church's ministers and numerous stories found in our archives. The genealogy of the Freeman, Gray and Hayward families, charter members of the church, was compiled by Mary Beth Wheeler.

Many thanks to the history team for thousand of hours spent putting this book together. To Bonnie Johnson, our church secretary, for additional proofing and just being there for us. Finally, thanks to Val Rogosheske, Carol Reid, and Jessie Harper for their work on congregational interviews and profiles, as well as to other Church members who wrote reports for our history.

Over the years, the Methodists in Minnesota
have had several names:
The Methodist Episcopal Church
The Methodist Church
The Northern Methodist Church
United Methodist Church

(See the picture timeline on page iv)

TABLE OF CONTENTS

GREETINGS FROM REVD WILLIAM F. MEIER, PASTOR	IV
MISSION STATEMENT	VI
DEDICATION	VII
ACKNOWLEDGMENTS	IX
TABLE OF CONTENTS	XI
FIRST 50 YEARS	**15**
PERIOD ONE - - 1863	16
PERIOD TWO - - 1863 - 1873	24
PERIOD THREE - - 1873 - 1889	29
PERIOD FOUR - - 1889 - 1896	38
PERIOD FIVE - - 1896 - 1909	41
SECOND 50 YEARS	**49**
PERIOD SIX - - 1907 - 1917	51
PERIOD SEVEN - - 1917 – 1930	58
PERIOD NINE -- 1934 - 1946	71
PERIOD TEN - - 1946 - 1957	83
THIRD 50 YEARS	**97**
CHAPTER ONE 1957-1963	99
CHAPTER TWO 1963 - 1967	107
CHAPTER THREE 1968 – 1971	111
CHAPTER FOUR 1972 – 1978	120
CHAPTER FIVE 1979 -1984	128
CHAPTER SIX 1985 - 1989	137
CHAPTER SEVEN 1990 - 1994	143
CHAPTER EIGHT 1994-1998	148
CHAPTER NINE 1999 - 2003	158
CHAPTER TEN 2004 - 2007	167
OUR SPACE	**175**
THINGS BEYOND WORDS	177
MORE THINGS BEYOND WORDS	187
DRAWN FROM FAITH	191
THE LABYRINTH STORY	192
HANDS TO WORK AND HEARTS TO GOD	193
FASHIONED FROM EARTH	193
THREADS WOVEN AND WORKED	193
HANGINGS	194
PARAMENTS	195
SEASONAL VISUALS: BANNERS, AND INSTALLATIONS	196
WORSHIP AND MUSIC	**199**
JOHN WESLEY'S DIRECTIONS FOR SINGING	200
SERVICE OF WORSHIP	201
HYMNALS	202
ORGAN	204
HANDBELLS	205
CHOIRS	206
ADULT CHOIR: A FAMILY TRADITION	207
MUSIC PROGRAM IN THE 1970S	208

- BRIDGE BAND HISTORY 210
- CHORISTER CHOIR... 211

OUR PEOPLE AT WORK 213
- BOARD OF TRUSTEES 215
- GRIP STORY 216
- JUNIOR HIGH METHODIST YOUTH FELLOWSHIP 221
- OUTREACH COMMITTEE 222
- PRAYER SHAWL MINISTRY 223
- SCHOLARSHIP PROGRAMS 224
- TRUST FUND 226
- WORSHIP COMMITTEE 229
- WOMAN'S SOCIETY OF CHRISTIAN SERVICE/ UNITED METHODIST WOMEN 230

PASTORS AND PEOPLE REFLECT 233
- OUR FORMER PASTORS 234
- ASSOCIATE PASTORS... 247
- PASTORS FROM THIS CONGREGATION 257
- REMINISEENCES FROM OUR CONGREGATION 270

THROUGH THE YEARS 323
- HISTORIAN - GERTRUDE GOVE 325
- A HISTORY OF PAST CIVIC INVOLVEMENT 326
- 150TH ANNIVERSARY COMMITTEE 328
- EARLY CHURCH RECORDS 330
- EARLY MEMBERSHIP 331
- EARLY BAPTISMS 334
- EARLY MARRIAGES 335
- MEMBERSHIP NUMBERS FOR THE LAST 150 YEARS 336
- SEMINARY 340
- THE SAINT CLOUD INSTITUTE AND PIONEER SEMINARY.. 340
- M. P. SATTERLEE'S STORY 342
- SCRAPBOOK 344

APPOINTED ONES 347
- STRUCTURE OF THE UNITED METHODIST CHURCH 349
- FIRST UNITED METHODIST CHURCH PASTORS 350
- ASSIGNED PASTORS... 352
- LIST OF ASSOCIATE PASTORS... 366
- PASTORS FROM THIS CONGREGATION 371
- RETIRED PASTORS ATTACHED 373

FIRST FAMILIES 375
- FREEMAN DESCENDANTS... 377
- GRAY DESCENDANTS 379
- HAYWARD DESCENDANTS 395
- MCCLURE DESCENDANTS 406

BIBLIOGRAPHY 415

INDEX 419

Growing our Legacy in Christ

150 years
1857-2007

The First 50 Years 1857-1907

Gertrude Gove

First United Methodist Church

St. Cloud, Minnesota

During First 50 Years ...

1855 Stearns County created. First local Protestant services held on Christmas Day – by Baptists. One Methodist minister serves Minnesota territory.

1856 St. Cloud incorporates. 35 voters choose first officers. City lots cost $3-$5 each.

1857 City population grows to 200-300. Rev. Pugh is sent to start Methodist work in St. Cloud; stays just a few weeks.

1858 Minnesota becomes a state. Ox cart trains on the St. Paul-Pembina trail rest at edge of town. Membership class of 11 organized in St. Cloud.

1859 July 4 temps in MN fall below freezing. Rev. Bowdish appointed to St. Cloud Mission. Second membership class of 13 formed.

1860 Lincoln elected president. The town has grown to 1000. Local Church has 31 members, no building. Methodists consider building.

1861 Pioneer Seminary and Institute opens. Farmland sells for under $1 per acre. Church membership reported at 51.

1862 Civil War and Dakota conflict stir local emotions. Homestead Act.

1864 Methodists dedicate their first building at 427 4th Ave. So. Project takes 4 months, 4 days.

1865 News of Lincoln's assassination delivered Sunday morning April 16, and is read from local pulpits.

1872 Sauk Rapids Methodists organize.

1873 January blizzard kills 70 in state. Ladies Aid buys lot on corner of 3rd & 5th for a new building. First building razed and lumber reused in the second.

1877 Great Grasshopper Plague takes local crops 4th year in a row.

1883 Gas lamps light local streets

1884 The Fifth Avenue church redecorated before hosting Annual Conference.

1885 First hospital built in St. Cloud.

1886 Tornado levels most of Sauk Rapids, some of St. Cloud. As many as 70 killed; rebuilding takes years.

1888 "Minnesota's Worst" January storm claims over 200 lives; many are children sent home from school.

1889 First mail delivery in city.

1891 Electric streetcars run to Sauk Rapids & Waite Park. Second Methodist Episcopal Church organized near Breckenridge and Cooper Avenues with own pastor.

1899 Mr. Tenvoorde buys first car seen in St. Cloud.

1904 Construction begins on granite wall around local reformatory.

1907 Mother's Day and Boy Scouts enter the culture

First 50 Years

INTRODUCTION: *A History of First Methodist Church* (1947 edition)

This is an honest attempt to write a true and complete history of the First Methodist Church of St. Cloud, Minnesota, from 1857 to 1947. The handicaps, however, have been many. Some are: the lack of complete files of Conference and local church records; lack of information concerning many of the pastors, Official Board Members and other Church workers; the discrepancy between the Conference and local church records and the lack of time for complete research.

The following references were used: The Annual Year Books of the Minnesota and Northern Minnesota Conferences; The St. Cloud Church Records; The St. Cloud Official Board Minutes; The *Mitchell Papers* at the Minnesota Historical Society; the *History of Stearns County* by W. B. Mitchell; and talks with old residents of St. Cloud or their descendants and with older members of the present Congregation.

Gertrude B. Gove

FOREWORD: *A Century Of Service* (1958 edition)

THIS HISTORY IS DEDICATED to the many pastors who have served First Methodist Church, St. Cloud, down through the century. It is the PURPOSE of this edition of the history of First Church to reveal something about each of the ministers who served this congregation and also to show the development of First Methodist Church as it conformed to the changing rules of the General Church. Mention of individual members of the congregation is not made except as they help explain this development.

"Each minister makes his particular contribution to the continuing life stream of the church and then, at the call of the General Church, moves on to another service in another community."- Russell A. Huffman

Information and pictures for this 1958 edition of the history have been obtained from the Church records, from letters and interviews with former pastors or their relatives and from the Minnesota Historical Society. Much of the cost of the pictures has been met by Earle Thompson and Gertrude Gove. Special assistance was given by Mrs. H. K. McCall, James J. Leigh, Mrs. Lloyd Lillestrand, and the Centennial Committee - Mrs. R. N. Jones, Mrs. Kurt Stai, Hillis Myers, and the Reverend Mr. Paul O. Metzger.

Engraving was done by the St. Cloud Engraving Company Inc.; duplicating by the Continental Press and Supply; typist, Bonive Pearson 1857 - 1863.

PERIOD ONE - - 1863

The first phase of Minnesota Methodism was that of Indian Missions represented by Samuel Spater who labored faithfully among the Chippewas from 1839 to 1855. The history of Methodist work among the white people in Minnesota began when the Rev. Chauncey Hobart was sent to the St. Paul and Minnesota district which then included all of Minnesota and much of Wisconsin. The first Conference ever held in Minnesota met at Red Wing[1] August 1856, in the chapel of Hamline University. At that time the Methodist work in Minnesota was divided among four Presiding Elders and David Brooks was given the St. Paul district. This included the St. Cloud Mission which extended from Clearwater to Winnebago Prairie[2] thus including the village of St. Cloud. John Pugh was sent out as a "missionary" to work in this field. One record states that he was in St. Cloud village May 20, 1857 and spent four weeks in and around the locality. Meanwhile the St. Paul district had been redivided by the Conference of 1857 and the Rev. Samuel Sterrett had been named the Presiding Elder of the Monticello district which included St. Cloud. Sterrett employed a Levi Gleason. Gleason was not a member of the conference so could not be "appointed." He no doubt came to St. Cloud village at some time during that year.

The April Conference of 1858 sent Gleason, now a probationer, and the Rev. Charles G. Bowdish, to Sauk River and Clearwater. Records show that there was a "class"[3] in St. Cloud in 1858 but do not tell who formed it. It may have been Pugh or Gleason or Sterratt or Bowdish or several or all. But who ever did it, the class was a good one. We find the following listed: Dr. Silas Marlatt, Ambrose Freeman and wife, Eli B. King, J. C. Wilson, William Hooper and wife, T. N. Berlin and wife, Mrs. Owen, and Mrs. C. Garlington and children.[4]

---

[1] 7-10 Aug 1856
[2] Near Sauk Centre, known on some maps as Winnebago Crossings [Red Ox Trails]
[3] p .1 1958 History Book "The Conference record of 1859 reports that St. Cloud had a "Class" of 11 members."
[4] Hobart, *History of Methodism in Minnesota*; St. Cloud Church Records; Conference Records.

The earliest membership records of the Methodist Church in St. Cloud show the first "class" joining in 1858 as being Ambrose Freeman, his wife, Jane, their children Thomas and Maria, John Fossett, Ann Garlington, William Hooper, Silas Marlatt, Jas. Williams, James C. Williams and Mary Wilson. By the end of 1859 Luellen Clark, Julia Crawford, Thomas and Mary Mann, John L. Thompson, Julia Owen, Mary Pierpoint, T. N. and Jane Berlin, Mary Garlington and daughter Margaret. John and Eliza Kotch had also joined. (See "Through the Years" section for more information on early members.)

A "class" in those days included only the most sincere and active church members. It was a testimonial and prayer meeting planned for the purpose of increasing the spirituality of the members. The pastor, or the class leader if the pastor could not be present, was in charge. Ambrose Freeman was the first class leader. Wayne Carver and S. H. Norris were later ones. Every member was expected to attend regularly and "habitual neglect wrought a forfeiture of membership." The class leader and pastor were very strict with the members and very frank to say and write what they thought of the members' conduct. The Books of Heaven surely will not contain any more caustic remarks than are found in the Class books of 1858-65. For example, A certain man was "doing tolerably well." Another was "too devoted to business to attend meetings." A third's name "should not be on the roll" and a fourth was "not known religiously."[5]

The first class is worth knowing more about. Ambrose Freeman came from Virginia, by way of Edgar County, Illinois, where the family lived for a time. They reached Minnesota in 1857. After the first crop was destroyed by grasshoppers, Ambrose moved his family to the village of St. Cloud so that he could earn a living at his other trade, that of brick layer and plasterer. They lived in Lower Town (at 312 12th St. South) and the house is still being used.[6] He was a "Shouting" Methodist of the Southern variety. His wife, Jane,

---

[5] Church Records
[6] in 1947 edition.

had been brought up according to the Episcopalian faith but she too was a Methodist by the time she arrived in St. Cloud, although a quieter one. The Freeman home was the center of all social and religious meetings of the Church and after her husband was killed by the Indians, Jane "carried on," training her daughters and son, Daniel, to be good Methodists. Their homes, too, were open to Church affairs and to traveling ministers.

Silas Marlatt came here in 1857 because ill health had forced him to leave Michigan and the medical profession for which he had been trained. He opened the first drug store in St. Cloud. It was in Lower Town, also, on First Avenue near the Teachers' College campus. Many a meeting of the Board was held in Dr. Marlatt's office. Later he moved to Middle Town, on Fifth Avenue at the Third Street corner. Dr. Marlatt, in 1863, married Miss Laura Gray, a sister of the mother of Mrs. Daniel H. Freeman. Both women were active Church workers, Mrs. Marlatt, at one time being Recording Steward. Dr. Marlatt was a true gentleman, quiet, unassuming, and scholarly, but retiring. Few knew him intimately but those who did had a friendship that was well worth the having. He lived until 1903.

Mr. and Mrs. Conway Garlington and children started from England for the United States. On the way the husband and father was drowned. Mrs. Garlington "carried on." She and her children took up a claim near St. Cloud. Later they traded the claim for the Bridgman house in Lower Town and there Mrs. Garlington kept an hotel. Her son, E. A., and her daughter, Margaret, later Mrs. McKelvy, became active Church workers.

T. N. Berlin was in St. Cloud in 1856 and was writing back to his friend, H. Z. Mitchell, in Pennsylvania, urging him to come out to Minnesota to live. Mr. Berlin helped many of the early settlers to build their first homes. He was a local preacher and in 1863 was in Fair Haven as pastor.[7] James C. Wilson, a sign painter, lived in Upper Town.[8] He was also very active in the church and served for a long time on the Board. He was the Recording Steward during the first years and also the Sunday School Superintendent, in

---

[7] (*Mitchell Papers*, St. Historical Society, St. Paul, Minnesota and Mitchell, *History of Stearns County*, page 1102)
[8] (above Empire Park)

1868.[9] Eli B. King and William Hooper lived in Neenah or St. Augusta, in 1858, but later may have moved into town.[10]

The first record that could be found of a Quarterly Conference was the one held at the home of Ambrose Freeman, July, 1858.[11] A Quarterly Conference in those days was quite an event. It was held every three months somewhere on the circuit. That was the time the Presiding Elder[12] reached the particular circuit on his vast district. The circuit at this time, 1858, included Neenah/St. Augusta, Winnebago Prairie and perhaps other localities around St. Cloud. We do not know how much of an affair the conference in the Freeman home was but the fact that a meeting of any kind was held indicated that Methodism was alive here, in 1858.

Another Methodist trait found early in St. Cloud was the "protracted"[13] meetings held in a house owned by John Ball, in February, 1859. This house[14] could hold one hundred and fifty persons and the St. Cloud Democrat says that it was "crowded." The preacher in charge was the Rev. Mr. Andrew J. Nelson who in 1857 had been sent by the Conference to Little Falls and Belle Prairie as pastor and principal of a school project that the Methodists had

John Ball home 1877, Lower Town
copy from Stearns History Museum, 25 Jan 2007

---

[9] (Mrs. D. H. Freeman; Church Records)
[10] (Mr. Hooper, in 1869, owned the Stearns House.)
[11] (Mitchell, 380.)
[12] Currently called District Superintendent
[13] (revival meetings)
[14] (just below the present Tenth Street)

taken over from Mr. and Mrs. Ayer, early missionaries. A. J. Nelson was a man of culture and education, also a man of energy and courage but circumstances caused the school project to fail. This probably accounts for his being in St. Cloud in 1859 and conducting revival meetings mentioned.[15]

In May 1859, Charles Bowdish was appointed as the first "stationed" pastor of St. Cloud. This was an important event in the history of the St. Cloud church. It meant that the Conference felt that the St. Cloud parishioners were strong enough and wealthy enough to support a pastor all by themselves and it also meant that the work at St. Cloud was important enough to warrant a preacher giving his entire time to the village alone.[16] Levi Gleason was sent to Winnebago Prairie.[17] In February, 1860, the first donation party given to a Methodist pastor in St. Cloud was held at the home of Ambrose Freeman. The St. Cloud Democrat says that the results were "substantial." At the annual Conference held that fall at Red Wing, St. Cloud reported 31 members.[18]

The first baptism was performed on Sunday, July 31, 1859, for one Margaret Remmel, no age given. The next three baptisms came on the first Sunday after Easter in 1860, all adults, with a second group of two adults and two young children baptized on June 10 the same year (five-year-old Trevanan Berlin and his two-year-old sister Julia). Allen F. Cassey, age three weeks, seems to have been the first infant receiving baptism on Sunday, Feb. 3, 1861. The whole congregation were witnesses. jbg

---

That year, the Rev. A.[Andrew] J. Nelson was sent to St. Cloud and Winnebago Prairie. In March of 1860, the Quarterly Conference had appointed a committee to consider the building of a church and school. By January, 1861, the St. Cloud Institute and Pioneer Seminary was in session with 33 scholars and A. J. Nelson, the Principal. This building was up on the hill above most of Lower Town, in what is now Central Park.[19] At that time all the land around was covered with beautiful oak trees. Near the Seminary stood the Everett School built in 1857, the Episcopal Church built in 1856 and the unfinished Baptist church. All of these buildings faced the East. Mrs. Jane Grey Swisshelm, the editor of the St. Cloud Democrat, says that the Seminary

---

[15] (Hobart)
[16] He lived, according to the 1860 Federal Census records, at the Garlington home in Lower Town.
[17] Indian reservation north of today's Sartell.
[18] (Conference Records)
[19] Barden Park today

was a handsome building with a cupola and a bell.[20] At the time the Seminary was opened, the work at Winnebago Prairie was discontinued so that Mr. Nelson could devote his entire time to St. Cloud.[21] He taught school during the week and then preached twice on Sundays.[22] The Conference of 1861 sent the Reverend Bartley [23] Blain to St. Cloud as pastor so that Mr. Nelson could spend his entire time with the school. In his one year as pastor and teacher, the Rev. A. J. Nelson increased the membership to 70.[24]

Relationships of the families of Freeman, Gray, Hayward and Marlatt are explained by family historian researcher, Mary Beth Wheeler of California, in the last section of this book called First Families. jbg

While St. Cloud Methodists seem to have formalized the need for a school and church in March of 1860, leading St. Cloud citizens had held organizing meetings to build such a school in the fall of 1858. As both a boarding and day school, it was to offer high school level classes and serve as an event center. The school opened with great hope just prior to the Civil War in January 1861 with an enrollment of 33. The first principal was the local Methodist minister who left to teach at Hamline after just a year with a staff of five in place. Former class leader S. H. Norris was sent to help in the seminary, a new pastor was appointed, the classroom space was adapted/converted for worship, and the Conference claimed ownership. "Swindle!" claimed local editor Jane Grey Swisshelm, in a growing public dispute. The well-intentioned staff could not continue enthusiasm or quality instruction. Classes continued with difficulty at least until the spring of 1865. See section, "Through the Years" for more of the story. jbg

---

[20](January and September, 1861)
[21] (Church Records)
[22] (St. Cloud Democrat)
[23] Church Records has Bantley, Conference Journals & Official Minister records have Bartley. He signed most of the records as B. Blain
[24] (Conference Records)

STATE OF MINNESOTA)
) ss.
County of Stearns)

    I, C. J. Bowdish, an ordained minister of the Methodist Episcopal Church, now stationed at St. Cloud in the County of Stearns and State of Minnesota, do hereby certify that according to and by virtue of the rules and discipline of said Methodist Episcopal Church, I have this eleventh day of August A. D. 1860, appointed Ambrose Freeman, William Hooper, James C. Wilson, Silas Marlatt, Trevanion Berlin, James R. Tralf and Edwin A. Jarlington, as trustees of the Methodist Episcopal Church lacated and situate in the Town of St. Cloud aforesaid.

    And the said Trustees and their successors, shall forever thereafter be called and known by the name of "The Trustees of the First Methodist Episcopal Church" of St. Cloud in the County of Stearns, Minnesota.

    Witness my hand and seal this eleventh day of August A. D. 1860.

Signed and sealed in the Presence of)
)
James M. McKelvy   )   C. J. Bowdish
J. W. Read   )

STATE OF MINNESOTA)
) ss.
County of Stearns)

    Personally appeared before me, this eleventh day of August A.D. 1860, C. J. Bowdish to me known to be the individual described in and who executed the foregoing certificate, and acknowledged that he executed the same free and voluntarily for the uses and purposes therein expressed.

                                                          James M. McKelvy
                                                            Notary Public
(Notarial seal, Stearns   Minn
    County, Minn.)
    Filed for record August 11 A. D. 1860 at 6 o'clock P.M.

Original copy of incorporation of Methodist Episcopal Church. Listed in the Stearns County Court house as Trustees of ..

The Conference of 1861 put St. Cloud in the Minneapolis district with the Rev. David Brooks as the Presiding Elder.[25] In November 1861, the women[26] of the church met at the home of Mrs. Julia (Charles) Owen and organized a Methodist Sewing Society. This group elected the following officers: President, Mrs. Nelson;[27] Vice President, Mrs. Ellen Thompson; Secretary, Mrs. Julia Owen; Treasurer, Mrs. Eliza A. Ball; Directors, Mrs. Elisa Ann Hooper and Mrs. Jane Freeman. [28,29]

In 1862, the Rev. Samuel Sterrett who had been a Presiding Elder came to St. Cloud and Winnebago Prairie as pastor for a year. Samuel H. whom I have already mentioned as an early class leader, was sent here to aid A. J. Nelson in the Seminary.

Josiah Hayward, the father of Mrs. D. H. Freeman, was now a member of the Quarterly Conference. "Uncle Josiah" was the genial host of the Central House.[30] He and his wife, the sister of Mrs. Marlatt, lived a long and useful life in the St. Cloud community. A.[Allen] E. Hussey[31] who had arrived from Ohio in 1856, was the Recording Steward at the Quarterly Conference about this time. [32] The pastor [33] reported 50 members at the Conference of 1863.

The early pastors were not always paid in produce. The February, 1863, donation party realized $105, nearly all in cash. [34] But most of the pastors had to live from hand to mouth and had to see that the hand did not go to the mouth too often.

Between the years 1848 and 1855, the Winnebago Indians were located in a reservation bounded on the south by the Watab River, on the east by the Mississippi, the north by the Crow Wing and Long Prairie rivers. The western boundary was a line drawn from the source of the Long Prairie River to the Watab. Winnebago Prairie was likely in the southern section of the reserve near today's Sartell. Originally from Wisconsin, the

---

[25] District Superintendent today
[26] original 'ladies'
[27] (probably Mrs. A. J.)
[28] (St Cloud Democrat)
[29] (Mrs D. H. Freeman says that this was the first of a number of Ladies' Societies which eventually became the Women's Society today. The women of one society would move away or die and the society would have to be reorganized. This happened several times due to the small and shifting population of the church.)
[30] (the forerunner of the Grand Central)
[31] Not listed in Church membership, but in 1860 US Population Census, Minnesota Stearns County page 12.
[32] (His son, Arthur, did the interior decorating of the 1910 church, which was the present one) in 1947.
[33] (Sterrett)
[34] (Mitchell History 1101-2.)

Winnebago had been pushed to a reservation in Iowa and then were moved again to Long Prairie. This reservation would not be a good fit, however, and in 1855 they would move to the Blue Earth Reservation. jbg

Period Two - - 1863 - 1873

David Tice

It was during the pastorate of the Rev. David Tice, sent by the Conference of 1863, that second period began. In May, 1864, a church "enterprise" was begun and in September, 1864, four months and four days later, the building was dedicated by Bishop Kingsley, assisted by the Rev. Jabez Brooks of Hamline University, and the local clergy, David Lowry of the Presbyterian, John Scott of the Baptist, and David Tice of the Methodist churches.[35] This building was erected somewhere between Sixth Street and Seventh Street and Third and Fifth Ave of today. We are told that it was built on donated lots and one was given by John L. Wilson, the Father of St. Cloud but we are not sure that meant they were given permanently.[36] We know that it was near the cemetery of that early day and that was near Seventh Street and Fourth Avenue.

The building was a frame structure of one story, with a cupola and a bell. The entrance was on the East as were all the buildings of Lower Town.

The choir sat on a slightly raised platform near the entrance with the pulpit at the other end of the room. Pews were in front and at the sides of the pulpit. A fine melodeon[37] with a good tone was put in this new building.[38] This building was erected in war time at war prices ($3,003.87)[39] and as the pastor had to raise the money by himself, he went East where there was more money.

---

[35] (Mitchell History 1107.)
[36] (The Register of Deeds files have not yet revealed the required documentation.) adt note: County of Stearns Land Records have no information on this building as of June 2007
[37] A melodeon (also known as a cabinet organ or American organ) is a type of 19th century reed organ with a foot-operated vacuum bellows, and a piano keyboard. It differs from the related harmonium, which uses a pressure bellows. It was first manufactured in 1854 by Mason & Hamlin of Boston, Massachusetts. It was useful as a substitute for the pipe organ, in particular, for practice. Picture and information from http://en.wikipedia.org/wiki/Melodeon_%28organ%29
[38] (St. Cloud Democrat, Mitchell History, Campbell Papers, Drs. D. H. Freeman.)
[39] Civil War prices

This church was the chief achievement of David Tice but it was not all that he did. At Conference in 1865 he reported 51 members, 110 scholars in the Sunday School and 30 Advocate Subscribers. This was the first definite mention of a Sunday School but it was a reorganized school so there must have been an earlier one.

About this time occurred the death of S. [Samuel] N. Norris who had taken over the work of A. J. Nelson, at the Seminary when the latter joined the faculty of Hamline University. Daniel Freeman and his sister, Lavisa, later Mrs. J. F. Stevenson, joined the church at this time. Wayne Carver was the class leader at this time. He later, 1866, entered the active ministry.

In 1865, the Rev. Charles Griswold was sent to St. Cloud where he served a year and then went on as Presiding Elder in the newly formed St. Cloud District which included St. Cloud, Monticello, Princeton, Clearwater, Rockford, Sauk Centre, Paynesville, Forest City, Winnebago Prairie,[40] Lake Mary and Alexandria. When Mr. Griswold left St. Cloud there were 41 members.

The Rev. Noah Lathrop, a talented preacher and a social gentleman,[41] came next as pastor, at a salary of $900. He was from Indiana and De Pauw University. He had begun his ministry in the Hoosier state and was in Minnesota when the first Conference was held, 1856. He served long and faithfully and even after he had been placed on the superannuated list[42] he took an active part in church work. He died in California.[43] At the end of his year in St. Cloud the number of members was 48. Sometime between 1869 and 1873 he was made a Presiding Elder.

The Rev. John R. Creighten served as pastor from 1867 to 1869. There were 40 members in 1869.

---

[40] Now Sartell, which was originally owned by the Winnebago Indian Tribe; resource Stearns History Museum
[41] St. Cloud Daily Times, Oct. .22, 1873
[42] Retiree list, Conference Journal
[43] Crosby's Scrapbook, St. Cloud Church Archives

Then came the Rev. William Wilson Satterlee who stayed two years. He was from Indiana, also. When he was seventeen years of age he joined the Wesleyan Methodists and was licensed to preach. He was a very helpful local preacher. Later, he joined the Methodist Episcopal Church and became a member of its ministry in 1867. St. Cloud was his second appointment. His son tells that they were living at Waseca when they learned they were to come here. They looked on a map and decided that between the "Saint" and the "Cloud" and the distance "up" this must be quite a "heavenly" place.

It is of interest to note that in the 1870 US population census, Rev. Satterlee's income was $200 a year. Their house was not only home for him, his wife and their five children ranging from 13 to 4 years of age, but a 65-year-old woman, Mrs. Gray; a female school teacher, age 24; and an 18- year-old male laborer. Their relationship to the family is not shown. [Probably Mrs. Gray owned the house, as the conference journals do not show a parsonage attached to this church. adt]

First Church archives contained an item printed in the *St. Cloud Times & Journal Press,* on October 5, 1931. The author, Marion Pease Satterlee, was the eldest son of the Rev. W. W. Satterlee. He was 12 when the family came to St. Cloud, then a town of under 3,000 persons and 14 when they left. The article was transcribed and is reprinted in the section "Through the Years." jbg

---

About the time that the Satterlees came, the State Normal School was established at St. Cloud. The Methodist Church (because of its location and the fact that it had Sunday School in the afternoons while the other churches had theirs in the mornings and the fact that a certain Miss Walker of the Normal School faculty could and did lead the music at the Methodist Sunday School sessions) became the church home for the Normal students and faculty.[44]

Prominent officials of the Church at that time were J. C. Wilson, whom we have met before, Francis Talcott, a pioneer jeweler of Lower Town,

---

[44] Satterlee in *St. Cloud Times* and *Daily Journal Press*, October 5, 1931, reprinted in "Through the Years" section of this book.

Thomas Gray, later President of the Normal School, John Hayward who in 1861 moved in from Winnebago Prairie[45] and W. B. Mc Intire and Frank Hanscome of whom nothing more is recorded.

William Wilson Satterlee, as a preacher, was clear and evangelistic. He took especial delight in the presentation of those truths relating to the higher Christian experiences. As a pastor, he was faithful and ambitious. He was a warm friend and like his Master, bore the griefs and carried the sorrows of his people. Few men have been the confidential advisor of so many as he. Satterlee was a born reformer. As a boy he was pointed out as the "little black abolitionist." Early in life he was interested in temperance and it was in connection with that that he was most widely known. After leaving St. Cloud, he was appointed in 1879, the agent of the Minnesota State Temperance Union and Missionary at Large. Still later he was appointed to the U. S. Grant University at Athens, Tennessee, as professor of Scientific Temperance and Hygienic Philosophy. This was the first chair of the kind in any institution of higher learning in the country. He occupied that position till his death.[46]

In June, 1870, there was a Sunday School of 138 scholars and, in 1871, T. J. Gray was the Superintendent. At the Conference of 1871 the pastor reported 92 members and 93 scholars.

Harvey Webb

In those days the pastor had to find his own residence. The new pastor of 1871, the Rev. Harvey Webb, did not think much of that plan. He writes, "Spent three days in search of a house in which to live and ten days hard manual labor repairing it and fitting it up for a parsonage. Had a house been in readiness, two weeks of valuable time would have been saved to the pastoral work. Eternity alone will reveal the loss to both the pastor and the people. I shall lose much valuable time this year by being located too far from my work besides the unnecessary tax of travel."[47]

Some time about 1871 Sauk Rapids must have been added to St. Cloud because the Rev. Webb writes, "I cannot in justice to myself or the charge, preach three times in each Sabbath. I could better preach every day in the

---

[45] Sartell area
[46] Conference Journal
[47] (Church Records)

week, one sermon. Either the morning service at St. Cloud or the Sauk Rapids appointment must be given up." At that same time the Board of Trustees resolved that the full time of the pastor was essentially necessary to the prosperity and growth of the Society at St. Cloud.[48]

In January, 1872, the Board was satisfied that the state of Brother Webb's health imperatively demanded a rest and they willing yet sorrowfully accepted his resignation and resolved to use their utmost endeavor to raise the balance due him. In April, 1872, a minister named F. A. Riggin was sent to continue the work. He was to receive $350 for the half year. He reported 74 members and 50 scholars at the Conference of 1872.

J. F. Stevenson was chairman of the Board at this time. He was born in Pennsylvania. In 1869 he came to Minnesota settling in Winnebago Prairie but soon came to St. Cloud where he built up what later developed into the Granite City Iron Works. He was a profound student of the Bible and kindred works. He received deep religious convictions when a boy and stayed by them all of his life. Almost as soon as he arrived in St. Cloud he joined the Methodist Church. Physically, mentally, and morally, Mr. Stevenson was a bulwark and tower of strength to the city, standing for the best as a citizen. His pastor, Dr. James H. Dewart, said at the funeral that Mr. Stevenson not only acted honest, he was honest. For years he was the main pillar of the Methodist Church and probably did more than any other man in St. Cloud to build up and sustain the Methodist work here. He not only gave liberally but he attended services regularly and induced others to do likewise. He was the kind of a person who could be very active and do much for an organization yet do it so quietly that others would not be conscious of it. He probably did not get as much credit for what he did as he might have had.[49]

The Board was very economical in those days. They urged that all the prayer meetings and teachers' meetings be held in the homes during the winter months. There was some sort of a Young People's society in 1872 because in April of that year the Official records show that the Y.P.C.A. was allowed to use the Church room on payment of twenty-five cents per week. By December of that year this group had turned itself into a Young People's Prayer Meeting.[50]

---

[48] (Records)
[49] (Mitchell History p 1078 and Mrs. D. H. Freeman)
[50] (Perhaps to pray for a softening of adult hearts)

Period Three - - 1873 - 1889

The Conference of 1872 put St. Cloud in the St. Paul district and sent the Rev. James T. Lewton here as pastor. The business of Lower Town had moved up beyond the ravine to Middle Town. The Methodists felt that it was time for them to move also. In February, 1872, there had been talk of moving the church building but the Board of Trustees had deemed it inexpedient to do so as the cost of moving and repairing and the purchase of a lot would cost the Society too much. But in April, 1873, the Ladies Aid had purchased Lot one of Block nine from the County Commissioners on the following terms- $100 down and $300 more in equal annual installments with simple interest of 7%. The plans and specifications cost $100.[51] This new building, using materials from the old, later became the east part of the 1910 structure. It did not have the colored glass windows that are there now [1947] and the interior may have been different but in size and shape was about as it is today. It fronted on Fifth Avenue. Until their own church was ready, the Methodists worshipped with the Presbyterians, the pastors, E. V. Campbell and J. T. Lemon, occupying the pulpit alternately, morning and evening.[52]

On September 7, 1873, there were no services in the Presbyterian, Baptist or Congregational churches because the pastors were taking part in the dedication services at the New Methodist church located at what is now Fifth Avenue South and Third Street. At that service over $1,000 was raised to pay off the indebtedness of the Society.[53]

The old Methodist Church is to be taken down and rebuilt on the old jail lot, near the Union School building. It will be finished off in gothic style, with corner towers. The entrance will be through the main corner tower. It will be 32 x 56 feet. Rev. Mr. Copp, of Sauk Rapids is the architect of the new building, and will superintend the work. Until their new house is completed, the Methodists will unite with the Presbyterians in their church.[54]

---

[51] (Church Records)
[52] (*St. Cloud Democrat*, April, 1873.)
[53] (*St. Cloud Times*, September 4, 1873.)
[54] *St. Cloud Times*, April 9, 1873

Harold Zosel's postcard collection, the foot bridge over the ravine

Postcard of the 2nd church, Archives of FUMC 1873

5th Ave So. Grand Central Hotel owned by the Haywards. 4th building on the right possibly Dr. Marlatte's drug store.[55]

A drug storefront on 5th Ave So.[56]

In October, 1871, the church was using script[57] for the running expenses. A year later, "penny collections" were started. A separate treasurer was appointed to take care of this. About 1872 or 1873 the church adopted the weekly envelope system of collections for the purpose of raising the pastor's salary. About this time there is mention of a sexton and his "salary" and "lucrative" position and his "duties." He was to receive $1.00 per week for ordinary services with the understanding that by ordinary services an occasional extra service would be included.

---

[55] Stearns History Museum Archives
[56] Ibid
[57] Script is any substitute for currency which is not legal tender, and is a form of credit. According to Wikipedia website. adt

Three women were on the Board now: Mrs. MeKelvy, (Margaret Garlington), Mrs. Melinda Hayward, (the widow of John Hayward, an earlier Board member), and Mrs. J. E. Bowing.[58] Mrs. Hayward was a sister of Mrs. Marlatt and Mrs. J. E. Hayward. Mr. and Mrs. Bowing came west in search of health for Mr. Bowing. They came to St. Cloud because Mrs. Bowing's sister Emma was here with her husband, J. F. Stevenson. All of these Official Board women were very active Ladies' Aid Society members, also.

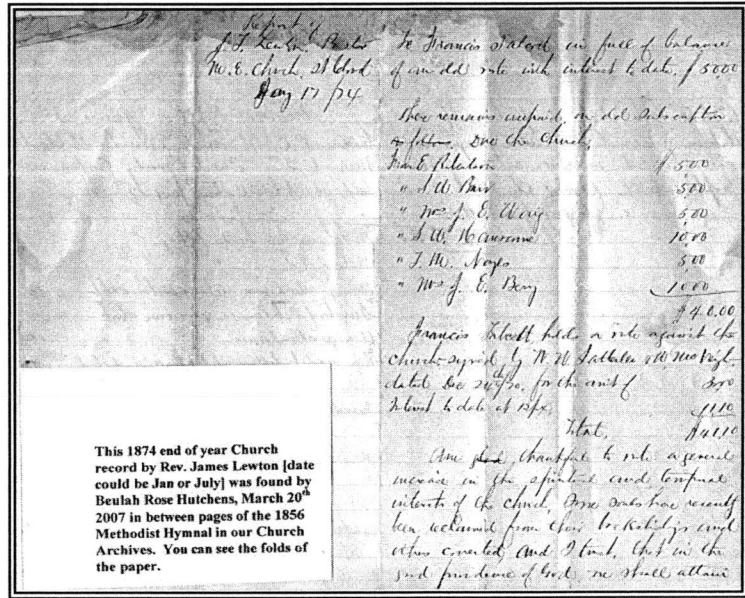

This 1874 end of year Church record by Rev. James Lewton [date could be Jan or July] was found by Beulah Rose Hutchens, March 20th 2007 in between pages of the 1856 Methodist Hymnal in our Church Archives. You can see the folds of the paper.

Lewton's page 2 of 1874 report

When Mr. Lewton came here there were 75 members and 50 scholars. When he left there were only 45 members and 55 scholars. Perhaps the building of the new church taxed the loyalty of the congregation too much.

The next pastor, the Rev. Horatio Southard Hilton, was very much discouraged almost from the beginning. He wrote in the records in the fall of 1874 that he found it almost impossible to get the Board together for a meeting. In May, 1875, he was forced to beg the officials for funds with

---

[58] (Records)

which to continue the work. In August, 1875, he wrote, "Unless the Lord send help speedily the Methodist Church must go down. It now lives by the inertia of its own spiritual stupidity."[59] There do not seem to have been very weighty matters to be discussed from 1874 to 1880. The Official Board held lengthy discussions about the church music but acknowledged that nothing was accomplished by such acts. Side walks and hitching posts were two other items of business taken care of by the Board.[60] When Rev. Hilton left there were 44 members and 65 scholars.[61]

Pew from 1873 building
First Church Archives

The Rev. J. W. [John Wesley] Klepper came in 1875 at a salary of $850 for the year with $50 for traveling expenses, and the Board's very gracious approval of his doing any outside work he could find and keeping the money for himself.[62] In December, 1875, the treasurer was authorized to make a financial statement for the second Sabbath of each month. Mrs. Marlatt was now on the Board. Several plans for systematic study of the Bible were discussed but nothing was decided upon although the Board agreed that such a course would undoubtedly be profitable as "we do not so fully as we should obey the injunction to search the Scriptures." In April the Sexton agreed to care for the church for one year for $1.00 per week, provided that the wood was furnished cut and thrown into the cellar and that he have extra pay for any extra work that he might do. The sexton's offer was accepted by the Board. The Rev. J. W. Klepper stayed only the one year and at Conference reported 32 members and 60 scholars.

John Wesley Klepper

The Conference of 1876 sent the Rev. Isaac H. Riddick to this charge and to Sauk Rapids. St. Cloud had been taken out of the St. Paul district after a year, 1872-3, and had been restored to the St. Cloud district. The pastor reported class meetings and young people's meetings and two Sunday Schools, one at St. Cloud and the other at Sauk Rapids. It is rather strange that the school at the Rapids was thriving because very early in the year the pastor

---

[59] (Church Records)
[60] (Records)
[61] (Conference Records) Conference Journals adt
[62] (Records)

gave up preaching there saying that the Sauk Rapids folks would not turn out on a week day evening and he could not give them a Sabbath appointment.[63]

That was the year that the Methodists and Congregationalists united their services. Mr. Riddick was of the opinion that St. Cloud was not strong enough to support several Protestant faiths and since the Congregationalists were without a pastor at the time he suggested through his Official Board that he serve two groups. This was accomplished in February, 1877. Both buildings were used, he preaching in one or the other church every Sunday. He tried to add the Baptist group to his combined flock but failed. His departure from St. Cloud after one year was regretted, according to the Recording Steward, Miss Mollie Ellis.[64] Our Methodist membership was not increased by this merger; however, as the Conference minutes show that there were only 32 members and 50 scholars in 1877.

The original Congregational Church, 4th St. and 5th Ave So., just south of the recently demolished Coborn grocery store. The wooden turret has since been removed and additions built on the back. During the 40's and 50's, it was home to Bethlehem Lutheran Church. In 2007 it found new life as a worship space for the growing Muslim population. jbg

The Rev. I. [Isaac] M. Marsh was sent to St. Cloud and Sauk Rapids in 1877 and St. Cloud was put back into the St. Paul district. The pastor must not have taken care of the religious needs of Sauk Rapids for in January, 1878, Mr. Hyke of that city, appeared before the Board requesting services. After a free discussion it was decided to hold evening services there until the next Quarterly Conference met. The Board voted to patronize Dr. Marlatt in buying lamps and oils.[65] Several plans for raising the pastor's salary, of $800, were discussed by the Official Board that autumn and it was finally decided to use the subscription method again but to put the entire business in the hands

---

[63] (Records)
[64] (Records) Those Congregational Church Records are in our Archives, and are documented with the 2007 office of the United Church of Christ, 122 W. Franklin Ave, Minneapolis, Minnesota.
[65] (Dr. Marlatt's store was opposite the Church at this time.)

of some one person if such a person could be found, and pay him for the work. J. E. Wing volunteered to serve and was duly elected.

James Edison Wing had come from Maine in 1863, with his family and had settled in Brockway Township, Stearns County. In 1866, he had moved to St. Cloud. From 1870 to 1871 he was in Ottertail City operating a saw mill but came back to St. Cloud in 1871, to stay. He was an active member of the St. Cloud Methodist Church. Other members of the Board at this time were T. [Thomas] J. Gray, the Sunday School Superintendent, J. E. Hayward, D. H. Freeman, and John Cooper. A word about the last two men. John Cooper came to St. Cloud from Anoka County after he had served in the Civil War. He was prominent in business, politics, and church. He married Mrs. Melinda Hayward. Both were very active in the Methodist Church. Daniel Freeman came to Minnesota in 1857 with his parents Ambrose and Jane Freeman. He did not forget the church that his father and mother had taught him to serve. He and his wife, Hortense Hayward, were both very active in the church and their home was often open to the Church meetings. Many a Church supper was served in the Daniel Freeman home on the "lap boards" that preceded the trays of today.

In August, 1878, the Superintendent of the Sunday School reported that the school was "very small but good what there was of it." At Conference that year, the pastor reported 43 members and 40 scholars but he apologized for the small number in the following manner, "There are no new people coming into town, therefore the churches are not increased by letter.[66] A few of our people have moved away leaving us the weaker." He reported that the relations were most pleasant between the Congregationalists and the Methodists. The union started by Riddick must have continued.[67] In October, 1878, the W.C.T.U.[68] was allowed to use the lecture room, Friday afternoons, for the purpose of giving temperance instruction to the children.

---

[66] letter of transfer from one class/church to another.
[67] (Records)
[68] Woman's Christian Temperance Union

METHODIST CHURCH, St. Cloud, Minn. Built in 1873. Picture taken in 1877 Remodeled in 1906. Union School in middle. Pat Kelly home at left.
DONOR: John B. Pattison

Mr. Marsh was from Nova Scotia and Salem, Massachusetts. In 1869 he came to Minnesota and served several charges before reaching St. Cloud. He was a man of fine abilities. His sermons were filled with instruction and attended with unction. He always gained the hearts of the people among whom he labored. In January, 1879, he was given a leave of absence for four months to recuperate his health. The Board tried to pay all of his salary in advance. In May, he reported back but the Board would not let him work. In spite of the absence of a pastor the debt was paid, the church was carpeted, and more hymnals purchased before Conference time. When the pastor went to Conference he was instructed to say that St. Cloud wanted a minister, again, and felt that it could pay $500. Records indicate Rev. Mr. Marsh was returned for another year. At the Conference of 1880, St. Cloud had 30 members and 40 scholars. Mr. Marsh was later sent to Richfield where he died in 1881.

In 1880, the St. Cloud Methodist Church was about as low financially, numerically, and spiritually, as it is possible for a church to be and still exist. Then came the Rev. M. O. McNiff, originally from New York. The pastors, Marsh and McNiff, differ as to the Sunday School. In 1880, Mr. McNiff wrote, "A few faithful ones have kept up the prayer meetings and the class meetings but there is no Sunday School." In January, 1881, there was a school with an attendance of 60 to 70. They were using the *Berean Lesson Leaf* and the *School Advocates* and the Teacher's Journals. The Rev. McNiff preached at Brockway and Sauk Rapids and had a class at Rice's Station. He felt that the group at Brockway needed a regular service as often as every two weeks but he felt that he could not go that often. Mrs. Marlatt was the Recording Steward. At the close of that year there were 83 members.[69]

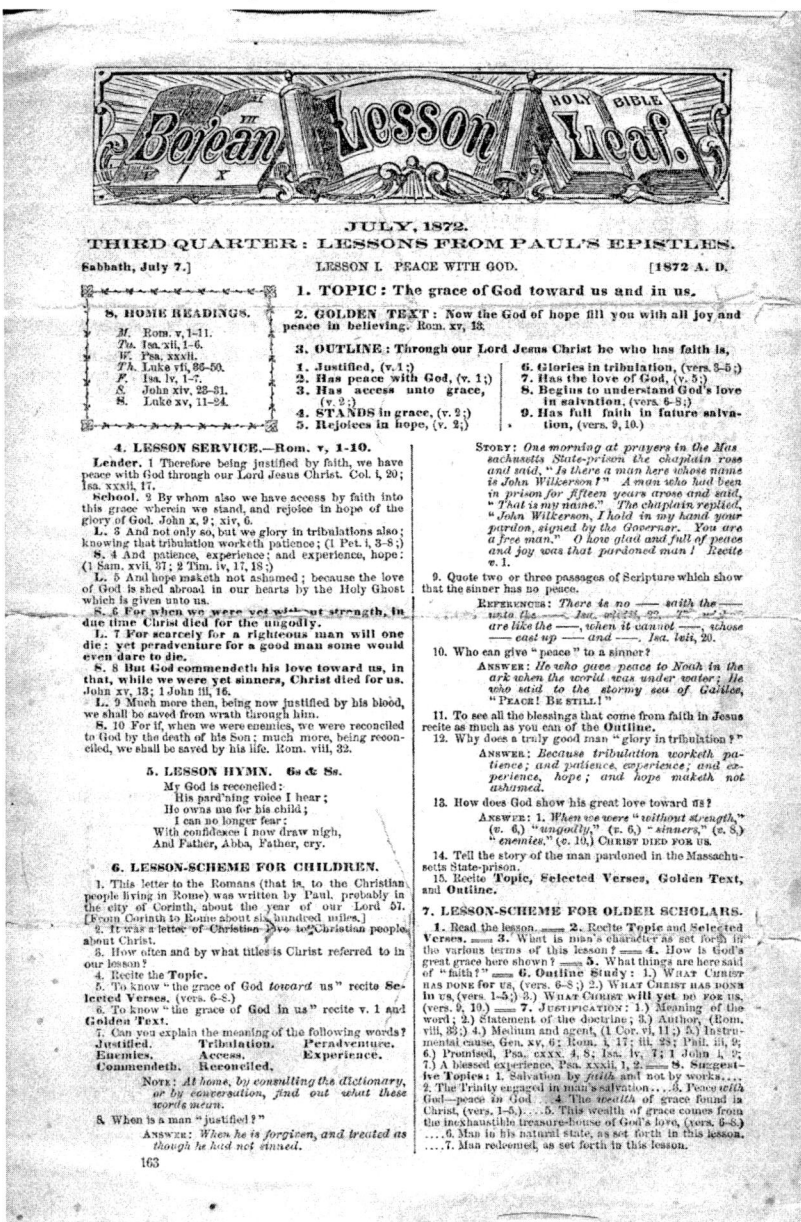

In 1881, a former Presiding Elder, the Rev. J. B. Starkey, was sent to St. Cloud as pastor. Things continued to improve. Even though the

---

[69] (Records)

membership decreased in actual numbers, the spiritual life of the congregation was much better. Mrs. Starkey, a powerful evangelistic singer, helped her husband put his sermons across.[70] A ministerial association was formed by the pastors of the Presbyterian, Baptist, Congregationalist, and Methodist churches. A. Orton was the Sunday School Superintendent. A Sunday School was organized at the Little Red Schoolhouse. Dr. Scruby (a veterinarian) was a new and very active member of the Board. It seemed as though the church had regained its morale. With its spiritual condition improved, the congregation began to improve the outward appearance. With paper and paint they renovated the building. That year there were no debts against the church. The Methodists even went into the real estate business. They sold the buildings on the rear of the church lot and also sold a lot that was owned by the church. At Conference in 1882, 46 members and 94 scholars were reported

During the years of 1882-4, under the guidance of the Pastors, Henry Frank and E. S. Ferry, the St. Cloud church increased financially and spiritually. There were 81 members and 90 scholars in 1884 and the St. Cloud Methodists had given very liberally to Hamline University.

W.M. Martin 1884-1887

Then came the years that the Rev. W. M. Martin was here. His pulpit was the red stand that later became a pedestal on the pulpit platform. (It served as a pulpit till 1890 and then was discarded. The Rev. J. A. Edwards found it in the storeroom, repaired it, and restored it to the church.) The marble top table came about that same time. The Presiding Elder reported that St. Cloud paid its pastoral support in full in those years. When Mr. Martin left after three years of service here, there were 95 members and 165 scholars.

---

[70] (Mrs. D. H. Freeman.)

The church continued to prosper during the time that the Rev. J. W. Briggs was here. In 1888 there were 114 members and 144 scholars and a year later there were 123 members and 125 scholars. Early in the year Pastor Briggs was compelled to leave, due to ill health, but the work was continued with the help of the Rev. H. S. Brace, a supernumerary[71] of the Central Illinois Conference.

PERIOD FOUR - - 1889 - 1896

In 1889, St. Cloud Methodist Church began another period in its history. The Rev. R. [Robert] R. Atchison came as pastor that year. Again the Methodists aroused themselves. The church building was remodeled, repewed, repainted (a cream color) and generally beautified at a cost of $1,222. The Presiding Elder said that it was a model of neatness and good taste and due to the persistent efforts of the pastor every dollar was paid before Conference time. Mrs. Bert Miller and Miss Blanche Gray (a cousin of the Haywards) gave the walnut pulpit. The Ladies Aid gave the pulpit chairs. Dr. and Mrs. Scruby gave the pews.[72] Mr. and Mrs. Harrison gave the folding chairs which were at first used in the class room and later used only for very large congregations. A large organ was purchased by subscription. The windows were changed and made larger and colored glass was put in due to the generosity of Mrs. S. Marlatt and daughter, Mrs. John Cooper, Mrs. Millie Akers and daughter and others. Miss Mollie Ellis gave the folding door between the class room and audience hall. A word about Mrs. Akers.

She and her husband, the Rev. J. M. Akers, came to St. Cloud from Pennsylvania, in 1869, in search of health for the husband. He evidently regained his health, because the next year he began preaching in Minnesota. He died in St. Charles in 1889, due to a nervous strain brought on by a powerful revival which he had conducted. His wife and daughter, Nannie, came back to St. Cloud to live near Mrs. Akers' sisters, Miss Ellis and Mrs. Bowing. All of these women were very active members of the St. Cloud Methodist Church.

---

[71] retiree
[72] (They are down in the Gymnasium, but where is the pulpit?)

The Sauk Rapids church had been closed for four years. The building had been damaged by the cyclone and the membership had become scattered and discouraged. In February, 1890, the Presiding Elder found a young man with grace and grit who was willing to go there and take his chances. He found that Mr. Atchison and his wife were willing to help him and even said that he should share with them until he got started. As a result the Sauk Rapids members were gathered together and reorganized and new ones were added. A flourishing Sunday School was started, a live prayer meeting was formed, and the church building was reshingled and repainted outside and in.

Meanwhile, even before 1889, out in the western part of St. Cloud, near the Osseo Tracks and along Breckenridge Avenue, a group of folks had become so interested in the work of the Church that they had rented the upstairs of the Stiles Artificial Stone Works (Concrete blocks) and held services there. Mrs. Stiles was a sister of H. A. Daniels, a prominent worker in First Church. The women of that community gave many suppers at 25c per plate to the Railroad men and the young people raised money by holding ice cream socials at which home made ice cream was used. A Sunday School and Ladies' Aid Society were formed and both thrived. A student preacher named Gaylord assisted them, as did Mr. Stiles. Mrs. F. K. Whitney lived out there for a time and taught in the Sunday School. After the family moved out near the Reformatory she still taught her primary class out in the West End, driving the six miles with a horse and buggy. There was an actual Church roll of members and it was a separate congregation in every way. The Conference recognized their enthusiasm by calling them the Second Church of St. Cloud and by donating $50 to them, and by sending them a pastor named D. S. Wigstead who was to take care of the Sauk Rapids work also. That year money was raised; a lot was purchased; and rocks were hauled for a foundation.

But the enthusiasm died down when, in 1891-2, their pastor, the Rev. A. W. Taylor, was called from them to serve at Browns Valley and the First Church pastor could not give them the attention they needed. The Rev. J. [James] H. Dewart transferred the members to the First Church and the Sunday School was kept more or less half heartedly until it died out. And so Second Church and its church building vanished into thin air. A Church of God evangelist came along later, and gathered up the religious fervour that was lying dormant and formed the Church of God congregation. The Conference Records tell the tragic story very graphically. In 1890 First

Church had 123 members and 170 scholars. Second Church had a Sunday School of 90 members. The next year, First Church reported 123 members and two Sunday Schools of 180 scholars and Second Church reported 24 members and 90 scholars. Sauk Rapids did not report. In 1892, First Church had 148 members and 196 scholars.

In 1891, the Rev. J. H. Dewart was sent to First Church, St. Cloud, which was then in the Fergus Falls district.[73] He was left with all the work at First and Second churches and at Sauk Rapids, as has been said, and was not able to do it all. West End suffered. The next year the conference gave Dr. Dewart just St. Cloud First Church and sent a supply to St. Cloud Mission, as Second Church was now called. Sauk Rapids was kept in the Duluth district and given to still another pastor. The five years of Dr. Dewart's stay in St. Cloud mark a period of very great spiritual prosperity for the St. Cloud Methodist Church. Perhaps the fact that he was allowed to stay here a longer time than had been the custom may account for this growth. Religious development of an individual or a group is dependent upon time.

Dr. Dewart was an excellent preacher and lecturer. His individuality coupled with analytical power brought him to conclusions notable for their  originality. Such convictions he set forth with a clearness which rendered him especially convincing as a preacher. His sermons were always centered around the application of the gospel more than upon the gospel itself. The result was that his teachings appealed to a class not often found within Church walls. He believed in a church which helped a person to live a better physical, mental, and moral life. Dr. Dewart had unusual success as a lecturer at the Reformatory. He was also a great believer in young people so he organized what he called the "Twilight Club," a society for neither the old nor very young. He was especially anxious to help the Normal School students of Methodist faith. He probably was seeking to do what the Wesley Foundation is trying to do today. Mrs. Freeman tells of entertaining the club, one hundred strong, at her home for suppers. She said that a certain play, "The Temple of Fame," won fame for that group and Dr. Dewart.

---

[73] (Sauk Rapids was in the Duluth district.) According to Conference Journals, St. Cloud was in the Minneapolis District.

The electric fixtures were put in during the pastorate of Dr. Dewart. A small organ was purchased, second hand, at a cost of $25. The Junior League gave a Pulpit Bible. Mr. George Crosby[74] was Sunday School Superintendent for several years in this period 1893-1900.

In 1894 the pastor reported 150 members and 275 scholars in three Sunday Schools. (Where were those three schools?) The Sauk Rapids pastor reported 26 members and 50 scholars. That year, 1894, St. Cloud was put back into St. Cloud District. In 1896, Pastor Dewart reported 118 members and two Sunday Schools of 230 scholars. (Dr. Dewart died in North Dakota, October 6, 1922, and the funeral was in charge of his life-long friend, Dr. G. H. Bridgeman, president Emeritus of Hamline University.)[75]

PERIOD FIVE - - 1896 - 1909

The Conference of 1896 sent the Reverend Lyman W. Ray[76] to St. Cloud and a supply to St. Cloud Mission. Mr. Ray stayed till March, 1898, when he resigned. His salary was $800 including house rent. At Conference of 1897, he reported 140 members and 230 scholars. There was also a Senior Christian Endeavor of 60 members and a Junior organization of 30 members. The Reverend F. E. Ross came in May, 1898, having been transferred from Moorhead. At the close of that year, St. Cloud had 168 members and 160 scholars.

In 1897 or 1898, a committee was appointed to raise the money and erect a parsonage but as far as we know there was no parsonage built until 1915.

Prominent church officials of this period were: D. H. Freeman, John Cooper, J. F. Stevenson, John Shaefer, George C. Hubbard, B. B. James, George Crosby, D. N. Taylor, M. L. Glaser, Mrs. Millie Akers, Miss Mollie Ellis, Mrs. L. A. Marlatt, E. D. Harland, Ed. Hammond, Dr. A. D. Whiting, Mrs. F. K. Whitney, E. A. Garlington, John Isely, Mrs. W. S. Hamilton, Miss M. L. Hill. The Christian Endeavor officers were: Flora Joslin, Blanche Bethel, May Davis, Agnes Ashley.

---

[74] Along with being the Church Historian, his scrapbook with the list of memorials is in our Archives, and a lot of information in Gertrude's writings were taken from this scrapbook. He owned a furniture store in St. Cloud before moving to Paynesville, Minnesota. SHM information.
[75] (Conference Records, 1923)
[76] Rev. Ray never signed the Church record book, he used a stamp with red ink. - adt

The climax of Mr. Ross' work came in July, 1900. The church building had been closed for a complete renovating. Special subscriptions managed by the Ladies' Aid met this bill. The exterior of the church was painted again, this time a drab green. It was reshingled for the first time since it was built in 1873. The interior was papered a neat shade of terra-cotta and the walls were stenciled with a heavy figured border in gilt and brown. The ceiling was divided into four large panels with border and scroll figures in the center of each. The entire effect was decidedly good and with other improvements such as painting, repairing, etc., the structure was vastly improved in appearance.

Then it was formally reopened by Bishop Isaac Joyce who preached in the morning in the Church and lectured on China in the evening in the Davidson Theatre. The Bishop was a man of striking personality, intense

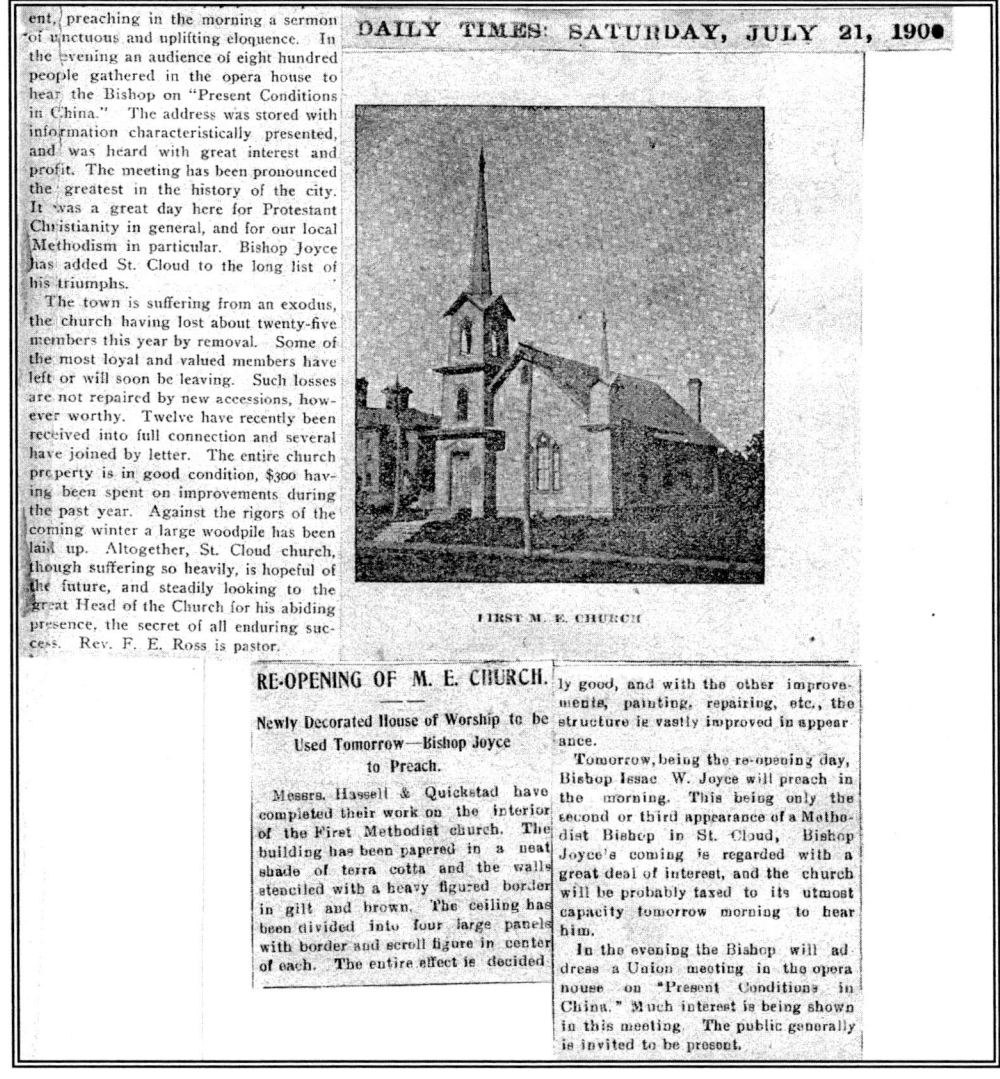

earnestness and tremendous energy. He had traveled extensively throughout the Far East so was very able to lecture on the subject. The St. Cloud papers of that time seemed to feel that this meeting was a very great one for St. Cloud Protestantism, in general, and St. Cloud Methodism, in particular. The Bishop was the International President of the Epworth League.[77] His presence in the city may account for the formation of the Joyce Chapter of the Epworth League in 1901.

The pastor wrote of the work at St. Cloud, thus "The town is suffering from an exodus, the church having lost about twenty-five members this year by removals. Some of the most loyal and valued members have left or will soon be leaving. Such losses cannot be repaired by new accessions, however worthy. Twelve have recently been received into full connection and several have joined by letter. The entire church property is in good condition, $300 having been spent on improvements during the year. Against the rigors of the coming winter a large wood pile has been laid up. St. Cloud Church, although suffering so heavily, is hopeful of the future and steadily looking forward to the Great Head of the church for His abiding presence, the secret of all enduring success." F. E. Ross.

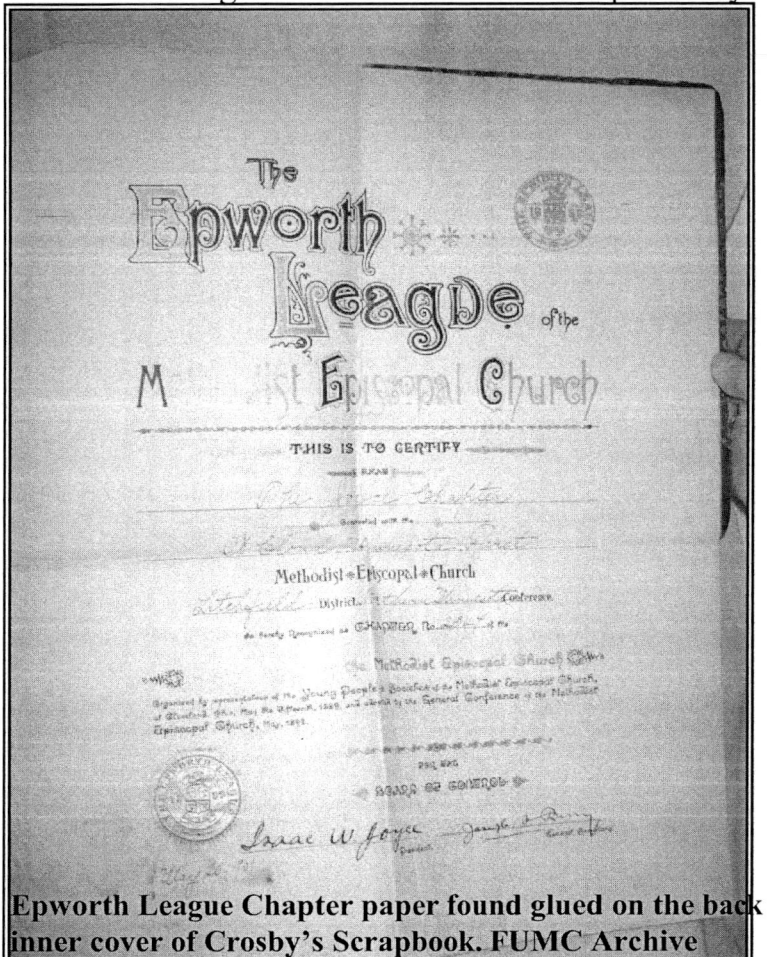

Epworth League Chapter paper found glued on the back inner cover of Crosby's Scrapbook. FUMC Archive

About 1900 the St. Cloud district was

---

[77] Epworth League was the youth organization of the Methodist Episcopal Church, a forerunner of the Methodist Youth Fellowship. adt.

renamed the Litchfield district. Did that mean that the Conference felt that the Litchfield congregation was doing bigger and better things than was the St. Cloud group? It is up to us to bring about a change of names again, in our favor.

The Conference Minutes from 1899 to 1904 were not read so we cannot give the number of members and scholars for those years. A preacher by the name of Charles W. Lawson was here after Mr. Ross left. The church was again painted and decorated and hard floors laid, the Ladies' Aid standing the expenses. A new organ was obtained.

In 1904, the Reverend Charles Wilbur Stark was sent to St. Cloud and remained here until June, 1906, when he left for a work that he was especially fitted for, the Anti-Saloon League work. He worked to compel the saloons to close at midnight Saturday night and stay closed all day Sunday. It was the law at that time but was not being obeyed. His success in St. Cloud made him famous and a large share of the credit of "putting the lid on" in Minnesota is due to the persistence and pluck of the Reverend Mr. Stark. No doubt he, at that time, was doing a very daring thing when he mixed his religion with politics.

Charles W. Stark

When Mr. Stark left, L. B. Schei, a graduate of Hamline University, was a supply here for the remainder of the year. When Mr. Stark came here, there were 133 members and 175 scholars and 16 Epworth Leaguers. At the close of his first year, there were 135 members and 160 scholars. At the close of his second year, he reported 180 members, 165 scholars and 145 Leaguers. Mr. Schei reported at the close of the year he finished, 171 members, 85 scholars and 34 Leaguers.

It was about this time that a very interesting coincidence occurred. Mr. James Binnie was the assistant Sunday School superintendent, his wife was a great worker in the Ladies' Aid Society, his son, Ernest, was president of the Epworth League and sang in the choir. His daughter, later the wife of J. E. Magnuson, taught a Sunday School class, his daughter, Bertha, later Mrs. Howard Leopard, was secretary of the Epworth League and pianist of the League and Sunday School. Miss Zelah Harland, later the wife of Ernest Binnie, was a League and Sunday School worker, Mr. Harland was the Sunday School superintendent, Mrs. Harland was a worker in the Ladies' Aid Society, Howard Leopard played in the Sunday School orchestra, Brant Leopard "did all the talking" in the Epworth League, Mrs. Leopard was the President of the Ladies' Aid Society, and Mr. Leopard was the fun maker at all the parties. Thus one church has done much to bring three families very intimately together.

Only evidence found of Schei being here. adt

The Reverend T. Stanley Oadams, was sent here in 1907 and stayed two years. When he went to Conference in 1909, he reported 185 members, 154 scholars and 80 Leaguers. One of the most interesting events of the church was the Colonial Banquet held in February. The custom began with a colonial social. The first one found on record took place in 1908 at the H. G. Smart home. It was usually a money making affair as well as a lovely party. Mrs. Oadams was a member of the Ladies' Aid that year. Other members were Mrs. Millie Ahers, Miss Addie Clark, Mrs. W. N. Bethel, Mrs. E. D. Hammond, Mrs. Wm Fasholt, Mrs. Ed. Harland (Mrs. Ernest Binnie's mother), Mrs. Shaefer, Mrs. E. Von Levern, Mrs. Margaret McKelvy, and Mrs. S. Marlatt.

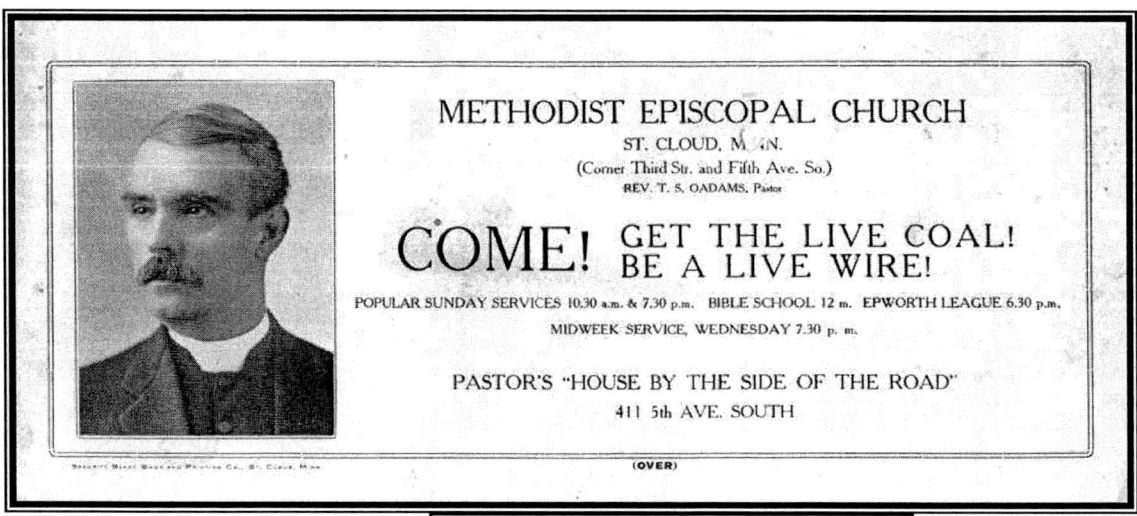

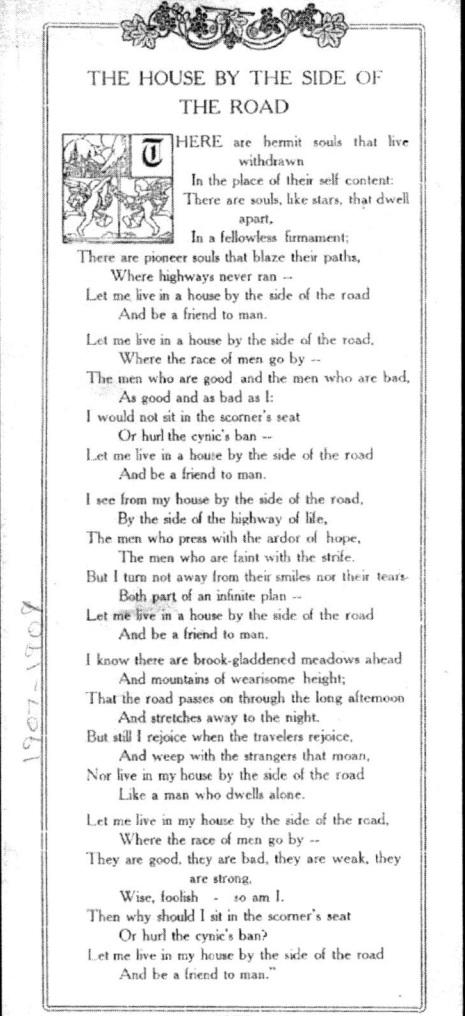

The back of the above advertisement.

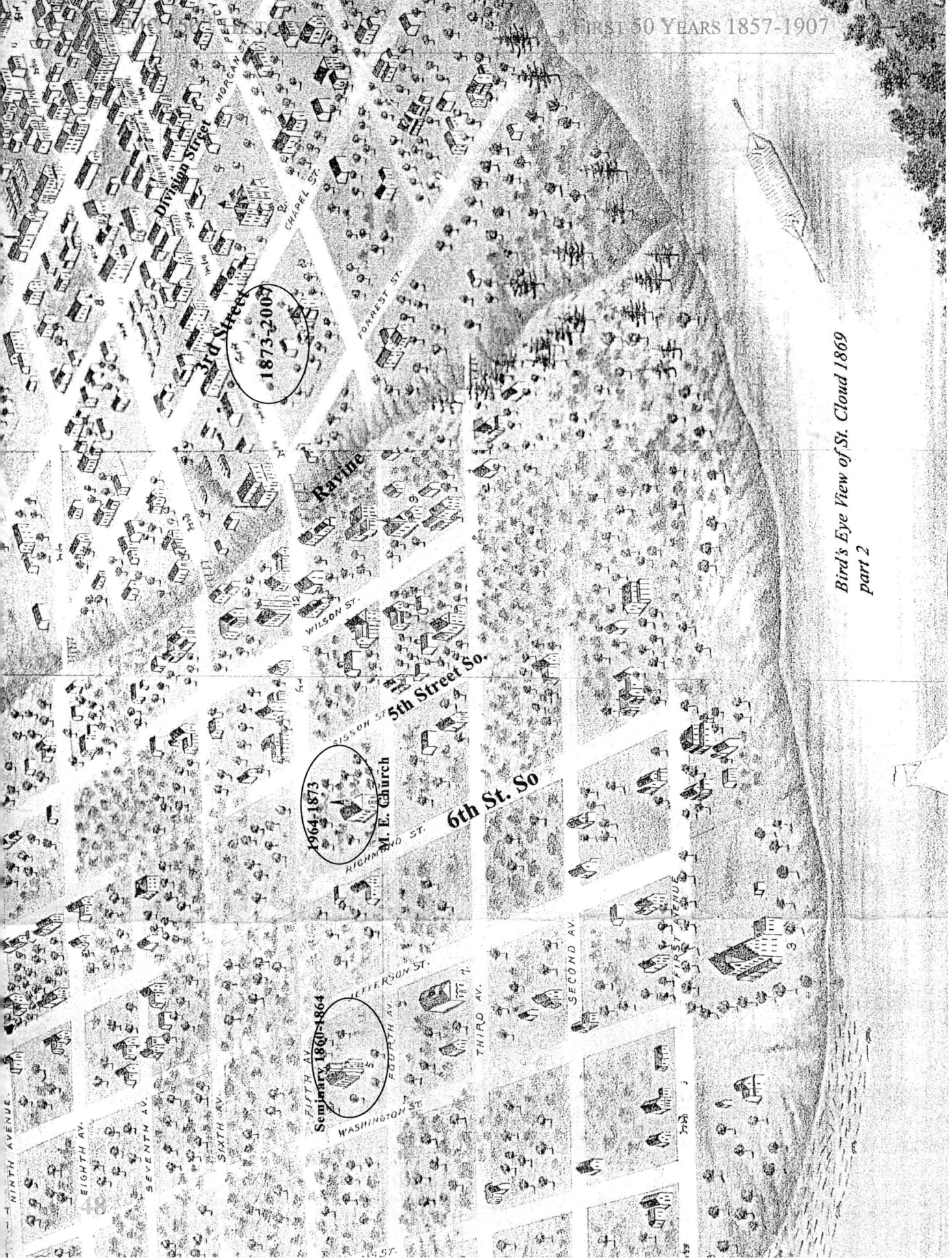

Bird's Eye View of St. Cloud 1869 part 2

Growing our Legacy in Christ

150 years
1857-2007

The Second 50 Years 1907-1957

Gertrude Gove

First United Methodist Church

St. Cloud, Minnesota

During the second 50 years ...

1908 First Model-T's are built.

1910 Church work begins in Waite Park; First Church plans new building with space for community gymnasium.

1911 Second building relocated on the block; new church built on the corner beside the old.

1914 WWI begins. A membership class is organized in Waite Park. New space dedicated when half the building debt has been paid.

1915 Salary for choir director is $4.00; pianist and custodian each $1.

1916 Parsonage and garage built on a lot just south of the church.

1918 Armistice ends WWI; Locally, flu takes lives of 72 in last 10 days of October.

1919 Waite Park Methodist Church lays its cornerstone. Women's Suffrage and Prohibition become law.

1920 First Methodist invites Hamline University to locate in St. Cloud.

1925 Blue Cross Society formed for young women; Ladies Aid has three active circles.

1928 Two seven-passenger cars hired to bring Sunday school students from outlying parts of the city.

1929 The stock market collapses; First Methodist grows.

1930 Sauk Rapids Methodists share pastor and some programs with First Church.

1933 Bank run has President closing U.S. banks for 3 days. 75th Anniversary celebrated in February. Balcony added to accommodate growing membership.

1938 Tensions increase between Germany and the U.S. 1914 building undergoes renovation.

1940 Armistice Day blizzard leaves 27" of snow at Collegeville.

1941 Pearl Harbor bombed; US declares war.

1943 Polio epidemic causes ban on large gatherings in state. Mortgage burned for the 1914 structure.

1944 Cost of living in U.S. rises nearly 30%.

1947 First Church has 90th Anniversary celebration, marked by a 33-page history by Gertrude Gove.

1948 First Methodist Church founds local Good Will Industries.

1950 Congregation votes to build a new sanctuary.

1952 Eisenhower and Stevenson both make campaign stops in St. Cloud.

1954 Contracts let for the new building; cornerstone is laid.

1956 Fourth building opens for use. Early centennial observances are begun, the old building raze

Second 50 years

PERIOD SIX - - 1907[78] - 1917

The Sixth period of St. Cloud Methodist history begins with the coming of the Rev. Frederick William Hill. When he came, there were 165 members on the roll. Before the year was up, the Congregation could see that there would be need for a larger building in the near future. The Conference records show that St. Cloud Methodist Church did grow rapidly in the years that Hill was the pastor. In 1911, there were 270 members and 275 scholars. Two years later there were 277 members, 441 scholars, and 45 Epworth Leaguers.

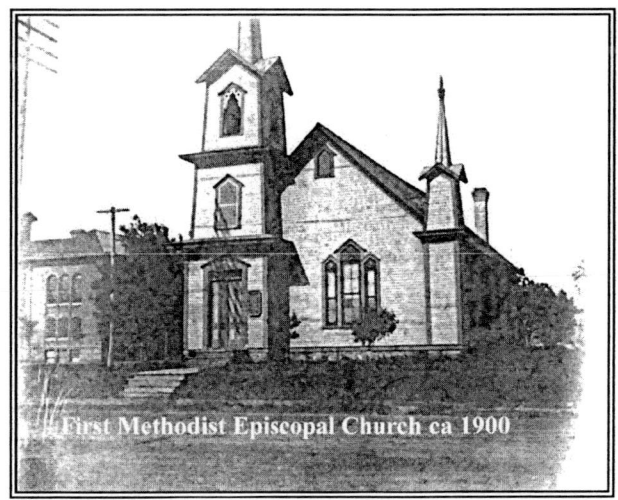
First Methodist Episcopal Church ca 1900

Early in 1910, the Society began to lay plans for the erection of a new church. In April, the first subscription was circulated. That spring, the Ladies' Aid Society purchased the lot next to the one on which the church was standing, 302 Fifth Avenue South. (The Official Board bought the lots on which the parsonage stands, later.) The Ladies' Aid Society also voted to raise $1000 toward the new church and parsonage. (They already had $246.37 in a fund for such a purpose.) Plans and specifications were obtained and then the opposition began. Some members did not want to use the old building in forming the new. Others did not want to build at all. Still others did not want to build as extensively as was planned. Many could not see that a church, to really serve humanity, must serve every day in the week and in more ways than by sermons and songs only. But eventually the disagreements were ended and the work was begun the next year, 1911. The District Superintendent, E. H. Nicholson, said at the Conference of 1911, "St. Cloud is building an up-to-date institutional church building with everything that will make it a religious and social center for the community. Good subscriptions to

---

[78] Editor Note: We divided sections by 50 years, which did not follow Gove's writings, so we will start with 1909. adt.

the amount of over $20,000 have been secured and a church that will be a credit to Methodism will soon be in operation."[79]

And so the Twentieth Century Institutional Church was begun. The old building was used as it was moved back on the same lot and faced north. The Epworth League room of the old was made into the Ladies Parlor of the new. The auditorium of the old became the chapel of the new. The architecture is of the Gothic type. The famous St. Cloud granite was used for the first floor wall and the second was made of cream color brick with red bricks for trimmings. The corner stone was donated by the Holes Brothers and the capstone of the gymnasium was given by Mr. Lilliquist. The first floor or basement contains a gymnasium and accessories. The second floor consists

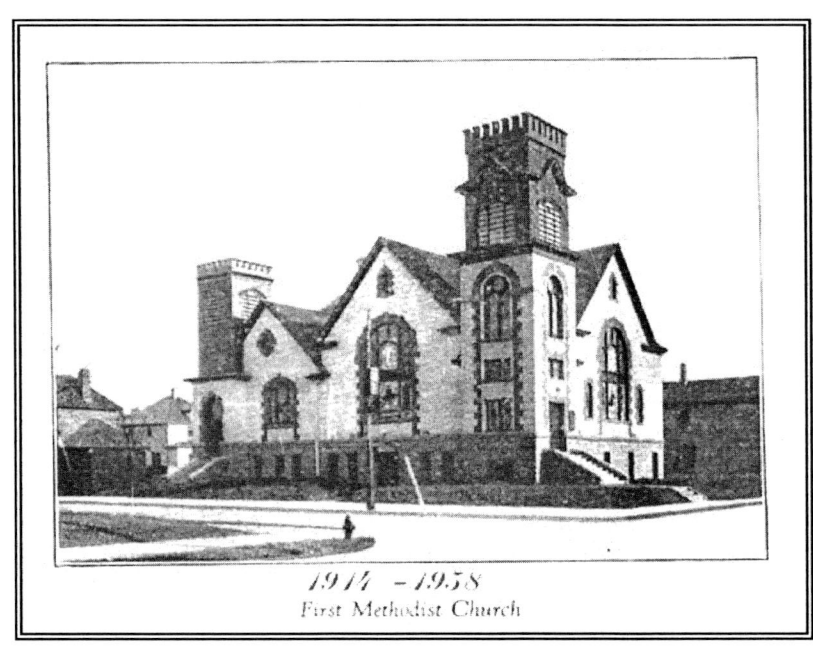

1914 - 1958
First Methodist Church

of a Ladies Parlor and a chapel, later called the reading room, social room, and Epworth League room, and the auditorium. Sliding doors separate the old and new parts of the church and can be raised or lowered as occasion demands. This edifice cost the congregation, which had a membership at that time of between 270 and 300, $18,000. The general contractor of the building was Henry P. Steckling. The stone work was done by W. J. Murphy and Charles Lease. F. H. Dam was superintendent of the construction. Arthur Hussey, whose father was an early Church member, did the interior decorating. The building committee was: H. G. Smart, Chairman E. D. Hammond, W. N. Bethel, Arthur Cooper, L. L. Erickson, the treasurer of the building fund. The Official Board at that time was made up of the following: L. C. Brown, H. G. Smart, J. W. Campbell, Dr. A. D. Whiting, W. N. Varner, Bert Bowing, H. A. Daniels, F. K. Whitney, William Fasholt, J. E. Barr, Dr. J. M. Farnham, Ed Harland, E. D. Hammond, M. J. Cleveland,

---

[79] (Conference Record)

W. H. Leopard, W. N. Bethel, John Jenson, Arthur Cooper and
L. L. Erickson.

The cornerstone was laid September 10, 1911, four hundred persons witnessing this impressive ceremony. Dr. E. H. Nicholson, the District Superintendent, assisted by Dr. E. A. Cook, pastor at Renville, a substitute for Dr. George H. Bridgeman, president of Hamline University, who could not be present due to illness, the local clergymen of the various churches, the building committee and the men in charge of the construction sealed within the granite walls a metal box containing a Bible, a copy of the last Conference minutes, a copy, each, of the *Northwestern Christian Advocate*, *The Epworth Herald*. The *St. Cloud Daily Times* and *The St. Cloud Journal Press* and a list of the persons who by their donations were making the church a possibility.[80]

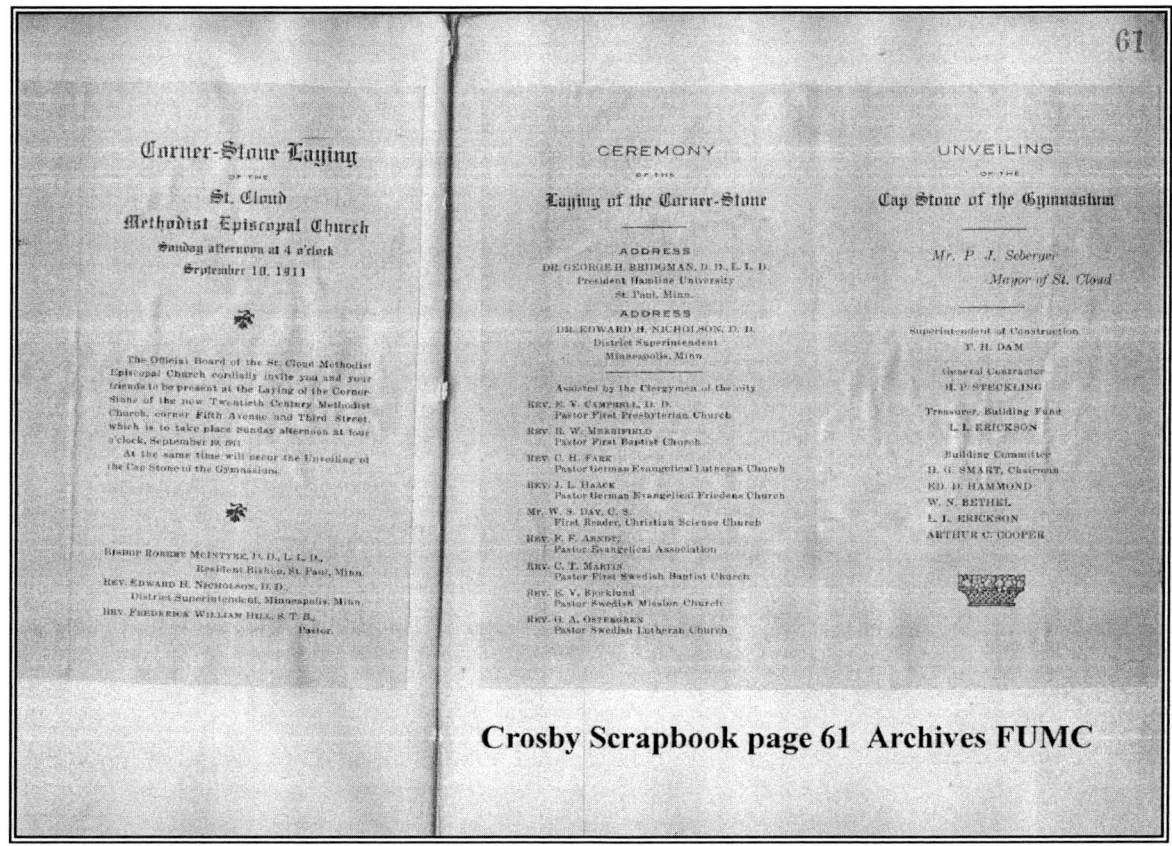

Crosby Scrapbook page 61 Archives FUMC

Then came the unveiling of the capstone of the Twentieth Century Institutional Church by Mayor P. J. Seberger. As the Methodists desired to

---

[80] The remains are in the vault of the current church building. They did not survive in any readable condition when it was opened in 1956. See picture p 93. -adt

serve the community-at-large through the gymnasium, it was very fitting that the first officer of the city should officiate at this service. (The plan of the 1911 Methodists has not been worked out exactly as they wished it to be, but groups interested in athletics are using it for basket and volley ball. The Sunday school uses it for class rooms, the church suppers are served in that part of the building and some of the Camp Fire and Boy Scout organizations meet there.)[81]

The old building was used for services all of the time between the spring of 1911 and the fall of 1912, except for about four Sundays when the Methodists met in the Baptist Church due to that Congregation's generosity. The new building was occupied by November 1912, even though the interior decorating had not been done and the pipe organ had not yet been installed, said the *St. Cloud Daily Journal Press* of that date.

On May 23, 1914, occurred the dedication services. At 9 A.M., the Official Board, the Ladies' Aid Officers, and the Sabbath School Officers met with Bishop Quayle. At 10 A.M., the morning service was held in the presence of a large congregation, which filled the auditorium and the chapel. A choir of some thirty voices under the direction of Mrs. J. A. Porter rendered beautiful music. Miss Claire Wilson was the organist. After the sermon by the Bishop an attempt was made to cancel all the debt. The church had cost $24,000 and all but $7600 had been paid. The Bishop raised $5,333 in about forty minutes. Then the Building Committee with H. G. Smart, as chairman, presented the edifice to the Bishop.[82] The doxology and benediction closed this very important service.

---

[81] p 18, 1947 History Book
[82] Today's custom is to consecrate a church building before the debt is paid, and dedication of the building is when the debt is fully paid. adt

In the afternoon a special service was held by and for the Sunday school. Mrs. William Morris was the Superintendent. The Rev. James Geer, a classmate of the pastor, and a former Superintendent, L. L. Erickson, were the speakers. Dorothy Steward, a daughter of Mr. and Mrs. Darius Steward, recited "Our Dedication," and a girls' chorus with Miss Ruth Allen as soloist, sang several numbers.

The seven o'clock Service was the Epworth League's hour. Miss Anna Holmberg (Mrs. Kurt Stai) was in charge. A former pastor, the Rev. Mr. Stanley Oadams, was the chief speaker. The evening service was opened by prayer by a former pastor, the Rev. Charles W. Stark. Nathaniel Quickstad did the solo work. Dr. W. H. Jorden, the District Superintendent, preached the sermon. Miss Marie Kothman was the organist, and Miss Bessie Fasholt was the musical director.

On the west and north walls of this sanctuary were two large stained glass windows picturing "Christ in the Garden of Gethsemane" by Hoffman and "Christ, the Good Shepherd" by Plockhorst.[83] There are four rose windows on the south wall. Only three have survived to this date: 22 April 2007. adt.

The *St. Cloud Daily Journal Press* of November 1914, gave the credit for the enterprise to the intelligent and harmonious and enthusiastic cooperation of the Official Board and especially to the Building Committee. The District Superintendent reminded the pastor and congregation that theirs was a great responsibility: "St. Cloud is the most strategic center on the district because it is located at the seat of the Normal School. With right vision and true enterprise this church may well become one of the most important in the Conference."[84]

But the church building was not the only achievement of the St. Cloud First Church during the pastorate of

---

[83] p 7 of the 1958 History Book
[84] W. J. Jordan, Conference Minutes, 1914

Rev. Hill. In every department of the Church's work, there was an increased interest in the work of the kingdom. The Sunday school, under the leadership of L. L. Erickson and Mrs. Morris, continued to increase in numbers as the Conference records show. The spiritual condition of the school was good, also.

Mr. Erickson went over to Sauk Rapids and stirred up a thriving school there. He, or some one, found a Polish local preacher by the name of Silco, who formed a class of Polish Methodists in Sauk Rapids. In 1914, when the Rev. A. F. Oliver was sent by Conference to Sauk Rapids, the membership jumped from a mere handful to about 110.

A class out in Waite Park (which was yet a suburb of St. Cloud) was beginning to plan for a church building, John Bensen having donated two lots. F. A. Ward, John Bensen, and Arthur Cooper were appointed by the pastor to act as a Board of Trustees for the Waite Park Methodists.

On March 27, 1913, Mrs. Lindsay of the Minneapolis Branch of the Woman's Foreign Missionary Society was present at the Ladies' Aid meeting of the First Methodist Episcopal Church and organized a Missionary society here, with the following officers: President, Miss Mary A. Ellis; Vice President Miss Addie Clark; Corresponding Secretary, Mrs. M. J. Cleveland; Recording Secretary, Mrs. S. M. Gilleland; Treasurer, Mrs. C. F. Wonder. Mrs. F. W. Hill was elected chairman of the program committee with Mrs. C. S. West, and Mrs. J. J. Newton her assistants. The first regular meeting of the Society was held April 3, 1913. By October 1914, the society had raised $183.32 for Missions.

Miss Ellis, the first president, was very active in the work. She had been a teacher in Pennsylvania before coming out to Minnesota to be near her sisters, Mrs. J. M. Akers and Mrs. J. M. Stevenson (the second wife of Mr. Stevenson). From reading the Church records we are sure she gave liberally of her education and talents to further education in St. Cloud. Now in 1913, she began to organize the children and young people into societies for the purpose of teaching them more about Missions. These classes were named the Little Light Bearers, the King's Heralds, and the Standard Bearers.

On May 23, 1915, the first anniversary of the erection and dedication of the Twentieth Century Institutional Church was observed with appropriate services. Dr. Jordan, the District Superintendent, was the speaker of Sunday morning. Mrs. Porter and the Misses Bessie and Maud Fasholt furnished the music that day. The Sunday school at this time was in charge of Mr. Irwin J. Orton. The Epworth League meeting was led by Miss Agnes Cooper. The evening service was a time of baptism and reception of new members, most of whom were members of the catechism class.

In 1910, First Church became the owner of several lots in Syndicate Addition, James F. Stevenson deeding lots 17 and 18 in block 3 on June 23, 1910, and Mary A. Ellis deeding lots 17 and 18 in block 1. On May 24, 1910, the Church purchased lot 2 in block G in Wilson's Addition, from Arthur E. Morgan, the consideration being $750.00. (Ellis gift was sold in 1919).

In 1915, Mr. Hill felt that he had accomplished all that he could in St. Cloud so asked that a new minister be found. William Chappell Lee of the Minnesota Conference was sent to St. Cloud by the Conference of 1915. An attempt was made to pay off the entire debt but it could not be done as a parsonage was wanted. In November 1915, the Board voted to sell some of the outside lots that the church owned. In June 1916, an undivided half of three lots in block 87, Lowry Addition, was sold for $462.50. By July 1916, $2,304 had been raised to build a parsonage. The building committee for the parsonage was A. C. Cooper, G. S. Smart, John Mattseon and J. W. Campbell. In August 1916, the North Twenty Feet of lot 3 in block G in Wilson's Survey were purchased from C. L. Atwood for $975.00. Meanwhile a subscription list had been circulated and a building committee appointed.[85]

The erection of the parsonage was the greatest piece of work done by the St. Cloud Methodists in 1915-1917 but mention of other things belongs here. Miss Bessie Fasholt led the choir for $4.00 and Miss Zim was pianist for $1.00. The janitor was receiving $1.00 per Sunday for two fires and $.75 for one, also $.50 for a mid week fire. His duties were minutely given. He must tend fires, straighten chairs before services, sweep the building, clear the sidewalks of snow and ice, and use sand or ashes on the steps to prevent accidents. The St. Cloud School Board had rented the church (all but the auditorium) for class rooms and later for athletic purposes.

---

[85] (The Conference Records speak of it as a fine brick building. Why, then, is it stucco, today?) p 19, 1947 History Book

When the Rev. Mr. Lee left St. Cloud there were 270 members, 310 scholars, and 65 Epworth Leaguers on the roll. Sauk Rapids was under the leadership of the Rev. F. J. Bryan, had 38 members and 83 scholars. In a year or so, Mr. Lee was made Superintendent of the Litchfield District, so he came to St. Cloud at least four times a year.

Rev. Wm. C. Lee and family 1915-1917 in their first automobile, background 3 McKelvy sisters. Lees lived with the McKelvys (city directory).

Archives, FUMC, St. Cloud
scanned Mar 2007

PERIOD SEVEN - - 1917 – 1930

Period Seven is what we might call a boom period for the St. Cloud Methodist Church. The events center on the Rev. George E. Tindall who was sent here by the Conference of 1917 and who stayed until the Conference of 1923. World War I days were winding down. His chief emphasis was laid upon evangelism. Class meetings were still being held at First Church; prayer meetings had not yet been given up; family altars were stressed; and revival meetings with the Baptist Church were a part of every year's program. Mr. Tindall's pastorate was also characterized by a general systematizing of the

Church work. Old debts were paid off and new bills were met as they came. On debt paying day, the entire indebtedness ($6,500) was met, the mortgage burned, and over $8,000 pledged on the Centenary (Methodist World Missionary project). A religious census undertaken by the Ministerial Association revealed 1026 persons

A.D. 1911 GYMNASIUM
In Current Garden, 2007 from 1912 building

who showed a preference for the Methodist Church.[86] Many more or less minor details were taken care of in true "methodical" manner. The church bulletin board was repainted; the inside front doorway steps, the steps from the auditorium to the waiting room, and the steps to the choir room were made over; the push ball table, which was not useful in the gymnasium, was sold; the "reading room of the Church was very comfortably fixed up by the Teacher Training Class"; a stereopticon lantern[87] and curtain were purchased; and improvements to the extent of $1800 were made in preparation for the Conference, which was to be entertained by the St. Cloud Methodists.

St. Cloud First Church attempted and carried out great things in those years. The Board of 1917 included George W. Clark, Ernest Binnie, Mrs. A. C. Cooper, Mrs. Charles West, Mrs. H. G. Smart, Miss Mary A. Ellis, Arthur C. Cooper, H. G. Smart, Mr. J. A. Matteson, J. E. Barr, Dr. J. M. Farnham, William Varner, F. A. Ward, J. W. Campbell, William Morris, J. Ed. Magnuson, M. J. Cleveland, Mr. Hoyt, H. H. Andrus, James Binnie, E. D. Hammond. The December 1920 Board included a few new persons: Charles Cater, J. E. Pramann, Charles Barr, G. E. Talbert, and Francis Lichtenberger. In April 1921, Rolla Sprague, Mrs. H. E. Hanson, and Mr. Irving B. Hoover were members. A year later, 1922, Charles Quinn's name was on the roll of Board Members.

On May 18, 19, and 20 of the year 1919, St. Cloud First Church celebrated the sixty-second anniversary of its founding. The Sabbath School "went over the top" in attendance and in benevolence. At the dedication of the church in 1912, the School had pledged $500. A special collection brought in $192, which took care of the $158 still due on the pledge. New hymn books entitled "Awakening Songs" were donated by the "St. Cloud Sammies," a class of boys taught by Miss Jennie Watt. At the morning service Judge M. C. Tifft, the Executive Chairman of the St. Paul area of the Methodist Centenary, gave an address entitled, "A Layman's Message on Stewardship." In the afternoon the laying of the cornerstone of the Waite Park Methodist church occurred.[88] The evening sermon was preached by Dr. Frederick E. Ross, a former pastor, from Columbus, Ohio.

---

[86] Church Records
[87] A **stereopticon** is a projector or "magic lantern," which has two lenses, usually one above the other. These devices date back to the mid 19th century, and were a form of entertainment and education, before moving pictures. From www.wikipedia.org
[88] (The details of this will be told, later.)

Monday evening was given over to a jubilee banquet at $1.00 per plate. The Rev. W. C. Lee was the toastmaster and the speakers were Dr. F. E. Ross and Dr. E. D. Kohlstead.[89] Tuesday was debt paying day. The entire indebtedness to the extent of $6,500 was taken care of, the mortgage was burned, and over $8000 was pledged for the Centenary.

Waite Park Methodist Episcopal Church, *St. Cloud Daily Times*, **28 Nov. 1919 p 6, col 1,2,3**

Another big project undertaken at this time was the Waite Park Methodist Church. $500 had been secured from the John Rorer Memorial fund which was probably money donated by a wealthy person by that name for the aid of struggling churches. A building was erected in 1919, probably upon the lots donated by John Benson [Bensen] a few years before.

The cornerstone was laid May 18, 1919 by the pastor, George E. Tindall, assisted by the two Sunday school superintendents, L. L. Bowers and Charles Quinn, Mayor Lee E. Welsh (who was also the president of the Waite Park Official Board), and the contractor, Mr. Dryfas. The speakers of the occasion were the District Superintendent W. C. Lee and Dr. Frederick E. Ross, a former pastor at St. Cloud. The dedication ceremony took place November 30, 1919. Bishop Charles Mitchell could not be present so the District Superintendent, W. C. Lee, substituted for him. Dr. E. D. Kohlstead was another speaker of the day. And so the John Rorer Memorial Methodist Church of Waite Park was built and dedicated to the Lord's service in a village of over 1000 persons, one-half of whom are Protestant. (Today [1947], the church is known as the First Methodist Church of Waite Park.) The Conference of 1919 sent the Rev. W. E. Peterson to be Mr. Tindall's assistant at Waite Park and at Sauk Rapids.

In February 1920, First Church felt so able to help finance a large project that they sent J. W. Campbell to the Board of Control of Hamline University to invite them to locate their institution in St. Cloud.

---

[89] (Rev. F. W. Hill was expected at this service but records do not tell if he came.)

Another great occasion of this pastorate was the entertaining of the 26th session of the Northern Minnesota Conference October 5-11, 1920. Bishop Charles Bayard Mitchell presided at most of the meetings. Mayor Mattson and the Rev. E. V. Campbell, the pioneer minister of St. Cloud, welcomed the visitors. The Presbyterian minister said in the course of his talk that although every drop of blood in his body was Presbyterian, he had had much in common with the Methodists. He had gone to a Methodist Sunday school, his college chum was a Methodist, he had preached his first sermon in St. Cloud in a Methodist church building and, to climax the whole story, his first child had been baptized by a Methodist preacher.[90]

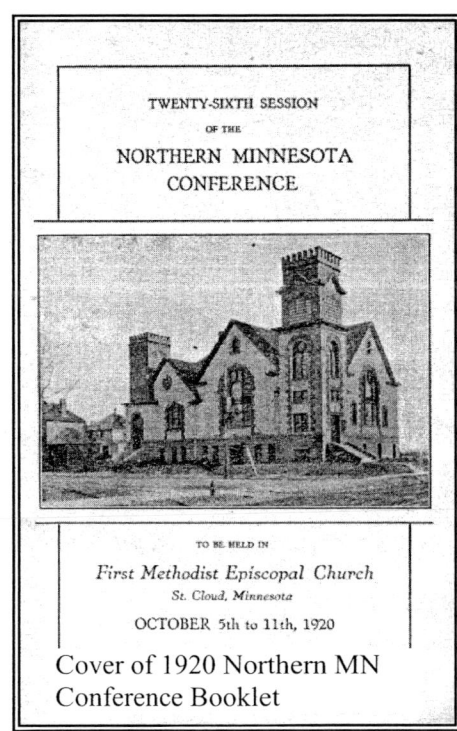

Cover of 1920 Northern MN Conference Booklet

Other speakers of the week were the Methodist preachers, G. G. Valentine, William Shannon, W. H. Jordan, W. E. J. Gratz, F. W. Hill, and George Mecklenburg; and the returned missionaries, Howard Musser and B. M. Jones. Two State Reformatory services were conducted by the Rev. F. W. Hill (who had been a preacher out there while in St. Cloud as pastor) and the Rev. William Shannon. Music was furnished throughout the Conference by Miss Bess Fasholt, the choir director of First Church, and by the Conference Male Quartet. Bishop Mitchell preached the Sunday morning sermon in the United Theatre. The pastor, Mr. Tindall, wrote of the week's services, "The Conference was most successful in every way and proved a

OUR COMING GUESTS [1920]

St. Cloud is to be honored with a week's convention of the Methodist conference of Northern Minnesota, which will include some of the ablest men of that denomination in the country. The Methodist membership is noted for its patriotism, its enthusiasm, its faith in the Great Father, and its helpful spirit towards the children of men. There is red blooded brotherly love in Methodism. The representatives of that great Protestant church will be very welcome in St. Cloud, and we are sure our citizens of various creeds will unite as one people in giving them cordial greeting, and in making their stay in the Granite City pleasant and profitable. They come on invitation of the Commercial Club, and are in that sense guests of the city, and St. Cloud has another opportunity of extending its unstinted hospitality.

St. Cloud Daily Times, 5 Oct 1920

---

[90] (*St. Cloud Daily Times*, October 6, 1920.)

Godsend to the Methodists in these tri cities."[91]

In November 1921, a District conference was held in St. Cloud, Bishop Charles Mitchell presided. Other speakers were Dr. W. H. Jordan, Dr. J. P. Jenkins, Rev. E. C. Reinke of Parker College, A. Z. Mann of Hamline University, Rev. Roy L. Smith of Minneapolis Simpson Methodist church and Dr. and Mrs. Hauser, returned missionaries. Thirty-three ministers and forty laymen were present.

Now a word or two about the Sauk Rapids work. In 1916, the Rev. F. J. Bryan was the pastor and Sauk Rapids had 40 church members and a Sunday school of 87 scholars. The next year Sauk Rapids had 38 members and 83 scholars. Rev. L. S. Koch was appointed to the Sauk Rapids work that year. But in March 1919, the Rev. Mr. Koch was removed to Sleepy Eye and the Rev. Mr. Tindall was appointed/forced to add the Sauk Rapids work to his own. The Conference of 1919 sent the Rev. William E. Peterson to assist Mr. Tindall at Waite Park, Sauk Rapids and St. Cloud. That same year, 1919, Sauk Rapids painted the exterior of their building white and calcomined (whitewashed) the interior and put in a new system of lighting and did not go into debt for any of it. They even reduced the debt of $800 by $500. In 1920 and 1921 the two ministers, Tindall and Peterson, worked in Sauk Rapids and then in 1922, the Rev. E. B. Service was sent to be Mr. Tindall's assistant and the Rev. T. B. Clark was given entire charge of Waite Park and Sauk Rapids. The Rev. T. B. Clark remained as pastor of the two congregations from 1922 to 1924. Then Rev. Raymond F. Mattock was appointed. He stayed for two years and after that the work was left alone more or less until 1928 when the Rev. G. E. Tindall was sent to Waite Park. Then the Sauk Rapids folks were cared for by him until ill health made it impossible.

When the Rev. G. E. Tindall went to Conference in 1918, he reported 250 members, 327 scholars, 40 Senior and 46 Junior Epworth Leaguers. The next year he reported 260 members, 301 scholars, 30 Senior and 22 Junior Epworth leaguers. The year the Conference met here St. Cloud had 323 members, 492 scholars, 25 Senior and 42 Junior Epworth Leaguers. A year after that, St. Cloud reported 318 members, 501 scholars, 40 Senior and 25 Junior Epworth Leaguers. Waite Park and Sauk Rapids together reported 93 members, 98 scholars and 21 Junior Epworth Leaguers. At the close of the year, 1923, St. Cloud had 230 members, 416 scholars, 40 Senior and 24

---

[91] (Journal Conference Records, 1921)

Junior Epworth leaguers, but the church was in a good condition, financially and spiritually.

In 1923, the Rev. H. W. Bell came to St. Cloud to work with the Methodists here. During his pastorate St. Cloud entertained the Epworth Leagues of the Litchfield District. District Superintendent W. C. Lee said that it was the best of all the good conventions he had attended during the past seven years.

The gymnasium was redecorated the winter of 1924-25. Screens to divide off the Sunday school classes were procured, thus giving more room. In June 1925, the windows over the pulpit were painted, thus taking away the glare and the mortgage was burned. In July 1925, the Church sent a young man to the Boy Scout Council at Itasca Park. Miss Bessie Fasholt was still the choir director. A new piano was purchased this year. Pastor Bell's Official Board these years included the following: Edwin Wendt, J. W. Pramann, Charles Quinn, William Morris, F. A. Ward, Harry Smart, M. J. Cleveland, E. D. Hammond, J. W. Campbell, Charles Cater, Mrs. Block, William Varner, and H. H. Andrus. Rev. R. F. Mattock was in charge of Waite Park and Sauk Rapids during the year 1924-25.

In 1924, St. Cloud reported 358 members, 428 scholars, and 65 Senior Epworth Leaguers. The next year, St. Cloud reported 396 members, 413 scholars but no Epworth Leaguers.

In 1925, Rev. A. L. [Andrus Laverne] Richardson was sent to St. Cloud and Rev. R. F. Mattock was returned to Waite Park and Sauk Rapids. Rev. Richardson's Official Board in December 1925, included the following: Charles Orton, Rolla Sprague, Ed Magnuson, W. E. Brown, Arthur Bluhm, A. R. Berglund, H. H. Andrus, E. D. Hammond, Edwin Wendt, William Morris, W. N. Bethel, Charles Quinn, Charles Cater, Charles Hall, and Julian McCutchan. That was the year that the pastor was allowed the help of a deaconess. Mrs. Augusta Luneman [Lunemann] served for two or three months. Mr. Westhaver was the Sunday school Superintendent. Charles Hall and H. H. Andrus were the Gymnasium committee of the Board and Mr. Hall was also doing Boy Scout work. This was the first time since the erection of the new church that mention was made of a pipe organ.[92]

That same winter, December 1925, the Blue Cross Society was organized with Miss Margaret Burmeister as the first President. This society with its three-fold purpose (religious, social, and educational) was formed to care for a group of young women in the church who could not attend the regular women's organizations because they were mothers of small children or business or professional women. One of the first funds started by the Society was a pipe organ fund. Every year the Society has added to that fund. The first president later became a Missionary to Japan and on her return to the United States in 1931 was a guest speaker at the Blue Cross banquet given that year.[93]

In 1926-27, the Ladies' Aid Society was divided up into three circles each to have its own social and money making activities. One circle was east of the River, another was east of Eighth Avenue, and the third was west of Eighth Avenue. On April 29, 1927, Circle Three presented a play, coached by Mrs. Kurt Stai, entitled, "The Strike of the Ladies' Aid." It brought out very vividly the great part the Ladies' Aid Society plays in helping the finances of the church. The great need of the church according to the skit was adequate Sunday school space.

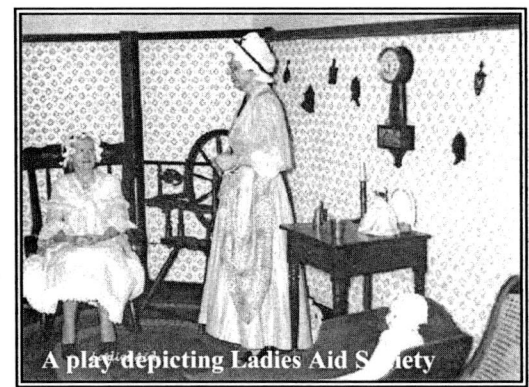
A play depicting Ladies Aid Society

The play[94] was well given but First Church did not build the needed rooms.

Charles Quinn

William Varner was chosen as the Superintendent of the Sunday school, Mr. Westhaver having moved away in January 1927. J. F. McCutchan was the chairman of the music committee and Mrs. Burlingame, the organist. Wednesday evening was set aside for choir rehearsal.[95] Charles Quinn's local preacher license was renewed and

---

[92] (There was a pipe organ committee, namely: Mr. Morris, Mr. Westhaver, and Mr. McCutchan, but no organ.)
[93] This organization celebrated its 25 years on 24 April 1950 with a small booklet written by Gertrude Gove.
[94] Copy is in the Church Archives
[95] In 2007, it is still on Wednesday evening. adt

Paul Evans and Clarence Nelson applied for licenses. Mr. Cater and Mr. Cleveland were authorized to sell the lots that the church owned in the West End. (Probably these were not the ones purchased by the Second Church group.) In April 1927, the pastor proposed that the church observe its seventieth birthday but no record of such a celebration was found.

At the conference, 1926, the pastor reported 350 members, 392 scholars, 46 Senior and 32 Junior Leaguers. In 1927, he reported 393 members, 342 scholars, 46 Senior and 32 junior Leaguers.

In 1927, the Rev. J. Arthur Edwards[96] came to St. Cloud. With him came the idea of "All Church Night" suppers and Colonial banquets and Vesper services, which became a part of the church program. He believed in advertising. He put a sign over the parsonage door stating what the building was and who the pastor was. The Church could not afford an electric sign so he secured an electric light[97] for the old sign on the church lawn. At Christmas time, a lighted tree was put on the front church lawn and a lighted star was placed near the top of the church. [He also repaired the red pulpit[98] of the Martin period and used it as a pedestal on the pulpit platform.][99]

1890 Walnut Pulpit Memorial Gift
Mrs. Bert Miller and Blanch Gray

At that time, the Men's Club painted the floor in the old part of the church and painted the chairs. The ladies, under the leadership of Mrs. M. J. Cleveland, made and put up the drapes, and the church purchased the wicker furniture and the lamps, thus making a very attractive and comfortable social room for the church. The kitchen was enlarged about this time, also, the men doing the work. The pulpit platform was enlarged to make room for the choir back of the pulpit and the platform in the social room was removed.

---

[96] Edwards was an Easterner who had served Minnesota charges since at least 1912.
[97] Ibid..
[98] Gove, 1958 History Book, p. 29 of Crosby's scrapbook with the list of memorials. 1890-1900
[99] Ibid.. [On the pulpit are three different dates as to when this was added to First Church. The scrapbook seems to be the best evidence of the date.]

The church adopted the budget plan and took out workmen's compensation. This was the time that Mrs. W. E. Brown was president of the Ladies' Aid Society, Charles Quinn was Sunday school Superintendent, Evelyn Hall was president of the Epworth League, and Charles Cater was treasurer of the World Service fund. Mrs. Burlingame was still the organist, but Miss Bessie Fasholt, in October 1929, resigned her position of choir leader. During these years a great effort was made to bring the Sunday school to the children of all parts of the city. Two seven-passenger cars were rented for $1.50 per Sunday and sent to the various parts of the city to pick up children and bring them to the First Church. This plan was started in the spring of 1928. By autumn, busses were running out to Pan Town and to the East side, also. The St. Cloud Methodist Sunday school placed third in the State, March 1930. A church census of the second grades of the public schools showed that the Methodist Church placed highest in preference. And still the Sunday school workers had to plead for more room, more adequate quarters for their work. Three plans were suggested to the Board. Use the gymnasium with movable partitions, build a balcony in the auditorium, or take down the old part of the church and build a new unit to the church with two or three stories arranged just for the Sunday school. But again no action was taken.

From Dorothy Stueve's Archives

At the conference of 1928, St. Cloud had 325 members, 445 scholars, 45 Senior and 10 Junior Epworth Leaguers. That Conference sent a former pastor, the Rev. Mr. Tindall, to Waite Park and Sauk Rapids and returned the Rev. Mr. Edwards to St. Cloud. Mr. Edwards, desiring to work in the East, had for sometime been negotiating for a transfer. The opportunity came in May 1930. The Official Board allowed him to leave and accepted in return the Rev. Harold E. Mayo, pastor of Calvary Methodist Church of Lewiston, Maine. Mr. Mayo preached his first sermon in First Church on May 18, 1930. At this time, there were 428 members of the church, 320 enrolled in Sunday school, and a small Epworth League.

Period Eight -- 1930 - 1934

Period Eight begins as one of growth and accomplishment. During the pastorate of the Rev. Harold E. Mayo, beginning May 1930, 405 names were added to the rolls. New people were sharing in the responsibilities as well as in the privileges of the Church. Mr. and Mrs. Mayo—conscientious, able leaders—gave of themselves unsparingly in promoting the various interests of the Church, welding them into a harmonious whole; establishing First Church as a "church where folks are friendly"; a truly metropolitan church; a social, civic, and spiritual force in the community.

In 1930-31, the Sauk Rapids Methodists were without a leader. Mr. Mayo, rather than let the work disintegrate, added it to his work at First Church. The Conference of 1931 named the Rev. Mr. Mayo the pastor of both churches. The Sunday school work was continued as before at First Church, the scholars being brought over by bus. Many of the Sauk Rapids members transferred their membership to First Church and came to St. Cloud to the morning worship service although there was still a building over at Sauk Rapids and services there on Sunday afternoons. There was a Sauk Rapids circle of the First Church Ladies' Aid. The merger seemed to be working out satisfactorily for both congregations.

Work among the Methodists in the Pan Addition was resumed. Mrs. J. M. [Norma] Dobson and others were responsible for a thriving Sunday school, which met in an old store building that had been converted into a chapel and community house. A circle of the First Church Ladies' Aid Society was formed there, also.

A circle of the Ladies' Aid Society was formed in the West End, also.

January 1933, the Quarterly Conference of First Church St. Cloud, and First Church Waite Park, requested the bishop to put the two churches in one charge with the Rev. Allyn Hanson (who had been appointed to Waite Park in 1932) associated with the Rev. Harold E. Mayo in a combined ministry. Mr. Hanson was to have direct responsibility for the Wesley Foundation which was organized in 1932 among the Teachers' College Methodist students.

At First Church, the aim was to put into action, among the entire membership, a unified church program. This meant attendance at the Church School, with its classes for all, so as to learn the Biblical truths. This also meant attendance at the worship services in order that the music and sermons may inspire the students to live the truths learned in the Sabbath School. And finally, it meant active membership in one or more of the various organizations which tend to develop leadership and character and lead to practical application of Christian truths such as the Epworth Leagues, the Wesley Foundation, the Boy Scouts, the Camp Fire groups (formed in 1930), the Men's club, and the various Missionary societies such as the W.F.M.S., the Blue Cross, the Wesleyan Guild (organized in 1931-32 to do for the young women what the Blue Cross does for those a few years older), and the children's groups.

The Official Board for 1932, which sought to carry out such a program consisted of the following:

TRUSTEES: W. H. Bethel, J. W. Campbell, Charles W. Cater, M. J. Cleveland, Dr. J. M. Farnham, E. D. Hammond, J. F. McCutchan, William Morris, J. E. Talbot.

STEWARDS: A. Atwood, Mrs. E. J. Binnie, A. F. Bluhm, J. M. Dobson, H. E. Dingman, H. B. Gough, Mrs. E. D. Hammond, Mrs. M. J. Cleveland, Anton Hartman, Theodore Jensen, Arthur L. W. Johnson, Dr. R. N. Jones, Paul Lund, H. H. Andrus, Dr. E. H. Orr, Dr. P. O. Pederson, D. D. Poulter, J. E. Pramann, A. L. Koep, A. L. Smith, Raymond Sherk, Rolla

Sprague, Mrs. Kurt Stai, D. M. Taylor, Earl Thompson, A. J. Van Alstyne, F. A. Ward, Edwin Wendt.

    RECORDING STEWARD: J. F. McCutchan;

    CHURCH TREASURER Charles W. Cater;

    FINANCIAL SECRETARY N. T. Bergquist.

    OTHERS on various committees: Mrs. J. M. Farnham, Mrs. H. H. Andrus, Charles Quinn (Local Preacher), John E. Talbot (Sunday school Superintendent), Rev. Allyn Hanson (Advisor of High School League), Mrs. L. D. Staples, Mrs. Edwin Wendt, Miss Svea Swanson, Miss Elizabeth Hebei, Mrs. F. A. Ward, Mrs. Mary E. Mayo, Miss Theresa Oatman, Miss Helen Cater, Miss Gertrude Soder.

    It was during this period of First Church's history that the Seventy-fifth anniversary of its birth was observed. The following were appointed to serve as the general committee: William Morris, Chairman Edwin Wendt, John E. Talbot, J. W. Campbell, and Mesdames E. D. Hammond, M. J. Cleveland, Kurt Stai, and J. M. Dobson.

    The celebration lasted over the weekend of February 17-19, 1933. At the Friday evening banquet, Mayor Phil Collignon, President George Selke of the State Teachers' College, and Rev. A. F. Malmborg, president of the St. Cloud Ministerial Association, were the guest speakers. Saturday evening was "History Night." Several members of the congregation, through the medium of dramatic skits written by Mrs. J. M. Dobson, presented various incidents connected with the activities of the church in years past. The Rev. A. L. Richardson, a former pastor, was the guest speaker. The Sunday morning sermon was preached by the Rev. W. C. Lee, another former pastor. The climax of the celebration occurred Sunday evening when the resident bishop, the Rev. J. Ralph Magee, preached the sermon.

    For years, hopes were entertained that a pipe organ would be installed in First Church, St. Cloud. During the pastorate of the Rev. Harold E. Mayo, the Official Board sanctioned the purchase of a small theatre organ which, with installation, was to cost $1100. A special drive was conducted, part of the money raised, and the organ installed. This purchase did not prove entirely satisfactory, however. It cost more than was planned (it was $1911 before all bills were paid), a theatre organ does not quite meet the needs of a church worship center, repairs for a second-hand organ are frequently needed, and often repairs and repair men cannot be found. However, the tone of the services has been lifted considerably due in large part to this organ and to the faithful and efficient organists, choir leaders, and music committee members. This list includes the Misses Winifred Chute, Margaret Mitchell, Constance Clokey, Jean Hammond, Ellen Jones, and Mr. A. C. Hayes as organists; Miss Irene Johnson, Mrs. James Carpenter, Helen Steen Huls, Orville Westhoff, Julius Whitinger, Mrs. Jean McCutchan Blair, and Shirley Hammond as Directors of Music; and Mr. and Mrs. Julian McCutchan and Mrs. P. S. Lund on the music committee. Special thanks must go to Julian McCutchan who has spent many, many hours working with this organ to have it ready for Sunday. This free service has saved First Church many dollars for repairs.

Because of the increased attendance at the Sunday services it was deemed necessary to erect a balcony in the sanctuary. This, too, has not proved entirely satisfactory as can be seen as one enters the room, but it has afforded added and much needed seating space.

The local women's work was organized into the Women's Guild. The purpose of this was "to unite all the women of the congregation into an effective whole for the development of Christian ideals and practices to the end that the kingdom of God shall be the more perfectly attained at home and abroad." The several circles of the Ladies' Aid Society, the Blue Cross Society, and the Wesleyan Service Guild had the same general officers and general meetings but each group retained its own identity, keeping its own officers and plans of work. The first meeting of this new organization was held October 17, 1933 with Mrs. Kurt Stai as the first president. One of the many interesting and worthwhile events sponsored by this Guild was the public lecture given by Mrs. Gladys Hasty Carroll, a well known author who was also a friend of the Mayos.

In the fall of 1934, a three-way transfer took place whereby the Rev. Harold Mayo was sent to a church in Cedar Rapids, Iowa; the Iowa man went to Madison, Wisconsin; and the Rev. Harland Chester Logan, DD, pastor of First Church, Madison for six years came to St. Cloud.

PERIOD NINE -- 1934 - 1946

INTRODUCTION

Harland C and Alice Logan

Dr. Logan preached his first sermon in Minnesota in St. Cloud Sunday, September 30, 1934. For eleven years, the Bishops and District Superintendents of Litchfield District, Northern Conference have favored St. Cloud residents by re-assigning Dr. Logan to this charge. These were years of depression and World War II – difficult times indeed! His experiences and those of his congregation through the years have been many. Always, through sorrow and happiness, sickness and health, depression and prosperity, peace and war, Dr. Logan has proved himself equal to every occasion, an excellent pastor, and a true friend to all.

St. Cloud was not privileged to keep Mrs. Mabel Logan for long. In October 1935, she passed to her eternal home. Although here a short time, her influence for good was keenly felt and her death was widely mourned. As a token of great respect for her Christian life, the women of the church through the Missionary Society have set aside in the name of Mrs. Mabel Logan a yearly gift of money for the education of Chinese women. A daughter, Miss Ruth Logan, served as a very capable and charming hostess in the parsonage until June 1937 when Dr. Logan was married to Miss Alice Lewis, a teacher in the St. Cloud Public Schools. Mrs. Alice Logan, too, has filled a large place in First Church. Her special contribution has been in the work with the youth of the congregation and her constant lookout for new people. Few pastors' wives are loved as much as is Alice Logan.

DR. LOGAN'S FIRST GREAT AIM

Dr. Logan, from the start, endeavored to weed out the inactive members on the church roll. His purpose was to make them active in this or some other church, or, if necessary, drop them from the roll (after the three years of inactivity required by the Discipline). Thus, for a few years, in spite of the addition of new and active members, there was a noticeable decline in the figures as reported at the previous Conference time. [See also "Through the Years."] For example, in 1934 there were reported 981 members, including 124 inactive. In 1938 (a middle year), Dr. Logan reported 600 active and 150 inactive making a total of 725. In 1946, there are 541 active and 72 inactive, thus making total of 613.

First Church, St. Cloud probably will never be a great church numerically (this is true of many of the Protestant churches in St. Cloud), but this smaller membership can be, and today is, very active and is holding its own very nicely. With the elimination of this "dead timber," First Church has been freed for action. The attendance has been growing steadily larger. The sanctuary is well filled each Sunday and two services are necessary at Easter (9:30 and 11 a.m.). Since the 1937-38 year, the Sunday worship services have been held at 10 a.m. during the months of July and August.

Of special interest is the fact that on the records is the certificate of transfer of membership from the Community Church, Shanghai, China, of Mrs. Joseph R. Dobson.

During all this period, the Sauk Rapids charge has been a part of the St. Cloud work. One year, Rev. F. J. Bryan assisted Dr. Logan, but during the other years the congregation has attended services in St. Cloud. The church building at Sauk Rapids has finally been sold for cash and the money transferred to our building fund.

DR. LOGAN'S SECOND GREAT AIM FOR FIRST CHURCH

Dr. Logan's second great aim was to make First Church financially sound. He refused increases in salary until the long-standing debt ($2575 in 1934) was paid off. With determined and concerted effort, the Official Board went to work. The Penny Share plan was adopted; Miss Elsie Gosswiller served as treasurer of this money; and on Sunday, May 30, 1943 the final mortgage was burned amid great rejoicing.

The needed repairs were not neglected during these years, either. Sometimes special drives were conducted (as for new hymnals and choir chairs), and once a generous gift from the estate of William Morris (formerly an active member of First Church) served as incentive for the congregation to accumulate enough more to redecorate the interior of the entire church. While this was being done, services were held in the Community Center (formerly the Unitarian Church). Everything was finished in time for the Easter services, 1938. Other improvements during these years include the railing on the front steps and the vestibule, reshingling of both church and parsonage, and remodeling and redecorating of the parsonage.

A budget was followed and as the years went by it was increased to include a definite amount to be set aside for permanent improvements, which might mean a new church structure. At the first Official Board after the burning of the final mortgage, the consensus of opinion was that it is good for a church to have a debt IF payment of that debt is not neglected too long. A committee was appointed to investigate the possibilities of remodeling First Church's building so as to make it a modern plant (especially helpful in Church School work). After a careful study, the committee headed by H. B. Gough reported in December 1944 that it was thought best to erect an entirely new structure to cost not less than $64,000. One-half of this amount must be raised within five years or the project would be abandoned. The Official Board and later the congregation (according to the Discipline) at special meetings called in December 1944, voted to accept the plans of the committee. Pledges were acceptable at any time but the special drive for money did not begin until December 1945. A year later (December 1946), $37,000.00 had been pledged (and some paid).

GREAT INCREASE IN BENEVOLENCE GIVING

One great change in First Church is the noticeable increase in giving toward benevolences. Entire credit for this must go to the pastor. Dr. Logan has constantly preached that no one can be truly Christian until he has world-wide vision and until he can pray for, love, and help financially all people of all nations and creeds everywhere. Each year more and more members of First Church are putting money into the benevolences side of the church envelopes. This habit is being emphasized in the Church School, also, with fine results.

In the ten years the offerings for benevolences have increased from $128 to over $1200 a year in recent times. This does not include the moneys turned in by the Church School and the Women's Societies. Nor does it include the special Lenten and World Communion Sunday and Dedication Day offerings which have always been large. During the 1944-45 year, the Methodists in Minnesota, in cooperation with the Bishops' Crusade, inaugurated the Minnesota Methodist Million Movement. St. Cloud's share in this was $2100 for the Crusade itself (rehabilitation of war torn areas), $610 for Hamline, $1700 each for the

Pension Fund for retired ministers or their widows and for the Methodist Home for the Aged. At Christmas time, First Church subscribed $2189 with $2000 paid by May 1945. At Easter 1946, the remainder of the drive was tackled with the result that over $700 was contributed. By Conference time 1946, $5300 of the total $6110 had been pledged.

The following financial officials have served well during these busy years: P. S. Lund, Allen Atwood, Clarence L. Pilger, and Lloyd Lillestrand as chairmen of the Finance Committee; Charles W. Cater as church treasurer; N. T. Bergquist, John Pramann, Merrill Johnson, Mrs. Lloyd Ohs, and Miss Leah Johnson as Financial Secretaries.

CONFERENCE CHANGES

The time for the annual conference was changed in the year 1939-40 from fall to spring. Thus the year 1939-40 was only eight months long. Yet all bills and obligations were met on time. Until 1938, the Rev. J. W. Lillico was District Superintendent of Litchfield District. For the next six years the Rev. Earl Baumhofer visited St. Cloud in this capacity. In 1944, the Rev. E. B. Cooney was appointed to serve this District. Delegates to the annual Lay Conference during these years have been H. B. Gough, Mrs. Augusta Lunemann, and again Mr. Gough. The Lay Leaders under the United Church arrangement (since 1940) have been first, Mrs. Augusta Lunemann and now Mr. T. A. Gustafson.

CHURCH LITERATURE

Increased interest in the church literature has also been a part of this pastorate. In 1934, there were only 33 subscribers to the *Christian Advocate*. In 1938 there were 65. In 1946 there are 102. Copies of the *Upper Room* to the extent of 100 or more are regularly distributed each quarter. Many prayer books and other devotional material have been sent to the men and women in the armed services. The women of the WSCS are reading literature printed for their special use. This amounts to 25 subscriptions to the *Methodist Woman* and 24 to the *World Outlook*.

THE UNITED METHODIST CHURCHES[100]

In the year 1940, the three churches the Methodist Episcopal Church, the Methodist Episcopal Church South, and the Methodist Protestant Church were merged into the Methodist Church. This brought about many changes in First Church, St. Cloud. Members had to accustom themselves to dropping such words as Episcopal, Epworth League, and Women's Foreign Missionary Society [WFMS]. They had to learn new words such as Jurisdiction (an extra Conference), Methodist Youth Fellowship [MYF, and Woman's Society of Christian Service [WSCS].

THE WOMEN'S WORK

Probably the greatest change noticed was in the Women's work throughout the world. This was a merging of every society and type of work of the women in the congregation into one great society known as the Woman's Society of Christian Service. This was not as difficult in St. Cloud as elsewhere because here (since 1933) was the Woman's Guild. The only real difference was that under the WSCS, the WFMS[101] is also a part.

The purpose of this new organization is "to unite all women of the church in Christian living and service; to help develop the spiritual life; to study the needs of the world; to take part in such service activities as will strengthen the local church, improve civic, community, and world conditions." St. Cloud women become members of this society by giving prayer, service, and annual contributions of money to the budget through membership offerings or dues or pledges or gifts.

St. Cloud's WSCS membership has averaged 100 each year. The presidents of this organization have been: 1940, Mrs. Julian McCutchan; 1941, Mrs. J. M. Lunemann; 1942, Mrs. Lee Welsh; 1944, Mrs. Vernon Morrison; 1946, Mrs. W. K. Norris. Mrs. E. A. Drews has been the efficient treasurer from the time the Guild was formed (1933).

---

[100] Gove uses the United for the uniting of US Methodist churches, in 1939, not the uniting that took place in 1968 of the Evangelical United Brethren and the Methodist Church.
[101] Women's Foreign Missionary Society

The WSCS through its various departments and committees seeks to bring cheer to all women of the congregation. Flowers or cards are sent in time of illness or death or great joy. Baskets of food and clothing meet the physical needs. Always a friendly hand is extended to the stranger. A large amount of money is turned over to the Church's treasurer each year for local work. This has averaged around $600 per year since 1933.

St. Cloud's Methodist women's share in the missionary work of the world amounts to around $225 a year. The study of missions in a special class each winter stimulates this giving. Mrs. Geo. Friedrich has been the teacher for several years.

The money making and the sociability angle of the WSCS are met by the five circles. These were once geographically arranged but now are divided according to the drawing of names by the chairmen of each circle at a meeting of the Society. This latter method seems to help the women become better acquainted.

The WSCS cooperates with several other Protestant churches in St. Cloud through the United Council of Church Women. This was formed by Mrs. Alice Logan and in 1944-45 she was the president of the group. The WSCS also joins wholeheartedly in the World Day of Prayer, which is held all over the world on the first Friday after Lent begins.

The Wesleyan Service Guild of Period Eight was merged with the Blue Cross Society, thus giving the latter society several very active workers. The Blue Cross Society is in a sense the evening circle of the WSCS. As individuals, its members may become members of the general society and attend the general meetings. As a group, also, the Blue Cross Society is a part of the WSCS. One-third of its dues goes directly to the WSCS Treasurer for work in the foreign mission fields. The Blue Cross Society strives, also, to do home missionary work and to help in the local church activities.

RELIGIOUS INSTRUCTION

In common with the trend of the times all over the United States in all denominations (if true figures are used), a noticeable decline can be seen in the attendance at the Church School (formerly called Sunday school). This is due partially to the lower birth rate during the depression years. In 1934, the pastor reported 530 on the Sunday school roll—all departments from the Cradle Roll through the Home department. In 1938 these were 425. In 1945 there are only 271 on the roll. At First Church, another reason was given for this decline. For several years it has been the policy of the school to not count a person enrolled until he has attended three times and also not to keep his name after three months absence. However, in spite of this clearing of the dead timber from the records, attendance at First Church at 9:45 Sunday

First Methodist Church, corner of 3rd Street and 5th Avenue, 1914-1956

morning has been good, regular, and steady. Also, too, the year 1945-46 records reveal a 20% increase in Sunday school enrollment.

The work of the Church School is divided into three great parts, namely the work with the children (Elementary); work with the Junior and Senior High School students (Youth); and work with the adults. For many years Mr. J. E. Talbot has faithfully given of his time as General Superintendent of this school. Mrs. Augusta Lunemann, Miss Blanche Atkins, and the Rev. F. J. Bryan have served well as teachers of the Women's and Men's classes. Mr. Charles Quinn, Local Preacher, has done such excellent work that, several years ago, the Conference gave him a license for life.

The Youth work includes all who are between the ages of 12 and 23. The same set of officers and advisors serve for the Sunday Morning Church School and also for the Methodist Youth Fellowship meetings held Sunday evening. Mrs. Alice Logan has been the excellent advisor of this group since the first (1940). During the year 1944-45, Miss Catherine Young assisted in this work.

The college young people, although theoretically a part of the MYF, are, in St. Cloud, working through the Wesley Foundation only. Dr. Logan, as pastor, is the Director. Through the years, the college advisors have been the Misses Elizabeth Hebei, Ruth Cole, Mamie Martin, and Irene Halberg and Messrs. Roland Anderson, Clair Daggett, and George Skewes.

In an attempt to serve the young persons who are older than the High School group and who do not attend Teachers College, a Sunday morning class has been held. Mrs. Alice Logan, Miss Charlotte Knudson, and Mr. George Skewes have, in turn, taught this class.

The 1941 and 1942 Conference Journals mention an orphanage sponsored or set up by First Methodist Church St. Cloud. adt

---

St. Cloud has been honored by the annual summer institute, which is held by the young people at Morris. For four years, Dr. Logan served as Dean of the Institute and for three years Mrs. Logan was Dean of Women. St. Cloud's MYF has been represented at Morris each year by young people who have been very active in the work thereafter. The Blue Cross Society and other groups have helped somewhat with the expense of this work. In 1945 and 1946, the young people brought home several awards for good departmental work during the years.

One of the best things Dr. Logan has done for St. Cloud is the inauguration of the Weekday Religious Education classes, which have been conducted on "released school time" through the Seventh, Eighth, and Ninth grades of Central Junior High and Riverview School at T. C. (Teachers College). The first year (1938), the Protestant students in these grades were divided by grades regardless of denomination. Dr. Logan taught all the Seventh Grades in the First Methodist church building. Since that year each pastor has taken care of the instruction of his own church children—all three grades—in his own church building. At our Church, the average attendance has been 50. Dr. and Mrs. Logan have been the teachers for this, with the assistance the last few years of Mrs. Lloyd Ohs and Miss Jessie Marshall.

Boy Scout Troop No. 1 of this city is sponsored by First Church. A Camp Fire group is sponsored by the Blue Cross Society. Neither group consists of Methodist youth only.

SPECIAL EVENTS

One of the notable events held at First Church was the observance of the Sesquicentennial of Methodism in the United States. At a church dinner held December 12, 1934, a history of the one hundred and fifty years of Methodism in the United States and in St. Cloud was given by Miss Gertrude Gove. Local persons, costumed appropriately, stepped into a large album as Miss Gove told how the persons represented were associated with this history. For example, the following were impersonated: Barbara Heck, Philip Embury, Bishop Asbury. Mrs. E. W. Wendt, Mrs. Kurt Stai, Charles Quinn, Dr. Logan, and Gertrude Gove acted as the committee responsible for this event.

In 1935-36, the Blue Cross Society led by Miss Ruth Logan and Miss Gove, staged a Parade of Wedding Gowns. Mrs. Kurt Stai as narrator explained the history connected with the lovely gowns displayed.

The Men's Club and Boy Scout Troop No. 1 were responsible for the successful Hobby Show a few winters later.

The February banquets, long a tradition at First Church, were discontinued when World War II came and rationing went into effect. However, the Men's Club and the Woman's Guild (later WSCS) held several enjoyable joint meetings.

Perhaps the greatest event, socially, for First Church, came on September 20, 1944, when Dr. and Mrs. Logan held Open House to all their friends. This marked a triple anniversary. Dr. Logan was seventy years young, he had completed forty-five years in the Christian ministry, and ten years in St. Cloud. That evening and the one following, many friends, both in and outside the congregation, called or sent greetings. A purse of seventy silver dollars, voluntary gift from the many friends in the congregation, was presented to Dr. Logan by Mr. Charles W. Cater, the church treasurer. The Men's Bible Class presented Dr. Logan with a fine Bible. Everyone was especially glad that among those present were Dr. Logan's daughter, Ruth, and her husband, Mr. Marshall Hulbert of the faculty of Lawrence College, Appleton, Wisconsin.

The purely spiritual occasions have been many. One outstanding one was the observance of John Wesley's Heart Warming experience, May 24, 1738. Others have been Dedication Sunday, Crusade for Christ Sunday, and the several Communion Services.

In keeping with the trend due to the war, special attention has been paid at First Church to flags. A committee headed by Miss Leah C. Johnson selected the lovely Christian and United States Flags, which now stand on the pulpit platform.

Throughout the war years, First Church has kept in touch with the men and women who have gone from this congregation into the armed services. Letters have been written by the pastor and by special committees; special literature has been sent; special prayer services before the Sunday morning worship service have been held. Mrs. James Dobson should be mentioned as very active along this line of church work.

At the Sunday evening service, November 12, 1944 (Sunday nearest Armistice Day), special honor was paid to all who had entered the Armed Services from First Church. A relative or friend lighted a candle for each of the 115 then on the Honor Roll. On the same evening a brief memorial service was held for three of these who gave their lives in service Jack Sanborn, Larry Jensen, and Boysen Jensen. On the Sunday nearest Memorial Day (May 27, 1945), another Memorial service was held. This time it was for Robert Wegner, Herbert Bastien, and Jerome Gross. Then on January 13, 1946, a memorial service was held for Robert Stai. At the present time, May 1946, there are 126 names on the Service Roll, seven of whom have made the supreme sacrifice.

In the near future the names of all who offered themselves to the service of their country in a military way will be engraved on a plaque similar to the one now hanging in the front entrance and which bears the names of the men who went from First Church in World War I.

FAITHFUL WORKERS

Reprint permission granted from *St. Cloud Times/Times Media*, for Monday, 31 Mar 1943 page 3, Col 2.

Many have faithfully served First Church during this period. Perhaps the list of Official Board and Committee Members as nominated for the year ending May 31, 1947, will reveal, sufficiently, the work at this time.

TRUSTEES—Allen A. Atwood, Charles W. Cater (also Treasurer), Clinton F. Hill, E. A. Drews, Dr. R. N. Jones, E. G. Opitz, J. F. McCutchan, J. M. Lunemann, John Talbot (also Superintendent of the Church School).

STEWARDS - Arthur Bluhm, John Bensen (also Secretary for the Quarterly Conference), Harold Campbell, Amos Crosby, Clair Daggett, Mrs. E. A. Drews, Mrs. J. M. Dobson, Harry B. Gough (also Lay Member to the Annual Conference), Miss Gertrude Gove (also Church Historian), Miss Edith Grannis, T. A. Gustafson (also Lay Leader), O. M. Hafferman, Mrs. E. D. Hammond, Earl Hoffman, Miss Leah Johnson (also Financial Secretary), N. L. Lillestrand, Mrs. A. Lunemann, Mrs. Charles Megarry, Mrs. William Megarry, Vernon Morrison, Hillis D. Meyers, Mrs. Lloyd Ohs (also Assistant Treasurer), Clarence Pilger, (Alternate Lay Member), John E. Pramann, Charles Quinn (also Local Preacher), George Skewes, W. E. Smith, Mrs. Anne Stai, Earle Thompson, Edwin Wendt, C. E. Ward, the Rev. F. J. Bryan (Retired), the Misses Svea Swanson and Elsie Gosswiller (Communion Stewards).

OTHERS—Mrs. E. J. Binnie, Mrs. R. N. Jones, Mrs. J. F. McCutchan, Mrs. Clarence Pilger, Mrs. Viola Topp, Mrs. Ina Wood, Miss Beatrice Ellis, Miss Blanche Atkins, Mrs. F. J. Bryan, Mrs. J. E. Pramann, Mrs. Robert Sovereign, Mr. Denis Moonier, Mrs. Denis Moonier, Mrs. Charles Emery,

Mrs. Frank Payne, Mrs. E. A. Seibert, Charles Stark, Mrs. Amos Crosby, Mrs. Walter Walker, Mrs. Earle Thompson, Dan Chamberlin, Lloyd Ohs, Wallace Scherfenberg, Mrs. Vernon Morrison.

Pictures of the 1914 building Sanctuary, from Earle Thompson's Slides

1914 Overflow room off of sanctuary

Chancel as it was in the early years; notice the old pulpit on the right

Chimes

The balcony window and seating

View from the chancel area

1950's picture includes current pulpit, lectern, and altar

TRIBUTE TO DR. LOGAN

Dr. Logan's work among St. Cloud citizens has been of such a nature that each year seems a climax. Yet each additional year brings something even greater that has been accomplished by First Church under Dr. Logan's leadership. His influence is felt throughout the city, also. It shows in the Ministerial Association, which each year seems to unite the various Protestant churches still closer, especially during the Lenten season and at Thanksgiving time. Church people, Protestant and Roman Catholic, know and respect Dr. Logan as a Christian gentleman. In civic affairs Dr. Logan stands high, too.

Deeds speak louder than words but even deeds fail to show how great has been the influence of Dr. Logan in St. Cloud's Methodist Church. We hope First Church will be able to "walk alone" and keep going forward even after he must leave St. Cloud.

PERIOD TEN - - 1946 - 1957

In the spring of 1946, Dr. Logan announced that he would ask to be retired at Conference time. With great regret the First Church congregation, the City of St. Cloud, and the Northern Minnesota Conference bade him farewell. Inadequate were the efforts made to show the appreciation of his work. First Church held public farewell parties at which time sincere tributes were spoken and a large "purse" was given for a radio to be chosen by the Logans. At the Conference, the Bishop and other clergy and laymen publicly acknowledged the great work done by Dr. Logan.

Dr. and Mrs. Logan went to their lake home in Shell Lake, Wisconsin but since September 1946, they have been "supplying" at Shell Lake. Those two neglected churches are indeed fortunate!

The Committee in charge of the Ninetieth Anniversary (1947) of our Church's existence includes all of the Seventy-fifth Anniversary Committee still in St. Cloud (J. W. Campbell, Edwin Wendt, John E. Talbot, Mrs. E. D. Hammond, Mrs. M. J. Cleveland, Mrs. Kurt Stai, and Mrs. J. M. Dobson). The Official Board added the following: the presidents of the Woman's Society of Christian Service (Mrs. Vernon Morrison and Mrs. J. M. Dobson) ; the president of the Board of Trustees (Dr. R. N. Jones) ; the Lay Leader (T. A. Gustafson); the Church Treasurer (Charles W. Cater) ; and Church

Historian (Miss Gertrude Gove). The Committee added the following: Raymond Stensrud, Mrs. John Bensen, J. Miller Lunemann, and H. B. Gough.[102]

From this point forward, the text is from Gove's second history, *A Century of Service.*

1946 -1955

The Rev. Mr. Russell Allan Huffman came from Willmar, an enthusiastic and progressive young man, just the person to help First Church push through to completion of its *Venture in Faith*. The constantly growing membership wanted to go ahead at once but emergencies arose. The ceiling in the social room had to be repaired at once. The centennial pledge was not yet met.

Finally, on February 20, 1950, came Pledging Sunday. Then in July 1951, the congregation voted to build the new structure on the site already in use. This meant the moving of the parsonage. Earlier the church had acquired one lot at 308 Fourth Avenue South but soon found that it would be impossible to purchase the adjoining lots. However, this was space enough for the parsonage. After more delay came the November 1951 "Parsonage Sunday" drive, which brought in enough funds for the moving, repairing, and remodeling of the house. The "new" parsonage was open to visitors early in 1953.

In 1954, the parsonage occupied the space where the new church was to be erected. Earle Thompson's slides and pictures documented the move from 5th Ave to its 3rd street location.

Parsonage on the move, Russ Huffman, Jr., remembers his sister, Susan, was in the house while they were moving it.

---

[102] See the next Insert for the paragraph that Ms Gove wrote as her finish statement for the 1947 edition of her history.

New home 3rd street.

Fourth Building

According to new church rules, it is impossible for a Methodist congregation to start building until more than one half of the estimated cost has been raised. So in April 1954 Dr. John Henry Soltman of the Methodist Board of Church Extension was hired to supervise the "104 weeks of sharing." A congregational meeting held June 30, 1954 authorized the trustees and building committee to proceed with the necessary contracts and loans. Contracts were awarded to the Conlon Construction Company and to the Bensen Plumbing and Heating Company, both of St. Cloud, and to the Cold Spring Electric Company. The architect was Virgil E. Siddens, then of the Louis C. Pinault firm.

Ms. Gove's 1947 history includes this information: The Building Committee consists of the following: Allen A. Atwood, Charles W. Cater, Mrs. J. M. Dobson, Mrs. E. A. Drews, H. B. Gough, Dr. R. N. Jones, Lloyd Lillestrand, J. F. McCutchan, Mrs. William Megarry, E. G. Opitz, Clarence Pilger, Mrs. Vernon Morrison, George Skewes, John E. Talbot.

Already a part of the money to be raised before any building is done has been subscribed and several thousand dollars have already been given.[103]

The cornerstone was laid November 21, 1954 with Dr. H. C. Logan presiding. Into the container for future generations to see went the following:
1. Bulletins (3) of this cornerstone-laying service
2. Bulletins (3) of Victory Sunday when pledges were taken for the Building Program Crusade; copies of the brochure announcing the Building Program Crusade; sample bulletins of June 13, 1954, announcing the congregational meetings for June 30, 1954, and July 11, 1954

---

[103] p 34 of Gove's 1947 History book.

3. Announcement of the election and organizational meetings of both the Board of Trustees and the Building Committee, August 22, 1954

4. Announcement of the actual date of beginning construction of New Building, September 28, 1954, giving list of members received last year

5. Announcement of the coming of Dr. Kagawa to St. Cloud, October 1, 1954 - October 31, 1954

6. Last Layman's Day Service

7. List of all contributors to the Building Fund since its beginning in 1943, including the names of all church school children who gave monthly through the Sacrificial Offering

8. A copy of the new Revised Standard Version of the Bible published in 1953, New Testament in 1946, and Old Testament in 1952, symbolic of the fact that the Bible is the basic foundation of the Church

9. One 1952 *Discipline of the Church*, symbolic of law and organization of the Church

10. *St. Cloud Daily Times* for Tuesday, August 19, 1954, giving pictures and story of groundbreaking and beginning of the Church

11. The *St. Cloud Daily Times* for Saturday, November 20, 1954, giving story of corner stone laying

1956 Building - Cornerstone

12. A History of *First Methodist Church, 1857-1947,* written by Miss Gertrude Gove

13. Current issue of *Upper Room*

14. Current issue of *Christian Advocate*

15. Copy of *The Methodist Hymnal*

16. Copy of the *Upper Room* prepared for the World Council of Churches meeting in Evanston, Illinois, in August 1954, in the various languages of the nations represented in the Council.

This new church was erected on the south part of the property at the corner of Fifth Avenue and Third Street South and faces the Avenue, 302 South 5th Ave. This virtually fireproof building is constructed of concrete, steel, and brick with stone facings modified by local granite at the entrance. The section erected in 1954-1956 consists of the worship center and, below it, the social hall and the ultra-modern kitchen, which the WSCS so proudly paid for in one lump sum (the result of several years of hard work). The educational unit, so badly needed, will be erected as soon as the money can be raised. A new drive is taking place in 1958.

Some of the modern helps for good devotional services held in the Nave are the ceiling of acoustical plaster and tile, the hearing aids in some of the pews, the thermopane-lined family room, and the public address system (the gift of Dr. and Mrs. E. M. Anderson), which carries the service to 480 in the pews, to 70 in temporary seats in the social aisle and the family room, and to 300 more in the Wesley Hall downstairs. Automatic heating and ventilation with zone temperature control eases the work of the caretaker, who is busier than ever because the church is in use most of the week now.

During the pastorate of Rev. Huffman, the two conferences, Minnesota and Northern Minnesota, were united again (1948). At that time, too, St. Cloud was put into the newly created Central District. For easier handling of the finances, the unified weekly system was adopted at First Church, pledges to local budget, missions, and the building fund being placed in the three sections of the one envelope each Sunday. Several years before the General Conference handed down the commission system, First Church, St. Cloud, had been operating under the Department (or Commission) plan.

A Church office was another new thing at First Church during this pastorate. The Blue Cross Society did much to help by giving, at various times, a desk, typewriter, typewriter table, file, and paper cutter.

Beulah Rose Hutchens tells about this room being used as an adult men's Sunday school classroom also. Pastor Huffman while working on the morning sermon, was listening to the group talking. He started to make a correction to the group discussion and leaned back in the chair that is pictured on the left and fell backwards onto the floor.

In 1948, First Church took on the responsibility of forming the St. Cloud Good Will Industries, which is now a semi-community project located at 21 Fifth Avenue South.

A "Discretionary Fund" was set aside to enable the pastor to meet emergencies that cannot wait for official action.

Choir 1950's Rev. Russell Huffman
Dorothy Steuve Collection

During the pastorate, three young men of the congregation became ordained Methodist ministers. They are Duane Lunemann (1953), Russell A. Huffman, Junior (1957), and Manning Van Nostrand (1958).

Great changes took place in the Sunday morning services. Preacher as well as choir were robed; candles and the cross appeared on the altar, which now occupied the center of attention; and pulpit and (an added) lectern stood at each side and nearer the congregation. (The use of acolytes was added in 1958.)

A new electric Baldwin organ was installed. Because two services were now necessary on Sundays, two choirs and even two choir leaders were required. Along with the increased membership came the need for more organizations, one of which is the Business Girl's Christian Fellowship.

In September 1950, Miss Dorothy Sacher, a trained youth worker, came to assist the pastor in the office and with the young people in the church and the Teachers' College (Wesley Foundation). The next two years, Miss Shirley Thompson was the youth director. In the fall of 1953, the Rev. Mr. Shigeo Tanabe, the first minister of Japanese ancestry to unite with the Minnesota Conference, came to St. Cloud as associate pastor and youth director. The arrangement was most satisfactory and great was the disappointment when the church at large, in 1954, requested his release so he could serve the Harris Memorial Methodist church in Honolulu, Hawaii. The new associate pastor, 1954-1955, was the Rev. Mr. Irving Palm, also well trained in youth work.

In cooperation with Methodism the world over, First Church showed the film *John Wesley* several times. In October 1954, in cooperation with other Protestant churches in St. Cloud, First Church presented Dr. Kagawa, that great Japanese Christian evangelist. There has been Methodist participation in the joint Thanksgiving and Lenten services and the Palm Sunday concerts held in St. Cloud. jbg

---

The Rev. Mr. Huffman brought distinct honors to the congregation by his leadership in important District and Conference committees. Great was the shock in 1955 when less than a month before Conference time, it was learned that the Bishop had a larger place for Rev. Huffman to fill and that that place must be filled that year. Reluctantly, First Church members bade farewell hoping that they would be able to finish the building program without their enthusiastic leader.

1955 – 1957

In 1955, the Conference sent to Rochester Rev. Russell A. Huffman; to Warren Rev. Irving Palm; and to St. Cloud, Rev. Russell Luther Hubbard, who had been district superintendent in the Duluth District. Rev. Hubbard faced a most difficult task, that of stepping into the midst of a building program and keeping alive the enthusiasm (expressed financially) that had held the members together. But the work was done so well that by December 1955, enough money had been raised, the contractor had turned over the keys, and the trustees and the building committee had unlocked the front door, switched on the lights, and taken possession at 302 Fifth Avenue South.

From Earle Thompson's photo collection, the following pictures of the construction of the 1956 building.

1914-1955 Building — First Methodist Church St. Cloud — 1955 December Building

Archives, FUMC

January 29 to February 3, 1956 was New Sanctuary Week. Bishop D. Stanley Coors, Dr. Edgar Ackerman, district superintendent, and Dr. H. C. Logan were present to assist the pastor. (Illness had prevented Rev. Huffman from being here, also.) Between the two morning services, the relief carving on the front of the building was unveiled. Virgil E. Siddens, representing contractor and architect, presented the building to Mr. Carlton Eckberg, chairman of the building committee, and to Mr. Earle Thompson, chairman of the board of trustees. The pastor released the veil and the congregation saw, for the first time, the carving, which St. Cloud sculptor Otto Dallmann, had chiseled from Indiana limestone. Mr. Dallmann explained, "The figures represent prayer all ages, anywhere. The child is praying and searching; the adult, strong in faith, guides and protects youth with prayer." During third special week, the building was used for several types of meetings. Holy Communion was

Dallmann's Wood Sculpture

administered, the MYF entertained the city-wide Protestant youth groups, the choir gave a concert, and the entire membership participated in a birthday dinner in Wesley hall.

All admired the natural white oak paneling, which is the background of the chancel and then turned to see over the main entrance on the west side of the building, the large memorial window. The artist, Silianoff,[105] says that the theme of the design is "Christ preaching about a just and loving God omnipotent, omniscient, and omni-present and that it is an attempt to give a visual identity to the intangible." Almost 2000 pieces of true antique glass consisting of approximately 200 different colors and thicknesses were fitted in by hand and joined together with lead comes to form the complete window.

On the wall of the narthex is another piece of relief carving by sculptor Otto Dallmann. This memorial gift from the friends and family of James Martin Dobson is made of Minnesota white oak. Against a background of mosaic tile, Christ stands looking down over the four churches St. Cloud Methodists have erected. A window of the newest church is made from a piece of wood assumed to have come from the original church. The theme of the carving is found in I John 5:11.

St. Cloud is 100 years

When St. Cloud celebrated its centennial, First Church entered into the week's activities with enthusiasm. At the Sunday morning service, honor was paid to about 30 long time members of First Church. Dates used were 1897-1920. In the city parade, the youth of First Church displayed a float and the pastor, Rev. Hubbard, astride his fine horse, represented a Methodist circuit rider.

1957 Circuit Rider, Rev. Metzger

March 18, 1956, First Church began its own centennial celebration with a two year financial program which would overlap into the first year

---

[105] Milcho Silianoff Studio of Greensburg, Pennsylvania.

of the second century of St. Cloud Methodism. During the summer of 1956, a Memorial Lawn committee headed by Miss Edith Grannis raised the funds necessary for the razing of the old building. At a Sunday service, honor was paid to those who had erected the old church and the church historian read a list of the papers that had been put into the cornerstone in 1914 but which weather had made unreadable in 1956.

On September 4, 1956, the St. Cloud Daily Times *ran an article and picture of the opening of the 1911 cornerstone. Left to right in picture: Rev. Russell Hubbard, pastor; Hillis Myers; Gertrude Gove and J. F. McCutchan (Stearns History Museum photo.) Items placed in the cornerstone had been:*
1. A small Bible
2. The Methodist Conference minutes of 1910 or 1911
3. A copy of the Christian Advocate
4. A copy of The Epworth Herald (youth magazine)
5. A copy of the St. Cloud Times and Journal Press
6. List of contributors to building fund. Folder from the Cornerstone laying was added at a later date by Mable J. Lillestrand, 1956

The 2nd photo opposite shows the contents of the cornerstone 50 years later. adt

Thanks to the Blue Cross and others interested, the two stained glass windows were removed and saved for the time when they will be made into pictures for the education unit. The 1917-1918 Roll of Honor, the cap stone of the gymnasium and the corner stone were also preserved for the future. By late fall, the corner at Fifth Avenue and Third Street had become a beautiful approach to an edifice valued at $250,000.

In October 1956, a great change took place in Methodist literature. The recently revised *Advocate* was made into a pastors' magazine and *Together* was published for the congregational reading. First Church, St. Cloud inaugurated the All Family Subscription Plan, which seems to be succeeding. In 1956, also, First Church began publishing a parish newspaper known as the *Methodist Courier*.

The Conference of 1956 sent the Rev. Mr. Malcolm E. Shattuck of Clinton to Waite Park church. In addition, he was to serve as associate pastor at First Church and take charge of the Wesley Foundation work. Mrs. George Skewes became the assistant director.

1957

The Conference appointments read: Rev. Hubbard to Monticello, Rev. Shattuck back to Waite Park and St. Cloud, and the Rev. Paul Otto Metzger to First Church. Mr. Metzger had served congregations at Detroit Lakes and at Hobart Methodist in Minneapolis and was at the time a member of several conference committees and boards. His contribution to St. Cloud and further information about the church building will become a part of the second hundred years history.

Paul O. Metzger's Vision in 1957

So ends a century of service - service to the St. Cloud community, service to the Methodist Church in Minnesota and throughout the world, service to the Church of Christ and to the Kingdom of God He inaugurated.
There have been discouraging years. But there have been good years, too. Today, as we look forward to the next century of service the future looks brighter than it has ever been. Our Church membership hovers near the 1000 mark. We are midway through a building program which, when completed, will give us excellent facilities to continue and enrich the Church's ministry. Another full-time person has been added to our staff. The ministers who have so faithfully served us across the years would rejoice to know that we are thus prepared to face the next century with confidence and hope and faith.

Walls came a tumblin down...

Making way for the new

St. Cloud First Methodist Church, 1956, 4th Sanctuary

Growing our Legacy in Christ

150 years
1857–2007

The Third 50 Years 1957-2007

Nancy Gundersen

First United Methodist Church

St. Cloud, Minnesota

During our third 50 years…

1957 Paul Metzger begins pastorate. First Church observes its Centennial, Gove does a second history.

1960 Education wing is dedicated.

1963 King delivers "I Have a Dream" speech. President Kennedy is assassinated. Ken Beck appointed pastor.

1965 Rev. Beck joins King's second march in Selma, Alabama. Custodians have to deal with 66" of snow in March.

1967 KSJR begins broadcasting from Collegeville; staff includes Michael Barone.

1968 Methodist and Evangelical United Brethren denominations join to become The United Methodist Church, adopt cross & flame logo. Martin Luther King, and Robert Kennedy are assassinated. "First United Methodist Church" becomes official name.

1969 Pipe Organ installed. Richard Collman is Minister of Music, Michael Barone, organist.

1973 Handbells and new wall hangings dedicated.

1975 Massive storm hits area Jan 10-12, takes toll on people & livestock. Some roads closed for 11 days.

1979 Rev. Horst begins tenure. Wesley Hall renovated; Grannis-Martin Fund established.

1981 Tower entrance added.

1982 125th Anniversary celebrated

1983 Summer pulpit exchange has English pastor here and Horsts in Torquay.

1986 Jacob Wetterling abducted.

1988 O'Connell "Tree of Life" dedicated Nov. 6, 1988.

1991 Persian Gulf War. Halloween Blizzard leaves 3' of snow.

1994 Katie Schneider-Bryan appointed; parking lot dedicated.

1996 FUMC becomes charter member of GRIP.

1998 Contemporary worship begins. Early service renamed Classic, second, Bridge. John & Janelle Kendall lead Bridge music team.

1999 Dan Schneider-Bryan joins staff.

2001 9/11 attacks. Labyrinth becomes part of Memorial Garden.

2005 UMCOR (United Methodist Committee on Relief) directs aid to Katrina victims in New Orleans. Congregation begins Visioning process.

2006 Staffing changes from two to four positions: lead pastor, part-time visitation pastor, Christian education, and youth directors.

2007 I-35W Bridge Collapses. 150th Anniversary marked. New Horizons ends its 30 year history. First Church votes to explore relocating/building. Bill Meier appointed lead pastor.

Preface and Acknowledgments

This history is intended to tell the major events of the church for the last fifty years. However, it is also a social history of the many church activities that occurred during this time, activities perhaps not as important individually as major events, but very significant to our memories of the time we spent together. Most of the material for this study came from the reports presented at the church's annual meetings--more formally called the Fourth Quarterly Conferences. Some came from the *Courier*, pastors' letters to the congregation, newspaper accounts, special First United Methodist Church publications, and people's memories. I had help in putting together this account. Lois Barron, Dorothy Stueve, Shirley Echols, and Jessie Harper read my drafts and questioned either my facts, my commas, or my wording when they saw a need. I thank them for helping make this a better history than it would have been without them.

Nancy Gundersen

Chapter One 1957-1963

1955: In the summer of 1955, Rev. Russell A. Huffman, who had lead the First Methodist Church of St. Cloud in a vigorous building campaign to construct a new church on Fifth Avenue, was transferred to Rochester, Minnesota. In his place, Rev. Rev. Russell L. Hubbard, who had been district superintendent in the Duluth District, came to St. Cloud to help finish the project. By December of that year, the new church was complete, and keys to the building were turned over to the congregation. In January 1956, the new church was dedicated. It was a spacious and bright building, with a high ceiling in the sanctuary, light wood, light bricks, and large windows. Downstairs was a fellowship hall, a kitchen, the minister's office, several Sunday school rooms, and some storage rooms.

May 1957 – May 1858: After being in St. Cloud for two years, Rev. Hubbard in the summer of 1957 was assigned to the Methodist Church in Monticello, and another minister, Rev. Rev. Paul O. Metzger, came to serve First Church. Before the St. Cloud assignment, he had been in Detroit Lakes and at Hobart Methodist Church. He and his wife, Phyllis, plus their children, Steve, Cindy, and Barby, were to stay for six years. It seems apparent that the congregation appreciated his talents and approach, as well as those of his wife. According to the Pastor Parish Committee report of 1958, "It is clearly evident that the welfare of the whole church and of the people individually are the constant concern of this pastor and of his wife."

In May of 1958, slightly less than a year after Rev. Metzger arrived, the church held its annual charge conference, and those responsible for the activities of the church wrote reports. These reports for the church year 1957-58 give us a feeling for the first year of Rev. Metzger's tenure.

At the time of the report, the church had 959 members, and the congregation was doing their work with around $47,000 in receipts. The pastor was paid $5,400, plus $450 travel expenses, and a parsonage to live in.

Besides Rev. Metzger, there was an associate minister, Rev. Malcolm E. Shattuck, who had numerous responsibilities. He was the pastor of the Waite Park Methodist Church, having been sent there in the summer of 1956. He also worked with the Wesley Foundation at St. Cloud State College, and served part-time at First Church. However, in the summer of 1958, the Annual Conference decided that he should devote himself full time to the Waite Park Church, and so Rev. Metzger was left without an associate minister. Fortunately, the church was able to hire Mrs. Florence Lund as a full-time education assistant, and she stayed for over four years.

John Scheel Custodian

There were three other staff members to assist with the work: Wilma Slobetz, church secretary, John Scheel, custodian, and Ruth Skewes, who worked part-time with the College Wesley Foundation. At this time, First Church had considerable responsibility toward the work on the campus of St. Cloud State College.

The church was a vigorous church, and had many lay officers, commissions, and committees. The Nominating Committee report for 1958-59 named the work bodies, many names familiar to Methodists today and some no longer used. Some examples are the Commission on Membership, the Commission on Education, the Commission on Missions, the Commission on Stewardship, the Commission on Recreation and Social Fellowship, and the Parsonage Committee. The Library Committee was formed in 1957. Previously the church had only a Good Literature Secretary, an odd title to contemporary ears. Over this was the Church Council, composed of all the leaders of the church.

Several things are of note. One is that, almost without exception, all married women are referred to by their husbands' names, not their given names. This practice was to continue until the women's movement and new social preferences did away with the practice (by 1974 records have fully gone over to the new practice). In addition, many of what we now call "committees" were referred to as "commissions."

Each committee and commission had a nicely filled out membership of workers. Undoubtedly not everyone was particularly active or came to all the committee meetings any more than they do today, but still one has the impression of a busy congregation.

The Sunday school was functioning well, with 215 children enrolled in the children's program, 112 in the youth division (ages 12-23 years), and 30 adults. On any given Sunday, about half of the pupils were in attendance.

There were also organizations within the church at this time. The Woman's Society of Christian Service reported 214 in their group, with an average attendance of 50 women at meetings. There were also small group meetings in circles. Members of the Woman's Society called on shut-ins (report for that year said that over 300 calls were made), had study sessions on mission topics and others, and earned and managed a great deal of money. For the year 1957-58, they had control of $10,518. $1,008 of this was sent to the District Treasurer, $5,741 was spent on local church activities, other small expenditures used up some more, and $3,747 was kept as cash on hand.

For the working women, there was the Blue Cross Society (later to become the Wesleyan Service Guild). They had 37 members that year, held regular meetings, and helped both church and community, particularly with financial needs. At this time the men's group did not seem to be very active.

There was, however, the Methodist Youth Fellowship (MYF) which was very active, with their retreats, rallies, a Christ Work Day, the Christmas candlelight service, and numerous other activities.

The various Protestant denominations in St. Cloud did some things together. Activities included a mission study on Japan that Methodists spearheaded a United Protestant weekly Lenten service, and the United Church Women's programs.

Some changes occurred during the first few years of Rev. Metzger's tenure. Most significant, the Building Committee was reactivated in 1957 to begin work on an addition to the church, the education unit (which would hold classrooms for the Sunday school, several offices, the church library/meeting room, the nursery, the choir room, and several washrooms).

According to the Building Committee's chairman, William Clark, in May 1958 the church had 408 pupils of all ages enrolled in classes, with an average attendance of 250. By 1960, he said, it was predicted that they would have 800 pupils. (In actuality they never achieved that high a number, but they did reach an average attendance of 270 by May of 1961.) In his minister's report to the same conference, Rev. Metzger commented that they already had $30,000 pledged to the new addition.

The church was growing during this time. Church attendance during 1957-1958 averaged 401 persons per Sunday. (Summer attendance was not included in this figure, as summers always showed a drop in attendance.) Rev. Metzger gave much credit to the Commission on Membership and Evangelism, headed from 1957-1958 by Glenn Carlson and then the next year and for eight years after by Woodrow Wilson and his wife, Eleanor.

Loyalty Dinner

Finances also were looking healthy. People were committed to their church. During the stewardship drive of 1957, according to Rev. Metzger, 85 men of the church were "actively engaged in solicitation" while the women prepared the loyalty dinners that accompanied this drive. The total of money pledged for the next two-year period was $109,877.

Several additional matters of interest during this time period: Arthur Bluhm, a worker in the Sunday school program, was honored in December 1957 for over 40 years devoted to Christian education. His daughter, Dorothy Stueve, remembers helping her father set up the church school classrooms in the fellowship hall of the old church early each Sunday morning. Former Sunday school pupil Rev. Marva Jean Hutchens remembers his warm smile and the candy he kept in his pocket for welcoming children.

Also, the church was taking an interest in the youth camp at Spicer (Decision Hills) and had contributed almost a thousand dollars to it. This camp was to figure significantly in the retreat and camp experiences of the church.

The choir acquired robes in 1958, and an electric organ was purchased for the church.

May 1960 – May 1961: By 1960-61, there is a record of a Men's Club sponsoring the Boy Scout Troop #1 (which met in the church), having a pancake supper, giving Bibles to the 4th grade children in church school, and sending work crews to Decision Hills.

Rev. Metzger was leading the church and at the same time doing much committee work for the Minnesota Conference. Mrs. Lund, the church's education director, was also doing work on both levels. Finally, the Pastoral Relations Committee in exasperation declared in their 1961 report to the local church conference that although the committee was proud of their pastor's and educational director's participation in District and Minnesota Conference work, "the pastoral relations committee feels that the District Superintendent and the Conference should be aware of the fact that although these are very capable people they are only human and a limit must be placed upon the amount of time required of them outside the local church." Whether this complaint ever made its way to official ears is unknown.

In the same 1961 report, the Parish Visitor, Ruth Skewes (who had been hired in August of 1960), said that she was doing 40-45 home calls a month, plus weekly hospital visits. The church called on all Methodists in the hospital, whether they were members of the local church or not. Fewer were than were not. She was also working with the Wesley Foundation at St. Cloud State College.

Rev. Metzger praised Ruth's work in its many facets, including "her endless goading of the minister to see people she has marked for a pastoral call." (He, himself, was diligent in that department, reporting in his first church year that he had made 345 hospital calls and 120 home calls.)

In 1960, the education and office wing was finished and was consecrated in May. Rev. Metzger said of it: "No one appreciates the spacious educational plant more than those of us who work in it week in and week out. It would be quite impossible for us now to give it up."

First Methodist Church 1960, with Education Wing

By the Annual Meeting in May 1962, Mrs. Lund, the Christian Education Director who had apparently been a great help to the church's program, had left to work for the Methodist Department of Publications in Nashville, and the church was left with neither an associate minister nor an education director. At the same time, the Minnesota Conference had decided that it wanted to have an ordained minister working with the campus Wesley Foundation, so they proposed sending a minister to St. Cloud to work with the Wesley Foundation half time and with First Church half time. Rev. Richard Lewis would come to fill the position. He would work with First Church's educational program and assist the head minister by preaching occasionally and doing some hospital visiting.

 Ruth Skewes would then give up her Wesley Foundation work and spend more time with the church, making her many calls as church visitor, putting out the *Courier,* sitting in on a number of committees, and teaching 8th grade confirmation.

The Parsonage Committee, which apparently was conscientious and had done much work on the minister's residence over the years, recommended to the congregation that they keep up the parsonage at its present level and start a fund to buy or build a new parsonage.

For the first time in quite a while, the Methodist Men held monthly dinner meetings, and the church had four certified lay speakers (men who sometimes substituted in other pulpits, as well as handling some other assignments for churches of the area).

Finally, in the 1961-62 year, the church offered space for a day care center for mentally retarded children, and planning work had begun, in cooperation with a local committee.

Library, 1961

May 1962 – May 1963: In the Quarterly Conference Report of May 16, 1963 (for 1962-63), one notes what had been somewhat evident for several years, a bigger push in Christian Social Concerns, a committee chaired by Florence and Ernest Stennes. According to their report, the committee kept the congregation aware of bills before the State Legislature, and Ernest Stennes attended a conference at Hamline University on how to lobby for the school bus bill and Sunday closing. The committee informed the congregation of the State's new fair housing law and the State Commission Against

Discrimination. They also urged the congregation to help support Rust College, a black school in Mississippi, which the congregation did.

Nationally, this was a time of social unrest, particularly because of racial tensions and a heightened sense of social injustice. Dr. Martin Luther King was leading protest marches. In August of 1963, there was a March on Washington where King gave his now famous speech "I Have a Dream."

The Commission on Missions also became involved with this social issue. They hosted a church choir from Rust College, and housed the choir in church members' homes. They also gave $400 to Rust College.

The Commission on Education and the Family Life Committee was also out in front on progressive issues They planned and executed a four-week sex education series for the adolescent youth of the church, which, according to the conference report, was "well received."

In April 1963, the Pastoral Relations Committee was notified that it was the Conference's intent to move Rev. Metzger to Hamline Methodist Church in St. Paul.

In Rev. Metzger's final report to the congregation, he had positive words for membership, which continued to grow; the church school, which "is effective"; and the youth program, which "shows increased vitality." He complimented the congregation for its good spirit and also for giving facilities to the Association for the Mentally Retarded for the operation of a day school.

However, he noted that church finances were rocky. They had, he said, enjoyed six years of few financial problems. With the building of the new educational addition, income had increased significantly five years before, then had remained at that level ever since, even though they had gained additional members and individual incomes had gone up nationally. Then, in the spring of 1962, they had had a lackluster finance campaign. As a result, Rev. Metzer said things needed to be handled soon before they became more serious.

Along with the notice that Rev. Metzger was needed elsewhere, the Conference recommended a possible successor to him. According to the Pastoral Relations Committee chair, Hillis Meyers, the committee met with the minister and had attended his church to hear him preach. They unanimously voted to accept him as the senior minister of the church. However, Meyers said, "Because of the many moves involved and the possibility of last minute changes by the Bishop and his cabinet... it is not advisable to disclose the man's name at this time." The man being discussed was Rev. Kenneth Beck, who would come to First Church and stay for 16 years.

CHAPTER TWO 1963 - 1967

May 1963 – May 1964: By the church's quarterly conference in May of 1964, Rev. Kenneth Beck had been the minister of First Church for a year. He was a friendly and hard working minister, very interested in theology and social issues both. He described himself as the church's "resident theologian" and encouraged significant congregational involvement in the matters of the church. His family consisted of his wife, Catherine who would become a professor of art history at St. Cloud State College, his son, Peter, and two daughters, Martha and Sarah. They lived in the church parsonage. Before coming to St. Cloud, Rev. Beck had been at Christ Methodist Church in St. Paul and the Methodist Church in Raymond, Minnesota.

The governing body of the church was the Board of Stewards. Its chairman was Carlton Eckberg, and the Lay Leader was Charles Emery. Membership was slightly under 1,000, and the church budget for the coming year was $67,214.

The church had the assistance of two part-time ministers, Rev. Donald Day, who was also the minister at Waite Park Methodist Church, and Rev. Richard Lewis, associate pastor, who was also directing the college's Wesley Foundation. Each had a one-fourth time appointment. Rev. Day and Rev. Lewis worked with Sunday school and the junior high/senior high young people.

One of the church's works in progress was the new stained glass windows for the sanctuary. The themes of the windows had been chosen by the Memorial Committee, and three of the windows were being made by their designer, Bronislaw Bak, an art instructor at St. John's University. One had been given by the Woman's Society in honor of their 25th anniversary.

A School of Missions had been held three Sundays in January, in cooperation with the Waite Park Methodist Church. The school dealt with mission work in

Southern Asia. This was the time of the Vietnam conflict, which may have influenced the part of the world that was chosen. First Church's former pastor, Rev. Russell Huffman, gave the keynote sermon, and an average of 90 persons were in attendance each session, a very good response.

The Commission on Membership and Evangelism was composed of four couples, with Woodrow (Woody) & Eleanor Wilson as the chairs. They made approximately 150 calls and brought 53 new members into the church in the 63-64 Charge Conference year. Each group of new members had an orientation session with Rev. Beck, and then he, Ruth Skewes, and the committee tried to help them become active in some part of the church's work.

The junior high MYF was having an interesting and thought-provoking year, advised by Dr. and Mrs. Roger Barrett and Dr. and Mrs. Alvin Schelske. Examples of their activities included speakers from the National Association for the Advancement of Colored People and Alcoholics Anonymous. They also saw films on inter-faith marriage and migrant workers.

For more active programs, they had a winter hayride, a roller skating party, and an income-earning spaghetti dinner, as well as a work day in the fall. The senior MYF was also doing interesting things, although their advisor, Rev. Lewis, commented that attendance seemed to drop off dramatically after students were confirmed.

The Woman's Society of Christian Service (WSCS) had 187 members and Wesleyan Service Guild had 41 members. Aside from WSCS's regular meetings, they served the summer coffee hour after church, a mother and daughter banquet, worked on Loyalty Dinners, and served dinners, luncheons, and coffee breaks to a three-day study session of Minnesota Conference of Ministers. If all of this cooking were not enough, they also made and packed 500 cookies at Christmas for mentally handicapped children in Cambridge School. Wesleyan Service Guild studied missions, had speakers, handled two church coffee hours, and made a special financial donation to the church.

The Men's Club held a pancake supper, sponsored the Boy Scout troop at the church, and donated money to church projects and needs.

In his report to the congregation in May 1964, Rev. Beck exhorted it to commit to a "greater ministry of service" in the St. Cloud area. The need for church laity to be involved in the world's work was to be a continuing theme of his ministry.

Rev. Lewis also spoke to the church's people: "The one thing that I like about working with this church is the chance to express new ideas. I do not expect everyone to agree with me, or I with them, but there is a chance to explore here that is lacking in other places."

May 1964 – February 1965: The summer of 1964, the church had a softball team in the City Church League, the first time in many years, and they won the championship.

In the fall, the church started a three-year series of classes for confirmation, a 7th grade, an 8th grade, and a 9th grade. They were held on Tuesday evenings. Meanwhile, the Sunday school classes started using the new Methodist curriculum. It was cheerful material, with special songs for the different age groups, brief lessons, suggested activities, and a church newspaper that children could take home and read with their parents.

The Day School for mentally and physically handicapped children continued to meet in the church.

There was a School of Missions held in January by the Missions Commission, headed by Ralph Sorenson, and $6,929 in total was disbursed from the church budget for benevolences (givings outside of local church).

In his annual report, Rev. Beck said, "We have a beautiful, functional, well-maintained building. We have a fine staff and many, many lay people serving effectively." However, he still believed more could be done by church members. "The laity is the laos, the people of God, but many do not know it. Many still feel that the ministers and other staff personnel are 'paid to be religious for them,' that it is the duty of the layman to pay, and of the preachers to pray--and teach, and recruit, and visit, etc."

1965: In 1965, there was money available for another large window, so the church was going to order it and eight small ones for the chancel. However, the window maker, Mr. Bak, said that it would look better to install all the small windows at once, so he gave the church credit for an additional eight chancel windows.

The parsonage committee was as usual busy. In 1965 they had painted the parsonage; and the chair, Robert Madeson, reported that next they needed to re-side and paint the garage.

There was talk that Rev. Day of Waite Park Methodist would be transferred, and that the Wesley Foundation wanted a full-time person. Hillis Myers, chairman of the Pastoral Relations Committee, told the congregation that his committee had been talking about having a full-time associate minister for the church, someone who would be responsible for education, among other duties.

The youth group went to Pine Bend in the summer of 1965 to run a children's Bible school, and there was an ecumenical youth group coffee house - the Back Way - in Wesley House (near the college campus). The three-year confirmation classes were still taking a toll on Sunday night MYF.

Since 1962, the church had been having nagging financial troubles. In the treasurer's report for the year 1965, Mrs. Donald Orth reported that the church had spent $82,574, $420 more than they had taken in for the same period.

1966: Because of financial troubles, the church started sending out monthly statements of pledge payments, which helped the money come in more regularly, but did not help the deficit, as 1966 was ended with a $804 negative balance.

Financial matters had not been helped by needed church repair. The House Committee (what is now the Building and Management Committee) had to spend $3,271 on the church building. The heating system had to be fixed, some painting needed doing, and bricks and the ceilings in the sanctuary and narthex were cleaned. As the chairman, Donald Allen said, their three thousand, plus expenditures were "more than a little over our proposed budget of $900."

In February of 1966, Eleanor and Woodrow Wilson made their final report for the Commission on Membership and Evangelism, as they were no longer going to be chairing it. Woody Wilson talked of their new members and of the hospitality of the Becks, opening their home to the orientation session: "I am sure that many of the new people leave with the feeling that they have known Rev. Beck and his family for a long time."

CHAPTER THREE 1968 – 1971

1968: In 1968, the Methodist Church united with the Evangelical United Brethren Church and became the United Methodist Church. Some things changed in the local churches, but much remained the same. There were now three Methodist churches in the immediate area, Waite Park, and Grace (formerly an EUB congregation).

The youth group's name changed from Methodist Youth Fellowship (MYF) to United Methodist Youth Fellowship (UMYF). The church women's group abandoned Woman's Society of Christian Service (WSCS) and took up United Methodist Women (UMW).

Rev. Beck had become very busy, aside from his traditional church duties. He had a variety of Conference responsibilities, including District Director of Social Concerns. He was president of the St. Cloud Ministerial Association, chair of the Board of Directors of Tri-Cap, secretary/treasurer of the Committee for a Sheltered Workshop, and a member of several other boards and commissions.

He was also involved in a radio ministry, as well as the securing of a site for a new Methodist church in the north section of town.

Rev. Beck had some help with the church responsibilities, in that Peary Wilson, an intern minister, had been assigned to the church. He worked with the UMYF, as they planned and executed various projects to earn money for their United Nations trip. They also had weekend retreats at Decision Hills, planned a canoe trip for the summer, and did a variety of other things. He also taught 8th grade confirmation.

Ruth Skewes continued to handle the *Courier,* sending out only about four a year because Rev. Beck and others had started writing letters to the congregation when something needed communicating. She also called on new

Methodists in the area. Where she got all the names is not certain, but possibly it was from referrals of other Methodist churches, probably from Welcome Wagon referrals, certainly from church visitors.

Membership as of Jan. 1969 was 1,095, and there was a confirmation class of 39. New members were added to the church, 129 of whom, including members of the confirmation class.

In this year, the Commission on Stewardship and Finance had been broken into two committees: Stewardship and Finance. William Bridges of the Finance Commission reported the spending of the church as being $81,216, with an overdrawn amount of $2,220. This had partly come about because of some big expenditures to maintain the church building. Expenses were partly helped by the church renting out several classrooms to the St. Cloud area school district.

A helpful organizational chart was included in the quarterly conference report for 1969. It showed the Board of Administration being composed of a representative from the Decision Hills Committee, the Pastor Parish Committee, the Trustees, the Nomination Committee, Finance Commission, Building Maintenance Committee, Audit Committee, Campus Ministry, New Church, and Day Care Center.

The second decision-making board was the Council of Ministries, which included a representative from the Board of Administration, the Lay Leader, chairs from Ecumenical Affairs Committee, Membership Committee, Mission Committee, Stewardship Committee, Finance Committee, Christian Social Concerns Committee, Worship Committee, Education Coordinator, Children's Division, Youth Division, Adult Division, Family Division, WSCS, and staff.

It is interesting that many of the reports to the March 1969 annual conference were made by commission chairs, but that the nominating committee's slate of officers for 1969-1970 had only committees on it. Names were changing. In addition, it appears that the former Stewards were now Members at Large. This may have had to do with the merger of two denominations with different names for things needing to agree on common practices.

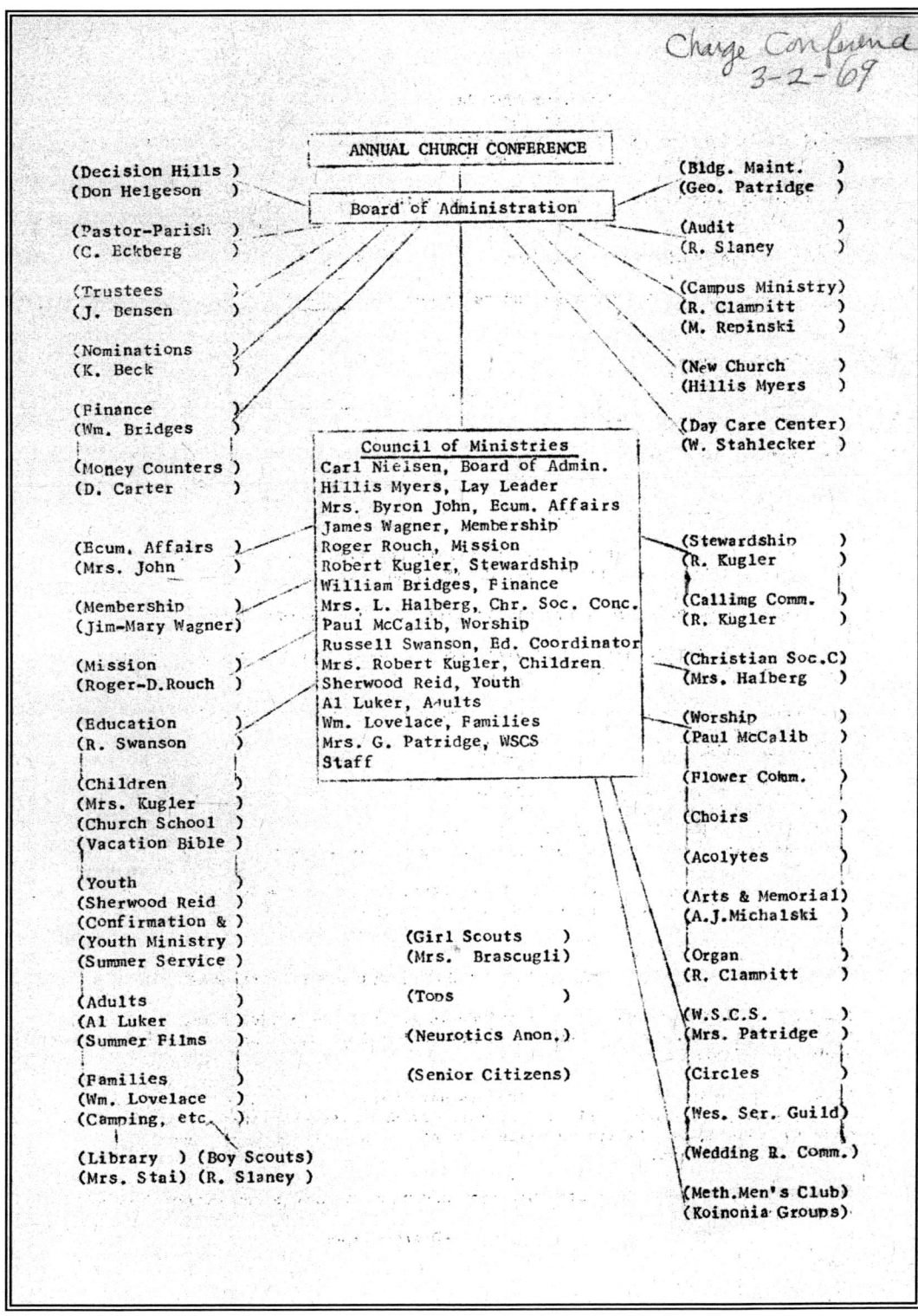

Betty Partch made the final report of the Parsonage Committee, as its work was going to be incorporated in a new Building and Management Committee.

The committee had not done a great deal of work to the parsonage, as extensive decorating had been done in 1967, and they were still paying for it. However, the Men's Club had purchased and installed carpeting in the parsonage dining room, kitchen, and bath.

The newly formed United Methodist Women had 166 members. Among their activities, they served five weddings and some coffee hours after funerals.

The Commission on Education, headed by Pauline Hopkins, held a church camping weekend at Decision Hills in 1968 and were planning another for 1969. As usual, vacation church school was held.

Another wrinkle in education happened at this time. The early church service was only 45 minutes long and then there was a half hour for adult classes and Talk Back (a discussion of the Sunday's sermon with Rev. Beck). The Talk Back was popular, but thirty minutes (minus getting-there/getting-settled) did not make for satisfactory classes. While this adult activity was going on, the children were in church school for 1 hour and 15 minutes.

Rust College was on the church's agenda, as the Christian Social Concerns Committee, with Dick and Mary Corliss chairing it, sent books to Rust College in Holly Springs, Mississippi. At the same time, the Wesleyan Service Guild was trying to exchange letters with the staff of the college. Their motivation was a hoped for "better understandings between people." Gertrude Gove worked on this.

The Missions Commission, headed by Kay Seeley, had a fine and varied year. In January, there was a program with an Ecumenical Dialogue Group, composed of a Catholic priest, a Lutheran pastor, and Rev. Beck. It is interesting that this activity was discussed at the annual meeting under "missions." Perhaps an uneasy feeling about possible connotations helped lead to the formation in 1969 of the Ecumenical Affairs Committee.

Then, also in January, a six-hour workshop for missions was held at the church, and in February Indian religions were studied (Hinduism, Buddhism, and Islam). This study topic may have come about because of church interest in the Lodhipur Institute in India.

Apparently, this led to the need for some Methodist denomination study, and Rev. Beck led a three-session class on Methodism. Finally, in the fall of 1968 the church was involved in a series of ecumenical services conducted in Waite Park, Sauk Rapids, Centennial, and St. Mary's Cathedral.

It is interesting to note that in spite of the financial problems of the church, they still gave $5,455 as their World Service apportionment and almost $4,000 in Advance Specials to various causes. As in past years, this giving was considered an essential part of being a church and not to be slighted.

1969: In mid-1969, Marvin Repinski had become the Methodist campus minister at St. Cloud State College, and he made a report to the church's annual meeting about his program and ministry. He had a weekly Tuesday evening program at the college, with either a discussion on a selected topic or a worship service. The group also made a yearly trip to some place that they had an interest in. In 1969, it was, as he said, to the "Deep South," an area of the country still deeply disturbed about integration.

Wesley Foundation had a singing group that performed at two of the church's services, and Rev. Repinski took students along with him when he went to other churches to be guest preacher. He commented that he was attempting to help students "to gain some positive view of the Institutional Church. It's not the most popular institution with students!"

On July 1, 1969, Rev. Richard Collman arrived in St. Cloud to be the church's associate minister. He was an energetic young man with a love for both ministry and music. In addition, he was a good fit for the young people of whom he was in charge.

In his report to the Annual Charge Conference of February 1970, Rev. Beck was able to report that the church was still growing, perhaps not as much as desired, but still a "fine accomplishment in a time of general decline." (Most of the mainline churches were experiencing membership loss.) The membership committee that year was headed by James and Mary Wagner.

They saw 88 new people join the church, including 23 confirmation students. At the same time, the church lost 61 members because of death, a move out of town, or lack of interest and attendance. Rev. Richard Collman continued with the church as associate minister, and Betty Partch was secretary. John Scheel was the custodian. Ruth Skewes handled visiting and administrative responsibilities.

William Bridges and his Finance Committee were working with the church's continuing and growing deficit. They had prepared a 1970 budget that would help reduce the debt. Rev. Beck concurred: "It is wise at this time to make necessary adjustments, before the day comes when we are so far in arrears that we must cut program staff or benevolence commitments in much more drastic ways."

Experimentation with the education programs seems to be a staple of First Methodist. The fall of 1969 was no exception, when the church started a

Sunday school with a goal that every church family would go to church on either the second or third Sunday for 2½ hours. Children would go to a class for this period of time. The youth and the adults would go to church, enjoy a coffee or juice break, and then go to a class on their particular Sunday in the month. (There would also be the 11 a.m. service each Sunday.)

On the first, fourth, and occasional fifth Sunday, there would be the standard two worship services (9:30 and 11:00 a.m.) and one-hour children's classes at the same time as each service.

According to Rev. Beck in the Feb. 1970 Charge Conference Report, the program had only "limited success." While there had been a commendable increase in youth and adult education, the children's attendance at first, fourth, and fifth Sunday classes was down dramatically. One suspects the schedule was confusing to parents because of its irregularity.

Youth ministry was also starting some new programs. A small Tuesday evening group had begun, led by Sherwood Reid, and the church was starting a coffee house in the youth room. There was also an informal group, which would meet weekly to do various activities of their choosing. Rev. Collman said: "I am confident that youth ministry is best done by and for youth - that is why we may be slow in getting going, but have a more engaging ministry in the long run."

The Missions Committee, headed by Linda and John Peck, held a large auction in a field on the north end of town, land that the Annual Conference had recently purchased for a new church. Those who attended remember lines of items stretched across the field and an auction that lasted well into the afternoon. That year the church gave a total of $18,393 to benevolence.

The Worship Committee, headed by Paul McCalib, had a great deal to handle. Richard Skewes, who was Ruth Skewes' son, resigned in December as church organist, and in January 1970, Michael Barone became the new organist. He handled music programs on St. John's Public Radio Station.

In addition, the Worship Committee was experimenting with some newer types of services on occasion. Rev. Beck said of this: "First, there is a certain risk involved every time we depart from the usual service, but it is a risk worth taking in order that our worship may be stimulating and encouraging to our faith. Second, most of the time we do stay pretty much with the tried and true--we are not really 'far out.'"

A new organ, a Wicks Pipe Organ, was installed in the fall of 1969. The Organ Committee, a subcommittee of the larger Worship Committee, was headed by Richard Clampitt. This committee spearheaded a drive for a new organ and oversaw its installation. The old organ was advertised, and went to the Lake Koronis Assembly Grounds. In this same year, a bell for the Church's tower was purchased, a memorial to a young man, Gary Davis. It came from a Capuchin monastery in Wisconsin.

In his annual report to the congregation, Rev. Beck also listed the various organizations using the church: the Boy Scout Troop #1 (John Peck, Scoutmaster), the Girl Scout troop, the Association for Retarded Children, the Community Day Care Center, the Hearing Loss Clinic, the Sight Loss Training Program, Neurotics Anonymous, and a number of other occasional users.

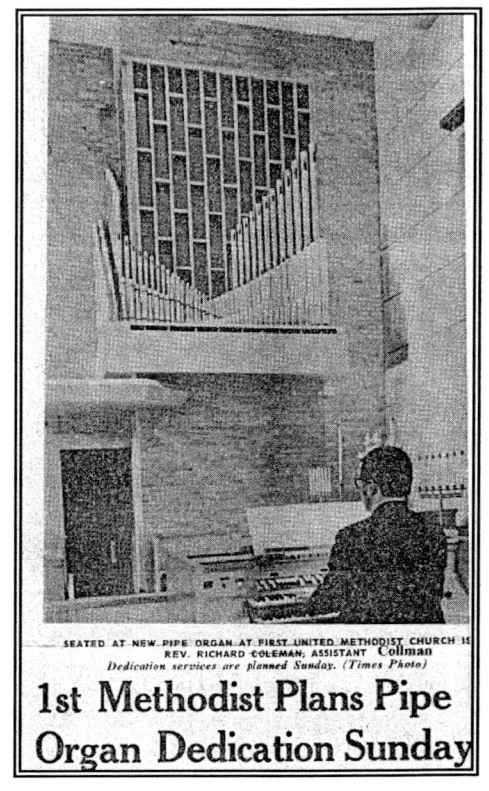

Permission granted by *St. Cloud Times/Times Media* to use the 14 Nov 1969 article page 12 Col 1.

There was some controversy about the church's practice of keeping its front doors unlocked and thus open to the public. On several occasions sound system equipment was stolen. Rev. Beck was a staunch supporter of an open church, and the Worship Committee at this point agreed with him that the doors should be kept open from 8 a.m. to 11 p.m., or until no one was in the building. There are stories of Rev. Beck coming over from the parsonage to lock the church up at night, often with the family dog, and of one occasion when he found a small flood in the church basement.

The Ecumenical Affairs Committee had been formally recognized as a local church committee in 1969 and was under the chairmanship of Joanne John. The committee decided to contact the clergy of 32 churches and parishes. Twenty-six of these contacts responded positively, and in September of 1969, there was a first community meeting, with representatives from nine congregations attending. Eventually this community group named itself the Layman's Inter Church Committee and started to meet monthly. They had as many as 18 churches and parishes participating. Among other things, a Pew Exchange was held in conjunction with the Week of Prayer for Christian Unity. Rev. Beck and Rev. Collman were both involved in this venture into ecumenism.

A November 2, 1989, concert at Orchestra Hall, Minneapolis, was called a "Joyful Noise: A Musical Birthday Gift to the Community from the Institute for Ecumenical and Cultural Research."

God surely has a sense of humor. When in the 1850's Boniface Wimmer was planning the foundation of Saint John's Abbey, he wrote to King Ludwig of Bavaria to ask for money, pointing out that the 20,000 Catholics in Minnesota had only 12 priests. "Without a doubt," he wrote, "many of our Catholic countrymen, as elsewhere, will succumb to the Methodist sect if they do not soon receive spiritual leadership and protection." Saint John's has more than fulfilled his vision, becoming a flourishing religious community that has provided leadership in the church, not just in Minnesota but through the country.

What Abbot Boniface could not foresee, however, is that Saint John's would become a center of ecumenism. Little more than 100 years after he wrote, the dreaded Methodists and other Christians from all over the world would join Catholics at the Institute for Ecumenical and Cultural Research to form communities of scholars to live, work, and pray together in an atmosphere of true Christian friendship. *Deus simper maio*, the theologians used to say: God is always greater and does more than we can imagine. We might translate: a God of surprises.

Patrick Sherry, Lecturer, Religious Studies

Department, University of Lancaster, Lancaster, England
provided by Joanne John

Rev. Collman in his Quarterly Conference Report praised the congregation: "I genuinely feel that this church is one of the most progressive and flexible in Minnesota, and I am grateful for the opportunity to work here and serve you."

Rev. Beck concluded his report with: "Along with my family, I have enjoyed the past seven years in St. Cloud. We are looking forward, the Lord, the congregation and the Bishop willing, to the continuation of service in your midst in the Name of Christ."

1970: A number of changes occurred in 1970. The Nominating Committee gave a report, naming committees for the period of June to December of that year because the Methodist Church was switching its organizational year over to a calendar year in 1971. The group FISH was being organized at the church (a volunteer assistance group that had people on telephone duty who were able to help with community callers' needs--an emergency ride to the doctor's office, a sudden and important need for a babysitter, the name of a St. Cloud contact organization, such as Catholic Charities, to call for help).

Finally, on January 1, 1970, members of the Wesley Foundation at St. Cloud State College became participants in the United Ministries in Higher Education a group composed of a number of Protestant denominations that united to facilitate religious activities on campus. Consequently, the organization no longer reported to First Church's annual meeting, and ties were somewhat loosened between church and campus.

Russ Swanson, who was working with Sunday school, said that his committee had decided to offer only one Sunday school, at 9:30 a.m., starting in the fall of 1970. He said that the numbers were too low to justify two sets of classes (and it was growing increasingly hard to staff two sets). They would still have adult classes at both 9:30 and 11 a.m. Ideally, the families with children would all come at 9:30 a.m., the adults going to their classes and the children to theirs. Then at 11 a.m. the whole family would go to church together.

Some of this undoubtedly happened and was a benefit to families with young children because now the adults could go to classes, knowing their children were busy elsewhere. However, what also happened is that families with children started preferring the 9:30 a.m. service, and the 11 a.m. service, which had previously been well attended, started to shrink to much smaller proportions.

Richard Collman married Katherine Kennedy in June 1970. Rev. Beck conducted the ceremony, and the church membership was invited to the wedding.

CHAPTER FOUR 1972 – 1978

1972: A new ecumenical project was underway in St. Cloud in 1972, the United Christian Development Effort. Along with the Methodist Church, the St. Cloud Diocese of the Roman Catholic Church, the Presbyterian Church, Peace United Church of Christ Salem Lutheran Church, and Bethlehem Lutheran Church were joined in a group effort to meet a need the clergy were seeing in their ministry. Fred Haverland was the church's representative on the working group.

Their goal was to provide some retirement housing for middle-income people of all denominations. Ministers and priests had become aware that St. Cloud at this time did not have enough apartments to serve older people. There were several special lower-income apartments for seniors in St. Cloud, but their income ceilings disqualified some people and disturbed others, who either didn't want to receive any government aid or perhaps didn't like to reveal their private finances to gain entrance.

An ecumenical adult education series was also meeting at Cathedral High School on Sunday evenings, and members of the church were encouraged to attend. At the same time, First United Methodist was holding its own adult education, with four different courses being taught on Sunday morning, and Lenten Seminars on Sunday afternoon. These Sunday afternoon programs were attended regularly by nearly 100 people, an excellent response.

John Scheel, the church's long-time custodian, retired after 17 years and was honored and thanked at a retirement party.

After Mr. Scheel's retirement, Jim Garven signed on as church custodian in 1972. He also started working with the youth. He went at it with gusto. He was involved with the United Nations Seminar for youth, he worked with the young people at the Pine Bend Mission (where they conducted a Sunday school), and he supervised a youth program that served hot coffee to drivers on holidays. The young people also served coffee some Sundays at church, went Valentine caroling, went on retreats and canoe trips, saw movies together and discussed them. Some of these events were shared with the 7th and 8th graders.

Worship and conversation about religious matters were also a part of Jim's program. Jim said, explaining his varied agenda of doing and of contemplation: "Through these happenings the young people encounter themselves, other people, nature, and God."

This was the first year of handbell music in the church. Natalie Slack owned a set of hand bells and assembled and conducted a boys' group of players, who performed frequently. Two other new additions were the use of lay liturgists in the worship services and quite a few musical groups and soloists from outside the congregation. Wally Miller was directing the Chancel Choir.

The Association for Retarded Children left the Church in 1972 to find more space for their program. Sometime after their leaving, Mary Theresa Anderson's Montessori School rented upstairs classrooms in the church and have remained since, although the school has recently changed owners.

In the same year, the Grannis Education Fund awarded three students with $400 loan/scholarship awards.

1973: The Vietnam War was nearing conclusion, and in January of 1973, Rev. Beck reflected in comments to the church's annual charge conference the uneasiness that he had felt during the past years as he spoke and demonstrated against the war, knowing that there were those in the congregation who felt very strongly that this was a necessary war.

He said that while he "would never intentionally alienate a fellow human being, for the purpose of Christian love is reconciliation," nevertheless, he believed that "some abrasiveness is inescapable if one is true to what he believes is right and good."

The year 1973 also saw Rev. Robert Kendall arrive on staff part-time to assist Rev. Beck. He was to be involved with the liturgy, new member visitation, drama in the church service, and occasional preaching. He performed some memorable Bible characters as part of church services.

At the same time, according to Carlton Eckberg, chairman of the Pastor-Parish Committee, "After due diligence, soul searching and cross-examination, we accepted the request of Ruth Skewes that she become a part-time employee limiting her visitations to the elderly. . ." The Committee commended her "for her many years of devoted and Christian service to First United Methodist Church for which we are most humbly grateful."

Ruth Skewes explained, in her own report as Parish Visitor, that "having reached the age of increasing self-interest and decreasing energies at just the right time to qualify for Social Security," she had chosen to reduce her workload. However, she was still going to call on hospital patients, those in nursing homes, and on shut-ins. She would also help with membership records. In 1974, one learns that she was also available to take shut-ins to doctor appointments, to the hospital, or back home. One wonders how much she really cut down her work.

This same committee redefined Jim Garven's role in the church. He was appointed Administrative Assistant, which meant being church business manager as well as supervisor of custodial work. He would also continue to work with the young people.

A second handbell choir was performing for worship, as the church had purchased its own set of hand bells. Catharine Van Nostrand's Cherub Choir was in its fifth year of performing.

In the middle of 1973, the adult choir director, Wally Miller, resigned and a member of the church, Tom Abbott - a music professor at St. Cloud State - took over the job when no one else wished it. There had been problems with a low number of singers in the choir and frequent absences. Tom appealed to the congregation to help put the choir back on a secure footing, new people joined, and the choir was able to provide music for the Christmas season.

In September 1973, Meals on Wheels started in St. Cloud. United Methodist Women joined with other church congregations to deliver these meals to homebound people. Some money was also contributed by them in order to help keep the cost of meals down.

Allen Brink, chair of the Missions Committee, reported that the committee had decided to put into its budget a one-fourth funding of annual expenses for a missionary overseas. This was a new expenditure for First Church, but the committee had learned that there had been a dramatic drop in Methodist missionaries overseas, primarily caused by lack of funding.

1974: The January 1974 Charge Conference brought a small, but significant, change to the church's official documents. Women were now uniformly referred to by their given names, not by their husbands' names. This new practice was undoubtedly a response to the women's movement.

In the fall of 1974, the church was trying something new with their Sunday school. Children were encouraged to go to church with their families for a short while and then leave to go to classes. During the time when children were present, there was often special music or a short children's sermon. Jo Tennison, Coordinator of Education, was an advocate for children coming to church to see what was happening. She felt there were some misunderstandings about church on their part when she heard one child ask another, upon seeing Michael Barone in his sandals and long hair heading into the sanctuary, "Do you think he's Jesus?"

Adult education took a successful, if humorous, turn in 1974. There were six dinner groups that met in members' homes, had a meal and then a discussion on a selected topics. About 55 people took part. The name of the program was Food and Thought--the acronym was FAT. Dick Corliss led the effort.

The church had acquired the use of two new musical instruments, a Steinway grand piano, belonging to Minnesota Public Radio, and a Rieger tracker action organ, which Michael Barone owned. Michael also started a Community Concert Series in the sanctuary in 1974. Among the performers were Deborah Dean and Ellen Phillips, two professional opera singers, who grew up in First Church.

This year also saw vigorous activity in the Building and Management Committee. All the pews were refinished, and the church steps at the north entrance were carpeted. The committee also recommended rental fees for using the building for non-members and non-church-connected groups. They, however, did not propose a charge for using either the sanctuary or Wesley Hall for funerals.

The building already had some paid tenants: the Montessori school, Tri-Cap Day Care Center, Weight Watchers, and a Suzuki Studio (violin playing for young children). The Tri-Cap program came in the winter of 74-75 and conducted a Monday through Friday program in the lower level of the church.

1975: In his January 1975 report to the Annual Church Conference, Rev. Beck announced that Dr. Kendall was leaving his part-time position and that the church secretary, Betty Partch, was also leaving. The church hoped to hire a new person to help with visiting, but they did not intend to search for another assisting minister.

The year 1975 brought an increasingly international flavor to the congregation, as the church became Parish Partners with the St. Luke Methodist congregation in San Juan, Texas. In December, 12 members of First Church visited the Texas church.

In addition, the church sponsored three young Vietnamese men, Khai, Huu, and Anh. At this time, many Southeast Asian people were refugees from the fall of South Vietnam and were needing to settle elsewhere in the world. Catholic Charities brought many families into the St. Cloud area, and Protestant churches were sponsoring people as well. A good number of these refugees later left to go to warmer climates or to be near families and other refugees. Texas and California were particularly favored spots, as they were warm. Some refugees settled permanently in the St. Cloud area.

There were changes in church staffing in 1975. Catharine Van Nostrand left the position of Music Coordinator, and Phyllis Schelske took a position as Membership Secretary, taking up some of the duties that Ruth Skewes had left. She kept the church membership records and made home calls to prospective and new members.

Dorothy Bluhm Stueve 1983

Dorothy Stueve was hired as well. She was to be the first official Church Hostess. In her report of the year's work, she said she hosted around 25 different events - potlucks, concert receptions, seminar luncheons, confirmation, weddings, Wednesday night suppers. She also occasionally helped with funerals. In the past, circles and other groups had done this work, but with more women returning to paid employment, woman power had been cut dramatically.

An additional financial request came to the church in 1975. Minnesota congregations were asked by the Conference to participate in the Pension Crusade, an effort to provide adequate pensions for retired ministers of the conference. First United Church pledged $20,000 toward this effort, and $5,755 was sent the first year.

1977: The first membership directory with pictures was published in 1977. This was particularly helpful to a church that had continued to add new members. Faces and names could be put together.

Rev. Evelyn Durkee began serving the congregation in 1977 as a part-time minister. Her work was to be diverse: working with the Social Concerns Committee and the Adult Education Committee, some church visiting, and occasional preaching. She was a member of the Iowa Methodist Conference, but her family was now living in St. Joseph, as her husband, Phil, taught at St. John's. She was the first ordained female minister to work in the St. Cloud area.

Rev. Durkee was particularly interested in current social concerns, and in her first year with the church she and the Social Concerns Committee worked on a variety of activities focused on hunger. One Sunday the committee held a food and hunger teach-in for four hours, with a vegetarian meal and films and workshops. On another occasion they held a workshop on simple living.

There were also a variety of adult courses held during Sunday morning, which Rev. Durkee was involved in. Thomas Park, chair of the Education Committee, said that the adult education program made "phenomenal improvement" that year. Rev. Durkee said of her first year: "The joy of my job description is its breadth and flexibility."

The Arts and Memorial Committee, chaired by Arlene Helgeson, was planning and beginning work on a memorial garden for the small front lawn of the church. In the fall of the year earth had been moved, sod laid, and a patio put down. Spring 1978 would see the planting of bushes and trees.

The altar was refinished in 1977, thanks to Betty Partch's work. Mert Hubbard, chair of the Building and Management Committee urged the congregation to spend more money on church maintenance so that the building could be kept up.

In 1977 the church mortgage was fully paid and on Oct. 16, was ceremoniously burned. Howard Matthias, chairman of the Board of Administration, concluded his 1978 charge conference report on the state of the church by writing: "We enter this coming year with our mortgage paid, our budget balanced and our Congregation enthusiastic. We have much to be thankful for."

October 16, 1977 was the celebration of 120 years. A booklet was found in the archives telling of this special event: "This congregation has been housed in four buildings during the 120 years of its existence, as depicted in the silk screen art form which grace the cover of this booklet, the work of Laurie Halberg." adt

---

Rev. Beck's report to the congregation this year dealt with a number of things, including the need to support the new Methodist congregation to be established in the northern part of the St. Cloud area and his relief that the church's financial issues had been somewhat brought under control. He shared his disappointment that he had not been able to inspire greater financial stewardship in the congregation, but said that he had come to realize that he was a "child of God," and still worthy, even if everything in his ministry did not go as he might wish.

1978: Two pledge drives were necessary in 1977-78. The first drive did not meet the budget that had been set, so the Church had several all-church meetings to explain the budget and hear membership comment. Then the Stewardship Committee had a second drive in Feb. of 1978 and met the budget.

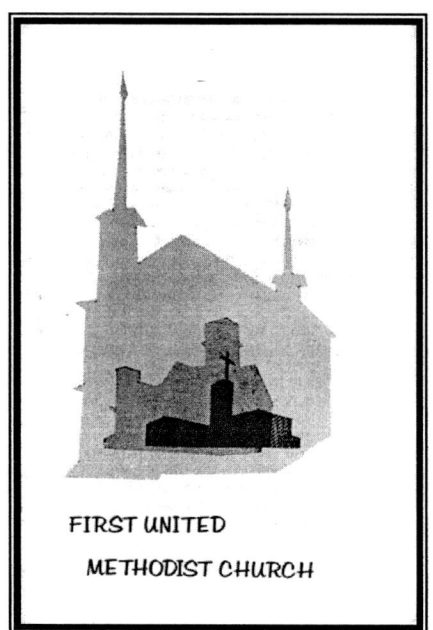

FIRST UNITED METHODIST CHURCH

In 1978, some of the parishioners from First Church transferred their membership to New Horizons United Methodist Church. Although this helped explain the church's membership dropping by around 70 people, the year had never-the-less been good for First Church financially. The year before there had seen a deficit of $2,585, and by the end of the 1978 it was down to $680.

The United Methodist Women always worked to keep attendance up at their monthly general meeting, and this year they tried a new course. They set the larger group's meeting time for 6:30 p.m. and served a buffet before the meeting. As there were nine circles and the larger group met once a month, except for summer, the responsibility for putting on the buffet was nicely spread around among the circles.

Mary Corliss chaired the Ecumenical-Social Concerns Committee responsible for introducing a Cambodian family to St. Cloud. The father, Chan Sakhon, the mother, So Yang, and two children were sponsored by the church. The congregation collected household items for the new family, and Mary helped them in many ways, including getting the adults registered in an English class and helping them to shop for groceries. The family did not speak English, and Mary did not speak Cambodian, but they managed to communicate enough for the basics.

The Church was exploring a Grannis-Martin Heritage Center, which they hoped to have in the room on the main floor used for the nursery. Both the Fine Arts and Memorials Committee and Rev. Beck were enthusiastic about having a room to house church books, including a collection of old books, with tables and chairs where people could read and study. As it turned out, this never was done.

A Task Force on Communication was chaired by Sam Wenstrom and asked to survey the congregation on a large variety of matters relating to how the church's procedures and actions were perceived. The results were basically very positive, which must have been pleasant for the Church to receive. In addition, there were some suggestions for changes.

Rev. Durkee continued her work with the church on a one-third time basis and enjoyed the opportunity to minister to the congregation.

In his report to the church's 1979 annual meeting, Rev. Beck spoke of the "challenging, demanding and satisfying" years he had spent in St. Cloud (over 15). He commended those who had worked in the church over the past year, both staff and congregation, and concluded with: "God has been good to us. May His benediction continue to sustain us in faith and love."

CHAPTER FIVE 1979 -1984

1979: The year 1979 was to bring change to the church. The Pastor Parish Committee, in consultation with others, had concluded that they wished the church to return to having a full-time associate minister. This would mean that the people holding part-time positions--present associate minister, youth advisor, education coordinator, and director of social relations--would no longer be employed. There would be a period of turnover, with the associate minister coming after the June Minnesota Methodist Annual Conference. The church also decided to fund a business manager. Charlotte Henningsgaard, a church member, started in May.

In addition, in January the church was looking critically at the Tri-CAP Day Care Center, which was using the basement of the church. The church's and the day care's use of the facilities were conflicting, especially in several classrooms, Wesley Hall, and the women's washroom. There had been complaints, and the Building and Management Committee said they were having a hard time keeping the church up properly. In a town hall church meeting held by the Board of Trustees, opinions were exchanged as to whether to renew Tri-CAP's contract when it came due. The no's prevailed. The day care center would, however, have some time to make their change.

That summer the new associate minister, Rev. Larry Hager, arrived. Soon after, Rev. Beck left for a planned trip to Africa, where his daughter Sarah was serving in the Peace Corp. Rev. Hager had to settle in quickly and learn the ways of the church as he was responsible for the ministerial duties. In addition, the important fall finance drive was in the planning stages.

The big change for the church came in August, when Rev. Beck returned to St. Cloud, traveled two days later to Lake Harriet United Methodist Church to interview for the position of senior minister (the previous minister, Dick Mathison, had died suddenly), and was offered the position. Rev. Beck had started his involvement with the Methodist Church at Lake Harriet, first as a youth and then, when in college, as a youth advisor. He and Catherine had been married in that church.. He decided to accept the appointment.

This, of course, was a shock to his congregation, which had routinely requested that the Minnesota Annual Conference reassign Rev. Beck to the St. Cloud church. However, Rev. Beck had served St. Cloud for 16 years, a long stay for a Methodist minister, and so in that way, the move was not entirely a surprise. Rev. Beck resigned his numerous local responsibilities (including a position on the St. Cloud School Board) and began the process of changing positions. For a short time, he was at both First Church and at Lake Harriet, and then in October, he left St. Cloud for his new duties.

Other things happened in 1979, aside from the changes in ministers. The Grannis-Martin Scholarship was begun, and a grand piano was purchased in the summer. Michael Barone and Arlene Helgeson learned of a 9-foot, used Yamaha piano being for sale, looked at it, and purchased it. They received member commitments for financing, and greeted Rev. Beck on his arrival back in St. Cloud with a new piano for the sanctuary.

In addition, there was some significant church renovation, partly thanks to money received from the estate of Gertrude Gove, which financed the Wesley Hall renovation. Dorothy Stueve commented in her report to the 1980 Annual Meeting that there had been considerable remodeling and painting the last year, along with significant turnover in janitorial help. She was eager to get back to regular living. She did, however, applaud the new dishwasher in the kitchen.

The lower level stained glass windows in the sanctuary were begun, as well as windows for some doors. Richard Haeg,[105] an

Dick Haeg is shown standing beside one of his latest stained glass creations — windows in the First Methodist Church in St. Cloud.

---

[105] permission to publish picture from St. Cloud Cathedral High School, *Crusader Companion* staff, published Volume 1, number 2, Winter 1982 p 5.

art instructor at Cathedral High School, was doing the work.

And there was the finance drive, planning for which started in June. There was a strong desire to have a very successful finance drive, as they had started the year with a $680 deficit. Jack Bensen agreed to lead the drive, and a retired minister with experience in such drives was hired as an advisor. Plans were made to contact members in their homes to receive their pledges. Ninety callers agreed to do visits, and $122,130 was raised in pledges, enough that they would meet the budget.

In November of 1979, Rev. Horst, his wife Locky, and their daughter, Elizabeth, arrived in St. Cloud and moved into the parsonage. Rev. Horst had previously served the Conference at Brunswick United Methodist Church (Crystal) and then in Northfield. In his report to the church's 1980 annual meeting, he noted that he had been serving only ten weeks at that point but commented, "I want to bear testimony to the cordial welcome you have given the Horsts. It has helped heal separation for you and for us."

After the Horsts arrived, there was a period of settling in, and Rev. Horst and Locky held numerous small group coffees at the parsonage to meet the congregation.

1980: In the spring of 1980, First Church decided to pay Rev. Horst a housing allowance rather than continue furnishing a parsonage. This method of handling clergy housing was becoming popular in the Conference because it gave the minister and his family the opportunity to buy their own home and to build up equity in it. Locky, with the help of Richard Clampitt, a member of the church, purchased a house at an auction held by the St. Cloud Vocational Technical College, and the Horsts moved in early summer. The parsonage was subsequently sold.

In the same spring, Ellen Deane Schwieger took her junior/senior high school singers, the Daybreak Singers, on a tour to sing at two nursing homes and at the Riverside Apartments (the apartments built by an ecumenical effort). Then, at the end of April, the Easter People (grades 3-6), under her direction, presented a musical, *From the Beginning,* at the church. They were accompanied by a 13-member youth orchestra.

Because of a new job with Minnesota Public Radio, Michael Barone resigned in October 1980, and Tess Kasling, our present church organist, began playing for worship. Ellen Deane Schwieger resigned in December.

1981: With the summer of 1981, Rev. Hager left the church to serve another in Howard Lake. First Church hoped to have a new associate minister assigned to them, but there was no one available. Consequently, the church hired several lay people to do some of the work that Rev. Hager had done. Joy Schwartz was selected to be Educational Director, and Carol Oleson, a member of the congregation, was hired as the Parish Visitor. (Not only was Rev. Hager not available to do calling, but Ruth Skewes had resigned as well and gone to live in Arizona.)

The church got a new roof in 1981, as well as insulation put into the roof. This cost almost $25,000, so to pay for it the church loaned itself some money from a bequest that it had received, the Halenbeck fund. Also considerable work was done on the heating system. The Gove Memorial Display Case was constructed in the tower hallway, and some changes were made in the building to comply with the fire codes. The family room at the back of the sanctuary was decorated to make it more inviting.

Another project for the church was arranging for a place that the youth could call their own. They had been given Room 101 in the basement, and, with the assistance of Joy Schwartz, had been working on various projects to earn money to decorate it. The United Methodist Women donated their profits from the fall rummage sale to the cause.

1982: To get an idea of the church's status after Rev. Horst arrived, one can look at records of the January 1983 Annual Meeting. 1982 was not a particularly enjoyable year for those working with church finances. The year's budget had been cut by $15,000 because the 1981 pledge campaign had not met its goal. Howard Matthias, chair of the Stewardship Committee, suggested to the congregation that it needed to increase its giving from the pledged amount so that some of the most "drastic cuts" could be reinstated.[106]

---

[106] Original picture used for the Dallman Sculpture and the 125th Anniversary celebration, copy in FUMC Archives.

Nevertheless, by the end of the year, the church seemed in fairly stable financial condition, as they had taken in more money than they had spent. However, as Michael Helgeson said in his report for the Council of Ministries, "a lot of time and energy was consumed by our budget problems." The total revenue collected this year was $169,381. Because of financial problems in the past several years, the church decided to propose to the congregation a 125th Anniversary Fund: special extra giving to provide a cushion for church needs. The congregation agreed to this.

Total outreach for the year (church's giving to needs outside the local church) was about $46,000. As part of outreach, the church at this time was helping a Cambodian refugee family and two brothers who were friends of the family adjust to an unfamiliar country and to St. Cloud.

A special committee was also planning a 125 Anniversary celebration for First Church. Everett Rasmussen and Helen Bensen were chosen as co-chairs. It would begin in May 1982 and run until May 1983.

Pictured on Wedding Bell Sunday in 1982 are couples married 50 years or more. L to R. : Carl & Edith Way, Mary & Charles Stark, Doris & Clair Daggett, Clinton & Margaret Hill, Earl & Dora Hanson, Carl & Minnie Peterson. Jim Garven at the lectern. Ken Beck and Michael Barone sitting in front of the group.

Joy Schwartz reported that in 1982 Sunday school attendance rose among elementary age children, with 120 children registered and an average attendance of 86. The church young people were involved in UMYF, although not as many as the church would have liked.

Archives
[108] Is called GRIP in St. Cloud, Minnesota

The youth had a much improved youth room, with carpeting, curtains, and a pool table. They also had a wide variety of activities: skiing at Powder Ridge, planning the Easter sunrise breakfast and service for the church, holding a rummage sale and car wash, caroling and taking Christmas cookies they'd made to church members, participating in a Camp Friendship work camp, and a variety of other things. Ken and Julie Dunlop were counselors, along with David Graham.

The Family Life Committee was active in 1982. There was a Winter Fun Day at Riverside Park, a Valentine's Party for young married couples, a family river canoe trip on the St. Croix River, a chemical use and abuse presentation, an Advent workshop, the Hanging of the Greens.

United Methodist Women had a membership of 167 women, with seven circles and a monthly dinner meeting of all members. According to chairperson Ellen Deane Schwieger, they helped finance the decorating of the youth room, managed funeral meals, and organized and facilitated an intercessory prayer group as well as handling numerous other activities.

In December 1982, the total membership was 1,007 members, with 54 new members (including 15 confirmation students).

Dick Haeg had finished his windows. The large windows were abstract and designed to illustrate Bible verses praising creation.

Carol Oleson, in the tradition of Ruth Skewes and Phyllis Schelske, was making her church visits, working with several committees, and trying to find rides for older members, as no buses were running on Sunday.

The period between May 1982 and May 1983 was celebrated as the church's 125th Anniversary. A special church dinner was planned for May 1982, and work on a 125th Anniversary history of the church was begun by Everett Rasmussen, with the assistance of Rev. Horst. The committee published a booklet, *125 Years of Continuous Faith: Rejoice, Amen,* in 1983.

In 1982, five guest ministers spoke at five different services. The opening service heard the District Superintendent, Rev. James Schneider. In June, Rev. Kenneth Beck returned to preach, in July former minister of First Church Rev. Huffman spoke. Then in August, Rev. Mark Haverland, who had grown up in the church, preached the sermon, and in October Rev. Duane Lunemann, another former young member of the church, gave the sermon.

There were other special Sundays as well: Confirmation Sunday (recognizing anyone who had been confirmed in the church), Wedding Bell Sunday (honoring those who had been married over 50 years, as well as members married in the church), and Historical and Memorial Sunday.

1983: In 1983, the celebration continued with an Honor All Men of Our Chuch and guest preacher Rev. Manning Van Nostrand, a son of the church. In April Rick Carlson, another son of the church, was ordained at First Church and preached the Sunday sermon. On Honor All Women of the Church Sunday, Rev. Marva Jean Hutchens, a daughter of the church, preached. Finally on May 15, 1983, there was an All Member Service with Bishop Emerson Colaw speaking and a presentation of an Anniversary Book (a scrapbook with all the events of the anniversary year displayed) to the congregation.

Shortly after, in the summer of 1983, Rev. Horst participated in a pulpit exchange with Rev. Walter Suffield of Torquay, England, for a six-week program.

Sometime in 1983, the church potlucks were begun, with those members of the congregation interested in dining with others signing up to be in groups of eight people. These groups then arranged for suppers over the church year, meeting at least once in each home. This tradition has continued up to present time, and valuable acquaintanceships and friendships have occurred.

In September of 1983, things were happening on the north side of town. The New Horizons United Methodist Church was dedicated, its members having spent a number of years in the Westwood Elementary School gym previous to its being ready for use.

Money was an issue in 1983, in that the newly started special Anniversary Fund had to be raided by $20,993 in order to meet the church's financial responsibilities.

Fernald House used by the Youth

1984: Parking had always been an issue at the church, although members had been able to use the City Hall parking lot (Former Central School playground) for Sunday parking for many years. In 1984, the decision was made to have some parking of the church's own. The Fernald House (the house next to the church, which had had a number of uses including being a parsonage and rental property) was taken down, and a small lot was constructed south of the church.

The Administrative Board also considered buying several nearby parcels when houses were for sale, but decided against it, partly because the church's finances were not strong at the time.

In 1984, the church again saw significant staff changes: several custodians left, as did two office managers, and the head secretary. These positions were filled, and Shirley Echols, a church member, continued on as a part-time secretary. A little later she filled the full-time position. Shirley Holzer continued directing the Chancel Choir.

The elementary Sunday school had apparently started awarding an attendance pin to children who had at least somewhat regular attendance, because in 1984 ten children received a yearly pin, and 17 children were awarded a two-year bar.

The Adult Education program for 1984, chaired by Evelyn Durkee (serving as a church member rather than paid staff), had several significant presentations dealing with sensitive subjects. One was the February 19 "Open Forum on Abortion," where a biologist (Wayland Ezell), a philosopher (Dick Corliss), a religious representative (Rev. Horst), an expert on the U.S. courts, and a

135

pediatrician were assembled to offer their viewpoints. Later in March, there was a three-session series on "Dying with Dignity."

Scholarships were given in 1984, as in previous years. Chair of the Scholarship Committee, Joan Clampitt, reported that five scholarships for $750 each were awarded from the Grannis-Martin Foundation, and six people received $400 scholarships from the Grannis Fund. Also in this year the first grant from the Stevenson Scholarship Fund (open to any local member of the congregation who was attending college) was awarded to Lisa Summers.

The Stewardship Committee in 1984 held an Every Member Commitment campaign. They sponsored a pizza party for UMYF members, who in return called church members to remind them of the upcoming Pledge Sunday. Personal contacts after Pledge Sunday were also made. By the time all the pledges were totaled, the amount was 8 percent over 1983's pledges.

A new group, United Singles, had begun. It was an ecumenical group, consisting of persons from the mid-20's to those past sixty. There were approximately 45 paid-up members as of the end of 1984, and the group met once a month in Wesley Hall. Unfortunately, this group did not have a long life span, as by the church's annual meeting in 1986 they had disbanded.

A bicentennial celebration of the Methodist Church in America was also held in 1984. The planning committee of ten people had assembled in November 1983, with Shirley Echols as its chair. The typical celebration things were done, thanks to considerable work by the committee.

A banner was made, bicentennial calendars were for sale, an offering was taken for restoration of Lovely Lane Church in Baltimore, Maryland, (site of the organization of the Methodist Episcopal Church in the U.S.) the St. John's Boys Choir came to sing, Rev. Beck came back to St. Cloud in April for Heritage Sunday, an ice cream social was held.

However, probably the most attention-attracting undertaking was a camp meeting held on the grounds of the Graham United Methodist Church in Rice. Methodist churches joining in the event were New Horizons, Becker, Clearwater, Clear Lake,

Picture owned by
Rev. Dr. Bob Kendall

Grace, Rice, and First Church. People were in costume, a circuit rider came on his horse (Rev. Kendall). There was hymn singing, an altar call, and a love feast. At the end of the day there was food.

Attendance was estimated at somewhere between 170-180 people. Shirley Echols, concluded her account of the year's celebration with, "That's It Folks: It'll Never Happen Again."

In 1984, Rev. Horst lead the United Nations-Washington Seminar for the Minnesota Conference, was chair of the District Board of Ordained Ministry and a member of the Conference Board of Ordained Ministry, and president of the St. Cloud Clergy Association, among his other outside activities.

CHAPTER SIX 1985 - 1989

1985: September 1985 saw Rev. Evelyn Durkee return to First Church as an associate minister. She again picked up work that needed doing: home visits, confirmation, Sunday school work, adult education, Bible study. Deb Robinson, a deaconess in the Lutheran Church, was hired to work with the youth, as Joy Schwartz had left.

A shared stewardship program had been started several years earlier. All members of the church were assigned to one of 13 work groups, and when it was the work group's month, members were called on to usher, greet, bring food for funerals and meetings at the church, do office work, visit for the church, and so forth. In 1985 Mary Wagner, Margaret Kline, and Ruth Sundby reorganized the groups and found people to serve as captains. With this system, some people who had never done work within the church became involved.

The United Methodist Women nation-wide began a four-year centennial celebration, and the Methodist Men in January of 1985 held a special organizational dinner, and heard a speaker, Jim Langer, a former All-Pro Football player. About 65 members and guests attended, and Harold Zosel was elected president of the group (which he has remained up to this day). That year they had the annual Pancake Supper in April, rather than in the fall.

Worship services went back to the 9:30 a.m. and 11:00 a.m. services. Coffee was to be served between services. A special feature in late 1985 was a New Year's Eve communion service, preceded by a dinner at Dick and Mary Corliss' home. Then the group moved to the church for dessert and the service.

The Advent planning committee arranged for a special Epiphany service. The three kings led the procession to the service, the bell choir played, and a small orchestra was directed by Bill Perconti, the church's business manager. Afterwards there was a King's Cake and a church potluck. Locky Horst was chairperson of the Worship Committee at this time.

The ministers were busy as well. Rev. Horst, in his message to the February 1986 church annual meeting, talked of the organizational work of the church and its demanding pull: "The organization always needs 'tuning,' securing volunteers is always necessary, money is always needed, administration is always demanding time and attention, committees are always meeting. The very importance of these concerns can keep us from being open to the renewal of the spirit of Jesus Christ at work in our midst."

Staff skit for Admin Board, ca 1985

Rev. Durkee spoke of her work and its enjoyable contact with all ages, from the children in Sunday school to elderly members whom she visited in their homes. She concluded her report with: "Altogether, the church within its own community and in its wider relationships offers exciting challenge to all of us. May we all deepen our love for the work and each other in the year to come."

1986: In the spring of 1986, the church conducted a spring second finance campaign because the annual fall campaign had not met the budget by more than $20,000. This second campaign yielded an additional $10,000 in pledges. There were 346 pledging units in the church at this time. At the end of the year, the total church membership was 933 members.

Bill Perconti resigned as business manager, and Shirley Holzer resigned as chancel choir director. Ruth Rawhouser was hired for Bill's position, and Priscilla Woodley for Shirley's. However, by August, Ruth had resigned to go with her husband to Germany for his work. Karen Kirt became business manager.

Rev. Horst, in his report to the church's annual meeting, congratulated the congregation on using their special donations as mission to others rather than putting the money into the general budget of the church. In his list of things he had done that year, he mentioned his radio ministry, *Word and Music*, Sunday mornings on WJON (which he has continued up to 2008).

1987: The biggest project to be tackled in 1987 was installing an elevator in the church. Sam Wenstrom, who had recently retired, was asked by Rev. Horst to lead a committee to do the project. After study and much conferring with others (where to put the elevator being a big issue), it was decided to build out the tower and put the elevator on the north wall by the set of stairs. The elevator selected was a sturdy one, and the whole project cost $100,000, much of which was hoped to be financed out of special donations to the elevator fund.

This was a significant contribution to accessibility. Those having trouble going up and down stairs would no longer be left out. Those in a wheelchair could get down to Wesley Hall without having to be carried. A handicapped bathroom was outfitted on the first floor of the church at the same time. April 1988 saw the dedication of the new elevator. Paying for it would continue for some time.

Before the elevator

Vacation church school was held in June, with Peace United Church of Christ and Newman Center joining with First Church. The theme was Walk in Peace, and the children designed their own peace T-shirts to wear for the week. The last day was International Day, with international foods for snacks and a peace walk from First Church to Peace United Church of Christ.

1988: The Sunday school continued in 1988 with a scheduling they had started earlier, having the first Sunday of each month be a special session for children, where all ages got together for a program. In March, they had a Lenten Fair with a seed-planting project and a butterfly-making craft. Sometimes there was a songfest. Another activity of the Sunday school was decorating a Christmas Sock Tree in Wesley Hall. Children brought new socks of all sizes for the tree, knowing that the socks would be sent to Appalachia after Christmas. Val Rogosheske was chair of the Children's Council this year.

The Men's Club had a successful pancake supper in April although a water main broke, and the City shut off their water 15 minutes before they were to start serving. The report of the event did not say how they handled this problem, but they must have, as they served 425 customers.

Pancake Supper
Ron Weaver & Harvey Tice

The Family Life Committee facilitated a fine assortment of happenings for a variety of ages. There was a Halloween party (with the youth providing a "haunted hall"), an Advent workshop, a family cross-country ski weekend, a Lenten Friends potluck, the family summer picnic, and a family Boundary Waters Canoeing Area camping trip.

The Adult Education Committee had an extensive and impressive list of programs in 1987: "A Day in the Life of a Missionary," "Homelessness in St. Cloud," "Women in Judeo-Christian Tradition," "Why I Left El Salvador," and other equally interesting titles.

An occurrence somewhat out of the ordinary happened when the church held a Refugee Dinner to help an El Salvadorian refugee family on its trip to Canada on the "Overground Railroad." $365 was collected for them.

Finally, the Joe O'Connell sculpture, a large wood and wrought iron piece, was almost finished and was to be hung on the north wall of the sanctuary. Rev. Horst explained how he saw as valuable what was a fairly large amount of money being spent on an art piece: "Art, including our fine music program, is 'holy waste' that feeds the soul and inspires the heart." Horst explained that the term came from Paul Tillich, who used it when speaking of the fine ointment a woman poured on Jesus to honor him.

The year 1988 saw the church purchasing a new computer system. Putting information into it and adjusting to it went on through 1989. Rod Heiser, Karen Kirt, and Ted Hansen spent numerous hours setting up accounts and putting information into the system.

The church's financial year went well in 1988, with a final total of $184,808 pledged (350 units). On pledging Sunday, members journeyed to the altar with their pledges, a ceremony that the chairman of the Stewardship Committee, Carl Nielsen, saw as helpful to a sense of shared stewardship. The church had a $600 cash carryover into 1989.

Beulah Rose Hutchens, who was the Church Historian, mentioned in her Annual Meeting report for 1988 that, "Several people have been very generous by sharing pictures, books, booklets and programs of our past. We are most appreciative of these mementos, and urge you to share, too." She also commented that the St. Cloud Daily Times generously featured activities of members of the church, and that this offered more material for the scrapbooks that she was keeping for church history.

1989: Rev. Horst commented in his report to the church's annual meeting in January 1989 that the church had suffered a loss, in that "calculations that led us to vote down purchasing the Roe house proved wrong." The house had been purchased by someone else, torn down, and now a convenience store occupied its lot. This meant that the property probably would not be available as a future church parking lot.

Rev. Horst also commented, as he had in several other messages to the congregation, that "we are not a neighborhood congregation," but were instead a regional church and needed to continue to offer exciting programs in order to make people willing to drive the extra distance in order to attend the church.

There were several family church recreational opportunities offered in 1989. A get together was held at Decision Hills in September, where 612 people from the church attended. A cross country ski weekend was held at Whispering Pines. There were also the usual church picnic, and an Advent workshop.

Interestingly, after many years of having Slave Days, where UMYF young people did chores for others and earned money for their projects, the name given to the activity was apparently looked at closely, rendered insensitive, and the event was renamed "Serving You."

In 1989, the church received the new hymnals that the United Methodist

1989 New Hymnals

Church had been working on, with an eye to including more contemporary music, folk music and international music, not to mention reconciling the Methodist and EUB traditions into a new common book. On the national level, "Onward Christian Soldiers" was looked at and judged perhaps too militaristic for a church dedicated to peace. However, the hymn was a very familiar and popular piece, and it was retained. On the November Sunday when the hymnals were to be dedicated, people were handed them as they came to the first service and took them to the pews to sing from. That evening a potluck supper was held followed by a hymn sing.

The church library was redecorated in 1989 and was used for numerous meetings, including adult education classes between services. This, unfortunately, caused some problems for the Library Committee, who noted that people were unable to come into the room between services and select books, since doors were closed, and people were reluctant to disturb others. This issue was somewhat solved by the committee putting carts of special books outside the library for people to browse through. However, this was obviously not full use of the library, and there didn't seem to be a good solution to the problem.

Chapter Seven 1990 - 1994

1990: In 1990 Deborah Robinson continued to lead an active youth program at the church, with the assistance of other adults. Youth helped in the church, went on retreats, held worship services in Munsinger Gardens and the woods at St. John's, had their spaghetti supper, and more. In 1989, she and her husband had adopted a baby daughter, and Deborah took a three-months' leave of absence. The records do not say how long she continued to work after this leave, but by January 1991, she had left, and another youth director had arrived.

By the church's annual meeting in 1990, Rev. Horst had been with the church ten years. In his message to the church, he pointed out that membership numbers for the previous year had broken the pattern of decline, even though the victory was small--six more people than the year before. The new total was 890 members.

Sunday school was involved in some new activities. Children learned about the Heifer Project, a program that purchased farm animals for people in third world countries, and the children sent their offerings to this fund. In December, the children performed a play to celebrate Christ's birth, *Angels and Lambs, Ladybugs and Fireflies*. It was a musical and had animals and insects telling about the birth of Christ. Costumes were made, and a fair amount of practice was required. All the Sunday school children could be in the play.

The Mission Committee voted in 1990 to sponsor Gordon and Ardell Graner, who were missionaries in Bolivia. One thousand dollars from the Anniversary Fund was sent to them. The sponsorship continues to the present.

Financially, 1990 was a hard year. Income rose only $1,000 from 1989, the church was still paying the debt on the elevator, and the city had assessed the church $5,500 for improvements, payable in 1991. In his January 1991 report to the annual meeting, Financial Chairman Don Helgeson proposed a special funding campaign to free the church from elevator debt and to help it recover from its pressing financial obligations.

In spite of 1990's financial troubles, mission giving was still high. Rev. Horst celebrated this giving: "It is one way we gave our life for the life of the world, one way we are the Church. We could keep that $80,000 - $85,000 for ourselves... But it would cost us our soul...."

1991: The chair of the Library Committee, Blanche Carlson, made her annual report in January of 1991. Normally this committee does not receive a great deal of attention. It selects books, it keeps them in order, sometimes advertises them: the expected work of a library. However, this year a dramatic note was introduced into their report: "We continue to ask, no--PLEAD, 'Anyone who has a United Methodist Church Library book at home, no matter how long overdue, to please return it....'"

This year the church was having a difficult time keeping the youth worker position filled. Cheryl Skalbeck was hired, she resigned, and Heidi Olson was then hired (who by September of 1991 had decided to go back to teaching, and the position was vacant once more). At this point, Jim Garven returned to the service of the church as a paid youth worker.

A lovely symbol and decoration was added to the church sanctuary in Lent: a mobile of white origami cranes, which hung near the lectern area. There were eventually 1,000 paper cranes, constructed by members of the church and the Sunday school. The cranes symbolized the desire for peace.

At the end of 1991, church membership was at 872 "full, active members." During the year a program of Fellowship Friends had been started to pair new members with established church members. This, it was believed, would help ease the transition from stranger into participating member. The same year, a letter was sent to 360 St. Cloud State University students telling them about the church and inviting them to participate. This letter, like other attempts to reach out to the college population over the years, met with limited success.

United Methodist Men and United Methodist Women continued with their activities. Of particular note, the United Methodist Women honored Cecyl Bemis and Carol Oleson as special members of the organization. The United Methodist Men surprised the congregation with two pancake suppers this year, one in the spring and a second in the fall (the traditional time for the suppers).

The first of Jim Hendershot's drawings for the church was hung in the library.

Rev. Horst spoke of church membership in his report to the congregation: "I believe what we do here at First United Methodist Church makes a difference in how people live their lives, conduct their work, make their decisions, live in their homes." Rev. Durkee spoke of the value of being members of a church as well: "When the major storms come and when special times of celebration arise in our lives we want others with us."

Rev. Horst's report for the year was basically positive, recognizing shortcomings of the church, but fully praising the attempts and successes of the last year. He did comment on the movement out of the south side neighborhood (or the planned move) of a goodly number of churches: Bethlehem Lutheran Church, St. John's Episcopal, Holy Cross Lutheran Church, and Granite City Baptist Church. What had once been the "church neighborhood" was no longer so impressively filled with houses of worship of the major denominations. On the near-north side, Holy Angels Catholic Church had also closed its doors.

1992: In January, the church started a trial program of serving one Saturday meal a month to the needy members of the St. Cloud area (other churches were participating on other Sundays). The Salvation Army, which fed people during the week, did not have meals on weekends.

Apparently serving Saturday lunch to the homeless and hungry was a mission that enough church members felt was a good thing, because the church was still serving late in 1992, dishing up between 75-100 meals each third Saturday of the month. It also continued to collect food for local food shelves in wooden boxes made by Phil Tennison and looking like little mangers. Both activities continue to the present.

A party was held in October 1992 to honor Evelyn, who had spent more than 30 years coaching acolytes. Her father had also been very active in the church, so she had a strong tradition behind her. At her party, some of the boys, now men, she had organized and instructed came back to honor her.

The Evangelism Committee, headed by Locky Horst, was particularly busy this year. They sponsored a conference on church growth for the church's Administrative Board, continued with Fellowship Friends, sponsored Name Tag Sundays (where people wore name tags) and continued organizing the potluck groups. On top of this, a new group, People Involved in Evangelism (PIE), was formed. They met bi-monthly for potluck and pie, and their mission was to call on first-time visitors to the church soon after the visit had occurred. At the end of 1992, church membership was up 15 people to 888 members, partly because of this extra effort.

Evelyn Durkee, Associate Minister

Money was still tight in the church, and the Finance Committee reported at the February 1993 church annual meeting, that in 1992 they had decided to make a Conference payment of the same amount as 1991, rather than a suggested raised amount. (In 1993, they returned to paying the full Conference amount.)

Gordon and Ardell Graner, the missionaries the church was helping to support, visited the church with their family in 1992. They gave a talk about their work and delivered a banner from the Bolivian Methodist Church. The evening of their visit, the youth group held an ice cream social.

Other things of interest taking place this year were a youth group lock-in at the Minnesota Zoo (certainly an interesting place to spend an overnight) and a weekly Bible study group, that was headed by Rev. Durkee and held before the 9:30 Sunday service. Some of the women of the church were also part of a bi-monthly group called Feminists in Faith, who met to learn about women's contributions to the faith tradition and to support each other's participation in the Christian church.

Rev. Horst spoke to the Church Annual Meeting of the need of the church to be (in the words of John Wesley), "the leaven of holiness," and to expand its involvement in community and the world. Horst reminded the congregation that "Wesley would have nothing to do with 'low demand' church life and neither should we."

1993: Another capital improvements project was accomplished in 1993, the acquisition of a second, larger parking lot for the church. Sam Wenstrom was chairman of the Board of Trustees and concerned about the church's lack of parking, both during the week and on Sunday. He and the board decided it would be desirable to purchase a red brick house across the alley for a parking lot. A carefully crafted campaign ensued to convince church members that this lot was necessary, and to convince the City of St. Cloud that this lot should be allowed in spite of it not being able to meet all City regulations.

In the end, a majority agreed that the project should proceed, the purchase was made, and the lot was ready to use in the fall of 1994.

The work of refinishing church pews was started in 1993, with Jim Wagner and Norm Huser overseeing the work. The United Methodist Men took their annual fishing trip and, as Harold Zosel said after a day of rough water and little or no fish, "This is usually a fun outing and all we need to do is build a little predictability into the weather."

In the winter of this year, the Adult Education Committee, headed by Ruth Knutson, sponsored a retreat at Decision Hills. Bob and LuBell Kendall delivered the program for the overnight on "Christian Ethics for Today." The occasion was an opportunity for good inspiration, good fellowship, good food, and some good outdoor activities (how much is not recorded, but Minnesota can be very cold in January).

United Methodist Women started the year without a president, not a desirable state to be in, but the previous board of the organization pulled together and kept the organization running during this difficult time.

A special Passover ritual was celebrated in the church this year. Flo Goodrich, a well-known St. Cloud actress and director, as well as an ambassador for Jewish culture and religion, came to the church and conducted a seder for members. Those attending ate small tastes of unleavened bread, horseradish, hard boiled egg, charoses (ground apples, red wine, sugar), and parsley as part of the ceremony. Then after the serious part of the evening was finished, there was matzo

House on current parking lot, June 1994
FUMC Archives

ball soup and other things that might have been served at a typical Jewish celebratory dinner.

Finally, Rev. Horst, in his minister's report for 1993, said of his experience in the ministry: "I have always been amazed that God has used me to preach the gospel and provide leadership in the church. It was God's call and not necessarily my choice. But being a minister is a privilege, one which I cherish and enjoy greatly as I serve among you." As it turned out, this was Rev. Horst's last report to an annual meeting of First Church. He retired in August of 1994.

CHAPTER EIGHT 1994-1998

1994: In February, after ten years of continuous service, Shirley Echols retired as church secretary. She had brought a desirable continuity to the church's work, and her presence in the office would be missed.

In August 1994, the church held a farewell dinner for Toby and Locky Horst, and there was a celebration of Rev. Horst's ministry. After the good-byes were said, the next day the church greeted their new minister, Katie Schneider-Bryan. She had served as campus minister for the United Ministries in Higher Education the year before. Her husband, Rev. Dan Schneider-Bryan, was pastor at the Kimball and Zion South Haven United Methodist churches. Previous to coming to Central Minnesota, both had served as pastors in the Twin Cities area for 12 years. The couple had two elementary-age children, Greg and Anna.

Although Ken Beck and Toby Horst had been frequently called by their first names by church members (informality had arrived in the church in the 1960's, just as it had in the rest of society), Rev. Schneider-Bryan almost immediately became known as "Pastor Katie" or simply "Katie." Perhaps it was her friendly manner, perhaps it was the long last name. At any rate, that's what happened.

Serious decisions were made in the church at this time. The Staff/Parish Committee decided that they wanted once again to have a full-time associate minister and hoped to have one assigned to them at the Minnesota Annual Conference in the spring of 1995. This person would take over the duties that Rev. Evelyn Durkee and Jim Garven had been handling--visiting congregation, working with education, working with the youth.

In addition, the church adopted a policy to give those working in it and the Montessori school children upstairs more security. Only one church door would be open during the day when no church programs were in session, the north door by the office. This was a big change because both Rev. Beck and Rev. Horst had been advocates of an open church. However, it was felt that the times required new measures.

Other things happened as well. The refinishing of church pews was completed, the new east parking lot was paved and ready for use, and the Board of Administration was renamed the Administrative Council. Bruce and Lori Wood became the directors of music, as Priscilla Woodley had left.

1995: The year 1995 was the first full year of Pastor Katie's time at First Church. Looking at it in some depth will give an idea of where the church was. At the beginning of the annual meeting in February 1996, those attending heard some statistics that District Superintendent Loren Nelson had shared with the area Methodist churches in an earlier meeting. Church members learned that the St. Cloud area had one United Methodist person for every 28,059 persons (1/2 the average in other Minnesota communities), and that the area had a high number of 18-34 year olds, many of these people renters and of medium income. It is known from studies, Rev. Nelson had said, that this group is traditionally under represented at churches, with only about one-third of them "strongly involved with their faith." Consequently, having a vibrant Methodist community in the St. Cloud area is more difficult than in many other areas of the U.S.

Membership was a mixed matter for First Church in 1995. The Evangelism Committee set a goal of contacting every first-time visitor to the church within 36 hours of their attending a service (in person if possible, otherwise over the phone). The committee contacted around 220 people in a year's time. Forty-three new members were welcomed into the church.

At the same time, this year saw a drop in recorded membership due to the church's contacting absent members and asking them if they wished to continue their membership. These were for the most part young adults who had left the family home and people who had moved from St. Cloud. The result was a withdrawing of 114 members and a more accurate total of 800 members in December 1995.

A big event in the summer of 1995 was the arrival of the church's new associate minister, Shane Burton, his wife Karen and son Patrick. Rev. Burton had just graduated from Garrett-Evangelical Theological Seminary and had been ordained in St. Cloud at the Minnesota Annual Conference. He had a friendly and open manner, great enthusiasm for the work, red curly hair, and past membership in a Christian rock band.

When Shane prepared his report to the church's 1996 annual meeting, he discussed the changes taking place in the church with new people and some new ways. He was planning for a workshop-based Sunday school program, and the Administrative Council had approved the idea early in 1996. He spoke of the church as it appeared to him: "There is such an incredible spirit of compassion present within this church....You reach out to the world is so many ways."

Worship was in the process of change at First Church. The 11 a.m. service was suspended for a period while the church decided what could be done to make it meet needs better. It had had low attendance for quite a while, partly caused by the Sunday school classes all being held during the same time as the early service. This

A potluck

made for a cohesive church, in that most of the members were meeting together every Sunday, but it left the second service with an embarrassingly small attendance. A committee was formed to try to better the situation.

At the same time, the Nurture/Membership Committee was involved in putting together numerous small-group activities in which church members could participate. There was going to a Twins game, a trip to see *Black Nativity*, put on by the Penumbra Theatre in St. Paul, an annual Christmas dinner for the congregation, and potluck groups. In addition, this group was organizing CARE, a group responsible for visiting home-bound church members and sometimes helping with special needs.

The Missions Committee under Dolores Keech was an active group. Among their numerous outreach projects were a Blanket Sunday, where $580 in offering was collected to help obtain bedding for those in need and Operation Classroom, where the Sunday school and congregation collected school supplies and sent them and two typewriters to areas where they were needed. Five people from First Church made a trip to the Red Bird Conference in Kentucky (a conference the Church assisted) to see the work that was happening there. In addition, money was collected and dispersed to various causes and groups throughout the year.

The Church and Society Committee, chaired by Julia Holscher, collected food all year for the Food Shelf at the Salvation Army. In addition, there was a special collection in November for those needing help with their Thanksgiving dinner, a Salvation Army Angel Tree in December, and the continuing Third Saturday Community Meals.

The Adult Council under the chairmanship of Ruth Knutson continued the discussion group after first service called "Coffee: Grounds for Discussion," and saw formed several new Bible study groups. There was a winter retreat on prayer at Decision Hills, which was led by Joanne John and Pastor Katie.

The youth had their activities, part of the year with Jim Garven and part with Pastor Shane. They held a spaghetti dinner at the church, held a Kaffee Haus once a month at First Church for youth who were 13-19 years old (in cooperation with New Horizons United Methodist), planned and carried out a Northeast District winter lock-in for youth from all over the District, and did a December cookie baking and selling project. In addition, nine youth and four adults went to Mountain TOP in July.

United Methodist Women finally had a president in 1995, Jo Ann Bridges. She reported at the annual meeting on their donations to Woman House in St. Cloud, to the youth's Mountain TOP mission trip, and to a family in the church who needed groceries. In addition, they visited shut-ins and served a Parent/Teen Banquet in February. There were five active circles.

The Men's Club had its fishing expedition and its November pancake supper, where over 500 dinners were served. They continued to donate money to projects for the church.

The Scholarship Committee continued its service this year with a fair amount of money to spend. The Grannis Memorial Scholarships were awarded for a total of $1,200. The Grannis-Martin Fund awarded 14 scholarships, dividing up $15,000. Finally, the Stevenson Scholarship fund gave out three scholarships totaling $525.

Of special note in the mid-90's were artistic creations for the sanctuary by members Mark and Maggie Brossoit and Pat and David Krueger. There were banners and in 1995 an Advent Village for worshipers to enjoy. One year for Christmas there was a Victorian house, one year a window frame

Two other things that affected the running of the church were new computer records and a shift in the terms of church officers and committee members to the beginning of the calendar year. It was felt that this would help with continuity of the work--having some experienced committee members busy with their work, who could integrate new members into the flow. Then, it was felt that the fall activities could begin quickly.

In her "State of the Church Report" for the year 1995, Pastor Katie talked of the many positive things that were happening in the church. She spoke of the need to "Continue to build trust in decision-making and mutual nurturing and empowerment of every person's gifts, as pastors and laity lead side-by-side." She also spoke of the need "to look outward to the guest in our midst, to include the new-comer and recognize future vitality is dependent on openness to the needs of the new and the unchurched in our community." These were to become two of the themes of her ministry, using everyone's special talents in joint ministry and being hospitable to the visitor.

Pastor Katie was putting her own talents to work in the church and in the community. She was on a Conference Board of Ordained Ministry Committee, was involved with United Ministries in Higher Education at St. Cloud State University, was a member of United Methodist Clergywomen's Association, and was a Girl Scout leader.

Wesley House UMHE
Woody Reed, Phil Durkee, Ted Hanson, Bob Kendall, Katie Schneider-Bryan

In the Annual Report for 1996, Dale Williams, chair of the Administrative Council, happily reported, "All our bills are paid including our apportionment for the second straight year, and there is money in the bank..." This was of course pleasant, particularly when the Church was replacing the roof over the education wing and paying for the new parking lot.

The Family Life Committee, Liz Inveiss chairman, conducted a fine number of events for the membership. There was the annual picnic in July, and in December a family craft session and potluck supper at the same time as the Hanging of the Greens. In September, during Rally Day for Sunday school, members of the committee set up an area for bubble blowing (an almost irresistible activity), and then at the Men's Club pancake supper, the committee offered face painting.

The Missions Committee continued with the World Church Service Blanket Sunday and with Operation Classroom, as well as a wide variety of projects. Three members of the church, John and Lois Barron and Dorothy Stueve went down to Louisiana in January to help with a Sager Brown project, working in a station holding relief supplies for disaster victims.

1996: At its annual meeting, the congregation adopted a budget of $270,000 for the coming year, cut down considerably from an initial proposal.

The Nurture Committee under Mary Wagner's chairmanship, had a large agenda of activities for members to attend. Groups went to a production of the Quite Light Opera Company, to the Twin Cities to hear the Canadian Brass at Orchestra Hall, went to two games, one at the Target Center and one at the Twins Dome. They also traveled to a Nativity pageant at the Hennepin Avenue United Methodist Church. In addition, they put on a 100th birthday party for Cecyl Bemis, a member of the church.

The summer of 1996 saw name tags assembled for all of the congregation. Members were asked to pick up their tags when they came to church, wear them to help others learn their names, and then deposit them on wooden racks made by Byron John.

A new children's program was started in the fall, a special type of Sunday school, where children were introduced to religious concepts through workshop activities. The program offered drama and puppets, art, cooking, music, Shepherd's Garden, computers, and audio/visual activities. Apparently this program, which the kids had voted to call Kids' Kingdom, was popular. According to Pastor Shane, in six months' time they had almost doubled Sunday school attendance.

The youth had a good year in 1996. Twenty-six people went on a mission trip to Mountain TOP in Tennessee, and UMYF held a monthly Kaffee Haus on Saturday in the First Church basement, open to youth from any denomination. According to Pastor Shane, there were as many as 200 youths on occasion enjoying the opportunity to get together. UMYF's leader, Pastor Shane, had a big year as well. He baptized his new son, Tucker, and joined a Christian rock group called the Church Nerds.

Pastor Katie, in her report for the 1996 church year, highlighted two special efforts of the church. One was the establishing of more small groups, including short-term "action teams." The other was a Gifts Inventory to find out the talents of church members and to better utilize these talents. The inventory was still in process as of the 1997 Annual Meeting. Pastor Katie spoke of the "God-given need to give through our God-given gifts." In 1996, the Mississippi River clean up was started as a special project about the same time of year as Earth Day.

The church membership was down slightly, from 800 members in December 1995 to 785 members in December 1996.

1997: A big push in 1997 was the beginning of GRIP (the Great River Interfaith Partnership). It was a local ecumenical organization, organized to encourage and assist people of faith in carrying out political action for the common good. At first clergy and laity met together and planned their new organization. Later they would branch off into two groups for the day-to-day work. This effort was particularly significant to First Church, as the church had long been interested in working with other denominations to break down the walls that religion had to some degree set up in the community. By this time, as opposed to the 1960's and before, the community was becoming more diverse.

This movement was connected to one in the Twin Cities, called ISAIAH,[108] and local people were given leadership training by a Gamaliel staff member, Greg Galuzzo. The first task the new organization gave itself was to do individual interviews, called 1-to-1 Interviews, where church members interviewed other members in order to better know the congregation and to ascertain what congregational members saw as the area's social problems.

In 1997, First Church composed its own mission statement, a list of core values, and a vision statement. The mission statement was "The mission of the FUMC is to create and build Christian community through inviting, forming, and sending faithful, active disciples of Jesus Christ." The core values and vision statement were more detailed, spelling out what this statement meant to First Church.

The church building needed repairs and renovation. Wesley Hall was once again redecorated. However, more needed to be done, major items such as a new roof. There was a decision to take out a mortgage in order to finance this work.

As to the year's finances, $3,544 more was spent than was taken in. The membership was at 752 members at the end of 1997, 33 less than the year before.

In the fall, Consecration Sunday was held at the Kelly Inn. It was a dramatic change from the usual church location, and the planners of the event hoped that it would encourage financial commitment from the members. A brunch was held afterwards, and people visited and enjoyed each other's company. The pledged amount to fund the church program for the next year did rise.

Pastor Shane Burton and Jim Garven started two Disciple Bible classes in the church. Books were ordered and a number of people started meeting once a week for serious study. The courses were popular.

The Church and Society Committee held its second Mississippi River Clean-Up and continued to be an enthusiastic participant in GRIP. They also promoted participation in the St. Cloud community's Random Acts of Kindness (where people at a certain time in February did special things for one another).

Also, someone from the committee was involved in a community group called Healthy Communities/Healthy Youth, a program coming from the Search Institute, located in Minnesota. Their research showed that whole communities were needed to help young people, that the nuclear families weren't enough. This sort of belief fit nicely with churches' philosophy, and many in the community and the church heard the message. The group in St. Cloud was short lived, however.

The Worship Committee facilitated the weekly church services during the year. In addition, they held a special Festival of Bells, with area bell choirs, including a noted Duluth bell choir, Strikepoint. The committee also continued to work on finding a new sound system and equipment for the sanctuary.

1998: Pastor Katie spoke of the good progress of the church in her report to annual meeting in January of 1998. She was in the process of finding a Director of Contemporary Music for the new second service. In addition, two Disciple Bible study groups were being led by Pastor Shane and Jim Garven, and the church had a start of a strategic plan to improve the physical facilities.

Pastor Shane Burton celebrated the accomplishments of the church: "I see our people at work in so many ministries." He also spoke of the frustrating inability to increase church membership. He suggested that inviting people to join with our church and serve on a committee might not be the type of invitation young adults were looking for. His perceptions, he said, were that "people don't want committee meetings, but rather want to be in ministry addressing their hearts' desire or passion. People want to be freed up for joyful service to the Lord!" He argued that "we need to reevaluate how we 'do' ministry."

In the spring of 1998, John and Janelle Kendall were hired to organize a contemporary worship for the 11 a.m. church service. They needed to organize their music team, design a contemporary service, and practice. The ministers would still be a significant part of the service (in fact Shane played drums in the group), but the music leadership would be done by the group, and there would be a lot of singing of the new music of Christianity. There would be some drama as well. It was hoped that this service would appeal to a group of people that were not coming to church at present.

There were a number of special occasions when the worship group performed (one of which was on a float in the community Wings Wheels and Water parade that summer), and they led one or two regular services. Then in September, the second service began. It was an exciting and musically compelling service. While it has never grown to anywhere near the size of the first service, nor was it expected to, it has an enthusiastic following.

The Worship Committee, working primarily with the traditional service, had a year of change. Bruce and Lori Wood left their work with the choir, and Edythe Williams resigned from directing children's choirs. A number of people stepped in temporarily to help, and then Mike Morey was hired to work with the

Chancel Choir from September to December. Elizabeth Inveiss was the interim children's choir director, and Nancy Seutter continued directing the bell choir.

The church also hosted music programs during the year, including a boys' choir from Australia that came to St. Cloud to perform in the America Fest International Singing Festival for Men and Boys, a 7-day occasion held out at St. John's. In addition, three St. Cloud churches, First Church being one of them, were assigned a resident composer, Robert Morris, to work for a period of a year to create six new anthems for them.

There was much work on the church in 1998. The sanctuary roof was replaced, a new boiler was purchased, the office was reconfigured, six ceiling fans went up in the sanctuary, a security system was put in, a new sound system was installed, two Sunday school rooms were remodeled, and a storage shed was assembled by the south side of the church.

On a smaller scale, the Children's Council held a shower for the nursery in order to collect some money and some needed supplies from the congregation. Things such as a small refrigerator, a sweeper and a CD boom box, as well as diapers, wipes, and snacks were obtained. Lydia Circle adopted the Family Room in the back of the sanctuary and handled wall painting, curtains, and a new carpet.

All this upkeep came at a price, of course. The church took out a mortgage loan for $415,000. This included a merger of the parking lot loan (at a lower interest payment).The fall membership campaign was successful, with special work done by Mary Beth Megarry and Doris Kelly.

In December 1998, Pastor Burton was reassigned to the Andover, Minnesota, area to work on starting a new Methodist congregation. His presence was missed.

CHAPTER NINE 1999 - 2003

1999: The year 1999 was about much more than money, but it certainly was about money. The church roof leaked, some water pipes were breaking, and a sewer line needed replacing. It was decided to start a new fund called the Carpenter's Fund to finance some of the immediate needs of the building and to have a nest egg for future needs. The congregation made pledges to the fund or made one-time donations.

Dottie Seamans had some cautionary comment for the congregation in her Administrative Council report to the annual meeting held in early 2000: "for two years the Administrative Council has passed unbalanced budgets and has succeeded in meeting all expenses. Finance committee cautions the Council against continuing in this venue."

Never-the-less, sewer pipe repairs needed to be made, and the digging up of some of the front lawn inspired a redesigning of the memorial garden and the installation of a walking meditation area known as a labyrinth. Both the garden and the labyrinth were financed with memorial money.

Those who were active with GRIP had a hopeful year. Members from the church participated in further researching the needs of the area, and in March an Issue Assembly was held in First Church for the entire GRIP organization. Approximately 200 people attended, and two items were selected for action: affordable housing and housing discrimination.

After more meetings and much informing and lobbying, GRIP held a community forum on affordable housing, where elected officials were invited. Some time after this, a governmental organization of the area cities (the Joint Planning District Board) voted to establish the Central Minnesota Task Force on Affordable Housing. The issue was now on governmental bodies' agendas. Marcia Summers and Val Rogosheske were intensely involved in this year's work, as was Pastor Katie.

Staffing was also in some flux in 1999. Rev. Dan Schneider-Bryan, Katie's husband, was the new associate minister. The church nursery was staffed by a paid person to give continuity to the experience for the young children, and the Chancel Choir had a new director, David Scholz. Bob Aigner, the administrative assistant, resigned in December. As a final difficulty, the weekend custodian position became increasingly difficult to keep filled.

The Mission Committee worked particularly hard this year to make the congregation aware of the mission work being done on local, national, and international levels; as well as trying to persuade church members of the continuing need for money to support this work. The church also heard from its sponsored missionary in Bolivia, Gordon Graner, who was in Minnesota.

The Adult Council sponsored a series of Coffee: Grounds for Discussion on the various denominations of Christian churches, and invited speakers to discuss the beliefs and works of their churches. They also studied Methodism for several sessions. A March retreat was held at Lake Koronis. There were in addition Men's Bible Study, a Thursday morning reading group, two Sunday morning classes, and a Wednesday morning group. Three sessions of Disciple classes were also being held.

Finally, the Men's Club had a very successful fishing trip in June. According to Harold Zosel, its president, "it was unbelievable!!!! We went to a new spot...had a new guide, a new weather man, and the fish were tied up and ready to bite!" This event was in contrast to a significant number of one-day trips that the group held over the years when the fish didn't bite, the waves were rough, the weather was cold - typical fishing experiences, but disappointing and hardly leading to stories about catching the "big one."

Under their new advisor, Pastor Dan, the youth were enjoying a full schedule of events. They went to Mountain TOP for their 1999 summer mission trip and held numerous fund-raisers to finance the trip. They met for breakfast on Friday mornings before school, they held a Kaffee Haus every third Saturday in the church, they served coffee for church every 2nd and 5th Sundays. And the 7th, 8th, and 9th graders attended confirmation, which was now called Wednesday Night Live.

Pastor Katie in her message to the Annual Meeting in January 2000 talked about the church's welcoming her husband, Pastor Dan, to the church, and of how they were a complementary team as his "personality and gifts for ministry are wonderfully different from mine." Dan spoke about his first year, "not only have I learned about the ministry and workings of a larger congregation than I have served in the past, but the many intricacies of being a part of a much larger leadership team."

2000: In 2000 several changes occurred. The church newsletter, the *Courier*, started a new format. Instead of continuing with the style of church bulletins, its pages were now 8.5" x ll" (a 17" x 11" sheet folded in half) and were laid out in an inviting style. Another change was the hiring of Julie Daniels to be the Church's financial administrator, a position she has held up to the present.

In winter, the Adult Council sponsored a retreat once again at Lake Koronis. The theme was angels, and there was an angel movie *(Michael)*, a talk on angels in the Bible, and a presentation on angels in art over the ages. There were also group discussions on angels, walks in the outdoors, and good food.

Sunday school had been lasting longer than the first church service for some time, but in 2000 it was decided to cut it back to the same time as the first service, with the children coming to the service for a time, participating in a children's sermon, and then going on to Kids' Kingdom until 10 a.m.

Early in the year, there was a statewide Methodist Youth Rally at the Holiday Inn, which the church's youth were involved in, and in the summer the youth went to Mountain TOP again.

The adults could become involved in some Sunday classes in March called "Soul Feasts." They were sessions on personal issues: grief, fair fighting, and deepening relationships. At the end of each session was a potluck.
Rev. Randy Johnson and Mark Bordewick conducted the sessions.

In late spring of 2000, the United Methodist Women offered what they called "Emma's Tea." It was a money-raiser for the Emma Norton Residence in St. Paul (a UMW residence for women), and was a typical "high tea" in the Victorian tradition. Both men and women were invited. Another UMW happening was a special thanks to Fern Michalski, who had been a food coordinator for church funerals for the last four years and had overseen 27 funerals.

The Methodist Annual Conference occurred in early June this year at St. Cloud State University, and Church members helped with its administration, as they had in other years. Not only was there a need for people to register and to host, but golf cart drivers were needed as well.

A Labor Day Family Camp was held in September at Lake Koronis Assembly Grounds, and Disciples Bible study started again, with two levels of classes. By the end of the year 2000, GRIP was lobbying for affordable housing in the area.

2001: The year 2001 is most associated by many people with the September 11 bombings of the two World Trade Center towers in New York, the Pentagon in Washington, D.C., and the failed White House attempt (the plane went down in a field in Pennsylvania). The minds and emotions of everyone were captured by this unthinkable attack. After it happened, the church members tried to make some sense of it, as did U.S. citizens everywhere.

However, before and after the attack, the church year unfolded, as years do, and not a great deal changed in the church's life, except people knew that the National Guard units and the Reserve would be called up to respond to this event, and this touched many, whether they knew someone directly involved or not. The U.S. and allies soon went into Afghanistan to clear out the Taliban. Forces remain there to this time.

The Bridge Service lost the Kendalls' talents in May. John and Janelle had served with their band for three years and needed more time to spend on their family. In June, Tasha Christensen was hired, and she proceeded to put together a new band to carry on. That summer the church youth went to North Dakota on a mission trip.

In the same summer, the memorial garden and labyrinth were finished. Stefan Helgeson, who had grown up in the church, designed the Memorial Garden, and Scott Danneman and a supporting crew did the landscaping according to Helgeson's plan. Scott was doing this as his Eagle Scout project.

Something new in the summer happened--what were called Faith Walkabouts, which consisted of a group that met for a walk once a month and enjoyed God's creation. There was also an ice cream social in the summer. The community meal on the third Saturday of the month continued, with various groups of the church (confirmation class, Bridge Band, choir, a cub scout group, etc., helping with the meal).

A small number of new people joined the church--the report from the Outreach Committee says they recruited seven members. The membership report says the church had 20 new members, so the confirmation class probably made up the 13-member difference. At the same time, some people moved away, and there were 22 funerals of members from the church community, a large number.

Beulah Rose Hutchens initiated having the pictures of the pastors of the church hung on a hallway wall outside the sanctuary.

Several name changes happened in 2001-2002. The speaker/discussion group between services went from "Coffee: Grounds for Discussion" to the shorter "Faith Forum" and "Church and Society" changed to "Faith in Action."

2002: In January 2002, the church took a big step forward in active service, voting to take part in the community Church of the Week program. This program provided emergency housing for those who were homeless during the winter and could not find a place to stay because all the regular shelters were full. Carolyn Garven was a particular supporter of this community initiative and explained what was needed from the church, both in physical needs and in volunteers to work the program. In March of 2002, the first people came to sleep at the church, with church members hosting each night.

In 2002, the south wall of the church needed repair, as did the sanctuary ceiling. A second Carpenter's Fund was initiated for this and for further maintenance of the church. Even with this fund, the church had a deficit of nearly $9,000 at the end of the year. And the proposed budget for 2003 had a $25,646 deficit. Financially, the church was going through some more hard times. Membership was almost the same as the year before: 698 members at end of 2002.

Some good times were never-the-less happening. The church saw new banners and paraments for Lent and Pentecost, and there were two children's programs, one a special Christmas program and the other a program at Pentecost.

Vacation Bible school was held with several area churches. Something new was tried for the 4th-6th graders, a two-day day camp. The first day the participants went to Minneapolis to the Hennepin Avenue United Methodist Church, the Minneapolis Institute of Art, and the Sculpture Gardens by the Walker Arts Center. The second day the group went to spend a day at Camp Koinonia.

On the last Sunday in September 2002, there was a special Celebration Sunday, honoring Pastor Katie's 21 years serving the United Methodist Church and Pastor Dan's 20 years of service. Both were recognized in the church service, and there was a special church dinner afterward.

Giving was a significant part of the church agenda. Aside from the every-year mission giving, there were several special collections. One was in October and early November, the coat drive for the Salvation Army. Over 75 coats, scarves, hats, and mittens were donated by the congregation. Then in December, the church had a Giving Tree, with names of people that needed Christmas gifts on it. Seventy-five people received Christmas gifts through the church's effort.

2003: Undoubtedly the most impacting occurrence of 2003 was the U.S. invasion of Iraq. The U.S. citizens and their officials were told that Iraq had frightening weapons — atomic weapons and biological warfare materials — a threat to the U.S. What was less spoken about was that Iraq held a vast store of petroleum, which was a vital resource for the world. Later it turned out that Iraq did not have such materials of war, but the U.S., Britain, and a small number of forces from other countries were in Iraq, beset upon by a variety of rebel groups. Both military lives and civilian lives have been lost, and continue to be lost, in this struggle.

The church held several worship services for prayers and thoughts on the war. In the nation, young people volunteered to fight, National Guard units and Reserves were once more called up, and for some of the U.S. citizens, life was badly disrupted.

It was both a difficult year for Pastor Dan and a satisfying one. Aside from the distress of Iraq, he experienced the death of his mother and also a bike accident, which caused serious harm to his shoulder and required an operation and some recuperation time. However, it was satisfying to take the youth group to Wyoming for a service project, and it was satisfying to have his daughter confirmed as a member of the church, as were her classmates from the church's 9th grade.

2002 Joy to the World

The children of the Church had their Sunday school experience made more enjoyable as well. Kathy Bies-Jaede, as Sunday school superintendent, worked decorating the Sunday school rooms, and wrote a monthly page for the *Courier* on opportunities and experiences of family groups and children. She also led the children's Christmas program, which was presented as part of the 9 a.m. service on December 14. Many others were involved in efforts for the children as well. One example was Lydia Circle, which assisted in painting the art room, and another was the Men's Club, which donated new tables for several of the classrooms. And there were the teachers and the people who recruited the teachers. Almost certainly others as well.

Early in the year, the church's long-time organist, Tess Kasling, was recognized for her 21 years of providing music for the church. The church considered itself lucky to have her talent and commitment for that period of time. That she was continuing made the occasion especially joyful.

The worship experience was enhanced by the choir donning new choir robes, and by numerous visuals, among them banners for Lent, Pentecost, and Advent. The artistic church members who worked on these visuals were Jill Haak, Karel Helgeson, Mick Benson, and Sharon Houg. Christopher Larsen was hired to direct the chancel choir in July 2003.

Val Rogosheske led an information class entitled "Love Welcomes All" in May. Its particular focus was on the church's welcoming of homosexual people to full participation.

Church finances were satisfactory this year, in spite of a "touch and go year from a cash flow point of view," according to Brad Schwieger, chair of the Finance Committee. Several special contribution campaigns and an excellent December giving helped. Also, pledges were up after the fall stewardship campaign, and there was a balanced budget for 2004, the first time in three years.

Pastor Katie had a full year of work in and out of the church building. Some of her outside work included being chairperson for GRIP's Spiritual Leaders Caucus, some brief devotional radio spots for a Christian radio station, membership on the board of Lake Koronis Methodist Camp, and being a writer for the United Methodist publication *Circuit Rider*.

In her report for the year Pastor Katie spoke of the worship service as being a place where people could "experience God's presence in order to be sent out each week to our needy world." She also spoke of the ministerial role during the moments of "births, deaths, confirmations, weddings, and the many unspoken passages in people's lives, in job loss, marital struggle, emotional needs, illness, and the ordinary stresses of daily life."

CHAPTER TEN 2004 - 2007

2004: Some attention-getting happenings occurred in the Church's life in 2004. A movie was receiving special attention from society and especially from Christians, *The Passion of the Christ*, directed by Mel Gibson. When the movie was released, Pastor Katie had some reservations about it — its concentration on only the last few days of Christ's life and the vivid and lengthy treatment of the torture Christ endured. She suggested that perhaps a Christian could skip this movie and donate the price of the ticket to the Easter offering instead! However, others felt that they wished to have the experience,

so a movie group was formed to go to a Sunday matinee and then to come back to the church to discuss what they had seen.

Another venture into uncomfortable territory came with the church's decision to offer a fall study entitled "Claiming the Promise: A Welcoming Bible Study on Homosexuality." This study was to be lead by Paula Tompkins, a church member and professor at St. Cloud State University, with the assistance of Val and Phil Rogosheske. Pastor Dan said of the upcoming seven-session study: "I'm edgy or anxious because this is not something we all agree on. I'm full of pride because we as a congregation are willing to bring our sometimes different ideas of rightness and engage one another."

The third attention- and emotion-grabbing event was a June separation surgery on the East Coast for two twins, Erin and Jade Buckles. The two little girls were grandchildren of David and Joan Ellens and had been born conjoined. The church offered prayers, some children made quilts for the girls, and members of the congregation were concerned. The separation surgery was successful, but was only the first of a number of medical procedures that the girls would need to go through as they lived as separate little humans.

There was fun as well in the church year. Although the youth were not planning a mission trip for the summer of 2004, they were already selling buttons to help finance their 2005 trip to Valdosta, Georgia. The youth also went on a canoe trip to the Boundary Waters with Pastor Dan, and the summer Bible school was held in the evenings at Newman Center. Once a month during the regular church year, the elementary age children had a "club" meeting themselves. There was the Kids' Kingdom Club for children kindergarten to 3rd grade and the Fun N' Son group for 4th through 6th grade. These groups had started the year before.

Several food-for-the-mind experiences were held for the adults. One was the Interfaith Dialogues, hosted by First Church and open to the community. One of the major participants in the dialogue was Dr. Joseph Edelheit, director of Jewish Studies at St. Cloud State. The other was Dr. John Merkle from the School of Theology at St. John's University. Also, the Faith Forum presentations and discussions continued. One interesting title was "What Are Social Principles? Why Would a United Methodist Want Any?"

GRIP had a satisfying year. As a result of a joint powers agreement between a number of local cities, some Life Cycle Homes had been built and were ready to be sold and lived in. GRIP had strongly advocated for this affordable housing program and was instrumental in it happening.

Three final things of note for the year 2004: 1) The church started a program where members could sign up for Automatic Withdrawal and then have payments of their pledges taken out regularly from their bank accounts. 2) The organ was being repaired in the summer, necessitating no organ for a number of weeks, 3) First Church started planning its 2007 celebration for the 150th Anniversary.

2005: First Church has always been sensitive to what was happening in the world outside its doors, and 2004-2005 gave everyone much to be concerned about. Four major natural disasters happened these years. First, there was the tsunami that struck south and southeast Asia in late December of 2004. Then at the end of August 2005, Hurricane Katrina hit the southern coast of the U.S. New Orleans was almost destroyed, as was much of the Gulf Coast in

Louisiana and Mississippi. In mid-September, Hurricane Rita roared into Texas and a little of Louisiana. Finally, on Oct. 8 there was an extremely destructive earthquake in Pakistan.

All of these events called for special contributions by the congregation and prayers for those caught in such a frenzy of natural forces. In St. Cloud, people packaged food for the relief efforts, including 20 people from First Church. Financial contributions to help were significant.

There was the continuing emphasis on membership this year, with four sessions of three classes each for potential new members. A core team of Fellowship Friends was developed to sponsor new members and to follow up with them during the first year of membership. Forty-five new people joined the church. At the end of the year, the church's membership totaled 687 people.

In 2005, the Resurrection African Methodist Evangelical Zion Church was invited to temporarily have their services, Sunday school, and an office area in the church while they pondered their next step toward getting their own facility. Their services were held in the sanctuary at 12:30 p.m. On several occasions, First Church and they shared meals together. Their pastor was Yolanda Lehman.

Glenna Cheney, chair of the Administrative Council, said of this sharing: "Two unique congregations with a common bond in Christ, were able to find ways to do their activities in the brick and mortar that sometimes seems ready to burst at the seams."

This year, the church started making prayer shawls. Women of the Church would meet together and knit or crochet the shawls. They were then given to newly baptized babies, to some who were married in the church, to those who were sick, to some older members, and to others suffering through trouble. The shawls were to wrap the recipient symbolically in Jesus' and the congregation's care and concern. Later there was some knitting of hats as well, and some making of slippers for soldiers fighting in Iraq.

The church started to examine its facility and program in a more intense way in 2005, trying to determine what would be best for it in the years to come. There was concern that only 11% of the present congregation had children of Kids' Kingdom age, and that a half of the congregation were 68 years old or older. There was also the ever-present worry about parking. What would the church do if City Hall left its location across from First Church, and the congregation could no longer use its lot on Sunday? The questions arose: "Would we attract new members if we were located in or near a growing neighborhood?" "Would additional parking make us more attractive to new members?"

First Church was one of five churches that were included in a Minnesota Annual Conference grant program to help them answer such questions about their futures. A coach, Dale Arendt, was hired to help facilitate the process of inquiry, and three teams were assembled to study the situation: 1) Renovation / Expansion Team, 2) Identity and Location Team, 3) Staffing / Programming Team. Meetings were held for the congregation to keep them apprised of the findings of the committees.

This was a year when money troubles were not large on the agenda. There was a surplus of money this year. Over $12,000 remained after the bills had been paid, and $35,575 had been pledged toward the new Carpenter Fund.

Both the church's custodian and secretary were new in 2005, and the church decided to give up on hiring a weekend custodian, and to ask the Building and Management Committee to recruit volunteers to staff the church during the weekends.

2006: The church continued to work on membership in 2006. The Outreach Committee had published a pamphlet on the church that was left around town, and they were working on a Web site. There was also the traditional follow-ups to any visitors who had signed the attendance pad. New members had their pictures displayed on a bulletin board outside the sanctuary. Sadly, in spite of these efforts, membership was down 33 people by the end of 2006. There were ten young people in the year's confirmation class.

The national level of the United Methodist Church was promoting new membership as well with a program called Igniting Ministry. There was a national ad campaign for the United Methodist Church and conferences to help train congregations to be more welcoming to new people. Churches could earn the designation "Welcoming Church" if they were doing certain specified things. First Church made adjustments where needed, filled out the papers and submitted them. (They were later accepted.)

Early in the year, the church held an adult education series on Islam. It ran for five weeks on Sunday nights and attracted about 100 people for each session, half from First Church, half from the larger community. Pastor Dan said of the sessions, "for me the value came in how part of the Islamic and Christian community spent time together listening to each other."

AnnElise Edeburn, a young woman attending the church, wished to work with the youth. She wrote a grant application to a program funded by Valparaiso University and received funds for such work for 16 months. Her program was called "The Table." Contributions from the congregation amounting to almost $10,000 also funded the program.

Resurrection AME Zion Church continued at First Church, but it was decided by First Church that they did not wish to make this a long-term relationship because of space considerations. (Resurrection Church had asked if they might continue using the church.) They continued in First Church through the middle of 2006 and attempted to finance a building of their own. However, their conference decided not to help them afford a building and to dissolve the church. Although First Church would have been pleased to have the congregation become members of its church, traditions were different, and Resurrection members did not join.

The church continued with active membership in GRIP. In September, there was an open meeting for the community, with Bishop Sally Dyck from the Methodist Church, a bishop from the Lutheran Church, and a Catholic bishop. All the religious leaders spoke, plus others, and the group decided that it wished in the next year to spend its attention on four different social issues: 1) Civil rights for immigrants, 2) K-12 public education, 3) Support for women's and children's shelters, 4) Support for a St. Cloud regional human rights office. Over 50 from our congregation attended the event.

Continuing to plan for the church, the Vision Research teams held meetings this year and in July and November, had Sunday brunches to explain to the congregation what they had learned. Seventy to eighty persons attended each event.

Kids' Kingdom continued to serve children, but leaders also helped the children serve others. The children took responsibility for putting up the May Food Shelf bulletin board, prepared treat bags for a 3rd Saturday meal, and made some children's blankets and knit caps for Anna Marie's Shelter.

171

In August 2006, the Administrative Board decided that the church would eliminate the position of associate minister and instead hire a full-time Christian educator, a part-time teaching and counseling pastor, continue with the Table staffing, and keep the present music staff. Although the church was sorry to see Dan leave, he was ready to lead his own church again.

25 Sep 2006 Church Picnic

2007: As it turned out, both of the Schneider-Bryans left. Late in 2006, Katie was asked to hold the position of Northeast District Superintendent beginning in July of 2007. She concluded her report to the 2007 annual meeting: "Through the next six months of '07, I will continue to give you my energy to create a good transition in this important time in the life of First Church. You have blessed me, taught me, seasoned me, and deepened my faith through your lives of faith. "

The next six months went by quickly with the 150th Anniversary celebration to look forward to. The committee, Dick Megarry chair, had been working for several years and had set the special anniversary event for Sunday, April 22. Many things preceded the special day. Karel Helgeson created vivid banners for the church with the United Methodist logo of the cross and flame, the motto "Growing Our Legacy in Christ," and the dates 1857-2007. A mug with the design on it was offered for sale, as was a pin with the picture of the church.

The old church office (next to Wesley Hall) was set up, with objects from the life of the church. There were many photographs, copies of annual reports, official books, some bulletin-making tools, an old desk chair used by the minister, an old typewriter, old account books and registries, pictures of previous churches, old collection plates. Annette DeCourcy Towler and Beulah Rose Hutchens were largely responsible for this accumulation, which helped make real the

History Display 1857-19

passing of years. There were also displays upstairs in the cases outside the sanctuary.

Finally, the big day itself, April 22. Bishop Sally Dyck preached the sermon, and after the service the congregation assembled at the Kelly Inn for an anniversary banquet. A fine dinner was enjoyed, and a program of pictures of the life of the church, along with an informative script was the entertainment. Byron John had made many wooden table centerpieces of the Methodist cross and flame for the occasion. Some friends of the church came back for the event, and it was a satisfying day.

Program, Kelly Inn 22 Apr 2007

Ironically, on the same day the church was celebrating, New Horizons United Methodist Church was voting to disband its church after 28 years of being a congregation.

Several anniversary concerts were held during the year, one being in late February with a group called Soul Cafe. Laura Caviani, who grew up in the church, played piano in this group. Later there was a March concert with the Apollo Concert Choir and Orchestra, some of First Church's choir, and several soloists from St. Cloud State University performing the Faure *Requiem,* under the direction of Steven Mick. He is First Church's choir director as well as Apollo's. In September, an organ concert was held in First Church's sanctuary, with organists Michael Barone, Charles Echols, and Tess Kasling.

On Sunday, June 10, Pastors Katie and Dan officiated at their final service at First Church, and after both worship services were over, there was a goodbye dinner held for them in the church fellowship hall. Then it was off to a new home in Duluth for the Schneider-Bryans and several weeks of interim pastors for First Church.

By July 1, 2007, Pastor Bill Meier and his wife Linda had arrived in St. Cloud, and he began his work as pastor of First Church. There were a series of meet-and-greet meetings in members' homes so that the Meiers and the congregation could meet each other. In addition, there was the work of gathering some new staff members and adjusting to a new church and a new minister.

On November 11, a special Church Conference was held, and a vote was taken on what would happen to the present church building. By a vote of 136 to 56, the congregation decided to pursue relocation of the church.

Growing our Legacy in Christ

150 years
1857–2007

Our Space

Janet Gray
Annette DeCourcy Towler

First United Methodist Church

St. Cloud, Minnesota

Come and find the quiet center
In the crowded life we lead,
Find room for hope to enter,
Find the frame where we are freed:
Clear chaos and the clutter,
Clear our eyes that we can see
All the things that really matter,
Be at peace, and simply be.[1]

Shirley Erena Murray

---

[1] *Faith We Sing*, hymn 2128, verse 1

Things Beyond Words

A person's first reaction when hearing the term "worship" is likely the experience of a Sunday morning service: the liturgy, preaching and music. These things are heard. Add to that experience the visual environment in which that happens: the architecture, the light, stained glass, sculptures, fabric arts, and drawings. Each reaches the heart in ways words do not. All combine for the deepest worship possible.

We have no records of how that might have been done in first or second buildings used by St. Cloud Methodists. That however changes with the third church built in 1914.

The 1914 building was home to several stained glass windows, two of which found new homes when the present education wing was completed in 1960. Both windows are of variegated glass on which details were added with paint, then fired.

One, based on a familiar painting by Plockhorst titled "Christ the Good Shepherd" is installed in the lower level meeting room.

The location of the second window is shown on a map of the current worship space found on the following pages.

The floor plan and accompanying key serve at least two purposes in this history project. Primarily, it a record of First Church's worship and meditation space in 2008. It can also be a guide for tours such as the one that follows.

Key to Sanctuary Diagram on Facing Page

A. Dallmann – Exterior Stone Sculpture
B. Dallmann – Bas Relief of Christ
C. Halenbeck Window
D. Bak Beatitudes Windows, (above organ in chancel)
E. O'Connell *Tree of Life*
F. Gove Memorial Display Case
G. Hutchens Stained Glass
H. Six Framed History Panels
I. *Christ in the Garden of Gethsemane* (1914 building window)
J-K Haeg – *Wilderness* Windows

a – e Haeg - Psalm Windows (lower south wall)
    a. "Blessed Are You," (above piano in chancel)
    b. "Mountains and Hills"
    c. "You Springs"
    d. "Sun and Moon"
    e. "Cold and Chill"

1-6 Bak - Windows (1-4 upper south wall, 5-6 upper north wall)
    1. Stewardship
    2. Mission
    3. Prayer and Worship
    4. Education
    5. Evangelism
    6. Christian Social Concerns

i-v Inserts
    i. Door to Stairwell
    ii. Doors to Education Wing
    iii. Doors from Tower Entrance to Fellowship Aisle
    iv. Doors from Fellowship Aisle to Narthex
    v. Hanging Panel in Nursery - Education Wing

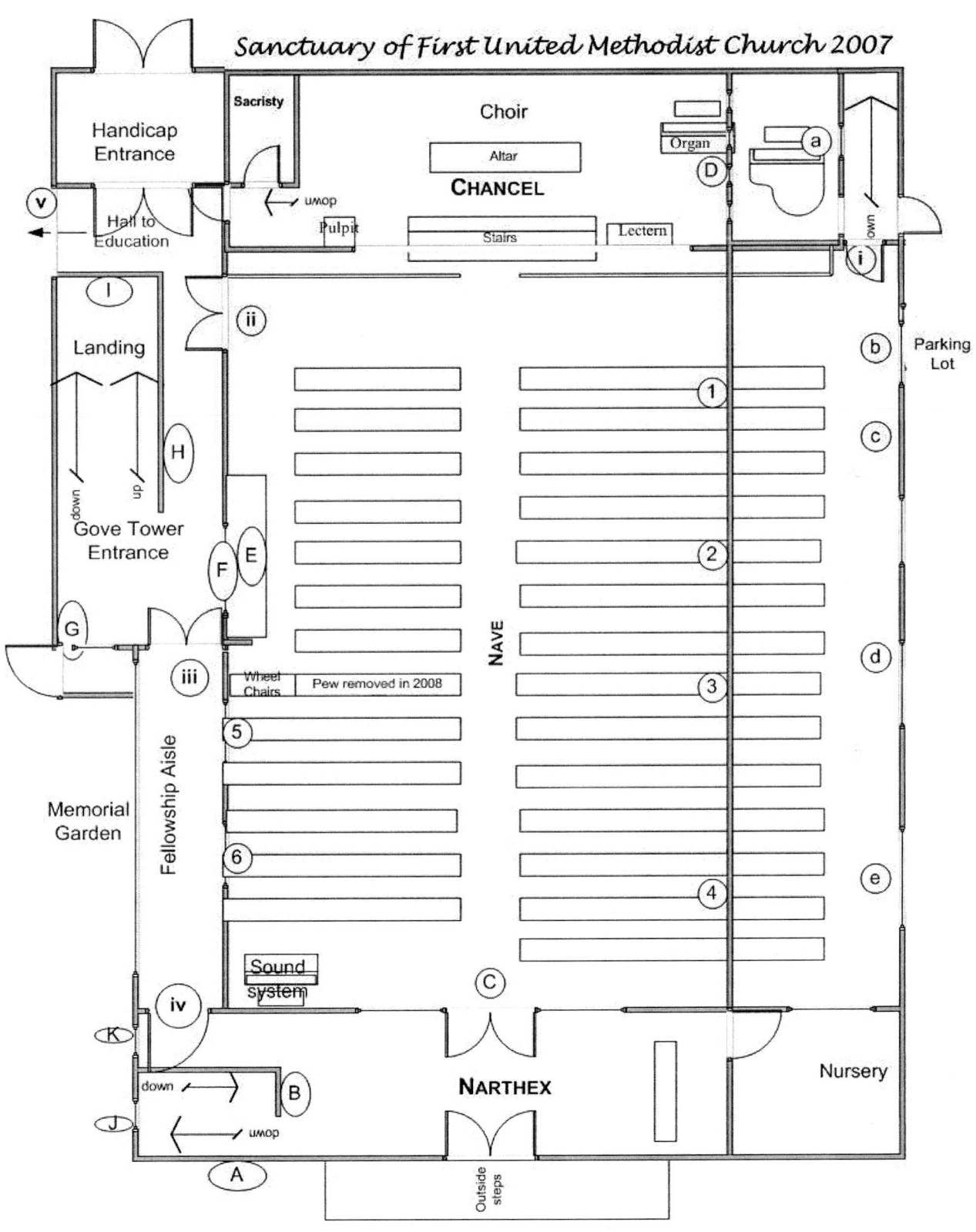

Our tour begins outside the building. Imagine you are standing with your back to busy Fifth Avenue South, having just walked up the steps to First United Methodist Church. On the outer west wall of the church is a larger-than-life bas-relief sculpture titled "Prayer." (A) The theme is reverence and consists of two figures – mother and son with bowed head and folded hands. The mother is looking down at her son and the boy is facing the large window above the church entrance. The garb worn by each of these two figures was especially designed so as not to designate a certain period of time.

"Prayer" was executed by a local artist, Otto Dallmann, who honed his skills at Cold Spring Granite while teaching art at Tech and Central Junior High schools. He retired from teaching in 1964 to focus on sculpture, and received world-wide recognition for his work. During the unveiling, Mr. Dallmann offered the following words:

The figure represents prayer all ages, anywhere. The child is praying and searching; the adult, strong in faith, guides and protects youth with prayer. ... This group will convey its message long after my chisels are idle and my hammer is silent.

"Prayer" was a gift by the Paradise family in memory of Annie May and Victor Paradise.

A large stained glass window, 20 feet wide by 16 feet high, is just above the entry doors. Passersby see it lighted at night. Our best view will come in a bit, when we are in the sanctuary, looking out.

One enters the narthex, or entryway, through a large set of glass doors. A second Dallmann bas-relief (B) hangs to the left.

This combination of white oak and mosaic shows

the four churches that St. Cloud Methodists built carved in the base, with Christ looking over them. Mosaic tiles highlight the background.

This carving served as the inspiration for bulletin covers during the 125th anniversary.

Two windows have been added to the north wall of the narthex in more recent years. One must look up or their beauty will be missed. These "hidden" windows represent Christ's 40 days in the wilderness, and are works by Richard Haeg. The panel to the left (J), over the stairwell, was given in memory of Fred Hoerber by his wife, Nan. The second piece (K) on the north wall of the entry is in memory of Gus and Anna Anderson.

Now step inside the sanctuary, walk down the aisle a bit, turn around and look up. There it is – a sermon in glass. (C) The 20 feet wide and 16 feet tall window glows even on cloudy days, and was in place when the sanctuary was dedicated in 1956.

"The Sermon on the Mount" is the title and theme of the twenty-panel west window. The window "establishes the style, stance, and tone of ministry which this church desires to offer to its community and the world" wrote Rev. Beck. "It portrays Jesus preaching the Sermon on the Mount ... to the first century disciples."

On completing the project, Pennsylvania-based artist Milcho Silianoff wrote that he "was inspired by the rhythms and order of God's creation and used a combination of curved and straight lines together with coloring to create a kind of 'modern visible poetry' to portray those words."

The artist used nearly 2,000 pieces of true antique-type stained glass consisting of approximately 200 colors, textures and thicknesses. Each was cut, fitted in by hand, and joined together with lead cames and mastic to form the complete window. The pieces are not uniform in thickness as a rolled glass would be, but vary from $1/8^{th}$ to $3/8^{th}$ inch, depending on the desired depth of color. The light-colored pieces are domestic, the dark imported. Reds contain gold, blues and cobalt. There is protective glass on the outside, which does not in any way distract from the view of the artistic window.

To many people, this is known as the Halenbeck Window as it was given in memory of Mrs. Grace Weiss Halenbeck and her parents, Rev. and Mrs. W. A. Weiss, by Dr. Halenbeck.

Now turn to face the front. "On entering the sanctuary, one is conscious of an inviting interior," wrote Rev. Hubbard of the church he had just come to serve in 1974. Window spaces on the north and south walls were filled with translucent glass, waiting for memorial gifts that were to come.

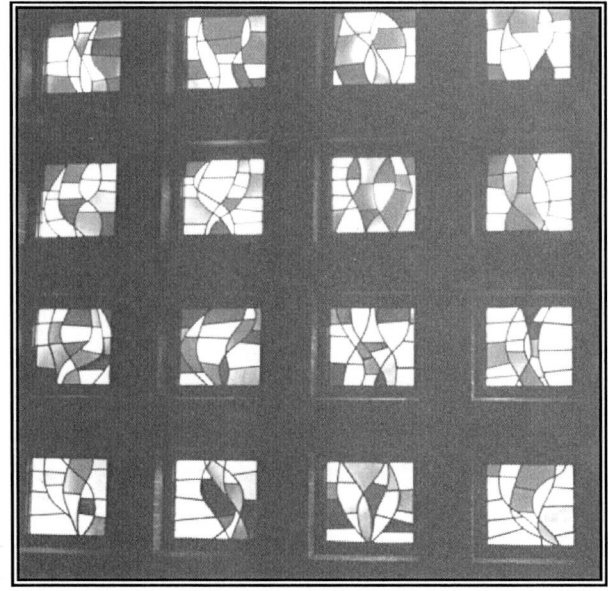

Look high on the south wall to the window lettered D on the floor plan, and those numbered 1-4. Those spaces were filled by Bronislaw "Bruno" Bak, artist-in-residence and instructor of Art at St. John's University, Collegeville, Minnesota, who designed the spectacular banner window for the Abbey Church there. They relate to the large stained glass window in the west wall in that they also interpret portions of the Sermon on the Mount.

The group of sixteen small windows in the chancel area is a development of the spirit of the Beatitudes, the beautiful joy of those who have a proper set of values, and who know that the way of Jesus is the way of sacrifice, but also of a fulfillment in joy. Bak's windows continue around the upper walls of the sanctuary as shown by numbers 1- 6.

1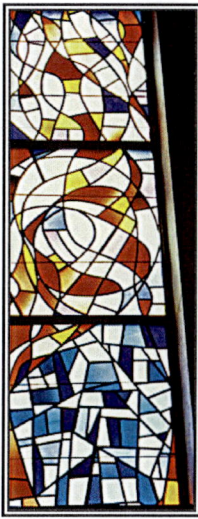

2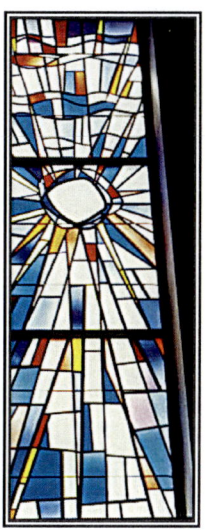

3

Stewardship The window nearest the nave is based on Jesus' admonition, "Don't let your left hand know what your right hand is doing," and is a clear call to the self-giving way of living, which was the hallmark of Jesus' own life. (Upper South Wall)

Mission "You are the light of the world, a city set on a hill can not be hid, nor do men light a lamp and put it under a bushel." Christ's teachings command us to be his people in a similar style and spirit. (Upper South Wall)

Prayer and Worship This window is devoted to worship as an integral part of the life of the Christian disciple and the Christian community. The text comes from Jesus' instruction to his disciples in the art of prayer, that part of scriptures known as the Lord's Prayer. (Upper South Wall)

183

4  5  6

Education The western most window in the south wall depicts the intermingling of the old and the new covenants in Christ's teaching, "I come not to destroy the Law and the prophets but that they might be fulfilled." (Upper South Wall)

Evangelism This window is based on the text "Enter by the narrow gate, for the gate is wide and the way is easy that leads to destruction." (Upper North Wall)

Christian Social Concerns The western most upper window is related to the text, "Not everyone who says to me Lord, but he who does the will of the Father shall enter into the joy of the Kingdom." (Upper North Wall)

A second St. John's University trained artist was the creator of the panels on the lower south wall of the sanctuary. From the front of the sanctuary on the lower level right-hand side are windows designed by Richard Haeg, an art instructor at Cathedral High School, who helped fashion Bak's banner window at St. John's Abbey Church. His work, identified by letters a-e on the map, expresses praises of creation as expressed in the Psalms. The design of window "a" was used for the logo on the church stationery from 1995 - 2007.

a. "Blessed are you, O Lord, the God of our fathers; bless the Lord, all you works of the Lord, ... Praise and exalt Him above all ..."

b. "Mountains and hills, bless the Lord; everything growing from the earth, bless the Lord."

c. "You springs, bless the Lord; seas and rivers, bless the Lord."

d. "Sun and moon, bless the Lord; stars of heaven, bless the Lord."

e. "Cold and chill, Bless the Lord; ice and snow, bless the Lord."

The wooden doors used to enter or exit the sanctuary contain stained glass inserts by Haeg. Each has its own theme, and is identified by letters i-iv on the diagram.

    i. Music: trumpets.
    ii. Communion: wheat and grapes.
    iii. United Methodist Church symbol: cross and flame.
    iv. Baptism and Christian Life: the water and the fish.

During a July 2008 telephone interview, Richard Haeg remembered being chosen to execute windows for First Church. He was selected from a group of 3-4 artists after submitting watercolor sketches of his vision to a committee that included Laurie Halberg and Catherine Beck. In addition to the lower windows on the south wall, he did the door inserts and two panels on the north wall of the entryway - a total of 22 pieces.

Mr. Haeg retired to his hobby farm in Collegeville after teaching art at Cathedral High School for 31 years. He has his studio there, where First Church's windows were created during his non-teaching time.

While a student at St. John's University, Richard was privileged to assist Bruno Bak with the magnificent banner window for the Abbey Church. Not long after its completion and all but one of the windows commissioned for First Church, Bruno Bak left for Chicago, and the stained glass studio at St. John's closed. The upper left window on First Church's north wall – part of Mr. Bak's commission – was only partly completed. It was Richard's honor to finish his mentor's work in his own studio.

jbg

Dick Haeg is shown standing beside one of his latest stained glass creations — windows in the First Methodist Church in St. Cloud.

More Things Beyond Words

The sanctuary tour focus now shifts from windows to walls and to the wood and iron sculpture marked "E" on the floor plan. The placement of the "Tree of Life" piece was an answer to a challenge caused when the education wing and tower entrance were added to the original sanctuary. A former window space was closed off and needed filling. Laurie Halberg remembers attending a trustees meeting not long after returning from his sabbatical in Italy.

> *It was at a meeting of the Trustees that the problem of filling a void in the sanctuary wall was being discussed. As a potter, I assured the other members that in no way would it ever be possible to match the bricks in color or texture. That bluntly stated, I went right on and said that if we were attempting to solve the void we should do it like the Duomo (Cathedral) in Florence. "We don't have Luca della Robbia anymore, but we have Joe O'Connell." That's the moment the seed was sown.*

Joe O'Connell on the left.

O'Connell responded with the black walnut and wrought iron sculpture "Tree of Life." Commissioned in 1986 while he was an artist in residence at the College of St. Benedict, the work took two years and received national attention, remembers former pastor Toby Horst.

It invites touch and contemplation. In Halberg's words,

> *Along the bottom the fingers of little children can touch the curl of a ram's horn and the pattern of feathers of the owl while it glances aside. They can cautiously put a finger in the jaws of a lion, and then wonder why a hand is clasped over the eyes of an angel. Does the woeful face in the corner hold a mirror to see his own image? Tess Kasling is there.[6] She's got angel wings. Joe is there: He's Judas, a business man adjusting his tie."*

"Tree of Life" was dedicated in November 1988. Rev. Toby Horst wrote an introduction to the piece for the bulletin that day which is shared here.

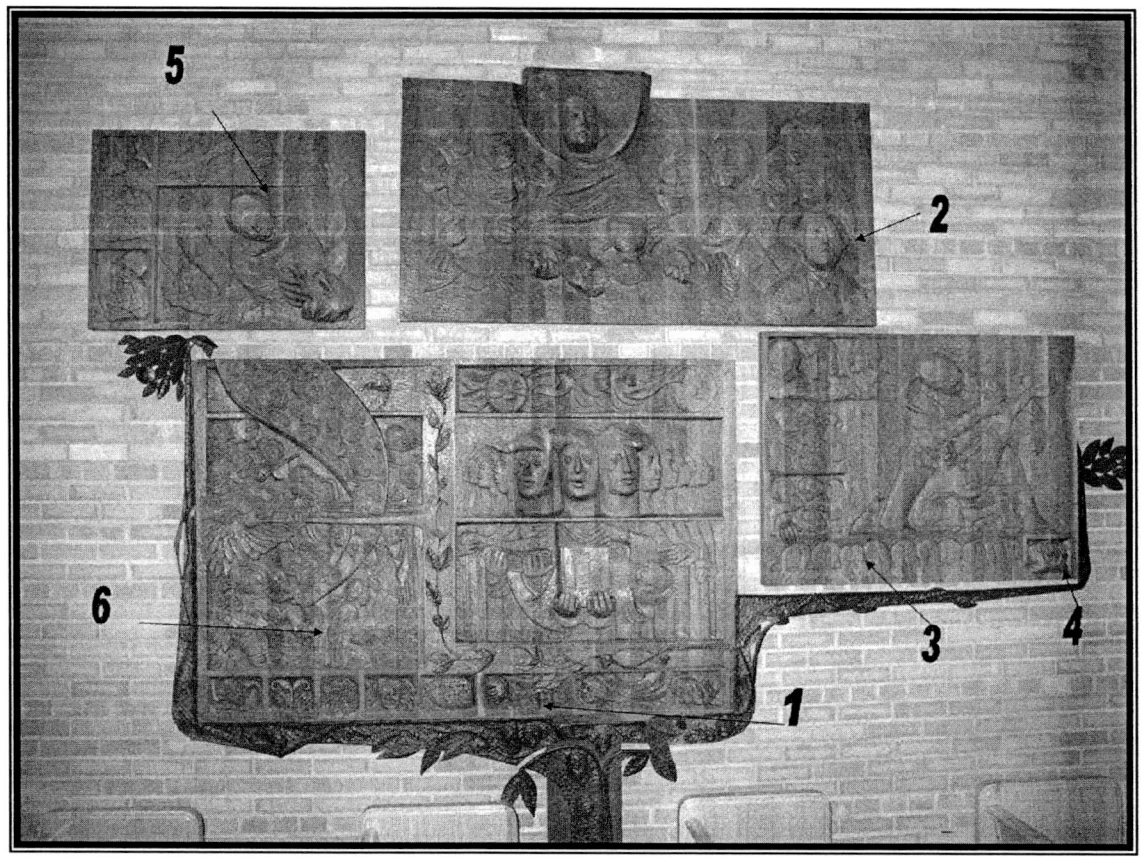

The iron trunk of the tree begins at the base of the sculpture and features a skull, reminding us of death, and apples, symbolizing life and creation. Vines reach out and entwine the four panels: the Last Supper, the Prodigal Son, the Good Samaritan and the music panel. Along the top of the sculpture the sun, moon and an angel all praise the Lord and his world. Along the bottom is a playful row of animals, just child-high for touching and enjoying [1]

Each panel is exquisitely carved and highlighted in the wood and bears the mark of its own uniqueness. In the Last Supper, we see John and Peter at Jesus' side. Judas is adorned in modern dress, suggesting that the concept of "selling out" remains with us yet today.[2]

In the delightful panel of the Prodigal Son, we see the series of events unfold: the gift of his inheritance, its waste and, finally, the degradation of the prodigal eating with the pigs.[3] In the lower right hand corner, we witness the clearly abashed face of the Prodigal's brother. [4] This parable is obviously illustrated with a touch of whimsy.

In contrast, the Good Samaritan panel haunts us with the images of the beaten man and his neighbors, who are desperately trying to determine their individual responsibilities, and with images which trouble us still today: those of starvation, prison life and the homeless.[5]

The music panel celebrates joyfully all our modern means of praise: our instruments, our voices, our bell choir. In addition, it includes the three Marys, steadfast at the crucifixion.[6]

Mr. O'Connell's sculpture is a beautiful, inspiring testament to our lives joined as one: in our shared history as Christians and in our united spirit as a congregation. The tree of life embraces us all.

Mick Benson has quietly taken on the job of regularly oiling the sculpture and the Dallmann piece to prevent drying and cracking.

The hall space connecting the sanctuary and education wing is the next stop. A display case (F), currently maintained by Beulah Rose Hutchens, features a frequently changing array of items, often of historical interest, and is a memorial to historian Gertrude Gove. Just across the way are six framed panels, (H) also featuring church history, which use photographs and calligraphy.

A few steps toward the elevator lead us to the newest stained glass window, based on John 6:48. Marked as letter G on the map, the lowest panel is at our feet. A short climb to the second floor gives a good inside view of the remaining panels, seven in all. The full effect may be best seen at night when the two-story ribbon of glass is illuminated for the busy world passing by. The window was given in memory of Warren Hutchens by his family. Photos on the left show details.

The same area leads to the stairs connecting the three levels of the addition. The first landing is the home for the second of the two 1914 building windows, "Christ in the Garden of Gethsemane," based on a familiar painting by Hoffman. (I)

We have now visited the spaces and places featured on the sanctuary floor plan, but there is more to see. The plan has an arrow in the upper left corner pointing to the education wing, where our tour continues.

The church nursery is the first large room on our right. One more memorial window hangs there. (v) It features three balloons, and was given in memory of Eric Gustafson by his young friends.

The last room we visit on the east side of the hallway is the library. It is fitted with bookshelves, comfortable seating, and a large table.

Library 2008 — The left hand photo looks south and shows the first two Hendershot drawings. They continue on the wall shown on the left on the second photo. Library shelving fills the far wall.

Drawn From Faith

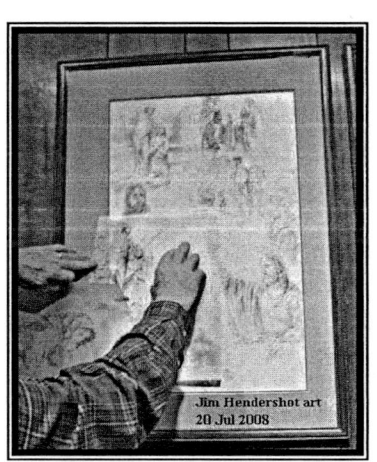
Jim Hendershot art 20 Jul 2008

Hanging in the church library are five framed panels of drawings by printmaker James Hendershot, of the art faculty at the College of St. Benedict and St. John's University, and member of this congregation.

One might describe the evocative pencil sketches as "drawn from faith." After receiving the commission from the church in the early 1990's, Hendershot tells he prepared by thoughtful reading of scripture and conversation with Rev. Horst. Over 135 images were first drawn on tracing paper, then manipulated over the drawing surface until the right relationships were revealed. White spaces are also important as they "leave mystery for the viewer," explains the artist. Only then were the final drawings realized on the sequence of five panels.

Mr. Hendershot also explains that the panels are a series, and together tell the story of Christ from annunciation to resurrection. As one stands in the library facing west, the panels read left to right around room, beginning on the south wall. In the first, one sees the annunciation, birth and flight into Egypt. The second tells of young Jesus. Moving to the west wall, the third panel focuses on his ministry. Images of the crucifixion and resurrection cover the surfaces of the fourth and fifth panels.

A sixth panel next to the library wall shows additional scenes for contemplation. Through the years, individual elements from the panels found their way onto bulletin covers.

We have now completed our walk to view permanent installations on and in First Church's fourth building. It is time to step outside again, to the corner, not far from where the walk began.

The northwest corner of the church property contains a memorial garden. It occupies the space where the 1914 building stood, and invites passersby to stop and rest. The focal point of the garden is a labyrinth, dedicated on October 7, 2001. At that time, a pamphlet was developed to explain both the history and use of this meditation tool.

The Labyrinth Story

Written with credits to many sources by
Rev. Katie Schnieder-Bryan

A labyrinth is an ancient circular diagram found in many cultures around the world. In its classical form, this sacred diagram consists of a single concentric circular path with no possibility of going astray. Labyrinths have been found in almost every religious tradition in the past four to five thousand years in such areas as Egypt, Greece, Italy, France, England, Peru, and North America. Walking the labyrinth is an ancient spiritual act and a physical meditation that is being rediscovered during our time.

Our labyrinth comes from the Christian tradition during the 12th and 13th centuries, and is a replica of the one in the floor of Chartres Cathedral outside of Paris, France. It was used in sacred devotions as substitutes for the pilgrimage to Jerusalem and for penance. The Chartres labyrinth is based on sacred geometry. It is composed of 15 concentric circles, and the center is shaped like a six petal  flower. This flower or lotus is based on a thirteen pointed star as a place of illumination. Like our lives, which at times move closer, then further away from God, the path has 32 turns going in, and 32 turns going out.

Our labyrinth and the re-landscaped garden area were made possible through memorial gifts to our church. May our labyrinth deepen our spiritual lives, and become an outreach ministry and a gift of peace and unity with God to our wider neighborhood.

HANDS TO WORK AND HEARTS TO GOD

Many things created to deepen the worship experience at First Church are not on permanent view, but are seen as the church year unfolds.

FASHIONED FROM EARTH

The altar in the chancel area often features a striking stoneware cross, fashioned by Laurie Halberg, ceramics instructor and former church member. He describes its creation process:

The slab of clay was prepared by hammering on the texture of a cracked, weathered slab of wood on to the clay which would be enriched with a wash of iron oxide after the first bisque firing. The reach of the arms of the (Tau) cross were simplified and its gentle curve allowed the imagery to perhaps even hearken back to the manger that cradled the Christ Child. An alpha and omega of Christ's life.

It was quite by chance shortly after the altar cross emerged from the first firing that a national show of liturgical art was announced to be held in Washington, D.C. ... It was indeed an honor to have the stoneware cross juried into the exhibition. With that credential added, I offered it as a gift to my church home.

THREADS WOVEN AND WORKED

Fabric arts – wall hangings; altar, pulpit and lectern hangings called paraments; and banners add to worship. Many artists have contributed – Merle Sykora and most recently Evelyn Lorenz, Karel Helgeson, and Jill Haak.

HANGINGS

Merle Sykora, fabric artist/weaver, was a colleague of Catherine Beck's when she taught art at St. Cloud State. He was invited to create hangings for the upper north wall, as well as sets of paraments. They were in place by Christmas, 1973. Sykora collaborated with a studio in Czechoslovakia,[2] using their patented technique in which silk organza was stitched onto a woven wool background, layered, torn and stretched. The left hand banner was titled "Spiryt" the right, "Rose." The artist wrote, "They are allegorical, enigmatic and purposely ambiguous so as to allow you the freedom to see what you will at any season of the church year or in any personal experience which might bring you to this place."

In 1996, after nearly 20 years of display, the hangings were in need of cleaning. Appropriately, Mr. Sykora wished to use a specialty cleaner in New York City and arranged for that to be done. Tragically, they did not survive.

For a time, the upper wall was empty, and the space waited. New hangings were to come from the hands of another fabric artist, Evelyn Lorenz, who shared these words:

The hangings on the north wall are titled "Reflections." They were inspired by the winter morning sun, shining through the stained glass windows, onto the opposite monotone brick wall. The design is taken from the colors in that reflection, the colors in the brick and the stacked organ pipes.

All the pieces are constructed of silk, appliquéd to a scrim and edged with pewter and gold braid. The special brackets and rods were created by Dr. Byron John. My muse was Jill Haak, whose encouragement and many trips to Minneapolis for silk, kept the spirit flowing.

---

[2] Vlnema Brno Studios. The unique technique was *Art Protis*. Source: Dec. 9, 1972 bulletin used for their dedication.

Paraments

"A new set of white paraments was received as a memorial gift. It was finished just in time to use on Easter Sunday (1983). Our plan is to replace some of the other color sets as memorial gifts permit," reads a paragraph in the minutes of the February 1984 Administrative Board meeting. This noted the first of four sets that member Merle Sykora, Professor in the Art Department, St. Cloud State University, was commissioned to create, to be paid for by memorials. The next was a fragile, green, hand-woven set done in rayon, since retired. The red and purple paraments that followed in 1986 and 1987 were hand quilted, then piece worked with silk.

In 1992, another set of white paraments was added. A gift of Mark and Maggie Brossoit in honor of her mother, the set features Hardanger embroidery on cotton fabric, and was first used for Christmas that year. Mary Johnson from Milaca, a colleague of Maggie's at Sauk Rapids-Rice High School did the stitching. "I do think they are some of the most beautiful paraments First Church has. I always loved seeing them," remembers Ms. Brossoit.

In the fall of 2004, Evelyn Lorenz was inspired to create a new set of paraments. Her notes on the process read:

> *The paraments titled "Extraordinary Times" depict the beauty of the Spirit flowing through the season of Ordinary Times. The inspiration for coloration and design is taken from the [first] three stained glass windows on the south wall of the sanctuary. The pulpit and lectern pieces incorporate the symbol of the flame of the Spirit.*

Both the wall hangings and the new paraments were given to the church by Evelyn and Don Lorenz.

Liturgical colors serve as reminders of the church year as seen in the changing paraments and hangings. Purple is used during Advent and Lent; black for Good Friday services. Christmas, Epiphany, and Easter call for white. Red symbolizes the season of Pentecost and All Saints Day, and green is used during "ordinary time," the weeks between other seasons.

SEASONAL VISUALS: BANNERS, AND INSTALLATIONS

During the late 1980's church friends Mark and Maggie Brossoit found a home for their artistry at First Church. Worshipers watched the development of color and symbols on a huge Ukrainian Easter egg (see page 198), a cascade of ribbons darkening through Lent, then exploding in white and gold at Easter, another of a thousand origami cranes calling for peace. Maggie recalls one of their largest projects was The Advent Village.

The background and buildings were in place for Advent One. Figures were added to the village each week - a baker, carpenter, weaver, homemaker, and then shepherds. On Christmas Eve, angels were suspended over the cave, and residents moved to see the new baby and his family. Maggie shared some memories:

One of the two years that we did the big village we had a bunch of angels we suspended over the scene, very near and even over the pulpit. As we were hanging them, we were expecting Toby, so we hung two right over the pulpit so that they would hang right in Toby's face. We asked him what he thought and, of course, he loved them, but then he thought a minute and climbed into the pulpit. Mark didn't even wait for him to comment. He just said, "Oh, Toby, don't worry about the two right in your way. Just give them a shove when you want to make a point. That's why they're made to swing."

I got to thinking that one booklet [membership directory] featured the Easter fabrics that we strung from the cross to the square colored windows up above the organ. I remember it featured all the fabrics – pretty. My other memories of that mostly involve fear! The ladder that FUMC had was the ricketiest thing ever. Since Mark was such a big guy, there was no way I was going to let him climb that nearly to the ceiling. So – that left me, and I hated every minute of it, especially when I had to get to the very top row of windows. Believe me, I had one arm wrapped around the ladder so as not to fall while with the other I tried to wedge the dowel holding the fabric into the window ledge. Every time I did that I was sure it would be the last, and everyone was going to feel so guilty at my funeral!! It's worth a good laugh now.

One Easter season I also remember doing a big fabric rainbow in front of the church that changed colors. I also remember that on the front wall, right next to the pulpit, Mark and I always did a wall hanging that changed each week, the colors darkening with the season until it was black on Good Friday, then white on Easter. A couple of years we also had a small tree we must have cut somewhere and stuck in a big bucket, which we covered. We hung ribbons of different colors from it (following the same scenario as the wall hanging). I remember that one Easter was flabbergasted because Mark and I had made the tree "bloom." We had bought lots of silk flowers and leaves and attached them, but we hadn't told him we would do that.

Many banners have been used to help us prepare for the seasons of the Church and special occasions. Some of the latest were the 150th Anniversary banners created by Karel Helgeson, which can be seen on page iii.

About 40 years ago, Joseph, Mary and baby Jesus found a home at First Church in the form of dressed, paper-maché sculptures created by Mechtild "Tilde" Ellis of Cold Spring, Minnesota. Ken Beck, then pastor, knew of her work through stoles she fashioned for him. When the original client for the statues chose not to accept them, Rev. Beck found a place for the "homeless family." Worshipers at First Church have seen them nearly every Christmas season since. One Advent, Joseph and Mary were displayed at the back of the social aisle, moving closer to the front each week as Mary's pregnancy advanced (with added padding), a worship team member remembered.

Holy Week 1990

Four Easters – Four Configurations

1956: Easter lilies flank the altar which is flush against the east wall. The removable center section of the communion rail serves as a kneeler by the altar. Choir pews are to the right of the lectern, under the lowered ceiling

Before 1968: The walnut cross has been added, no stained glass windows.

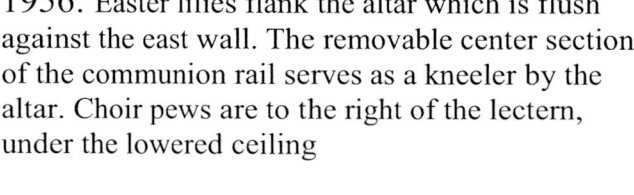

1990: The altar has been brought forward, and choir stalls moved leaving space for both organ console and grand piano. The wall cross has been lengthened; both stained glass and the Wicks pipe organ are now in place.

2007: Full choir, full pews, small orchestra and children's sermon time.

Growing our Legacy in Christ

150 years
1857-2007

Worship and Music
Annette DeCourcy Towler

First United Methodist Church

St. Cloud, Minnesota

John Wesley's Directions for Singing[1]

I. Learn these tunes before you learn any others, afterwards learn as many as you please.

II. Sing them exactly as they are printed here, without altering or mending them at all; and if you have learned to sing them otherwise, unlearn it as soon as you can.

III. Sing all. See that you join with the congregation as frequently as you can. Let not a slight degree of weakness or weariness hinder you. If it is a cross to you, take it up, and you will find it a blessing.

IV. Sing lustily and with a good courage. Beware of singing as if you were half dead, or half asleep; but lift up your voice with strength. Be no more afraid of your voice now, nor more ashamed of its being heard, than when you sung the songs of Satan.

V. Sing modestly. Do not bawl, so as to be heard above or distinct from the rest of the congregation, that you may not destroy the harmony; but strive to unite your voices together, so as to make one clear melodious sound.

VI. Sing in time. Whatever time is sung be sure to keep with it. Do not run before nor stay behind it; but attend close to the leading voices, and move therewith as exactly as you can; and take care not to sing too slow. This drawling way naturally steals on all who are lazy; and it is high time to drive it out from us, and sing all our tunes just as quick as we did at first.

VII. Above all sing spiritually. Have an eye to God in every word you sing. Aim at pleasing him more than yourself, or any other creature. In order to do this attend strictly to the sense of what you sing, and see that your heart is not carried away with the sound, but offered to God continually; so shall your singing be such as the Lord will approve here, and reward you when he cometh in the clouds of heaven.

---

[1] *United Methodist Hymnal*, p vii, 1989 edition. from John Wesley's *Select Hymns*, 1761

SERVICE OF WORSHIP

The worship service is the Church's coming together as a congregation to praise the Lord. The traditional style of worship, which Wesley prescribed, is one of the reasons Methodists are called Methodists: we have a designated method for conducting worship. This service has definite elements in a specific order. There is a call to worship, a hymn, an invocation, a call to confession, a general confession, a prayer for pardon (or else words of assurance), the Lord's Prayer, an act of praise, an anthem, the Scripture lessons (at least one reading from Old Testament, one from Epistles or Gospels), the affirmation of faith, the collect, the pastoral prayer, the offertory, another hymn, the sermon, an invitation to Christian discipleship, a final hymn, and the benediction. Every Sunday these elements play out in a completely traditional service.

However, some present-day "traditional" services do not include all these elements. Pastors can be flexible in what they select in order to achieve a meaningful service. Our church has seen both very traditional services and less complete, yet traditional, ones.

Whether completely traditional or not, this type of Methodist service typically has an organ and a choir. Generally the minister and the choir wear robes. There is an altar and lighted candles.

A contemporary Methodist service, such as First Church's second service, does not follow a strict pattern at all. Innovation and simplification mark such a service, along with modern Christian music and typically a band, a guitar, or a small musical group, plus a limited number of singers to lead the congregation. This type of service is more likely to use small plays, dance, and dramatic impersonations. Participants may wear more casual dress.

Whether traditional service or contemporary, Methodists observe the traditional Christian year: Advent, Christmastide. Epiphany, Lent, Eastertide, Pentecost, and Kingdomtide.

MUSIC

Music is important to most, if not all, Methodist services. Some churches may have fairly basic music: congregational singing, a choir, an organ or piano. However, church music can also be elaborate, using bell choirs, a variety of instruments, small orchestras, and bands.

First Church's music tradition leans to the more elaborate, with paid choir directors and organists with excellent credentials, challenging pieces of music, and a variety of instruments. In addition, the sanctuary has good acoustics, and concerts have from time to time been staged in it.

HYMNALS

Methodists have used songbooks for much of their history. The first Methodist hymnal, printed in 1856, was a small book with a black cover. It had one soprano line of music with the first verse written under the notes. The rest of the verses were written below. Charles Wesley's hymn "O for a Thousand Tongues to Sing" was the first hymn in the book, as it is in the present-day hymnal. Charles Wesley wrote hundreds of hymns, and they helped spread Methodist theology as well as contributed to Methodist worship.

Each verse in the hymn was indexed. An 1872 Bible-study lesson had a hymn verse written to sing. When one found the tune in the old hymnal, the verse was the fourth one, but easily found because of the index.

In 1909 a new hymnal was produced. It had a green cover and full scores, like present hymnals. Another new hymnal was published in 1932 and then republished in 1939 when different branches of the Methodist Church merged. All hymnals since 1932 have responsive readings, orders of service for communion, confirmation of new members, baptism, marriage, burial, dedications, and suggestions for worship.

During this period, there was a Cokesbury Hymnal that had many songs from the tent meetings/revival time, which was used for singing sessions other than formal worship. Also a Sunday school hymnal was available.

Starting in 1960, a revised hymnal was in the making, and by 1964 the hymnal was finished. There was a desire to include more hymns from the Cokesbury Hymnal, as it would no longer be published. For many of the pastors and organists who had memorized the hymns and numbers from the 1930's hymnal, there was a new learning curve. For the first time the hymnal could be ordered with a red cover. By 1968 the Methodist Church and the Evangelical United Brethren had merged, so this hymnal became the hymnal of the United Methodist Church (although other hymnals were used as well).

The present hymnal was released in 1989, with some hymns special to the Evangelical United Brethren tradition, music from other cultures and lands, and contemporary music. Amens were removed and lyrics were no longer gender specific. The cover had the Cross and the Flame logo on it and could be ordered in a number of colors.

The 1989 hymnal is unique to Methodism, in that it includes other languages, non-gender-specific wordage, and hymns chosen by committees of diverse people, both ordained and lay, musical experts and interested members of congregations. The Methodist tradition previously had been to use only hymns approved by the General Board of Bishops, Wesley, and long tradition.

An example of the hymnal's inclusiveness is hymn number 57, "O for a Thousand Tongues to Sing." It is also hymn number 58 and 59. The tune is the same, but each version is in a different language. Another inclusiveness issue was that of gender and the former practice of referring to God and humans always with a masculine pronoun. The new hymnal tried to be sensitive to this issue and to use both masculine and feminine pronouns when it seemed acceptable, to talk about "people" rather than "mankind," and so forth. Christmas carols were the hardest to change to non-gender, as copyrights are hard to change. So at the bottom of hymn 218 where one finds "It Came upon the Midnight Clear," there is a note that tells singers that "all" may be substituted for "men."

1909　　　　　　1932-1939　　　　　1964-1966　　　　　Current 1989

Organ

From early in First Church's history, there was some kind of instrument to provide music for the services. First Church used a melodeon in their original church building, later a reed organ, a theatre organ, an electric Baldwin organ, and now the Wicks pipe organ.

First Church is one of a few churches in St. Cloud still to have a pipe organ. This organ, like many other pipe organs, can be updated with a new stop (set of pipes/14 ranks) added to the range of pipes. This organ was installed when Rev. Richard Collman, a trained organist, was the associate minister and the person responsible for the Church's music. Richard Clampitt, a member of the Church, was instrumental in helping the Church acquire the organ. Michael Barone later became the Church organist and added his own portable one manual tracker organ to the sanctuary.

Because of the acoustics in this church and the ability to move the Wicks organ from one place to another, this church was used in the late 1980's for concerts by organists from various churches. Many other musical events have been held here.

On October 14, 2007, Charles Echols arranged with Tess Kasling a concert for the Church's 150th Anniversary. Michael Barone returned and played, as did Tess and Charles. There are other organists currently in the congregation, Julie Lindquist, Nancy Seutter, and Annette DeCourcy Towler, whose talents have been used off and on in the last 25 years.

A Yamaha grand piano was added in 1979. This piano has been used regularly in both services. As with most of our musical instruments, funds from a special collection and memorial monies were used to finance it.

Handbells

Roni Trulson

In 1973 the handbells were added to the musical instruments and were dedicated on December 9, 1973. The service program noted: "A set of English handbells has been given to our church to honor the memory of Edward A. Drews and May J. Drews. They were members of this congregation from the time of their arrival in St. Cloud in 1927 until their deaths in 1965 and 1973. These memorial bells have been given by Mrs. and Mrs. Merrill Johnson and the family and friends of Ed and May Drews."

The First United Methodist Church handbells were cast by the Schulmerich Company of Pennsylvania. They fit in three cases, and cover three full octaves (low C to middle C to two octaves above middle C). In 2002, a D bell was added above the 3 octaves, a gift from Joan Clampitt. Two octaves of melodic chimes were added in 2006.

Bell Choir Christmas Leona Nash director

The original group of ringers was called the Drews Handbell Choir. Members were Ken Christie, Phillip Hines, Jim Nielsen, Mike Olson, John Stenger, and Leslie Tix. Senior Handbell choir members were Lynn Anderson, Sue Ezell, Sue Land, Lorraine Matthias, Jennifer Olson, Betty Partch, Mabel Retherford, and Randy Retherford. The first bell choir director was Natalie Slack, and the original practice time was Sunday evenings at 7 p.m.

The bell choir has had several directors over the years, Leona Nash, Natalie Slack, Catherine Van Nostrand, Ellen Deane Schweiger, Shirley Echols, Nancy Seutter, David Scholz, Christopher Larsen and the current director, Steve Mick. The bell choir has performed at area churches, nursing homes, and regional bell choir events. Current members are Michelle Hedgren, Tess Kasling, Annette Towler, Roni Trulson, Angela Trulson-Lindsey, Carolyn Tufte, Teresa Colgan, Kim Colgan and Nancy Stigaard. Long-time members have been Roni Trulson, Angela Trulson and Annette Towler.

Each person plays three or four bells depending on the music. Angela Trulson-Lindsey has been known to play 8 – 10 bells during some pieces. In 2002, a D bell was added to the bells by Joan Clampitt. In 2006, a set of melodic chimes was added to the bells. In 2007, new table pads and covers were made by Arlene Towler and Nancy Stigaard. Nancy also made a banner for the tables. These were memorials.

27 Jan 2008 Prelude FUMC Bell Choir

Handbells have a colorful history. They were invented in the 17th century in England when neighbors of bell towers were tired of listening to long change-ringing rehearsals. Handbells permitted the rehearsals to take place in the spirited warmth of pubs. Furthermore, belfries were cold, drafty places and ringing tower bells was hard work. Handbells were first brought to the United States around 1840. They were popularized by P. T. Barnum as a circus attraction. Then they were introduced into the vaudeville circuit.

In the 1940's, people began ringing handbells in American churches. Handbells were first manufactured in the United States in the 1960's. There are over 10,000 handbell choirs in North America. Approximately one percent of these are community groups and the rest are affiliated with churches and schools.

Catherine Van Nostrand shares additional bell choir insights in her account found in this section.

Choirs

When did First Church choirs start? No answer has been found, except for information referring to concerts and choir directors. The first pictures we have are in the former (1914) sanctuary, showing the choir during a service, with Russell Huffman as pastor. Miss Leona Nash was the director. David Van Nostrand and John Barron were in this choir.

Leona Nash Choir Director

Many choir directors in recent years either have been the Apollo High School choir directors or a music faculty from area colleges. A high quality standard of church music keeps this group coming back to share their talents with God and his people.

2008 Choir
Steve Mick director
Tess Kasling organist

In 1969, there were three choirs, Cherub, Chorister, and Chancel. All rehearsals were on Wednesday nights, as has been the practice since about 1927.

ADULT CHOIR: A FAMILY TRADITION

David Van Nostrand

When I was in high school I sang in our First Church choir with my dad and brother, who were basses, and my mom, who was a soprano. The time was in the early 50's. The conductor at the time was Leona Nash. I remember some of the other men. Ralph Sorenson and Charles Stark were basses with me. Ralph was a guidance counselor at Tech High. I delivered Leona's newspaper over on Eighth Avenue South. Fred Haverland sang tenor and was a friend of mine and also my dad. His wife, Ruth, also sang I'm quite sure. I also sang in chorus at Tech and when I went on to college at Grinnell I sang in men's glee club and chapel choir. Some of my fond memories were the tours we did in college.

When I returned to St Cloud in 1968 and joined the church, I also joined the choir and have enjoyed singing in it ever since. Many of the members have similar experience as I and sang in college and also sing in other groups. In my opinion we have a fine tradition of good choral music in our church and have had several fine directors over the years, usually from the college or high schools. The music we sing is classical, such as Bach and Handel, and contemporary, such as John Rutter.

My wife, Catharine, who was a music major and part of the music staff at First Church, and I sang in other church choirs along the way, including a Baptist church in Boston while I was in medical school and Minnehaha Methodist church in Minneapolis. We have three daughters who are all active in our church music. Two of them work in church music now, while the third sings on a regular basis in the Twin Cities. Laura Caviani, our oldest daughter, now has a regular gig at Hennepin Avenue Methodist Church.

Music Program In The 1970s
Catharine Van Nostrand

Catharine Van Nostrand joined the First Church staff about 1969, first as director of children's vocal choirs, then also as Coordinator of Worship and Music and director of handbell choirs. Catharine had a degree in music education and previous experience directing choirs in Baptist and Presbyterian churches in Massachusetts and Minnesota. She served at First Church until 1978.

The Coordinator positions were initiated during Rev. Beck's ministry, and included also Coordinator of Education (Jo Tennison) and Coordinator of Youth (James Garven). Catharine, Jo and Jim comprised a staff of laypeople with expertise in their individual areas, and met weekly at Monday morning staff meetings with Rev. Beck, secretary Betty Partch and others.

Catharine's job involved advising the Worship Committee, planning hymns and anthems to complement chosen scripture/sermon topics, ordering new choir music and many other tasks.

One Sunday, Catharine facilitated an experimental worship service, and asked congregants to form a circle all around the edges of the sanctuary, face each other and hold hands. According to her daughter Laura (Van Nostrand) Caviani,, herself a professional musician, "Mom was ahead of her time - to actually have people participate [in the service]."

As children's choir director, Catharine held regular rehearsals with youngsters, age approximately 8 - 15, including at least two of her own daughters. It was a challenge to choose music that the kids would be able to sing and would enjoy singing, while also having it fit into the liturgical theme of that particular Sunday.

Laura remembers one Sunday the anthem was "All Things Bright and Beautiful," and choir members held colorful scarves as they danced all around. Choristers learned to use simple rhythm instruments, such as finger cymbals, and those who played other instruments, such as flute and recorder, were encouraged to occasionally play an obbligato.

About this time a very synchronistic event occurred: church member Mrs. Drews wanted to donate funds so the church could purchase a set of English handbells. But who knew how to direct handbell choirs? Fortunately, Sam and Natalie Slack moved to St. Cloud, and Natalie not only had expertise, but owned a set of bells. Funds were donated, the church purchased a three-octave set of bells, and the Drews Handbell Choir was born.

At first, Natalie invited only junior-high boys, whose voices weren't yet ready for singing choirs, to play the bells. Eventually, handbell choirs were opened to youth and adults of all ages and both sexes. Natalie carefully instructed ringers to always wear clean white gloves so their hands wouldn't tarnish the brass. After Natalie left, Catharine took over the handbell choirs, and wrote an original bell composition titled "Montage," which was performed during one service.

Rev. Richard Collman came to First Church in 1969 as associate pastor. Richard, Natalie and Catharine co-founded and co-directed a week-long Junior High Worship and Music Camp at Koinonia, a United Methodist site near South Haven, Minnesota. Campers sang, played Natalie's bells and their own instruments, learned how to find their way through the hymnal and enjoyed the lake. On the last night of camp, they gave a concert for parents and friends.

The 1970s were an active and colorful time musically at First Church, with new ways to coordinate music and worship.

Bridge Band History

By: Drew Sevcik and Tasha Christensen

When you look back on the 150 years of First Church, the Bridge Band is one of the newer additions to the life of the church. It got its start in 1998 when there was a desire to experiment with a contemporary service. The first leaders of Bridge Band were John and Janelle Kendall, and the associate pastor, Shane Burton, was one of the founding members. In order to spread knowledge of First Church and their new contemporary service, the band participated in the 1999 Wings, Wheels, and Water Festival Parade in St. Cloud and made pens and magnets to leave in well-traveled, conspicuous locales around town.

Through the years there has been a diverse number of vocal and musical talents in the Bridge Band including guitars, bass, percussion, keyboard, violin, and saxophone. In 2001, the band changed over with a new leader, Tasha Christensen. An open membership has attracted music lovers of all ages, from high school and college students through retired community members. Always looking for ways to spread God's Word through song, the Bridge Band enjoys learning new contemporary Christian music and also crosses over into popular music that relates to the message. The band is a mix of members from the beginning years (including Drew Sevcik, who has

participated since the band's inception) and newer musicians who were added more recently. They are a fun, music-loving bunch; in fact, some members also sing in the Chancel Choir at the traditional service. As we reach this milestone anniversary in First Church's history, the Bridge Band looks forward to extending a welcome to new members and carrying their ministry into the future.

CHORISTER CHOIR

By Edythe Williams

The children of First United Methodist Church had an opportunity to be part of a children's choir from 1988-98 under the leadership of Edythe Williams and daughters, Leanna and Priscilla. During this time, Annette Towler also accompanied the choirs part of the time, especially as the student helpers went off to college.

We divided the children into two age groups, Chorister Choir (Grades 4-6) and Cherub Choir (Grades K-3). This allowed older children to have

opportunity to sing in two- or three-part harmony. Liz Inveiss lead the younger group during part of that decade. We tried rehearsals after school, during 7:30 p.m. activity time on Wednesdays, and finally settled on meeting after the early Sunday service. Our members came from such a variety of communities that finding a week-night or after-school rehearsal time was not feasible.

The two choirs had the goal of learning about music and singing, as well as serving their church in musical worship. We alternated choirs each month so they would have ample opportunity to sing for a worship service.

We also had some fun social times and summer picnics during the year. During this era, we tried to incorporate teen and college musicians with the choir anthems whenever we could. For a brief time, we had a teen vocal ensemble but never enough interest for a choir.

A church really should always make the opportunity available for children to tell the love of Jesus through music.

FUMC 150TH HISTORY — WORSHIP AND MUSIC

Growing our Legacy in Christ

150 years
1857–2007

Our People at Work

First United Methodist Church

St. Cloud, Minnesota

OUR PEOPLE AT WORK

BOARD OF TRUSTEES

Bob Holscher

The Board of Trustees is entrusted with the responsibility for the oversight and management of the church building(s) and all real and personal property of the church. This board consists of nine members that elect their own officers and rotate three new members each year to a three-year term.

The Trustees play a major role in the life and on-going ministry of the church by continually updating facilities. Major duties include:
- Keeping all deeds, documents and legal papers and providing signatures for all legal papers.
- Maintaining and reviewing a policy and budget for use and maintenance of our church.
- Securing and reviewing adequate property and liability insurance.
- Maintaining a parsonage (if applicable).
- Ensuring all facilities are accessible to all persons.
- Receiving of all bequests, grants and trusts made to the church.

First mention of the Board of Trustees in our historical documents is dated August 11, 1860, and concerns the incorporation of First Methodist Church. Major projects over the last 150 years involving the Trustees include:
- 1864 - Construction of the first Methodist Church near corner of 4th Ave. S and 4th St.
- 1873 - First church is dismantled and lumber used to help construct second church on corner of 5th Ave. S and 3rd St.
- 1894 - Electric lights added to church.
- 1911 - Second church moved to back of lot and construction started on third church in same space. Construction included a large basement gymnasium.
- 1916 - Parsonage is built where existing sanctuary is today.
- 1953 - Parsonage is moved two blocks to make space for new fourth church.
- 1954 - Cornerstone laid for new church, which is completed in 1956.
- 1956 - Funds are raised to demolish third church. Two stained glass windows are stored to be used in future education wing.
- 1959 – Construction begins on education wing.

- 1988 – Elevator is added to church.
- 1993 – Parking lot is completed.

GRIP Story

Jim Towler

The Great River Interfaith Partnership (GRIP) arose out of the justice concerns of the people of the area churches. The purpose of the new group was to confront the base causes of poverty, discrimination and violence, which continued to surface in the community. The first informal meeting was held on May 23, 1996. At the first GRIP Public Assembly in May of 1998 at St. Mary's Cathedral, the *St. Cloud Times* included this report:

> *The community of churches seek to be a thermostat that determines the temperature and not a thermometer that reports it, said the Rev. Katie Schneider-Bryan of First United Methodist Church. "We are the people we have been waiting for," Schneider-Bryan said. Schneider-Bryan asked the 13 churches and agencies that publicly announced their commitment to GRIP to take the next step with the organization: Participate in community organizing training, anti-racism training, outreach training, citizenship outreach, leadership training and GRIP fund raising. (St. Cloud Times 5/17/98)*

Twenty-five of the 400 persons in attendance were from First United Methodist Church (FUMC). A central theme for GRIP has been "We do together what we cannot do alone." A short statement of purpose for GRIP/ISAIAH was developed in 2005 as follows:

> *It is our purpose to Transform Society from Isolation to Community,*
> *from Abundance for a Few to Shared Abundance for All,*
> *from Fear to Hope,*
> *from Racial and Economic Injustice to Racial and Economic Justice.*

Pastor Katie Schneider-Bryan was a significant founding leader of GRIP, both among the pastors of the area churches and in our congregation. There are other leaders in the congregation as well. Rev. Randy Johnson has chaired the Spiritual Leaders Caucus (pastors). Now he is president of GRIP and vice president of ISAIAH. Randy is a counselor for Catholic Charities and since 2007 has been a part-time pastor at First Church.

Mark Jaede has given significant leadership to the Diversity Task Force, including current negotiations to create a regional human rights office. Val

Rogosheske was a leader on the GRIP task force dealing with housing discrimination. Marcia Summers served throughout the life of the Affordable Housing Task Force. Diane Bublitz has served on the GRIP Executive Committee and Training Team.

Both Diane Bublitz and Jim Towler, as Core Team chairs, have served on the GRIP Planning Group. Howard Smith and Gordon Snyder have participated in the Living Wage Task Force. Marcia Summers and Jim Towler have regularly served on the Public Education Task Force. Other members of the congregation's Core Team have worked within the congregation for GRIP and its goals.

Following GRIP's initial organization in 1996, One-to-One in-depth conversations took place in 1997 and 1998. GRIP members visited with individual church members of their congregations. This was done to find out the desires of people for their congregations and for their community. More than 120 persons were visited at First United Methodist Church in these One-to-Ones. In 2003 this surveying was done with a different format - house meetings - including one at First Church. The listing of community needs identified by the churches revealed a public agenda which needed to be addressed.

GRIP's basic strategy involves rallying people in the congregations to support justice issues, creating proposals for ordinances or laws, and working with public governing bodies - city councils, commissions, the state legislature - and the people's elected representatives. GRIP attempts to bring about change to our human systems, rather than organizing charitable work, as important as that is.

Public assemblies are held each year to lift up issues for action and to invite public officials to step up to these challenges. In 2004 and 2005, five hundred to six hundred persons from the churches attended each assembly, with 35 to 40 persons from First Church in attendance.

How GRIP confronts the issues varies. Significant numbers of persons from the congregations attended and testified at city councils and planning commissions, and engaged public officials in conversation about the issues. Further, our people were among those who attended joint city council events and candidate forums. They also visited state legislators in St. Paul. In 2006 there was training for participation in political party caucuses to raise justice issues. Task forces are formed around each of the issues. Engaging new supporters and training leaders are regularly on the organizational agenda.

GRIP has not pretended to alone do justice work and has joined with a variety of allies, inside and outside the faith community. GRIP has counterparts in the Minneapolis-St. Paul area, all of which were organized as ISAIAH in 2000. Each of these groups has worked on issues of importance to their communities, and they often have worked together on issues involving the State of Minnesota. GRIP has worked through the ISAIAH network to increase funding for K-12 public education and battered women's shelters. Other issues in ISAIAH's agenda have included quality public transportation and the Dream Act, to enable immigrant children who graduate from high school to receive in-state tuition. ISAIAH is associated with the Gamaliel Foundation, which encourages interfaith justice networks around the nation and fosters training events for leaders.

In 1998 the first issue that drew the local churches' attention was housing discrimination in St. Cloud. That year it was verified that discrimination against people of color, single parents with children, and people with disabilities was commonplace among landlords in St. Cloud. GRIP organized the passage of an ordinance in 1999 that mandates landlord education and consequences for those found to be engaged in discriminatory practices.

In 1999 GRIP leaders began a three-year campaign to address the critical shortage of affordable housing in the adjacent five-city area. This resulted in the 2002 Joint Powers Agreement on Life Cycle Housing between St. Cloud, Waite Park, St. Joseph, Sauk Rapids and Sartell, which required that 15% of all new housing built in each city over the next five years would be affordable. This Affordable Housing issue drew prolonged public attention, bringing large number of GRIP supporters to city council chambers and planning commission meetings.

On a hot 2003 summer day at FUMC, persons from the various congregations and one non-profit chose three new issues: 1) Diversity: Hospitality/Acceptance/Understanding, 2) Economic Development: Living Wage, and 3) Education: Funding for Public Education.

In 2003 a Living Wage Task Force for GRIP sought to bring the adjoining cities in the St. Cloud area into common guidelines on the state's JobZ program. This program awards tax incentives to businesses starting up or expanding in exchange for the commitment to create a certain number of jobs at a given minimum wage. GRIP sought to help the cities develop a common wage standard for jobs in businesses that received tax credit subsidy and a living wage standard that is formula based.

The Diversity Task Force first addressed concern about racial profiling in law enforcement, which had surfaced as a problem in St. Cloud. After much effort in organizing the minority community and negotiating with the police department, a Community Policing Agreement was arrived at. On Sept. 8, 2005, this agreement was celebrated at the NuWay Baptist Church. Present were Police Chief Dennis O'Keefe and members of his department, representatives of the minority community, and GRIP people. The Diversity Task Force then turned its attention to advocating for a regional human rights office to serve the adjacent cities and three counties.

GRIP, through its Public Education Task Force, helped bring people in congregations to support the passage of the levy referendum for School District #742 in 2004. This referendum dealt with the basic needs of the schools. GRIP was a partner with others in this effort and was given some credit in helping passing the referendum.

In 2005 GRIP widened its public education concerns, mobilizing persons within the congregations to support an increase in funding for K-12 public education from the State of Minnesota. This was done by means of group presentations in the congregations and a letter-writing campaign targeted at legislators. Over 60 letters were generated from FUMC alone. The result not only increased the percentage of educational spending in the state budget beyond the governor's proposal, but did so without forcing cuts in Minnesota Care, which provides health insurance for the poor and lower middle class. The ISAIAH portion of the larger education coalition was firm in its insistence that other social funding should not be sacrificed for educational increases.

In 2007 the public education effort supported a standards-based funding approach to public education so schools can more adequately address the educational needs of the broad range of students in the state, including socially disadvantaged students.

In 2006 GRIP sponsored ten breakfast presentations of the Mind the Gap study, with an added focus on St. Cloud area data. The Itasca Group, a

Minneapolis-St.Paul study group composed of business, education leaders and some government leaders, found that their area would face a shortage of educated workers to take the place of those who were retiring. Although having a significant population, the Twin Cities had many undereducated citizens.

The St. Cloud area data on near-future employment changes and educational deficiencies among the socially disadvantaged paralleled the Twin Cities data. GRIP churches were paired with businesses, and FUMC was paired with Creative Memories. A total of 50 people, including business and city leaders, were in attendance, 30 from our congregation.

In the fall of 2006, GRIP took the lead in helping NuWay Missionary Baptist, an African American congregation, find a permanent home in St. Cloud. This was done by confronting subtle racism and being persuasive at City Council meetings. A re-zoning change made it possible for the congregation to purchase a building suitable for their needs.

At each GRIP Public Assembly, public officials (city, county, legislative) are invited to commit to supporting the issues selected for action. These persons are briefed ahead of time on what they will be asked to support. There have always been officials that have been willing to step up before the audience in support of issues. Others have chosen to be present but not step up, or at least not on all issues.

At the September 2006 Public Assembly before 750 persons at Bethlehem Lutheran Church, candidates for public office were invited to commit to working with GRIP. As a part of this assembly, discussions were held between the legislative candidates and persons from their districts. Bishop Sally Dyck of our Minnesota United Methodist Church was among the speakers, along with the ELCA Lutheran bishop and the Catholic bishop. A state officer of the Unitarian-Universalists also took part.

A line from the prophet Isaiah (Isaiah 58:12), often used by GRIP/ISAIAH, summarizes the purpose for these endeavors: "You shall be called repairers of the breach, the restorer of the streets to dwell in."

Junior High Methodist Youth Fellowship
(Late 1950's Early 1960's)

Mary Beth Megarry

During the 1950s and for a number of years thereafter, the 7th, 8th and 9th graders joined together in their own special group, Junior High Methodist Youth Fellowship (MYF), for fellowship, learning and service. They gathered on Sunday afternoons in Wesley Hall for their regular meetings, which included Bible study, refreshments and fun!

Sometimes the Junior High MYFers developed and performed special programs on the Wesley Hall stage that were related to their studies. Their families were their admiring and proud audiences.

In the early 1960s, the MYFers agreed that it was important for them to raise some money. They organized a spaghetti dinner fundraiser that became an annual event for more than two decades. To give Wesley Hall the atmosphere of a candlelit Italian cafe, they painted and posted a paper mural on the back wall of the Wesley Hall stage, and they made centerpieces by placing candles in bottles that were decorated with drippings of candle wax. To be sure that the food would be delicious, they recruited their mothers to do the cooking. In Italian folk costume, the MYFers sold tickets, waited on tables and, as strolling musicians, entertained their guests.

When Rev. Kenneth Beck came to serve First UMC in 1963, he initiated a field trip to Minneapolis for 9th graders prior to their confirmation. It was an event that enhanced their learning experience about God's world and the faith community. He took them on tours of the Hennepin Avenue Methodist Church, the Basilica of St. Mary and the Temple of Israel.

Always ready for fun, in the early 1960's, the Junior High MYFers sponsored the first dance ever held in Wesley Hall. They invited their friends to join them for a couple hours of enjoying refreshments and of dancing to their favorite recorded music.

A good time was had by the 7th, 8th and 9th graders of Junior High MYF through fellowship, learning and service.

Outreach Committee

Carl Bublitz

open hearts
open minds
open doors

As we celebrate our 150th Anniversary during 2007, the Outreach Committee of FUMC reflects upon our rich history and looks forward to actively serving the St. Cloud Area into the 21st century. Our faith community's philosophy of "Open Hearts, Open Minds, Open Doors" is manifest in Outreach's goal to embrace cultural and ethnic diversity in our mission of sharing God's love for all as a welcoming congregation.

Formerly, the current two committees of Outreach and Nurture were a combined committee called Membership & Evangelism. Today each committee reflects slightly different purposes of attracting new people to our church (Outreach) and building and nurturing relationships within our congregation (Nurture).

Currently, Outreach hosts four to five "newcomer gatherings" per year. This two-part orientation is offered to those new to our faith community who are considering membership. These gatherings serve as an introduction to the history, doctrine and uplifting spirituality FUMC has to offer. Each participant is encouraged to actively participate in this orientation and to conduct a self-assessment of spiritual gifts. The spiritual gifts assessment helps foster spiritual growth and empowers new members to become active in the life of the church through gratifying service and fulfilling participation in various ministries. Throughout Outreach's involvement in welcoming new members, our goal is to follow the model of "Inviting, Forming and Sending" disciples of Jesus Christ.

Prior to taking vows of membership during worship, new members may attend an Outreach sponsored breakfast and become acquainted with their Fellowship Friends from the congregation, who accompany them during the church service. The process of matching Fellowship Friends with new members helps create a welcoming atmosphere and makes new people feel connected. Outreach and Nurture committee members also sponsor various church outings and encourage members to attend a variety of family-friendly activities and experience the fellowship of our faith community.

Outreach's role of helping FUMC be a welcoming congregation will continue to change as we adapt to new challenges. In the last couple of years, Outreach became responsible for arranging Sunday greeters and continues to provide follow-up contacts of new visitors by phoning, letter writing and visiting. Outreach also encourages current members to reach out and welcome visitors and to make new acquaintances through practicing the Rule of 3 (in the first three minutes after worship, I will seek out and greet people I do not know) and the Circle of 10 (I will greet everyone who comes within 10 feet of me on Sunday).

The Outreach Committee has recently been helped by the United Methodist Igniting Ministries program. Igniting Ministries helps congregations update church facilities and procedures to become more welcoming to those actively seeking a church home and to meet the needs of the unchurched. Outreach submitted documents to Igniting Ministries to request certification as a Welcoming Congregation and received our certification in 2007. Resources are available from Igniting Ministries to help congregations reach out to others. Our church has updated our website and put advertisements in the local newspaper, Susan Dean's Newcomer Service church directory, and the telephone Yellow Pages.

PRAYER SHAWL MINISTRY

Arlene Towler

Shawls have been made for centuries to symbolize shelter, peace, comfort, and beauty. Here at First United Methodist Church, St. Cloud, our Prayer Shawl Ministry began in April 2005 under the leadership of the Care Committee. Twenty women responded to the call to knit or crochet in afternoon or evening groups the first and third Thursday of each month. Prayers are lifted with the sound of clicking needles, bringing friendship and love with each stitch. Meditation, conversation, and laughter are all part of this ministry.

We have given shawls to console the grieving, comfort those who are ill, and bring hope to those in despair. Joy is expressed as a baby receives a shawl when baptized.

When a shawl is completed we have a prayer to bless it. The end result is that both the recipient and the knitter are blessed.

Scholarship Programs

Beth Megarry

The congregation of First United Methodist Church is proud to offer scholarships to persons of all ages and walks of life, who follow in the United Methodist heritage of life-long learning. The scholarship funds are designed to assist United Methodist students in their college and/or seminary training. Because of the foresight and commitment of several church members, four funds have been established in thanks for God's gifts and blessings to them, or in memory of loved ones. They are the Grannis Memorial Education Fund, the Grannis-Martin Memorial Education Fund, the Stevenson Memorial Education Fund, and the Doreene E. Cater Scholarship Fund.

Grannis Memorial Education Fund. Miss Edith Grannis, who died on December 26, 1969, bequeathed funds in her will to First United Methodist Church for the creation of a scholarship fund as a memorial to her father, Samuel Higbee Grannis, and to her mother, Armenia Jane Grannis. The Grannis Memorial Education Fund was officially given its name on January 27, 1974.

The Grannis Memorial Scholarships are given to students with a Minnesota connection who are entering or currently attending a seminary and who plan to work in a United Methodist ministry. The awards are originally made as loans with one-third of the outstanding loan balance forgiven for each year of service to the United Methodist Church.

Edith Grannis served as the head librarian at St. Cloud State College (now State University) from 1922 until her retirement in 1955. She was a member of First United Methodist Church for over 50 years.

Grannis-Martin Memorial Education Fund. The Grannis-Martin Memorial Foundation, Inc., was established as a result of the will left by Miss Mamie Martin upon her death on March 27, 1979, at the age of 89 years. The foundation was named after Miss Martin and her best friend, Edith Grannis, who had bequeathed a sizeable portion of her estate (household belongings and personal effects) to Miss Martin.

Miss Martin was a member of First United Methodist Church for over 50 years. She was the library assistant to Miss Grannis at St. Cloud State. The two of them constituted the entire permanent staff for the library services at the college from 1927 until 1955.

The Grannis-Martin Scholarships have the same conditions as the Grannis Memorial Education Fund.

Stevenson Scholarship. The Stevenson Memorial Education Fund was established by the will of Robert F. Stevenson, who was a life-long Methodist until his death in 1982. He lived in St. Cloud almost all of his life.

Mr. Stevenson attended college at the University of Minnesota. He became a credit manager for International Harvester Company and in 1922 was their branch manager at Cedar Falls, Iowa. A short time after that, he returned home to manage the family business, which was to become known as Stevenson's Auto Service and Wholesale Parts Company, located on Fifth Avenue North and First Street, St. Cloud. He and his wife, Adelide (Dunn) Stevenson, were married for nearly sixty years when she died in 1972.

Awards from the Stevenson Memorial Education Fund are given to college students who are members of First United Methodist Church, St. Cloud, Minnesota.

Doreene E. Cater Scholarship. The Doreene E. Cater Scholarship Fund was established in 1996 through the gift of her husband, Donald Cater, in memory of her long, dedicated service to education in St. Cloud and of her commitment to Christ and his work through First United Methodist Church, where she was an active member.

Doreene Cater attended Drews Business College and then worked for the Triple A Agriculture office in St. Cloud, the Ideal Granite Company and then for 38 years with School District #742 under four district superintendents as office manager in the administration office. She was an active member of First United Methodist Church and participated in a variety of career-related organizations. Doreene died on April 30, 1989, just a week after she and Don had celebrated their twenty-third wedding anniversary.

Awards from the Doreene E. Cater Scholarship Fund are given to students who are members of the Minnesota United Methodist Conference and are entering their sophomore or higher year of college work.

These four scholarships have helped many students over the years. A new scholarship was introduced in the fall of 2007. The **Ruth Skewes Eakin Scholarship Fund** was established in memory of Ruth Skewes Eakin, who died in 2001. The scholarship grants will be awarded to students who are St. Cloud State University undergraduates and members of a United Methodist church in Minnesota. Ruth and her first husband, Dr. George Skewes, served as advisers to the Wesley Foundation at St. Cloud State for many years. Beginning in 1960 and continuing throughout the 1970s, Ruth was the parish visitor for First United Methodist Church.

The congregation of First United Methodist Church considers it a privilege to assist students as they work toward their goals in higher education.

Much of this biographical information was taken from a summary written by Russell Madsen in 1991.

TRUST FUND
Marcia Summers

The purpose of the First United Methodist Church Trust is to receive bequests, memorials, and other planned gifts and use them "to enhance and expand the charitable, educational, religious, and social outreach programs and total ministries of First United Methodist Church of St. Cloud."

A program on wills, estate planning and congregational trust funds held on September 19, 1988 with 29 attendees was the first step toward developing a congregational trust fund. Following that, a task force of Glenn Carlson, Jean Eckberg, Lois Fredrickson, Scott Johnson, Larry Lafler, and Harold Zosel developed a Resolution to Establish the First United Methodist Church of St. Cloud Trust Fund, which was approved by the congregation on April 13, 1989. Its structure included an endowed Perpetual Fund in which the principal was retained and a Ministry Fund from which both principal and income could be used "to enable the further growth of our church, its ministries, and stewardship opportunities."

A Trust Fund Committee of five, chaired for many years by Harold Zosel, developed a brochure with the theme "Reaching beyond annual church budgets to glorify God in new ways" and began a long process of attempting to build awareness of the fund and promote bequests. In 1991, this included a Wills Survey of the congregation and a Living Wills program presented by

Karen Kleinschmidt and Alice Frechette of the St. Cloud Hospital. In 1998, the Trust Fund received legacy gifts from Adella Opitz and Erma Coughtry, which were later used for a sanctuary sound system and the memorial garden.

The Carpenter Fund was established after a mortgage loan of $150,000 was obtained May 7, 1998, to cover costs for major building repairs combined with the outstanding parking lot loan. In 1999, a Carpenter Fund Planning Team from Finance, comprised of Bob DeHaan, Paul Gauerke, Don Helgeson, Doris Kelly, Jean Madsen, Mary Beth Megarry, Leanne Olson, and Pastor Katie Schneider-Bryan, developed its design and the first campaign for Cornerstone Gifts and three-year Builders pledges for June 1, 1999, to May 31, 2002, using the theme "We are all Carpenters in God's House!"

While the primary purpose of the Carpenter Fund was to pay off the loan, the committee also chose to prepare for future building needs or major improvements by including an endowed Reserve Fund in its design. This Reserve Fund would be built up at the end of each fiscal year by placing in it 50% of the balance remaining from annual pledged receipts which had not been needed to cover the monthly loan payments. The other 50% would be applied to mortgage reduction.

A second Carpenter Fund campaign received three-year pledges from June 1, 2002, to May 31, 2005, and a third campaign, with the goal of paying off the loan during the 150th Anniversary Celebration in 2007, received two-year pledges and one-time gifts from 2005 to 2007. By January 1, 2006, the loan had been paid down to $22,893, and the Reserve Fund had built up to $11,589 in the endowment and $4,840 of earnings.

In October 2001, a new Planned Giving Team was organized to revitalize the Trust Fund and clarify its relation to other types of planned gifts to FUMC, such as the Carpenter Fund, memorials, and scholarship funds. This team, co-chaired by Don Helgeson and Marcia Summers, included Mert Hubbard representing Trustees, Richard Megarry representing Memorials, Jan Bensen, Dottie Seamans, and Pastor Katie Schneider-Bryan. Extensive consideration resulted in the development of a new Trust Agreement with a revised structure, including four component funds in the Trust:

> **Ministry Fund**–an endowment fund from which only the earnings can be used to support FUMC ministries

Carpenter Fund–providing funds for mortgage payments and future major building repairs and improvements

Special Gifts and Memorials–gifts which may be designated for a special FUMC program or identified need, and memorials either designated for a specific purpose or undesignated to be used at the discretion of the Memorials and Fine Arts Committee

Dedicated Funds–legacy gifts established with a minimum gift of $10,000 and a written agreement with the donor defining the fund's purpose and disbursement policy. The existing Grannis, Cater, and Stevenson Scholarship Funds were incorporated into the Trust as Dedicated Funds.

After an open information meeting on April 9, 2002, the Trust Agreement was approved by the Administrative Council and a special congregational meeting on April 18, 2002. Funds in the Trust are invested by the Trustees of First United Methodist Church.

The Trust Fund Committee developed a new brochure with the theme "Create a Legacy" and an acorn-to-oak tree logo designed by Karel Helgeson. This logo was also used in a series of bulletin and *Courier* articles publicizing the Trust Fund and suggesting various ways to give.

In 2003, Jan Bensen and Marcia Summers presented a Faith Forum on the Trust Fund. In 2005, a letter and trust fund brochure were mailed to members over 50 with a survey requesting information on their intentions for bequests in their wills or other legacy gifts to FUMC.

An initial Ministry Fund gift of $5,000 was received in 2002. Gifts from Aural Greenstreet and Jessie Harper established the Greenstreet Dedicated Fund, and on March 16, 2006, an agreement was approved by the Administrative Council that $500 would be available from this fund each year, beginning in 2006, for the purchase of music for worship and/or stipends for special musicians. A bequest from the estate of Joan Clampitt was also received in 2006.

While the process of building the FUMC Trust Fund has been a slow one, we continue to try to educate the congregation on how their will and estate plans can express their faith and deepest values. Legacy gifts will enable them to be good stewards using assets they have been blessed to accumulate to perpetuate the ministries and outreach efforts of First United Methodist Church beyond their lifetime. "Great harvests grow from seeds planted in faith."

WORSHIP COMMITTEE
Jan Brinkman

The Worship Committee works to develop the entire worship experience. We work with the pastors to develop a thematic presentation for the different seasons of the church liturgical calendar. We use our actual worship services (one traditional and one contemporary), scriptures, music, visuals and artwork in the sanctuary and throughout the church to depict these themes.

We have been blessed with wonderful musical talent at our church. The worship committee supports the music staff and musicians in any way necessary.

We are blessed with talented people who can create and develop the visuals representing these themes. We have used banners, an Advent/Lenten window, a Lenten Sunburst, a Celebration Tree, paraments, wreaths, greens, trees, stars, balloons, flowers, streamers, fabric, breads of different countries, cornucopias, and candles.

The worship committee also does many behind-the-scenes tasks. These include coordinating monthly head ushers, lay readers, acolytes, communion stewards, funeral hosts, wedding coordinators, custodians for weddings, baptismal stewards, and soundboard operators. We care for and change the paraments in the sanctuary. We provide ongoing chancel care, including monitoring and ordering supplies, plant and flower care, brass cleaning, audio and soundboard needs, and organ and piano care and maintenance. We also evaluate and provide feedback on recent worship services.

We have enjoyed having hard working, active, creative and devoted members on our Worship Committee, who share their talents with all the members of this congregation.

WOMAN'S SOCIETY OF CHRISTIAN SERVICE/ UNITED METHODIST WOMEN
Carol Jones

The past fifty years have brought us many memories of projects and events that the members of the Woman's Society of Christian Service (WSCS) and then United Methodist Women (UMW) have worked on. It seems that most of those projects involved serving food, with the purpose of raising money for missions - international, national and local. Many others were service projects and donations to First Church.

The history of WSCS/UMW is impressive. The women of the organization have fulfilled their statement of purpose in every way. It has taken many Marys and Marthas to keep the organization going the past fifty years. We have had wonderful leadership from our presidents and their boards, with help from the committees and circle members. We have called on other women of the church to help on some of our projects, and they have come forward.

Membership was at a high in 1960, with 222 members. This number began to decrease in 1964. One explanation of this decrease given at the time was that it was "due to the number of employed women." The present day membership is 75. In 1972 a young mothers' circle was added, with a baby sitter hired in the nursery. This brought in 22 new members.

The 1960s included the Loyalty Dinners, summer coffee hours, mother-daughter banquets (remember the wedding dresses?), and Cherry Pie Day, where a pie-cutting pattern was used to ensure that every piece was the same size. 500 cookies were baked for the state school in Cambridge, and food was served for weddings and funerals.

The 1970s brought us the Christmas Bazaar as a fund-raising replacement for Cherry Pie Day. Meals on Wheels started in St. Cloud in 1973, and many members signed up to drive meals to community members who needed this service because of age or medical conditions.

The 1980s found each circle doing special projects. Deborah Circle served a Birthday Dinner, with seating at twelve tables decorated for each month. Rebecca, Susannah, and Rachel Circles held a Sweet Shoppe at the Men's Pancake Supper. A rummage sale and Country Store craft sale were added, with a special children's room. The children could shop for presents for their family for a price of 50 cents to a dollar. UMW Sunday was also celebrated.

With the 1990s came Pennies for Children, the Parent-Teen Banquet and our first funeral coordinator, Fern Michalski. UMW also helped Minnie Peterson with her making of many, many mittens - mittens that were knitted and donated for the Country Store. Minnie lived in a nursing home at this time, and made mittens as her contribution to the UMW and to the Church. UMW women furnished her with the yarn to construct extremely warm and sturdy mittens.

The 2000s brought us a White Elephant Sale and a Bake Sale, that were held in conjunction with the men's Pancake Supper. We continue to schedule the popular Bake Sale and also provide a SERV catalog sale, where we offer beautiful handicraft made by men and women in developing countries.

WOMAN'S SOCIETY OF CHRISTIAN SERVICE PRESIDENTS

1957 Ruth Haverland
1958 Ruth Haverland
1959 Lois Fredrickson
1960 Priscilla Dean
1961 Ursula Emery
1962 Marge Cook
1963 Marge Cook
1964 Betty Partch
1965 Betty Partch
1966 Charlotte Henningsgaard
1967 Charlotte Henningsgaard
1968 Liz Patridge
1969 Liz Patridge
1970 Liz Patridge
1971 Deanie Olson
1972 Deanie Olson

UNITED METHODIST WOMEN PRESIDENTS

1973 Mary Wagner
1974 Polly Medin (Jan.-Aug.)
　　　Ardis Hines (Sept.-Dec.)
1975 Ardis Hines
1976 Dorothy Stueve
1977 Dorothy Stueve
1978 Bea Huser
1979 Pat Tonnell
1980 Pat Tonnell
1981 Ellen Deane Schwieger
1982 Dorothy Stueve
1983 Dorothy Stueve
1984 Dorothy Stueve
1985 Dolores Keech
1986 Mary Corliss
1987 Mary Corliss
1988 Mary Corliss
1989 Anna Mary Leeseberg
1990 Anna Mary Leeseberg
1991 Anna Mary Leeseberg
1992 Dorothy Stueve
1993 Dorothy Stueve
1994 Mary Corliss, Kelly Wischmann, Dorothy Stueve, Jo Ann Bridges (rotating)
1995 Jo Ann Bridges
1996 Jo Ann Bridges
1997 Ellen Deane Schwieger
1998 Kelly Wischmann
1999 Kelly Wischmann
2000 Kelly Wischmann
2001 Kelly Wischmann
2002 Jessie Harper
2003 Dolores Keech
2004 Dolores Keech
2005 Dolores Keech
2006 Dolores Keech
2007 Dolores Keech
2008 Kelly Wischmann

Growing our Legacy in Christ

150 years
1857-2007

Pastors and People Reflect

First United Methodist Church

St. Cloud, Minnesota

Our Former Pastors

Rev. Katie Schneider-Bryan

Lead Pastor: 1994 - 2007

My sermon for you, the people of First United Methodist Church, was in the middle of your 150th year. I was blessed with 13 years of ministry with you, and blessed to grow in my own faith because of yours. The last image I used in that sermon was the Hebrew scripture on Elijah and the starving widow and her son. In that story the widow dares to use up all her jar of meal to feed the hungry stranger (Elijah) and in so doing, the jar of meal never runs out. It seemed a fitting story because again and again, I witnessed how you defied apparent scarcity and believed in abundance to make a difference in each other's lives, in the St. Cloud region and in God's world.

One of the first adventures of risk during our years together came in 1996, when we began to explore how to create a new and different style of worship for our second worship experience. A core group, including our associate pastor, Shane Burton, helped create a new and different welcome to those who weren't sure the church was "for them." The Bridge Service was created, and it was as if we mixed a bit of grain like that widow, and watched the bread rise. The commitment of the musicians and leaders of that service has been enormous.

Abundance in hospitality was poured out in housing the homeless in our Church of the Week ministry and in Third Saturday Meals, both of which are ministries of charity. This complemented your passion for justice, which helped lead to the creation of GRIP, of which our church was one of the founding members. This faith-based community organization continues to be a force for justice in our region, as political leaders and activists have learned to pay attention when GRIP speaks. I cherish those times when hundreds of us gathered to speak out for the voiceless. I also appreciated the opportunity to work with other clergy across our region on issues that mattered to us all.

Your passion for mission continued the long legacy. I recall that in 2005 you raised, beyond our budget, over $100,000 for mission. We tackled world hunger in the Heifer Project in the "great fifty days after Easter" that year, and virtually every group in our church found ways to raise money to buy an ark of animals to lessen the stark realities of world hunger. There were four-year-olds who were amazed to see that one glass of lemonade at their little stand brought five dollars, other children made garden bees, and everyone chuckled as a young alpaca clip-clopped down the aisle in worship to remind us of the ways we would help families around the world experience hope and warmth and an end to hunger. That spring alone, with a matching gift, we raised $8,000 to buy an "ark and a half"! Another $8,000 was raised later that fall in response to the tragedy of hurricanes like Katrina in the South. A fine Care Team for lay visitation was developed, and there were prayer shawls and mitten trees and countless bags of groceries donated in love. You have a heart for mission and a passion for justice, which is part of your legacy and, I pray, a vital part of your future.

You continued to make your building your launching pad for ministry as you house the Montessori Preschool, upgraded heat and rooftops (ask Jim Wagner and others), and created a beautiful and unique outdoor labyrinth in the memorial garden, a constant reminder and invitation to be people of prayer on this winding journey of faith. You found delightful ways to step up in stewardship, from First Fests to Phantom Brunches, to a phone call from "God" in the middle of worship. I am thankful for the humor and joy I experienced as we endeavored to be Christ's Body, together.

I was blessed to work with fine staff throughout the years, excellent in leadership and gifts, in music, education and administration. We all made each other stronger, which is the essence of being Christ's body. Nine years of our ministry together included a unique chapter of leadership as a "clergy couple," when Pastor Dan, my husband, was appointed to serve here with me. Our children, Greg and Anna, were blessed to grow up in your midst. It was a privilege for Dan and me to bless the bread and wine together, and to serve you, God's people. Dan continued the strong tradition of youth mission trips begun by earlier leaders, and put a new twist on Wednesday nights with the youth, which we all came to know as "Wednesday Night Live." A grant developed by our newest staff member, AnnElise Edeburn, helped strengthen our wider ministry to our youth, and their families. Meanwhile a grand group of volunteers continued to guide our Children's Ministry, from the Sunday Kids' Kingdom, to Christmas programs and wonderful hands-on projects for mission. We worked hard to expand our small adult groups for faith formation, and among the groups I was blessed to lead was our Oasis group. Many other groups were made possible with fine lay leadership.

This congregation has had a long legacy for fine worship, including excellent music with Tess Kasling and others, and the use of art to develop the theme for each season and Sunday of the Church Year. New paraments and stunning wall hangings were designed and sewn by Jill Haak and Evelyn Lorenz during these years, and other new artwork all reflected the power of art to inspire. Scholarships continued to support and touch the lives of students, and new gifts given to our Carpenter Fund moved us forward in good stewardship of our building and parking lot and in offering new programmatic ministries with bequests and other legacy gifts. Our mantra was to be those who stepped up to tithing, in intentional, proportional, and joyful ways. Your passion to be hospitable included becoming a Welcoming Congregation through Igniting Ministries. You continue on an intentional journey toward welcoming each person, whatever their sexual orientation, while also learning about our Muslim brothers and sisters in the wake of 9-11.

As Lewis Carroll put it, "it's a poor sort of memory that only works backwards." You dared to "dream forward" when we began to ask hard questions about our location and focus for ministry, and a superb Visioning Team emerged. Thousands of hours of research, prayer, discussion, and more prayer are leading you to consider a new place to continue the legacy of 150 years as the people of First Church. You are brave to believe that the church is not the building, but the people. I dare to lift up the fine leadership of Jim Davis, Lay Leader, and Glenna Cheney, Administrative Council Chair. There are far too many others to name, and too few pages to do so. Each of you leaves your mark for God's sake.

I close with a vivid memory. It was a moment of baptism, when little Samuel was in my arms one Sunday morning. As I held him and poured the waters of grace upon him, he reached for me: both of his little hands went up to my face, caressing me, and in that moment, the world as God imagines it, was real. There was an audible sound in the pews, as we caught our breath together, for it was a moment of blessing, and grace and beauty, flowing from his tiny hands, not only to me, but to us all. The waters of baptism have flowed a hundred times, the bread and wine been shared, through the gathered body of Christ called First United Methodist Church of St. Cloud. I was blessed to serve among you, and look forward eagerly to watching how you will continue to "grow your legacy in Christ."

Your sister on the journey,
 Katie Schneider-Bryan

>Permission granted by *St. Cloud Times/Times Media* for use of this picture and article, 11 May 1997, page 5b.

FAMILY PORTRAIT: THE SCHNEIDER-BRYANS

Sundays are hectic for clergy couple

Kimball family can relate with parishioners trying to cope with busy schedules

Family portrait is a look at one of the families that makes Central Minnesota unique.

♦ ♦

The family: Katie and Dan Schneider-Bryan live near Kimball with their two children, Greg, 13, and Anna, 9, who both attend Kimball schools.

Their background: Katie, who grew up in Faribault, and Dan, a native of southern Illinois, met while studying for their master's degrees in divinity at Garrett-Evangelical Theological Seminary on the campus of Northwestern University in Evanston, Ill.

They married in 1981 and both served in several churches throughout the Twin Cities for 12 years. They moved to the St. Cloud area in 1993, when Dan was appointed to lead two small churches: Kimball United Methodist in Kimball and Zion United Methodist in South Haven. He serves as the pastor for both.

Katie made the move north when she was appointed lead pastor of First United Methodist Church in St. Cloud in 1994. She now makes the 22-mile commute each day from their home near Kimball.

A "clergy couple": In church jargon, the Schneider-Bryans are what is called a "clergy couple." Yet, they don't envision ever working together at the same church because of differing interests in parish settings. She is more interested in serving a larger city church like First

TIMES PHOTO BY JASON WACHTER

The Rev. Katie Schneider-Bryan with her husband, the Rev. Dan Schneider-Bryan, have two children Greg, 13, and Anna, 9. Katie is pastor at First United Methodist in St. Cloud, where this photo was taken. Dan is pastor of Methodist churches in Kimball and South Haven.

REV. TOBY HORST

Lead Pastor: 1979 - 1994

During my fifteen years as the minister of First United Methodist Church, there were various accomplishments. The church took on a somewhat different self-image from being "poor" to being financially able. The organ was expanded (Richard Clampitt memorial), stained glass was expanded (memorials), the Life of Christ drawings by Jim Hendershot were added, the Joe O'Connell walnut wood sculpture was commissioned and completed (it received national attention). The church maintained an open door policy as a convenience to the congregation and visitors (for prayer, quiet and meditation) and a "rest stop" for the homeless. In addition, the church was made available to a variety of community groups for meetings and activities.

The Graners became our sponsored church missionaries in Bolivia, and Janet and David Trettel spent some time working in Bolivia. Cliff and Betty Johnson went to Mexico under church sponsorship. In addition, the percentage of the church budget devoted to outreach and mission increased. Two parking lots were added. The church went from a parsonage to a housing allowance. Richard Clampitt accompanied Locky in buying the Vo-Tech house at an auction.

While money for scholarships was available, John Eckberg gave the program "legal legs." With Sam Wenstrom's leadership, an elevator was installed. A 125th Anniversary celebration was chaired by Everett Rasmussen and Helen Bensen, and Glenn Carlson worked with United Methodist professional stewardship leaders to secure a 125th Anniversary Fund. The Third Saturday Meal (for the community's hungry) was begun, and Tony Michalskiand John Barron were early coordinators of Meals on Wheels.

The church organization was expanded, resulting in greater involvement in decision making. Shirley Echols and Charlotte Henningsgaard handled the office with professional skill. Evelyn Durkee made "peer calls" part of her visitation ministry. Jim Garven listened well, worked effectively with the young people and established an annual mission trip. Church school enrollment increased, as did the church membership, after some years of falling numbers.

Considerable emphasis was put on the church year, resulting in Maggie and Mark Brossoit's and Patricia Krueger's banners, a congregational Advent calendar, the Advent workshop and the delightful Epiphany festival. Fellowship opportunities, such as Lenten Friends and potluck groups, were important, as was the PIE (People Involved in Evangelism) outreach to non-members. Ecumenical work included the groundwork for GRIP, and special services of worship. The highlight of our ecumenical activity was the neighborhood churches' Vacation Bible School.

I enjoyed serving Christ and His Church at First United Methodist Church and the many opportunities provided for work in the Lord's name.

1983: Pastor Horst

1988: Horst, Durkee

MEMORIES OF A MINISTER'S WIFE

Locky Horst

When the Horsts arrived in St. Cloud in November of 1979, it was an easy experience in some ways and a not-so-easy one in others. Because First Church still had a parsonage, there was no need to house hunt. Also there were only three members of the family at home -Toby, Locky, and Martha - and daughter Martha was agreeable to spending her high school junior year in a new school.

At the same time, without their former larger family (Sara, Scot, and Mark were on to their own lives), Locky realized that they would be missing some of those instant community connections that come with school activities, such as band concerts and sports.

In a bit, Locky decided to go to St. Cloud State to get a degree in special education, as jobs were scarce in her areas, biology and elementary education. An incident that stands out in her mind happened fairly early in their St. Cloud time when she and Toby were having church gatherings at their house. On this occasion she also had an evening class at the University. She hurried home to serve coffee and cookies, but in her haste, slipped on the ice. She went down, her head hit the ice, her glasses flew off, and she said that for the first time in her life, she literally saw stars, along with having a strange liquid feeling in her head. However, she picked herself up, went home, and served coffee - no trip to the emergency room. Now she shakes her head at such duty-bound behavior.

The next spring the church congregation voted to give the pastor a housing allowance instead of furnishing a parsonage. This would allow the family to build up some equity in a home and meant a new house was needed. The Horsts moved into their new house on July 4th, the first house the family had ever owned.

Locky did do some teaching in her new specialty: two years full-time in District #742, a long-term substitution in Holdingford, some work in Milaca. However, there were always things to do with the church as well.

Her first leadership role was chairing the Worship Committee. Her committee, aside from doing all the traditional jobs of the group, had a liturgical dance workshop, and included some dance in Sunday worship. On New Year's Eve, the committee sponsored a dinner and a service of communion at the church. Locky said in her report for that year, "It was a great evening of fellowship and a beautiful way to start the new year."

In 1986 she continued chairing the Worship Committee and in addition directed a children's choir. In 1989 Locky assumed the responsibilities of chair of the Memorials and Fine Arts Committee.

Then it was on to heading the Evangelism Committee in 1992, where, among different committee happenings, the PIE Committee (People Involved in Evangelism) was formed. The group met bimonthly for potluck, pie, and planning. Their purpose was to welcome new people to the church going out and calling on first-time visitors. Church membership went from 873 members in December 1991, to 888 members in December 1992, and 908 members in December 1993.

Locky said of all of her church work, that she was never made to feel that because she was the pastor's wife, she had to assume those responsibilities. She was able to freely give her time and talents.

Heritage Sunday, 1999, Rev. Shane Burton, Rev. Toby Horst, Locky Horst, Rev. Ken Beck, Catherine Beck, Rev. Katie Schneider-Bryan

REV. KEN BECK

Lead Pastor: 1963 - 1979
by Catherine Beck

Impressions of First Church, St. Cloud – 2007: A "welcoming church" before there was a campaign to make United Methodist churches in Minnesota "welcoming."

First Sunday, July 1, 1963: Ken and Richard Lewis"), campus minister. People in pews chuckling at Ken's jokes. Al Schelske, principal of College Lab School, inviting our children, Peter, Martha and Sarah, to enroll at the school. (We had hoped for this.)

Helen Bensen inviting us to stop at the Bensen home, an 1860's house, anytime. We stopped on our way back to St. Paul that afternoon. It was the first of hundreds, maybe thousands, of such visits either surprise or invited.

Thursday, July 5, 1963: We officially move into the lovely prairie-style parsonage at 308 Third Ave So. We all loved that house. In the evening, Fred Haverland invites us to have supper at his Kay's Restaurant and Hotel after a busy moving day.

Late summer, 1963: Lunemanns gave us collie shepherd puppy, Shiloh.

Early December, 1963: Church maintenance man, Mr. Scheel, invites us to cut our own Christmas tree on his farm in Graham, Minnesota. A beautiful day but 22 degrees below zero. Sarah says the snow was up to her waist (she was seven years old), so Ken carried her across a large field of cornstalk rows. Peter and Martha carried the tree back to the car. We never again bought a commercial tree. Later, we cut our trees on Jack and Helen Bensen's farm.

July, 1964: The first "Go and See" tour. Ken takes a group of young people (college and high school age) in three private cars on a trip to see the U.N. and the Methodist building across from the U.N. Later, the tour was enlarged to include parents, chaperones and interested adults in large buses, with a side trip to Washington, D.C. and the Methodist building across from the U.S. Capitol. The Methodist centers in both cities provided programs of lectures and tours of the U.N. and other buildings. In this same year, Catherine starts to teach Art 121 in St. Cloud State Art Department.

March 7, 1965: First Selma, Alabama, Civil Rights March. Call goes out for clergy to go to Selma for a second march, which, hopefully, would be peaceful rather than violent as the first one was. It was Ken's 43rd birthday.

March 8, 1965: Ken was President of the Minnesota Council of Churches. He went to Minneapolis for the regular meeting of the Council, which appointed him to go to Selma. He left from the meeting on a midnight plane.

March 9, 1965: Ken marched with Martin Luther King and many other clergy and nuns to the Edmund Pettis Bridge in Selma, a peaceful event, both symbolic and historic. The group disbanded and Ken came home. Later, a third march ended in Montgomery, Alabama, the original planned ending.

March 28, 1965: 500 people march in deep snow to Civil Rights Rally in St. Cloud. Rev. Beck and Rev. Nor Schoenheider lead the procession.

June and July, 1965: Catherine teaches for eight weeks at Rust College, a Methodist college for blacks in Holly Springs, Mississippi (established in 1866). The UMW sponsored me.

July, 1965: Ken and Dick Lewis start tradition of First Church young people and adults conducting a vacation Bible school and youth group at Pine Bend Methodist Mission on the White Earth Indian Reservation near Lengby, Minnesota. Later, Bethlehem Lutheran young people joined with the Methodists.

Permission to publish picture and article, *St. Cloud Times/Times Media*, 29 Mar 1965 page 1, one of two photos

243

1965-1979: Family camp at Decision Hills Camp near Spicer, Minnesota. Fun and study for all ages and home-made ice cream on the final evening – even Shiloh attended.

Late 1965: Catholic Forum meets at First Church in first Roman Catholic-Protestant church service. Principal of St. Cloud Cathedral High School brought his school choir and school orchestra, and he delivered the sermon. This was the first such meeting in St. Cloud, which came as result of Pope John XXIII and Vatican II Council meetings. Father Godfrey Diekmann of St. John's Abbey was a Council member. After the service everyone went to the social hall for coffee and later to meet in small mixed Catholic-Protestant groups to talk as friends. Later a study book came out and Living Dialogue groups were formed.

Summer, 1966: Beck family spends summer in Europe. Parsonage is redecorated. When we come home, we hang our three large framed Bill Ellingson works, which combined civil rights and Vietnam War themes in multiple wood block prints. We had all new-member meetings at our house (three for each new group). Ken said that if they could spend three evenings under these works, they could join First Church. No one ever refused.

Ken is most remembered for his late night visits - if you left a light on, you might receive a visit. One woman called him "Night Rider Beck." But he was always welcomed - no door was ever slammed in his face - part of the St. Cloud "welcoming church."

All three children were confirmed at First Church, and all three children graduated from Tech High School. Martha was married at First Church, Peter at Bethlehem Lutheran. Martha's two older children were baptized at First Church.

1967: Institute for Ecumenical and Cultural Research established at St. John's Abbey, Collegeville, Minnesota. Ken and I were invited to attend evenings to discuss papers produced by scholars from all over the world, many of whom had been friends of ours before we all came to the St. Cloud area. It was a wonderful experience to hear very intellectual discussion of subjects we had not approached for years. Many of the scholars attended First Church while they lived at the Institute, and our children became friends with them and their children, some of whom attended school with our children while they were at the Institute.

Spring 1969: Sarah spends January to July at girls' high school in England while two English girls spend January to April with us.

March 7, 1972: Carlton and Jean Eckberg hosted a surprise 50th birthday party for Ken on a very snowy evening. Dee and Laurie Halberg, Merle Sykora, Hillis and Marie Myers, Ruth and Fred Haverland attended.

1972: Supreme Court decision on Roe vs. Wade. The Sunday after the decision was announced, Ken gave a sermon on the subject and how he felt about it. At the end, there was absolute silence and then a standing ovation - the only one of his life. Everyone knew the decision would result in the end of most of the Living Room Dialogue groups (one still does meet in St. Cloud) and a lot of the friendship between Catholics and Protestants in our area. Hopefully we can one day return to the joy of the day the Catholic Forum met at First Church, St. Cloud.

1972 – 1979: Vietnam War - Ken changes from belief in containment policy to definite anti-war policy. Helps with anti-Vietnam War marches and rallies. President of Tri-County Community Action Program, an anti-poverty program for Stearns, Benton and Sherburne Counties. Helps establish a handicapped workshop (under the Poverty program), which provided work for the participants, help for business and some housing for workers. Finally, he helped establish a Y.M.C.A. before he left St. Cloud.

Summer 1972: Ken and Catherine spend summer in Greece, Israel and Turkey.

1973: Gertrude Gove, retired St. Cloud high school history teacher, and Catherine publish a book, *The History of St. Cloud as Seen in Its Houses*, sponsored by the local chapter of Delta Kappa Gamma, a national education organization.

September to December 1973: Danish college student stays with us and attends St. Cloud State College.

1975: Ken elected a member of the St. Cloud School Board.

1975: Mechtild [Tilde] Ellis of Cold Spring makes first set of stoles for new ordinands for Minnesota Conference of the United Methodist Church. In addition, Mechtild (fabrics - St. John's), Merle Sykora (fabrics - First Church), Laurie Halberg (ceramics - First Church), Richard Haeg (glass - St. John's), and Joseph O'Connell (sculpture and prints - St. John's) all contribute to beauty of First Church building.

January - June 2004: Martha became a scholar at the Institute for Ecumenical and Cultural Research, working on a book about Plato. That January, Ken and I and Sarah drove up to Collegeville (31° below zero that night) to hear her presentation. (Christmas 2006, she presented me with her three-volume set of books on her project.)

March 2006: Ken dies, and his funeral is held at Hamline United Methodist Church, across from Hamline University.

Extra thoughts: Ken asked me one day if he dared play "Morning Has Broken" on a tape as part of his Sunday sermon. Since St. Cloud had always been open and welcoming to new ideas and new people, why not? He played it, gave his sermon, there were compliments. Now "Morning Has Broken" is in the Methodist hymnal. Other people must have liked it, too.

At the time Ken decided to change his attitude about the Vietnam War from containment to outright opposition, he asked Carlton Eckberg, Chairman of the Pastor-Parish Relations Committee, if he should resign as pastor of First Church because many people might be unhappy about his attitude. Carlton replied, "We, as a congregation, pay you to help us think about key issues in our world and our lives as you see them. We can agree or disagree but you must continue to help us, not quit when we need you."

I will always remember Ken and Shiloh every night at midnight heading out to run over to church (rain, shine or blizzard) to lock up the building. Only at midnight would the welcoming church lock its doors.

Associate Pastors

Rev. Dan Schneider-Bryan

Associate Pastor: February 1999 - June 2007

I knew a little bit of what I was getting into when I was invited to become a part of the staff at First. Katie, your lead pastor and my wife, had been serving First Church and commuting from our home in Kimball, Minnesota, where I was serving the Kimball and South Haven United Methodist churches. It took some coaxing to get me to think about moving as I was very much enjoying my ministry there. But the prospects of being a part of First UMC, of living in St. Cloud, and of being able to purchase our own home convinced me.

Being a part of a larger church was a new experience for me, and Pastor Katie was very much a part of how well this experience took shape. From the beginning we recognized our very different styles of ministry, and Katie, through her graciousness, made room for my gifts.

Being a part of First UMC called out the best from me. Preaching in the beautiful sanctuary with the variety of people in our congregation was a marvelously enriching experience. I very much appreciated the care taken in our worship. I had never served in a congregation in which music and the arts are so richly interwoven into the fabric of the church service. For someone whose only experience with music is singing louder than the person next to him, I was inspired by [Kasling], the choir, Bruce [Wood], David [Scholz], Steven [Steve Mick], the leaders of the Bridge Band and many others. They created a sacred space that inspired me as I prepared and preached. Sorry I don't have enough room to tell you a story here.

Although I was not the usual age for a youth minister, youth ministry was a significant piece of my activity at First. So many contributed: parents, the many Wednesday Night Live Guides, the adults who went on mission trips, and of course all the youth. During my time we changed the look of confirmation and began to call it Wednesday Night Live. We asked youth from 7th - 9th grades to come for an hour and a half. With anywhere from 30-45 present on any given night, we had some great times at what was more like a variety show than a class. Here are just a few words to describe WNL: Dumb - Dumbs, Mountain Dew, Fear Factor, "God is a Loving Parent who wants to be close to you," "John, what did you put in that drink?" "Hats off, two feet on the floor," "I want you to take a look at this video," the Ru-Ah chant, the Crosses at Decision Hills.

Youth mission trips changed a little. After two trips to Mountain TOP in Tennessee, we began to use the resources of Group Work Camps to travel to different areas of the country, including North Dakota, Wyoming, Georgia, West Virginia, and Michigan. Mission trip experiences are what many youth talk to me about later in their lives. One of the things First Church can be very proud of is its support of these trips. Each year it cost $10,000 to fund a group of youth and adults. In our time together, we not only met, but exceeded, these fund-raising goals.

There are so many other things to comment on that I hesitate to mention just one more. But I will. I felt privileged to have the opportunity to teach a variety of different classes. The Disciple classes and the Companions in Christ were growing experiences for me as a teacher. My thanks to all those who put up with my poor spelling on the handouts.

It is so very difficult to summarize eight years of your life in a few hundred words. I enjoyed being around your children and watching them grow, talking with folks both before and after worship, kidding around about the Gopher/Husky hockey rivalry (it's just as difficult remaining a Gopher fan just one block from UMD). I was so fortunate, so privileged, to serve with you in the times we shared. I look forward to hearing more of the stories of your great future.

REV. EVELYN DURKEE
Associate Pastor: 1975-1979, 1985-1995

Evelyn Durkee graduated from Union Theological Seminary in New York City in 1966. She married a fellow seminarian, Phillip Durkee, and they went to Germany for a year after graduating. It was "an adventure" Evelyn says and also an opportunity to learn German. They did odd jobs to earn their way.

Then Evelyn served as a Wesley Foundation campus minister in Iowa City from 1967-73 while Phillip went to graduate school. During this time their daughter, Rachel, was born and they adopted their son, Chris. Evelyn became a deacon in the Iowa Methodist Conference in 1973 and an Elder in 1975. She then served a combined ministry to Wyoming and Oxford Junction Methodist churches in Iowa.

After the family moved to the St. Cloud area in 1975, she was hired to work part-time with Rev. Beck and to handle much of the work that an associate minister would do - education, confirmation, calls on new members and the elderly, occasional preaching, serving as liturgist, conducting funerals and weddings. She was the first woman to serve as a clergy person in Stearns County, and she was one of the people who helped the church's sponsored Cambodian family adjust to their new country. Evelyn continued working for the Church until the spring of 1979, when the church decided they wished to have a full-time assigned associate minister rather than a part-time minister and several lay workers.

Later, when Rev. Horst was lead pastor, and the church's associate pastor had moved to another congregation, she returned to work for the church for a second time, from fall 1985 to fall 1994. Along with Jim Garven and Deb Robinson, she worked with the youth of the church. She also had numerous other committees to assist, such as Education, Adult Council, and Family Life Council.

Another role that gave her satisfaction was her work with the elderly: visiting, giving occasional rides, taken communion to them and, if they wished, a tape of the past church service. She pioneered peer visits to the elderly, taking an older person with her on a visit to another older person.

In 1994, after Evelyn left her employment with First Church for the second time (again the church decided they wished a full-time associate minister), she served the United Church of Christ in Aitkin. Later she and Phillip moved to Minneapolis, where he died in 2007.

Besides being a minister and a family and community member, Evelyn is an enthusiastic traveler, a friend to those from other countries, an English as a Second Language teacher (retired), and an advocate for social justice and human rights.

Interviewed, Nancy Gundersen

Evelyn & Phil Durkee can't pass up coming to the Pancake Supper

REV. LARRY HAGER

Associate Pastor: 1979 - 1981

When I think of First Church of St. Cloud, I think of these things:

1. Committed, capable lay leadership who took pride in their church and were fully prepared to support it not only with their time and gifts, but their imagination and creativity as well. I can only wish that other churches I've served could have matched those qualities. They have not.

2. I recall with fondness some of the characters. First, of course, is Ken Beck, whose originality and curiosity fostered the same qualities for First Church's members. I also think of the parish visitor, Ruth Skewes, who was genuinely concerned, gently reminded me of pastoral care needs, and loved her church. I fondly recall the enthusiasm that Jim Garven always conveyed in whatever he did: an enthusiasm I did not always match, but then few ever did. And then there was the irrepressible Mike Barone, whose expectations of music set a high bar for everyone, whose nature was challengingly interesting, and whose mission was to educate people to new tastes in music.

3. The youth I served were particularly creative. One student was studying the harp, others could plan elaborate games of Capture the Flag involving bicycles, and I recall a particular Halloween party the youth planned for the Sunday school that was reviewed by the teachers as being too effectively scary for the children. Given the youth's creativity, I was not surprised.

Recall, if you will, the trip to New York City in 1981 when the youth made their own travel and room arrangements, and I helped arrange a schedule that combined pleasure (we went to Mama Leone's and a Broadway show) with visits to ministry centers such as Covenant House (a shelter for youth in the Times Square area). We also visited Fort Apache, a police station in the South Bronx. I believe the highlight for many was revealed when some of the youth displayed pictures of themselves behind the steering wheel of Rolls-Royces and Bentleys and Masseratis: the show room for said cars was near where we stayed.

4. Also, there was always an appreciation for the arts and beauty. This was partially related to the tastes engendered by Mike [Barone], but just as much influenced by Catherine Beck and members who appreciated beauty. I think of the Helgesons and the Halbergs, and many others. For example, I

remember a dramatic presentation of banners hanging from the ceiling in the sanctuary as one approached the chancel.

I hope as First Church of St. Cloud approaches its future, it will testify with the same creative, fearless spirit I discovered when I was there. If we trust in God, we can trust in ourselves. Peace be to you.

Larry Hager service on the patio. 1980

Larry Hager 1979-1981

REV. MARV REPINSKI

Wesley Foundation, Associate Pastor: 1973 -1974

Greetings! Thank you for the sweet invitation to participate in the memory book: the "trail of joyful tears and smiles"! Here is my collection of events, personages and examples from the PAST.

First: The "past" is, in its gentle reminders, always with us. So the 150th celebration will be in the NOW!

Second: My life was shaped in the years in ministry in the St. Cloud area, hopefully for the better!! Shaped and styled by people, programs, the passion of caring and the potential that was always affirmed in the church, the college and the community.

Third: the Beck family, Ken and Catherine were to me like they were to hundreds. They were a deep well of inspiration and an example of living out a spirit of justice, biblical Christianity and an appreciation (so learned) of the arts. Pastor Beck was a splendid example of clergy appreciation: to our colleagues across the area - including magnificent contacts with students and faculty and administrators at St. John's and St. Ben's; Catherine's many presentations (how many slide shows?) throughout the Minnesota Annual Conference were a growing experience to MANY!

Fourth: Although my appointment, while in St. Cloud, was to the campus ministry of the college, a "sub relationship" was to First UMC. Assisting in youth confirmation and study groups; times in the pulpit and at the lectern and how many social times?...on and on….

Five: Tri- CAP comes to mind. One of the leaders, Fred Haverland, involved so many of us. That was one part of the social conscience that has always been a part of Methodism in St. Cloud.

…Many thanks for your work, you folks creating the memory/history book.

REV. RICHARD COLLMAN

Minister of Music, Associate Pastor: 1969 - 1971
First UMC, St. Cloud, was my first appointment out of Yale Divinity School, and I had both a challenging and enjoyable time from 1969-71. It was challenging because I remember Ken Beck changing the worship and education hours around, teacher training, a youth group from the late 60's that defied authority pretty well, a coffee house downstairs in the church and a heavy romance that first year with the woman I had met only the previous April at Yale! Katherine Kennedy moved to St. Cloud just after I did and was assistant personnel director at St. Cloud Hospital. And a new pipe organ was going in along with some staff changes too.

In spite of challenges, and sometimes because of them, those two years were also very enjoyable. Wonderful persons, intellectual stimulation, Marv in in campus ministry, "Talk Back" to sermons in the kitchen, our marriage on June 20, 1970. We still have the beeswax candle the Benedictine Sisters from St. Joseph made us! Tilde Ellis and her fabrics, an art show of Sister Naomi Wygant that stimulated Steve Helgeson's photography, the hospitality of the Helgeson family for youth events, the commitment to justice and social issues by Ken and others in the congregation, the Munsinger gardens. Rich and heady times. Thank you all for helping to get the feet of that young associate minister wet and ready for ministry in other places!

REV. DONALD DAY

Waite Park Pastor, First Church Associate Pastor: 1964 - 1966
I had the joy of serving First United Methodist Church as its Minister of Children's Education from 1964 to 1966; however, two decades earlier I was served by its congregation.

In the fall of 1949, I enrolled as a freshman at St. Cloud Teachers College. Having been active in my local church, I readily started participating in the young adult Sunday morning class at First church in, what seemed to me, an imposing two-story building. Along with some other men from the Selke Dormitory, we were picked up by Professor George Skewes and his wife, Ruth, to make certain we were part of the church. They were also advisors for the Wesley Foundation, so I became well acquainted with them. We grew to appreciate each other so much that the following summer when they went to Europe, their dog spent the summer with my family.

Rev. Russell Huffman was pastor at that time. His son, Russell, Jr., Duane Lunemann, Manning Van Nostrand and I were all freshmen together and were later all ordained members of the Minnesota Annual Conference.

I was drafted into the Army and when discharged went to Hamline University. Through strange circumstances I became the president of the Minnesota Methodist Youth Fellowship. In the spring of 1953 I found myself meeting with Reverend Huffman, asking him if there were any students at St. Cloud Teachers College who would be willing to serve on a conference youth team that would spend a year strengthening youth fellowships across the state. In his own persuasive way, he pointed out that I was as well situated as anyone to do that. Soon after I dropped out of college and entered the most defining year of my life. My becoming an ordained minister began with that conversation.

After serving the Waite Park Methodist Church for three years, I was asked also to serve at First Church as Minister of Children's Education on a part time-basis. My wife, Virginia, and I were gratified by the opportunity. I richly appreciated the wealth of dedication and ability that existed within the congregation. The responsibility to secure and work with the teachers and leaders of Sunday school was always stimulating. The support and guidance of Pastor Kenneth Beck was a blessing to a new minister. And an experience I value particularly was being one of the leaders of the well-structured confirmation program. The youth from Waite Park were included in this. What lively and bright youth filled the classrooms.

One closing story about First Church that, along with my childhood church, molded my life. One day my kindergarten daughter, Annette, was with me at the church along with her younger sister, Elizabeth. She was explaining to Elizabeth the office-set up, showing her their daddy's office, the secretary's office and then Pastor Beck's office. She informed Elizabeth, "He's the chief minister - he has carpet on his floor." The circle is complete - Annette is now a member of First United Methodist Church.

Lewis   Day   Beck

PASTORS FROM THIS CONGREGATION

Rev. Marva Jean Hutchens

The people of First United Methodist Church of St. Cloud, Minnesota, have been very influential in my faith journey. Anniversaries provide a wonderful occasion for celebrating the memories that have shaped so many faith journeys and for renewing commitment for faithful discipleship in the future. Thank you for the invitation to bring to mind some very special people.

One of my earliest memories is of gathering for the opening of Sunday school in the basement of the old church. Mr. Bluhm, who was the Sunday school superintendent, was always there to welcome all the children. He was so kind and seemed so tall, and usually had candy in his pocket. One of my favorite songs was "Step, step, step, step going to my church…" which we would sing and step with great vigor. Mr. Bluhm would just smile and nod his head as we sang and marched. I still have the Bible that he signed when we were given Bibles in third grade, and show it to the children we present with Bibles in my church.

Mrs. Way (Edith) was one of my Sunday school teachers. It was fun in later years to see her volunteering at registration for Annual Conference sessions.

Don Dean taught our fifth grade class, which was in the new church. It was during that year that his wife was killed in a car accident. It amazed me that he finished the year teaching our class. Although I don't remember the curriculum he taught, I do remember how he modeled the strength that comes in time of grief from being surrounded by a faith community.

Dick and Mary Beth Megarry were the MYF leaders. As youth, we didn't realize how blessed we were to have such caring people investing in our lives. There were some very fine spaghetti dinners with authentic candle wax drizzled on ketchup bottles for centerpieces and wandering troubadours to entertain the guests.

Leona Nash, the adult choir director, invited some high school girls to join a summer women's ensemble. She modeled the gift of inclusion.

Growing up in the church, we were blessed with influential pastoral leadership. I was confirmed by Rev. Paul O. Metzger. Rev. Kenneth Beck came while I was in high school. He modeled living out the faith within the church and within the community, and was a strong leader in the ecumenical movement and in civil rights. He was the one who first asked me if I had ever considered going into the ministry.

My "home church" has provided many gifts for my ministry. It was a sort of comfort that my first appointment was serving with another child of the St. Cloud Church, Rev. Duane Lunemann. Even though when Duane was going off to seminary, I was going off to kindergarten, we did know common friends from St. Cloud, which provided some common roots as we worked together.

I pray that as I serve churches, I will convey a genuine caring for the children that Mr. Bluhm gave us. I pray that youth in my watch will know the support of adults that Dick and Mary Beth shared with us. And in my current appointment, I pray that I may be to the people of Grand Rapids what Ken Beck was to the people of St. Cloud.

Thanks be to God for the people of First United Methodist Church!

REV. DUANE LUNEMANN

My Home Church
First UMC, St. Cloud, Minnesota
With a tinge of Hubris & Appropriate
Glorification of Old and Dear Memories

Duane J. Lunemann

Though I ultimately became a Methodist minister, I was baptized a Lutheran in the small town of Braham, Minnesota, where my father and mother were teachers in the schools of Braham-Grasson. When I was born, my father, J. Miller Lunemann, was the superintendent of schools there. In the depth of the Depression, two new teachers were needed and Dad said to the school board (his close friends for life), "You could use my salary for hiring those teachers." Sometime after, dad quit that job and decided to raise chickens on the home farm in St. Cloud. Dad soon discovered, however, that he could not support a family on egg money.

Dad knew the St. Cloud Superintendent, H. B. Gough. Mr. Gough indicated my father could possibly be hired when a job teaching math opened up. Mr. Gough was a member of First Methodist and took a keen interest in my entering the ministry. He sent a remarkable letter of recommendation to Garrett Seminary.

I remember Rev. Dr. Harlan C. Logan, his shiny black shoes - and one of his minister friends, who visiting, sat in the front pew one Sunday and said loudly "AMEN!" twice. I remember Dr. Logan's friendly smile, and the really nice way he talked with me on the phone when I called to ask the page number of a church membership class lesson.

I remember Mrs. Hammond, who stood at the inside door near the steps going up to the balcony every Sunday. She'd say, "Hello Duane" with a really real smile. And those steps up to the balcony were one-way, the narrowest I've ever seen, with a turn near the top. I remember how the balcony creaked. Especially when the new minister, Rev. Huffman, filled the church so folks had to go to the balcony. I remember Mr. Talbot, who reigned in the Sunday school office for lots of years. And Mr. Bluhm, who was our Sunday school leader. I can still see his hands: huge, masculine, weathered hands.

Ah, and her comes Mrs. Binney. One of her Sunday school lessons is still hooked in my mind..."full measure" means you can usually get another strawberry in the box if you just shake it ever-so-gently.

You will see in church files my Grandma Gus (Augusta) in a choir photo, with her flapper dress showing below her choir robe. I admired my Grandma Augusta. She was a daughter of the old timers, but she flew to the defense of our new liberal minister, Russell A. Huffman. He stayed here as long as he wanted, building the new church, until he was needed in Rochester, where he built the magnificent Christ Church.

I remember Roland Anderson, teacher of math at St. Cloud State College and a counselor, with his spouse, at a Sunday night student group, which met at their house on 5th Ave. Andy flew B-24's. He received wide-spread recognition, one day predicting to the second the moment wheels would touch down after an over-the-Atlantic flight.

Bill Megarry, along with many other church members, attended a Sunday night once-a-month affair called "the potluck." I recall Mr. Megarry sitting in a corner easy chair and explaining how he had participated in building the highway to Alaska. He talked about the mud, so thick you could hardly walk, and the cold, the challenges, the isolation and the need to stick together.

Now, Mary Megarry was a lady whose face beamed when she looked at people. She ran a Dairy Queen, as did my father-in-law, Rudy Strand. Once my mother, Myrtle Lunemann, rode to Minneapolis with Mary in her big Buick down highway 10, a highway the Megarrys had constructed. Mary said to my mother, "My! This road is rough!"

I was proposed for a Local Preachers License by the pastoral relations committee of this church, H.B. Gough, presiding. Rev. Russell Huffman spoke in support. I was approved by vote of the committee and handed on to the Central District Committee. Wonder of wonders, two more ministry candidates quickly came forward, Russ Huffman, Jr., and Manning Van Nostrand, whose father was a professor in psychology at the College. Russ and I went to Garrett, actually roomed together for a year, after which, as I recall, Russ transferred to Iliff Seminary in Denver. Manning went to Boston Theological Seminary, graduating with a Ph.D.

As I left St. Cloud to go to Evanston, Illinois, one of the last people I talked to was Charley Quinn. Charley had, as they say, "the map of Ireland on his face" - and the distinct sound of the Irish in his voice. He had helped me learn how to serve communion. At that last conversation, he handed me four books, all published a very long time ago in Ireland. I still have them - signed Charles Quinn - with some notes indicating these books came from his hometown and home church in Eniskillen, Ireland, a place where John Wesley did extensive labor.

Now a memory of my great friend, Sanford Wenstrom. I once suggested that a fitting nickname for him might be "Sam," and the name stuck. I performed the marriage service that joined Sam and the wonderful Maxine. Ask Sam to tell you the story of that marriage service.

> Bless us, O Lord,
> and this your church,
> which we receive
> from your bounty
> through
> Jesus Christ,
> Amen.
> Amen.

Rev. Duane Lunemann, pulpit, third building before 1956.

REV. MANNING VAN NOSTRAND

by Bernice Van Nostrand

Manning Van Nostrand III received his seminary degree at Boston University. He came back to Minnesota and served the Bethel and Cedar churches on the weekends. During the week, he worked on a Master's Degree in educational psychology at the University of Minnesota and did counseling in the General College.

Manning E. Van Nostrand

At Conference time, he was assigned to the Mahtomedi UMC. His next appointment was as Associate Pastor at Wesley Church in Minneapolis.

Manning wanted to work on a Ph.D. in Social Ethics at Boston University so transferred to the New Hampshire Conference and served the Salisbury, Massachusetts, church.

Next, Manning and I went to the Hampton, New Hampshire, church as he continued his Ph.D. studies. During this time, the early 60's, Hampton Beach experienced a number of riots. The Hampton Beach Project was formed and given Federal funding to stop the riots. People from the church, town, United Nations experts, State Police and college students worked together to make Hampton Beach a peaceful place again. Manning co-chaired this committee as well as served the Hampton Church.

We returned to Minnesota to serve the Owatonna UMC. Manning earned the doctorate degree and taught several classes in business ethics at Mankato State while serving the Owatonna Church. Next we served the Golden Valley Church.

We then went to Albert Lea. While in Albert Lea, Manning was one of 50 U.S. Methodist preachers who were invited by the Australian Methodist Church to come and be a Preaching Missioner. This was before the Australian Methodist Church and Presbyterian churches became the Uniting Church of Australia. Each Preaching Missioner went to three churches during the month he/she was in Australia.

Several years later, we went back to Australia to serve the Wavell Heights Uniting Church in Brisbane, Australia, for one year and then worked for the Queensland Synod, giving workshops on church growth all across that very large state.

We came back to Minnesota to serve Central Park UMC in St. Paul. Then we served the Stillwater UMC and later the yoked parish of Little Prairie, Castle Rock and the Moravian Church in Northfield.

Permission granted *by St. Cloud Times/Times Media* for this picture and article, 8 Jun 1955 p 4.

REV. DR. RUSSELL A. HUFFMAN, JR

Remembering the Beginnings of My Methodist Ministry
- And the First Endings….

Huffman Russ Sr and Jr.

As a former member, whose life now spans half of the 150 Anniversary Years, I congratulate all of us, especially the current members of First United Methodist Church, for not only maintaining but advancing a Methodist Ministry in St. Cloud since before The Civil War. I pray that you are still committed to preserving those qualities of Methodism centered on a disciplined quest for the Truth that may lead to an ever-widening circle of inclusion for the whole earth's boundless kinship.

If your heart is as my heart, give me your hand!

I also appreciate the opportunity to contribute to this written history, revisiting 75 years of mature memories and childhood images. Now I can see clearly how my careers in the ministry and medicine evolved within the nurturing influence of "family" – in the home, church, school, and community. And, long before my father began his St. Cloud pastorate, I knew of my good fortune to be a member of this parsonage family. Although my parents never pressured me toward a specific career, my decision in St. Cloud to begin my life's work as a Methodist pastor is inextricably linked to my parents and their high calling to the Christian ministry.

The Reverend Dr. Russell A. Huffman, Sr was for me and so many others the answer to the age-old supplication: We would see Jesus! He had the gift of an extraordinary intellect, able to synthesize complex philosophical or theological thought from which he created a down-to-earth reality that even a child could understand. Yet from his "Call to The Lord's Work" at age 16, through more than 60 years as an ordained Methodist minister, my father walked in humility and lived the constancy of a faithful seeker after Truth.

One thing he said that I have always remembered: "Things are not true simply because Jesus said them – Jesus said them because they are true!"

Like my father, my mother, Winifred Terry Huffman, grew to adulthood in rural America within solid Midwestern family values. Her strong-willed, socially responsible, religious mother and her remarkably wise and well-read father created a fertile environment in which to learn and grow. This extended family guided and sustained me when I lived with my maternal grandparents on their family farm during my father's seminary years and almost every summer from early childhood through college. My mother trained in business long before it was seemly for a woman, and that competence would later allow her to transcribe and edit my father's spoken word into printed manuscripts. She, of course, brought so much more to their grand alliance than tangible business skills. She had a refined and gracious manner, an unconditional respect for everyone, and a lifetime of continuous learning. She was for many of that era the "perfect" minister's wife.

Our family moved to St. Cloud, directly after World War II and our time as the minister's family of First Methodist Church would prove to be my parents' finest and most productive pastorate - and my decisive years. I began St. Cloud Technical High School as a terrified sophomore "newbie" and the "Preacher's Kid." However, my newness faded quickly in a wave of welcoming families in church and school, and lasting friendships that are still vigorous after more than 60 years.

Like many of my Tech High classmates, I continued my education at St. Cloud State Teachers College ("TC"), now St. Cloud State University, enrolling in the fall of 1949 as a pre-med student. At a time when the average minister's salary was significantly under $10,000 per annum, underwriting the cost of a private college was prohibitive for my family. So, attending a good school that was affordable - the annual tuition at TC was, as I recall, less than $100 a year - was essential. Of course, going to TC did allow me to live at home with my parents' continued support and - not insignificantly - my mother's willingness to apply her business training to the next generation and transcribe my dictation for college assignments. Although I worked part-time at the St. Cloud radio station, KFAM, as a staff announcer and disc jockey, I also participated fully in college life including intercollegiate athletics, acting roles in several college theater productions, and a wide array of social activities. By the time I finished college, I had made my decision to enter

Garrett Theological Seminary on the campus of Northwestern University - my father's alma mater.

At Garrett I smashed mind first into the New Orthodoxy that was completely discontinuitous to my philosophy of religion based in a responsible social gospel, a way of thinking called "the scientific method," and a Christ-led reality of the human condition. I was about to give up on this "neo-orthodoxy" when I met a second-year student who was disgruntled after spending his first seminary year at Iliff School of Theology at the University of Denver. He called Iliff "an atheistic school"! Immediately I realized that what I had found in my year at Garrett was certainly not the faith of my father's - maybe I could find it at Iliff? And I did find a theology integrated with the whole of life - a theology congruent with what I had learned in my parental home. I felt that I was where I should be, in the accepting and familiar milieu of rational thought at Iliff.

Over the years, I have rarely been asked, "Why did you become a medical doctor and specialize in psychiatry?" The questions were more often: "Why did you leave the ministry?" That answer, like much of life, is complicated – and I am not sure even after full graduate training in psychiatry and almost half a century of living that I understand the various forces vectoring my change to medicine. However, I am able to identify some of the issues and events that pushed me toward leaving, including a progressive realization that my ministry was not to be the same as I remembered my father's pastorate in the ideal of my growing-up years in our St. Cloud Methodist parsonage where I was never the minister, but the very privileged and skillfully protected "minister's son."

As I entered my first pastorate in 1956, no issue had more affect on me and my ministerial career than the civil rights movement, that challenged both our American democracy and our Christian faith. In the next few years, we faithful United States citizens were to witness historic events igniting in Little Rock, Montgomery, Selma, and Birmingham and their effects in small-town Minnesota. I heard the leaders for social justice, including the Reverend Dr. Martin Luther King, Jr., just released from a Birmingham Jail, plea to all Americans - especially those of us calling ourselves "Christian" - to take action and be set free from the enslavement of intolerance and racism. I took action as I thundered from the pulpit on "The Myth and Fallacy of Race!" and wrote epistles calling for "a strong stand" against this Evil by The Methodist Church and the other Christian denominations.

I might have learned to overcome the American Church's not responding (in my view) appropriately to the global issues of our time, had not the lifestyle of a local pastor continually chafed at my sense of self. Even living in a parsonage all of my early life, I had never confronted the expectations of literally "hundreds of bosses" - each with their own individual vision of who I should be as pastor. In the first few years, my sense of self withered to a pale reflection of a man trying desperately to please everyone.

However, I did feel an increased confidence through working with individuals in pastoral counseling, and began to develop a strategy for continuing my service by combining the ministry and medicine to serve the psychological and emotional needs of Methodist clergy as an American board-certified psychiatrist. When I discussed this ministry with my parents – as always throughout my life - I had their full support, and they helped me refine my thoughts and develop an operational plan that included talking to my district superintendent (D.S.).

When I approached my D.S. with my proposal to seek appointment in a student charge near the University of Minnesota, where I could serve part-time and give a congregation the benefits of a fully ordained minister while beginning to explore combining careers, I felt my superintendent hardly listened to my vision before he called in his counterpart from the contiguous district. Both men had known me most of my life and were long-time colleagues of my father. Their combined response came as a complete surprise: "We do not give out student pastorates to someone leaving the ministry, only to someone going into the ministry. And finally, becoming a psychiatrist will take you at least eight more years of rigorous medical training including medical school, internship, and a specialized residence in psychiatry - We just don't think you could ever make it!"

My rage was complete, intense, and long-lasting. Now, looking back over the last 47 years, I realize the enormity of God's mysterious gift - my extreme anger! I made a deep abiding pledge that night: No matter what happens - I will not fail! What I have always termed my righteous anger carried me through the many dark nights and doubt -filled days of medical and psychiatric studies, military service in war-time, and clinical practice from the Mayo Clinic to Europe and from the South Pacific to the rural homes of Native Americans in Alaska.

While I still carry a sense of the Christian ministry throughout my personal and professional life, the symbolic ending of my formal ministerial career came on a crisp winter Sunday in Fargo, North Dakota - Christmas Day 1966. The Vietnam War was raging and our family was fortunate to be together for the Christmas holidays in Fargo, where my father was senior minister at the First Methodist Church. My own family and I were literally on our way from Montana, where I had served a medical locum tenens, to Pensacola, Florida, for training-duty as a United States Navy flight surgeon – and, my father asked me to give the sermon on that Christmas Sunday. My sermon was titled "Walk Softly - and Carry a Big Pillow," as I attempted to give voice once again to the eternal Christmas message that God's answer to the needs of this world was to create "a family" and "Give unto us A Child..." But it was my father's introduction of me, not my sermon, which has stayed vividly in my memory for more than 40 years.

As he strode to the pulpit for the introduction, attired, as was his custom, in a black robe for anonymity from fashion and a stole signifying the Yoke of Christ, I was intensely aware of the sole ministry and dignity that my father always brought to the worship of God. I was proud of the ministerial bonds we shared in that Sunday worship service, appropriately reflected in my own black robe and stole. My father said: "I have known the speaker of the morning all his life. And, I could tell you some intriguing stories about him (laughter) or describe his many accomplishments. But, I will do what every parent does - introduce their child to the world. So, this morning on this Christmas Sunday, it is my honor and privilege to introduce to you the Reverend Dr. Russell A. Huffman, Jr - my son - and, my friend."

Permission granted for use of this picture & article by *St. Paul Pioneer Press*, St. Paul, MN. 14 Jun 1953 page 13, Column 2.

Rev. Mark Horst

When my family moved to St. Cloud, I was already in seminary. I had decided in 1977 that I needed to take the time to understand what God wanted from me, and it seemed that theological study was one way to get at that. So off I went to Yale Divinity School. I spent a couple of summers back in St. Cloud and always enjoyed worshipping at First Church. I was fortunate to receive some scholarship money from the Grannis Fellowship through First Church, and I deeply appreciate your long-time support of ministerial students.

After completing seminary in 1981, I worked on a Ph.D. in theology. After graduating in 1985, I was appointed as an associate pastor to Excelsior UMC. From 1989-1994 I served Fairmont Avenue in St. Paul. From 1994-2006, I was the senior pastor of Park Avenue United Methodist in south Minneapolis. This past summer [2006] I was appointed to serve the congregation in Stillwater.

When I think about how God has worked in my life, I can only say "the steadfast love of the Lord never ceases, his mercies never come to an end."

REMINISEENCES FROM OUR CONGREGATION

Note on Profiles of Church Members

These profiles might be rightly dedicated to all those church members, living and dead, whom we did not include here. We knew we could not include everyone because of space and time issues, but we would have liked to. Certainly we believe that the life of the church is made up of everyone's contribution. We decided to include only living members of the congregation, representatives of the church at this immediate period of time. They either wrote their own pieces or were interviewed by Val Rogosheske, Carol Reid, Jessie Harper, or Nancy Gundersen.

Nancy Gundersen

~John and Lois Barron ~

Lois is a native of the area, having grown up in Clearwater. John, on the other hand, grew up in South St. Paul, and came to St. Cloud to attend college at St. Cloud State. While in school, he sang in the First Methodist Church choir, and he met Lois on a blind date. They were married in the Clearwater Methodist Church.

John and Lois lived in East St. Paul for 11 years and were members of the Christ Methodist Church in Maplewood. Ken Beck was the minister and even then called on people late at night. This was, of course, not the only time their paths would cross. Then in 1965, the Barrons went to Granite Falls, where John taught mechanical drafting at the vocational college for seven years.

In 1974 the Barrons returned to St. Cloud, and now Rev. Beck was minister of First Church. It was a pleasant reunion. However, when New Horizons was in its beginning stages in 1978, the Barrons were charter members and attended it for a while, as they were living in the north metro area. They later returned to First Church.

While living in St. Cloud, John commuted to St. Louis Park for 11 years to work for a hearing aid company, and Lois served as a secretary for a number of St. Cloud State University offices. They are now both retired.

Both of the Barrons have assisted the church by taking on tasks needing doing. John was the coordinator of Meals on Wheels for about five years, and he is at present one of the money counters for the Church offerings. He's served on committees, helped with the pancake supper, and gone fishing with the Men's Club. He says, "That's about the only time I go fishing. I buy a license for one trip."

Lois has served on a number of committees also, including Missions, Finance and the 150th Anniversary Committee. She was the chair of the Pastor Parish Relations Committee when Pastor Katie was hired, and during Pastor Katie's time worked in the church office when they were between secretaries or needed a substitute.

Some interesting mission activity both the Barrons engaged in was going down to Sager Brown in Louisiana to help with the United Methodist Church Council on Relief (UMCOR). They went with friends and others from their Twin Cities church to help fix homes and even to assist in constructing a new house. Several years before, Hurricane Andrew had gone through, so there was plenty of work to do. The stints were for two weeks, and the Barrons did this for three years. One year Dorothy Stueve participated as well.

The Barrons have three adult daughters: Laura, a graphic designer in New Prague; Linda, working with cardiac telemetry at the Mayo Clinic in Rochester, and Mary, a language arts teacher at Apollo. They had one son, Paul, who died in a motorcycle accident in 1980. There are seven grandchildren.

For recreation and additional service, they belong to the St. Cloud Area Senior Fun Singers, through Community Education. During the Christmas season, they are particularly busy with concerts in senior residences.

~Mick Benson and Jessie Harper ~

My husband, Jim, and I, with our infant son, Steven, came to St. Cloud from Carlton, Minnesota, in 1952. Jim worked for the Singer Sewing Machine Company, but was soon transferred to Fergus Falls, Minnesota, and then to Minot, North Dakota. As Minnesota people, we were not happy campers in northern North Dakota, and we were thrilled to be transferred to St. Cloud in 1957.

We built a house in St. Cloud, and all seven Harper children grew up in that home, attended Washington and Garfield elementary schools, South Junior High School, and graduated from Technical High School. The nearness of St. Cloud State College enabled me to complete degrees in social science and sociology, and I was able to complete a doctorate at the University of Nebraska. When Jim died in 1983 from complications following an automobile accident, I was already teaching sociology at St. Cloud State University. I continued this inadvertent career until I retired in 1994.

Because our roots were in small Presbyterian churches in Northeastern Minnesota, Jim and I affiliated with First Presbyterian Church when we came to St. Cloud. Several of our children were confirmed there, and we enjoyed worshiping with many friends. However, during the volatile Vietnam and civil rights era of the '70's, we transferred to First United Methodist Church, and First Church has been my church home since then. Jim; my mother, Aural Greenstreet; and I were in attendance almost every Sunday.

Mick's family had an affiliation with First Church while he was a student at Saint Cloud State College. Following graduation, Mick and his wife and children lived in Windom and Albany, where he taught secondary art.

After Mick was divorced and I had lost Jim, we met and later were married in First Church in 1986. Mick and I lived in south St. Cloud from 1986 until 2005, when we built a patio home in Sartell. Our ties remain with First Church, where Jessie has been a member for 36 years and Mick for 21 years. In retirement Mick continues his work as a watercolor painter. Jessie enjoys several reading groups and amateur quilting. We like gardening, and have been blessed with opportunities to travel a good bit, both overseas and in the U.S. Together we have nine children and twelve grandchildren. Therefore our prayers are for world peace, and for health that is good enough to allow us to visit children and hold grandchildren.

~Bill and Jo Ann Bridges~

Jo Ann and Bill came to St. Cloud in Oct. 1956. They came from Iowa City, Iowa, to the St. Cloud Veterans Hospital. Bill was an occupational therapist, and he says he came from being a member of a two-person department in Iowa, to being the head of a 37-person department in St. Cloud. He did this work for 16 years, and then, until he retired in 1987, was the assistant to the medical director of the Hospital.

Jo Ann worked in offices until 1961 when the Bridges adopted their daughter, Risa. The family increased once more in 1963 when they adopted their son, Craig. Then Jo Ann was an at-home mother until the children were older. In

1980 she took a nursing assistant course and was employed at St. Benedict's Center for ten years. She says of that time, "I loved working there. . . .[and] I did a good job."

Bill has been involved in many activities of the church. He was the chairman of the Finance Committee for eight years during Ken Beck's time and says, "I don't recall as long as I was there that we ever met our budget." But, he adds, the membership always seemed to come through, and the church bills got paid. And, he points out that First Church always had a strong tradition of giving over and above that of meeting their own expenses.

Among his other church chores, Bill chaired the Building Management Committee during Rev. Horst's tenure. Bill also says he was head of the dining room "forever" for the Men's Club's pancake supper. However, this last year he turned the duties over to someone else. As Bill says of his own advancing years, "Eighty-one years - that's enough."

Jo Ann meanwhile has been on numerous church committees, as well as being a valuable member of the Church's women's group, both on the local and the district level. She is a life member of United Methodist Women, a recognition for the contributions that she has made. She remembers that the second year she was part of the group, she was chair of Cherry Pie Day. She worries about the organization now, as its membership ages. She says, "It's difficult… A lot of us aren't active any more."

Both have been Methodists for a long time: Bill was born Methodist, and Jo Ann was baptized when she was nine years old. When they came to the Methodist Church in St. Cloud, they became good friends with another Methodist couple, Woody and Eleanor Wilson, who had arrived in town almost at the same time. The Wilsons were the sponsors for the Bridges' daughter, Risa, and were extremely active in First United Methodist. Both the Wilsons were on the membership committee for a long while, either heading it or as members, and they did numerous other things as well.

The Bridges remember other church members too. Bill says, "Mary Megarry, she was one of my favorite people." Her family was involved in construction, and apparently Mary drove truck. They also remember Priscilla Dean, a young mother of the church, who, as Jo Ann says, was "so outgoing and bubbly." Priscilla died in the 60's from an automobile/bike accident, and this was very hard for church members to handle. They also remember Paul

Metzger. He baptized both of their children. Both agree he was a "brilliant man."

Their children, like everyone's children, grew up. Risa now lives in New Hampshire with her husband, Larry. She works in the arts and is presently managing director of Northern Stage in White River Junction, Vermont. Craig remained in Minnesota, making his home in Ramsey. He has worked in graphic arts for 25 years.

~Virginia Brown~

Four generations of Virginia Brown's family have attended First Church. Her grandparents, William and Julia Farrand Varner, moved from Belle Prairie to St. Cloud in the late 1800's and were members of First Church. Her parents, Leslie and Helen Johnson Varner, were members, and Virginia joined the church with the confirmation class of 1934. After she and John Brown were married, their two children, Robert and Barbara, were baptized and confirmed in First Church. Her grandson Ross was baptized here as well.

In spite of such a long record of church membership, Virginia and John were not married in the church. They decided to wed when John came home on leave from the service in the early 1940's. However, the church was locked, and Dr. Rev. Logan was on his two-week summer vacation. Fortunately they knew of a retired Methodist minister, Rev. F. J. Bryan, and he married them in his home.

They went back to Texas, where John was stationed, and Virginia found employment as a secretary for the American National Insurance Company. They spent their first two years of married life there. Then Virginia was expecting and went back to St. Cloud for the birth, while John shipped out to fight. He and his group were in Hawaii when they heard that the war was over. So John returned to St. Cloud and his wife and new baby.

John, whom Virginia calls "Johney," worked for Kemps Ice Cream Company and traveled throughout the state. They bought a house in Waite Park and were part of the Methodist Church there. John sang in the choir and served as lay leader. He arranged with First Church to employ Waite Park's minister, Rev. Day, part time so that he could supplement his Waite Park salary.

When the Browns moved back to St. Cloud, they again became part of First Church. Virginia joined Dorcas Circle and found that half of the members knew her mother. She heard little stories about her parents from these older women. Virginia was a faithful worker for the women's activities.

Virginia lives now at the Riverside Apartments, the complex that Rev. Beck, other St. Cloud pastors, and church members from First Church and other churches joined together to build. She says that her father and mother rented one of the first apartments there, and when her father died, someone hired a bus so that everyone from the apartments could go to his funeral.

John died in November 1991. Virginia's daughter lives both in Richmond, Minnesota, and in Arizona; and her son lives in Elk River. She has four grandchildren and four great grandchildren.

~Carl and Diane Bublitz~

Carl and Diane joined First Church in 1994 with a strong commitment to having a two-way flow. They wanted to serve others through the church, and they wanted the church to fill what they saw as a need in their lives.

Diane grew up an ELCA Lutheran in Wisconsin. She was quite involved in the church up to age 20. Her mother used to say, "As long as you put your feet under my table, you will go to my church!" When Diane left home, she left the church for 20 years! She worked for Lutheran Social Services, West CAP,[1] the State of Minnesota and the Private Industry Council 5. More recently, she returned to school to study accounting, and passed the CPA exam. Currently, she is Director of Operations for Bethlehem Lutheran Church

Carl grew up in the Methodist Church in southeast Minnesota. He has always enjoyed the outdoors and has worked 30 years for the DNR, currently at an area office in Little Falls. He and Diane met in the early 80's in Minneapolis during a ski trip with mutual friends.

Diane laughs when she admits that it was important to them to have a minister marry them, even though neither one of them was attending church at the

---

[1] Community Action Program

time. Soon afterwards, they moved to St. Cloud to make their commute times more equal.

That was a difficult time, as they had much less contact with their friends in Minneapolis, and were not yet connected to others in St. Cloud. At the same time, they decided that the "spiritual piece" was missing in their lives. So, they visited several churches, and settled on First Church. Instrumental in that decision was Mary Wagner reaching out to them, even making a visit to their home.

In their service to the church, they decided to act as a team. The first committee they joined together was the Church and Society Committee (now known as Faith in Action). Carl influenced the committee to do an Adopt a River project, which provided an opportunity for a wide variety of ages to get together on Earth Day to pick up litter on the Beaver Island Trail and in the Mississippi River. They did that for five or six years, with a total of over 1,000 pounds of litter removed. Carl fondly remembers a picture of Bob Holscher holding a big tire that they fished out of the river, a symbol, he says, of "reversing careless actions and treasuring God's creation."

They also joined GRIP, and helped on numerous community actions. Diane served as chair of the committee for several years, and held leadership positions with the area-wide organization. For the past three years, Carl served on the Outreach Committee, which deals with how to be intentional about welcoming visitors and new members. Diane had an interesting take on how their membership in First Church helped her change careers. She was not happy in her other job, but leaving work and going to school for two full years was a major step. She and Carl attended a year-long Disciple Bible study with Pastor Dan. Diane says, "That class created a calmness and allowed me to believe that all would be ok if I took this risk."

~Sharyn Clark~

Sharyn Clark moved with her family from Atwater, Minnesota, to Sauk Rapids in 1968. Her husband joined the staff of the Sauk Rapids public schools as junior high school principal. Their three children, Heather, Jonathan, and Jill all attended Sauk Rapids schools.

Sharyn was raised in the Evangelical United Brethren Church. When she and her family moved to Atwater where he was a teacher and administrator, the

Methodist church just across the street from the school became their church home. The Methodist connection continued when they moved to the St. Cloud area. In St. Cloud, she and her husband joined First United Methodist Church, where the children attended Sunday school and were confirmed. Sharyn was involved in teaching Sunday school and in attending an evening circle with other young mothers. Sharyn recalls carpooling from Sauk Rapids, transporting children to church events.

In 1980 Sharyn began selling real estate as a full-time occupation. As her children grew up and her life changed, she was less active in the church. More recently she has returned to church activities, and has served on several committees, including Finance, Stewardship, and the Care committees.

Sharyn lives in Sartell. Her three children are married, and all live in the area. This enables her to visit them, and to attend events with her six grandchildren.

~Jim and Jan Davis~

Jim and Jan Davis came to St. Cloud in 1989, after having lived in a number of different towns. Neither was from a Methodist background, but they agreed that when they arrived in a new town, they would attend whichever church seemed to fit them best, rather than selecting a church by denomination. For a few years, they attended another church in St. Cloud, and then joined First Church when Katie arrived. Jim was drawn also by the quality music.

When Jim and Jan came to First Church, their family was grown and on their own. They have a daughter, Kristin Kummer, who lives in the area with her husband and five children; and a son, Todd Davis, who lives in Eau Claire, Wisconsin. He and his wife have three children.

Jim is into his fourth year as Church Lay Leader. Consequently he was a natural choice to be facilitator of the church visioning process after the grant to hire a church facilitator ran out. It was also a good fit in that strategic planning is part of his job at CentraCare, where he is Vice President of Operations.

Jim believes "the [visioning] process was so helpful as we reviewed our situation here . . ." Although there was a desire by some to get to discussing solutions quickly, those guiding the process were determined that the group would thoroughly investigate the present situation here and the probabilities for the future before they went to solutions.

When the congregation voted in the fall of 2007 to explore relocating the church, Jim says, "That was huge." And he was happy that the "yes" votes were considerably more than the "no" ones - that meant a consensus of sorts had formed. Of the outcome of the vote, Jim says, "I really did not have a clue," and Jan adds that there was "a lot of anxiety before the vote."

Jan has been busy in the church and elsewhere as well. She has a special education background and has worked in the elementary schools. In fact, some of her pupils attended their wedding. When she came to St. Cloud, Jan had a job at the Stearns County History Museum as their first education coordinator. She now volunteers there.

Jan has been active in the church, particularly on the Faith in Action Committee and speaks with enthusiasm of their projects. One in particular involves adopting several Talahi Community School families at holiday time. The first year the committee decided to adopt three families. They asked for financial help and received it from the Men's Club, WSCS, the Table, and Wednesday Night Live, as well as the congregation. Jan says they were overwhelmed by the response.

This, however, was not the end of the project. The committee had to get information as to who were in the family, what was needed, and sizes. Then it was to the stores to find these items, at the same time committee members were shopping for their own families. The committee has done this for two years and plans to do it again this year.

One additional project of the Davis family: They do a Third Saturday meal once a year, along with their daughter and her family. Their last meal was boneless pork loin slices, grilled, a delicious treat they enjoyed providing.

~Charles and Shirley Echols~

Ten years as a church secretary should make one an expert. I'm not sure about expert; however ten years working with good people makes one a blessed person.

Shirley and Charles Echols, along with their daughter Julie, arrived in St. Cloud in the early 1970's. Charles had been hired to teach music at St. Cloud State College, and Shirley took care of the family, which soon grew to include their son, David. Shirley came from a Methodist background and met Charles, whose father was a Presbyterian minister, when he was on the music staff of a church she attended in California. Charles was playing the organ and working on his doctorate in music.

Although Shirley attended First Church regularly, Charles soon became St. Mary's Cathedral music director and organist, which caused him to be occupied elsewhere on Sunday mornings. And for a time, Shirley was too. She sang in their choir, as she had grown up singing in choirs. She tells about those days. First she would take Julie over to the Methodist nursery, then go to St. Mary's with David, hold him while she sang, and go back to First Church to pick up Julie.

The Echols joined First Church during the time of Ken Beck. By 1983 Shirley was directing the handbell choir, at this point, all adult women. Although Shirley had never directed or played in such a choir, she had been interested in one that played at her California church and had closely studied how they performed.

Sometime in late 1983 or early 1984, Shirley became a part-time secretary at First Church. This was early in Rev. Horst's time. By 1985, Shirley was the head secretary. She continued in that role for ten years and gave some stability to the office, which had a continuing turnover of staff. As Shirley says, "Mercy, I can't even count them all now."

She says that in spite of the turnover, "We had a good time with our staff ... we used to do things together." They went to ball games, lunch, plays, and staff birthday celebrations. Shirley remembers one morning breakfast to celebrate Jim Garven's birthday. He forgot to show up! She says that Toby was responsible for that sociability, as he started the tradition.

Some church members may remember the staff performing at a number of the church annual meetings.

Many things happened in the office in the ten years Shirley was there. She remembers one occasion when she came to work on April 1, and found all the office desks and file cabinets with their drawers pulled open and paper strewn around. She recollects that she didn't panic nor call the police, although she certainly was startled. A little later, Bill Perconti, the church's business manager, came in and confessed that he had done it as an April Fool's joke.

Other things of a more serious nature occurred as well. People would come into the church with some basic needs. They would be traveling and out of gas. Or they would need a place to stay or some money for food. Shirley says that Rev. Horst would converse with them to try to determine if their story was true. If he determined that it probably was, then a voucher would be given for gas, or one would occasionally be handed out for a motel room. People were sent to the Salvation Army if they needed a meal.

Another significant memory of Shirley's was the U.S. Methodist Church's bicentennial celebration, the planning for which began in February 1984. Ministers and representatives from the surrounding Methodist Churches came together to form a committee for an area-wide celebration, and Shirley became its chair.

After 25 years, Charles retired from playing organ at St. Mary's and from the University. Shirley continues to serve the church through work on committees, and now their daughter, Julie Daniels, is the church's Financial Administrator, working in the same office as her mother did not too long before.

~Dave and Joan Ellens~

Joan and Dave Ellens are a couple that the church would have difficulty doing without. Dave has worked with the Building Management Committee for years, including serving as chair. He has been involved in many fix-it projects at the church and has enjoyed the work for "the companionship ... being with the guys." One project he particularly remembers is stripping the sanctuary floors of wax and redoing them. He volunteered many hours during that project.

Joan says that she has been on the Nurture and Care Committees "forever," and has done much congregational visiting. She enjoys the people she goes to see and says of her service, "I've learned to be more patient because of people I've visited . . . and to be more understanding." Sometimes she and Dave go together. They also deliver Meals on Wheels and have been part of Disciple and Companions in Christ classes in the church.

Joan is a longtime member of First United Methodist Church. Her family moved to St. Cloud in 1952 when Joan was a high school sophomore. She later had the opportunity to help pack the cornerstone for the new church with newspapers, bulletins, other tokens of the time. She remembers being joined in the task by Dave Van Nostrand, Winness Anderson, and Dick Skewes.

Both Joan and Dave earned teaching degrees at St. Cloud State and were married in the new church by Rev. Metzger. They then went to Sheboygan, Wisconsin, for six years to teach: Joan, elementary and Dave, biology and driver's education, as well as coaching basketball. Diane (DeeDee), Melissa, Bruce and Michael were born there.

Then back to St. Cloud, where Dave worked on a master's program before beginning work as an admissions counselor for the University. Joan taught in Sauk Rapids and St. Cloud before beginning a new job at SCSU supervising student teachers. She then earned a master's degree in counseling. She worked at Rocori High School as a guidance counselor for 19 years.

Melissa, their youngest daughter, was born in St. Cloud. Now married and living in the state of Virginia, she and her family have received much attention these last few years because in 2004 conjoined twin girls were born to her and her husband. They were separated four months later and received national attention from television and newspapers. Joan went out East for the operation, but broke her ankle the first day she was there and so came back to St. Cloud. First United Methodist was concerned about the twins as well and later held a fund raiser to assist the family in modifying their home to accommodate Erin, who uses a wheelchair. At this point both Jade and Erin are doing well, as is their older sister, Taylor.

~Lois Fredrickson~

Lois Fredrickson, at the time of this interview, was one of the older members attending First United Methodist Church. She drove herself to church, arriving early so that she could park in front of the church, and sat regularly with friends in a pew on the south side of the sanctuary.

Lois and her husband, Ray, came to St. Cloud in 1948. In 1950 they bought a home near Technical High School, where Lois lived until recently. Ray, who was a salesman for Gamble Robinson, died in 1973. Their two children grew up here and both attended St. Cloud State College. Susan is now a retired teacher in the Denver area, and Richard lives in Kaiser, Oregon. Lois grew up on a farm near Bryant, South Dakota. After graduating from high school in 1932, she attended business school in Minneapolis and then became a secretary at University of Minnesota Hospitals. After she and Ray married, they lived in Minneapolis, Rochester, and Wadena before settling in St. Cloud. They joined First Church in 1949, and Lois has a wealth of memories of church activities since that time.

Lois' father kept a diary from age 18. The diary was continued by her mother, and finally by Lois herself. An important date in her diary was November 21, 1954, when she recorded that they "laid the cornerstone of the new Methodist church." Among the vivid memories about building the new church were the very many things church women did to raise money to help make mortgage payments. According to her, "We always said the women raised the money and the men spent it."

There were dinners served to many men's groups in town. Also, women served nickel dinners for church members and townspeople, and invited the community to Cherry Pie Day to celebrate Washington's birthday in February. Most wives did not work outside the home, and Lois recalls taking the children along to the church as they made pies, set tables, or peeled 50 pounds of potatoes. One gets a picture of women, young and old, who were constantly busy with church activities.

~Jim and Carolyn Garven~

Jim and Carolyn Garven moved to St. Cloud in 1969. Carolyn secured a position teaching first grade in the Sauk Rapids school district, and Jim began a degree at St. Cloud State. Jim had been raised in the Missouri Synod Lutheran Church, but his relationship with Ken Beck influenced both him and Carolyn to become members of First Church.

Carolyn taught elementary remedial education, then spent many years as Coordinator of Secondary Special Education. She retired in 2000, after a long career in the Sauk Rapids Public Schools. Because of the respect she had earned, Carolyn was urged to file for the St. Cloud City Council and was elected to represent East St. Cloud in 1999. This year (2008) she started her third term on the council.

Jim and Carolyn began their church activities as volunteers with children and youth. Eventually Jim was employed as a full-time youth worker, while Carolyn continued as a volunteer. There were many children and youth in church during the 1970's and 1980's, and lay persons were very involved in programming for them.

For example, First Church started the Pine Bend program, a vacation Bible school for Indian children, on their home reservation. Upwards of 30 students from First Church and neighboring churches participated in the program each summer. Fern Michalski and Pat Tonnell were among the women who worked diligently in a rather primitive kitchen, cooking for both children and workers, while Jim and Carolyn and other adults carried out programming. The program continued for many years and provided experiences for numerous young people.

An important activity for youth and adult sponsors was a United Nations tour. This tour began as a Methodist Conference-sponsored project, but eventually First Church had its own tour, conducted frequently enough to allow every First Church young person who wished to participate during their high-school years. When Toby Horst became pastor, he led UN tours that again were Conference sponsored.

Jim and Carolyn remember the great variety of programs they led or participated in for First Church youth during the 70's and 80's. Several are EYE (Ecumenical Youth Encounter), with thousands of kids from many churches; Urban Plunge (a week in the Twin Cities doing a mission project); skiing trips; Youth Council; movies; weekend retreats; Sunday night classes; spaghetti dinners; and canoe trips. More serious activities were confirmation classes, Easter breakfasts and Sunday morning Bible studies.

Jim and Carolyn continue in church activities today. Jim occasionally teaches classes at First Church, and Carolyn is a member of United Methodist Women and works with Church of the Week in the winter. They both particularly enjoy golf, where Carolyn's skill is quite intimidating. She began the game as a seven- or eight-year-old, and was a member of West High School's winning teams in the Twin Cities.

The Garven have two daughters, Stephanie and Cindy; four granddaughters and one grandson. All indications are they will continue contributing to the church and to the St. Cloud area for a long time

~Janet Gray~

I moved to St. Cloud in 1942 with my parents. My father, Arnold Borsheim, supervised a National Youth Administration project that would later become Brainerd Hall, located just west of the Teacher's College football stadium. My mother, Ruby, was a homemaker/seamstress, and I was a student at Riverview Lab. Our church home was Bethlehem Lutheran I did not know about the Methodists until much later in my life.

The first time I remember being inside the Methodist building was for the funeral of a Tech High School classmate, killed by a tornado. Within a few years after that, both Bethlehem Lutheran and First Methodist embarked on building programs.

After high school, I was one of two female biology majors at St. Cloud State. My chemistry lab partner that first quarter was a good-looking young man from Elk River by the name of David Gray, and we soon began dating. His housemates were Methodist, their girlfriends were Methodist, and soon I was attending Wesley Foundation gatherings. Directors Shigeo Tanabe, then Irving Palm welcomed me. A month or two after the new sanctuary was in use by the Methodists, two good college friends held their wedding there; David and I were attendants.

For the next twenty years, I was a "preacher's wife," first in a student charge in Colorado, then Atwater, Little Falls, and finally Crookston. After the painful death of our marriage in the late 70's, I moved again to begin life on my own in Melrose. With no Methodist Church in town, I would have to drive to wherever my new church home would be. I was drawn to St. Cloud, a larger congregation where I would not have an expected role. Mom was in St. Cloud; I had known the Becks for years. The choice was obvious. As it turned out, I joined the church the month Ken Beck learned he was to move.

Let me go back to the mid 1960's. My husband and I had a modest cabin on a small lake southeast of Park Rapids where many of our neighbors were fellow clergy. Wives of three of the families had been high school "best friends," and each had married a minister. All the couples had modest places on 100 foot lots within 800 feet of us. Richard and Barbara Mathison were our immediate neighbors. She drove; he read and wrote sermons for his Lake Harriet Methodist Church, and was dying of heart failure. It was Richard Mathison's death in 1978 that created the vacancy Ken Beck was appointed to fill. Toby & Locky Horst became part of that circle of friends, and also had property on the same quiet lake.

By November, 1978, I was driving in from Melrose for choir rehearsals - both chancel and handbells - and for Sunday worship. I knew the interstate well! For several years I was on the worship committee, adding another round trip.

Just over twenty years later, Mother and I decided it was time to share a home, and moved into a patio home built "just for us" something she never dreamed was possible. She kept on at Bethlehem, as I did at First Church. Mother died in March 2002.

I am most thankful for the support and inspiration found through the life of this congregation. It has become my spiritual home.

~Ralph and Nancy Gundersen~

Ralph and Nancy have been with the church since they first came to St. Cloud in 1964 with two preschool children, their son, Mark, and their daughter, Lee. Ralph was working on his doctorate in entomology and had been hired to teach biology at St. Cloud State College. Harold Hopkins was the Biology Department chairman then, and he and his wife, Pauline, the Partches, the Goehrings, the Coulters, and the Grethers - all from the Department - belonged to the church. Although Nancy came from a Congregational background and Ralph from a Lutheran one, both had attended Hamline University, so liked finding a Methodist Church.

Nancy was soon teaching Sunday school upstairs in the church, and Ralph was in a room off Wesley Hall teaching older children. Nancy remembers music time, when three-, four-, and five-year-olds all met around a piano to sing before they went to their individual activities. She also remembers making containers of an inexpensive play dough out of flour, salt, water, and food coloring.

A year or two after this, Nancy was asked if she would lead a circle. This startled her because she was new and not very experienced. However, being a former teacher and needing some sort of adult activity, Nancy agreed and was soon immersed in circle activities. It was a good time and an easy way to make friends of all ages. After a while, she realized that many of the women had already been circle chairmen, and that they were glad to have someone else assume the responsibility.

One memory she has of those years is being a waitress for Cherry Pie Day and wearing a costume of a white dust cap, matching shoulder scarf, and an apron. The dust cap did nothing for anyone's appearance, but it was fun to be part of a very busy day.

Ralph has been on numerous committees, including Finance, Memorials, and Scholarship, and has been a faithful worker for the Men's Group pancake supper. For many years, Woody Wilson would telephone in the fall, and then Ralph or Nancy was reminded that pancake supper was around the corner.

When Mark was in high school, he was part of Jim Garven's UMYF and enjoyed Jim's imaginative activities, as well as the thoughtful times. Mark was also in Boy Scouts at the church when John Peck was scout master. Lee was married in the church by Rev. Horst.

~Laurie and Dee Halberg~

We arrived in St. Cloud in 1963, a few months after Ken and Catherine Beck came. Our children grew up in the church, were confirmed there, and the oldest was married there. We both were involved from the beginning and did everything, from teaching Sunday school, serving on numerous boards and committees, being lay leader (Dee), and doing art work and landscaping (Laurie).

Laurie is pleased that his monolithic stoneware cross, often placed on the altar, contributes to worship. He was on the Fine Arts committee and the Board of Trustees when he introduced Joe O'Connell to the church and suggested he might be commissioned to do a piece of art that would cover the space on the north sanctuary wall. The congregation supported this, and in 1988 the four mahogany panels - joined with forged iron - became the "Tree of Life" relief, a priceless treasure for the church. Joe once told Dee that the thing he hated sculpting most, was hands. Sometime, look at the number of expressive hands in that relief! His art reflects the humorous and the devout, both very much part of his personality.

We particularly remember the leaders early in our membership: Carlton Eckberg, Hillis Meyers, Jack Bensen, etc., for their wisdom, humor and patience with training some of us youngsters. Dee remembers sitting in on a meeting one night where we were voting on a controversial issue, and another member, having sat through numerous votes and amendments said, "We're just going to have to keep voting until we get it right!"

First Church went through some interesting and difficult years in the late sixties and seventies. The whole country was divided and inflamed over the civil rights movement and the Vietnam War. During this time, Ken answered the call to march at Selma. There was division in the church, as well as the community, and emotions often ran high. Still, it was at times like this that we were reminded anew that the role of the church was to challenge the status quo when injustice was taking place, and that to be faithful often meant discomfort and unpopular stands.

Ken Beck was grateful that the board insisted on providing him an open pulpit, as were we. He shaped our thinking for years. We might add that he was not only well read and an advocate for Christians using the head as well as the heart, but he always put his interests and money where his mouth was.

We didn't realize how fortunate we were to be part of First United Methodist Church until we left St. Cloud. It took us five years to find a church that was as open and challenging as it was during the years we attended. Best wishes on this new history project.

~Don Helgeson~

Don grew up in the Presbyterian church, but married Arlene Mittelstadt in the old First Church sanctuary in August of 1950. The young couple then moved back to Minneapolis, where Don was working on a master's degree in business at the University of Minnesota. In March of 1951, they moved back to St. Cloud and Don joined First Church.

Even though Don was busy with his business, Golden Plump Poultry, Inc., he was active at First Church from the time he joined. He first helped on the Building Committee, which was planning for the new church, that would go up next to the old one. Don also helped with fundraising for the new church. Don doesn't remember very much angst associated with the move next door. The old church had many problems, and the new church was much admired. The fact that they were right next to each other made the good-byes to the old church more gradual.

In addition to working on the Building Committee, Don taught Sunday school for a few years. Dr. Logan had just retired, and Russell Huffman was the minister. Later, Don also did several years of confirmation teaching.

Don has also served on the Finance Committee for many years. It's been interesting for him to see professional accounting practices evolve over the years and the effects of computers. In addition, Don served on the Conference Finance Committee for a number of years. During this time he helped revise the pension system and was able to see the broader financial perspective of the Conference.

Don assisted with some Men's Club activities, especially the Pancake Supper, which was a pretty good fund-raiser for the church. The fact that Golden Plump donated eggs for the event helped!

Don and Arlene had four boys: Mike, Stefan, Scott, and Glen. They were active in the youth group, and several of them volunteered at Pine Bend. One year, Arlene went along to cook for the group. This was a huge job, because she not only cooked for the First Church youth and adult leaders, but also made a lunch for all the young participants in the day camp. The job was made tougher by the rather rough facilities in which to work. So Arlene was exhausted when she got home.

Arlene's cooking skills did not extend to pies, however. One family story that always brought laughs is the one about the year the women's group was having a cherry pie sale and insisted that the pies be homemade. Arlene found herself quitting the group rather than admitting that she didn't want to make a pie! Her particular interest was in the arts, and that is where she contributed to the church.

Don has appreciated the leadership of the ministers of the Church. Ken Beck had a significant influence on him; many good conversations had the effect of liberalizing both him and Arlene. Ken frustrated Don on the tennis court with his steady lobs to the baseline. He would just wait for Don to make a mistake. Later, after Ken left First Church, Don would see him at meetings of the Hamline Board of Trustees, on which Don served for 16 years.

Don and Arlene did a lot of traveling, but it was not sitting-at-a-resort vacations. Their trips involved adventure, exercise, and learning. Many ski and bike trips were taken, and in 1978, they climbed a mountain in Nepal. They often shared pictures at church, and Arlene showed a Sufi dance.

Arlene died suddenly in January 2005. Several years later, Don married Sue Shepard.

~Mike and Karel Helgeson ~

Mike and Karel are St. Cloud natives. Mike is the son of long time members Don and Arlene Helgeson and was baptized in this church in 1952. Karel went to St. Peter's Church and Grade School, and then to North Junior High. It was then that she first visited First Church, when JoAnn Ferrario invited her to a youth group hay ride. She felt that this church was warm and welcoming from the first. Later, she also visited to hear Peace March speakers during the Vietnam War years.

Mike's earliest memory of First Church is sneaking into the educational wing while it was being constructed. He was about five years old at the time. He has good memories of growing up in this church. The MYF was a large, active group. He remembers having fun with Barb Klein, Doug Binnie, Peter Beck, Mark Patridge, Dave Nielsen and Steve Harper. There were retreats at Decision Hills with Rev. Lewis ("Revy Eddy") and Rev. Beck.

There was a canoe trip to the BWCA with Rev. Lewis ")that could have turned out badly, as he had little experience camping. Luckily, a good number of the boys were Boy Scouts! Many of this MYF group were pioneers in the Pine Bend mission program. They would drive around in a station wagon picking up youth from the reservation until they had packed the car, and then return to the program site for singing and activities and lunch.

Mike and Karel both graduated from Tech in 1970, but didn't date until two years later. They happened to meet downtown one summer when they were both dressed up, he for a job, and she for an interview. Mike asked Karel for a date for the very next night! In the fall, Mike, a junior at Gustavus, left for Vienna for nine months. Karel had finished an R.N. program and had worked for a year at Methodist Hospital in Rochester before working in downtown St. Paul.

When Mike graduated from Gustavus, he was working with his dad in the poultry business and was to live in Jakarta, Indonesia, for two years. What better company than Karel? So they married in December of 1974. Their marriage at First Church was one of the first in which Ken Beck was joined by a priest to celebrate the union.

When the Helgesons returned to first church, Mike's international perspective made him a natural for the Missions Committee. It's been the work that he has been most interested in through the years. He has also served on the Council of Ministries (now the Administrative Council and was chair of the Scholarship Committee.

Mike has helped First Church in other ways as well. He would bring a drill from the feed mill and hook it up to a paddle to mix the pancake batter for the pancake supper. And since 1977, he has provided the Christmas tree for church. The first year, it was so big that when it was set up, Rev. Beck looked like a bird in the branches as he was preaching!

Karel has helped in numerous ways at First Church. She helped in the nursery and taught Sunday school. Working with Cathy Danzl on the Youth Education Committee, Karel remembers putting on pageants, such as It's a Small World After All. Karel also was on the Memorial Committee and the Adult Education Committee.

While working on the Worship Committee, Karel was deeply influenced by Rev. Katie Schneider-Bryan. Karel said, "Katie introduced me to the concept of visuals being a part of the mission. I hadn't thought of it in that way. It gave me confidence to display what I made."

The family enjoyed retreats at Decision Hills when the kids were young and appreciated all the relationships that were formed then. "You don't realize then that it will end and just be a good memory."

Mike and Karel have helped many people form good memories at First Church.

~Mert and Nancy Hubbard~

Both Mert and Nancy grew up in Long Prairie on dairy farms, and their families were friends. After they were married, they came to St. Cloud in 1958. Mert worked with Northern Wire Products, a manufacturing firm, for about 37 years, the last half as co-owner. Nancy served as an executive secretary at a number of places, St. Cloud National Bank being the longest period. Later they started a business, Flexible Pipe Tool Company, and worked together for four years. They sold the business when they retired.

The Hubbard's have three sons, Kevin, Mert, Todd and Neil. All were confirmed at First Church. Kevin and Neil now live in the Twin Cities area, and Todd lives in St. Cloud. The Hubbard's have two grown granddaughters.

When the boys were younger and involved in church programs, two of them at separate times went to New York and Washington on the United Nations trips. Kevin was shocked to see people sleeping on the streets and a drug user with tracks on her arms.

Neil had his own experience to remember. He and several others went exploring New York and ended up in Harlem, where they apparently looked lost. A young black man came up to them and told them that they shouldn't be there, but that he would stay with them and help them get the right bus back. His kindness impressed Neil.

Mert has worked hard in the church. He served a stint as chair of the Board of Trustees, was on Building Management Committee, was the chair of the Board of Administration, was on the Finance Committee. Nancy has served two terms on the Missions Committee and two on the Worship Committee.

The Hubbards have a church story that they tell with amusement. One Sunday Pastor Katie suggested that people move around in the church, not just sit in the same place by the same people all the time. The next Sunday the Hubbards decided to sit on the other side of the aisle and ended up in the spot where the Helgesons traditionally sat. A little later, just before the service started, the Helgeson family whisked into the church, headed for their pew, and found the Hubbards sitting there. Arlene exclaimed, "You're sitting in my pew!" Of course the Hubbards didn't move, so the Helgesons sat one pew forward. Arlene and Nancy would laugh about this afterwards, this jolting out of accustomed ways.

Both the Hubbards have done volunteer work outside the church. On her own Nancy began collecting gently used books for underprivileged children in 2006. The St. Cloud Reading Room Society, of which she is a member, began supporting her project in 2007 under their literacy program. The over 2,000 books she and they collected went to Talahi School, Anna Marie's Shelter, and the Boys and Girls Club. When she travels to California in the winter, she works with children in the schools, primarily assisting children who are learning English.

Mert also works on community projects. He has assisted with projects for Red Cross, Chamber of Commerce, and Top Hatters. He also is involved with SCORE, a program where experienced business people counsel small business owners.

Nancy sums up the fondness the Hubbards have for this church, "I love this church - it's my church." She says the church is "a community that you become part of."

~Beulah Rose Hutchens~

Beulah Rose and Warren Hutchens came to St. Cloud from Iowa in 1946, he to teach business courses at Technical High School, and she to soon be the mother of twins. They first lived several blocks from the church in an apartment house on 7th Ave. So.

Soon after they arrived, Beulah Rose had church visitors, Ursula Emery and Juanita McCutchan from First Methodist. They probably knew she was Methodist from the Welcome Wagon, a service that visited new families, gave them information about St. Cloud, brought small gifts from town businesses, and recorded some information about the family, including religious affiliation.

The visiting committee invited the Hutchens to church. Although Beulah Rose was, as she says, "very pregnant" with her twins, the Hutchens went to church several times before Marva Jean and Marvin were born in October.

The Hutchens continued attending the church, and later for several years, Beulah Rose was responsible for the cradle roll. When a baby was born to someone in the church, she would visit the new mother, and put the baby's name on a ribbon hanging from a picture of a baby in a cradle. This hung on a wall of the church. Later she also would chair circles from time to time. Finally, up to the present time, she has put together scrapbooks for the church and thereby helps to preserve the history.

Beulah Rose remembers when her twins started Sunday school. Edith Way was their first teacher at church, and Arthur Bluhm was Sunday school superintendent. She remembers Mr. Bluhm as having a kind and welcoming manner, and she remembers the candy he had in his pocket to welcome children to the church.

As the years went by, two more sons, Marlin and Marlowe were born into the family, and Warren was busy with vocational education, helping to start first the vocational college in an addition off of Technical High School and then at a new building on the north side of town.

Because at that time District #742 would not employ married women in the school system, Beulah Rose was not able to continue her kindergarten and primary teaching career. However, after the children were in school, she did substitute teaching.

Beulah Rose also had an influence on city affairs. She was appointed to the St. Cloud Planning Commission. This was particularly significant to the town's history, in that she was the first woman appointed to that commission. She served for 15 years.

Beulah Rose testifies that it is indeed true that Rev. Beck was a surprise visitor in the evening. She says that Warren would come home from working at the St. Cloud Technical College around 10:15 p.m. or so. Then sometimes at 10:30 p.m. the doorbell would ring, and Ken and Catherine would be at the door for a visit.

After retiring, Warren and she traveled the United States, seeing all parts of the country. It was a happy time. Warren died 13 years ago. Their daughter, Marva Jean, is an ordained Methodist Minister in Grand Rapids, two of their sons live in Brooklyn Park and one lives in Illinois.

~Byron and Joanne R. John~

When Byron and Joanne R. John arrived in St. Cloud in 1964 with three small children, Keith, Carl, and Elizabeth, they needed to find a church home. They first attended a church of their former tradition - but not quite!

In an orientation class for membership, they learned the Bible was interpreted and taught literally, a doctrine with which they did not agree. They visited

First Church but were told by an usher there was no nursery and were directed to the crying room. Fortunately, soon after they became acquainted with Arlene Helgeson, who assured them there was a nursery and that the congregation was enthusiastic about their new minister, Rev. Ken Beck, who had a strong interest in social justice. That is how the Johns came to First Church.

Byron, a pediatrician by profession, says over the years he has "been on many of the committees," but particularly on the Building Management Committee. However, he particularly enjoys contributing with his woodworking. He has made the name tag holder stands in the sanctuary, the cabinet around the sound board in the back of the sanctuary, extended the choir risers, built the food offering box by the library, and made the table decoration crosses for the Church's 150th Anniversary Dinner.

Joanne R. has enjoyed working in the past on the outreach, adult education, and worship committees. She also has participated in several groups, as well as GRIP. She says, "The average church member does not realize how much work goes on behind the scenes." She took classes at United Theological Seminary in New Brighton, Minnesota, because of a growing interest in images of God and biblical language, primarily in relation to gender, and continued with the work to earn an MA in theology.

~Robert and LuBell Kendall ~

The Kendalls' ties to First Church began in 1972 when, Bob says, "I was Ken Beck's flunky" - a part-time assistant who called on members, assisted as a liturgist, and occasionally preached. During that first year Bob, a professor of speech communication, taught part time at both St. Cloud State and the University of Minnesota (where he completed his dissertation). He also worked one-third time at Mound United Methodist Church as an associate pastor. [See pastor's section for all places Bob served.]

Bob remembers that first year as a time of the Vietnam conflict. Some people expected pastors to avoid political topics in their sermons. Since Ken did not adhere to that idea, a few of First Church members migrated to the Presbyterian Church, where the pastor pretty much avoided speaking of the war. At the same time, Bob recalls with a chuckle, there was a sudden influx of ex-Presbyterians at First United Methodist. He also remembers the joy of working with two young couples who were struggling with their faith at that time. Both couples are active participants at First Church today.

In 1982 as empty nesters, LuBell and Bob moved to St. Cloud. Although their children grew up in the Monticello church, eventually their son John and his wife, Janelle, were instrumental ("Pun intended," quips LuBell) in starting the Bridge Service here at First Church.

During his more than 50 years of ordained ministry (13 years as pastor in three different states), one of Bob's interests has been religious drama; he has portrayed at least 19 different characters - among them, Jonah, whom he performed in a drama at First Church with his son Dean. (It was by Wolf Mankowitz and was called "It Should Happen to a Dog.")

LuBell feels that among the most meaningful First Church activities are the small potluck groups, which provide a way to meet and know people better. Additionally, both were deeply impressed by the way this congregation came together in its response to the Heifer Project a couple of years ago.

Retired since 1992, the Kendalls keep busy traveling, spending time with their family - scattered from St. Cloud to the Michigan upper peninsula to Baltimore - and remaining very involved with First Church, the community, and their residential co-op. They can sometimes be spotted in remote places, where Bob officiates at the weddings and funerals of family members, colleagues, and/or their children.

~Ruth Knutson~

Ruth Knutson is a quiet force in whatever circles she travels. Ruth Carlson grew up Methodist, one of eight children in Farmington, Minnesota. Her parents were active in the church, her mother as the pianist, and her father as the treasurer. She was a member of the Epworth League, the predecessor of the MYF.

Ruth's interest in social justice dates back to her childhood. She remembers her church being in sympathy with Ghandi's work for peace. She also remembers her mother always having a meal for any hobo that knocked on the door during those depression years, even though times were tough for their large family too. The family also welcomed the black Rust College singers into their home when they needed a place to stay while on tour.

Ruth married Russell Knutson, and they lived in Mississippi afterwards, where she worked in a library. Ruth was warned not to go to a storeroom upstairs, as that was where the black custodians took their breaks. She ignored that advice, and became friends with her coworkers.

Russell and Ruth had two daughters, Katherine and Martha (Imani). Tragedy struck when Russell died in 1958, and the girls were only three and four years old. Ruth returned to the University of Minnesota, where she got a teaching degree with kindergarten and primary license. During those days, Ruth said, it was "one day at a time; I didn't dare think of the next day."

She interviewed for a job in St. Cloud with Kermit Eastman, and believes "the kids got me the job!" She told Mr. Eastman that she would have to bring the children along. They sat quietly reading and coloring during the interview. Ruth admits that she used bribery that day for about the only time of her parenthood, promising the girls a treat if they behaved!

When she and the girls came to St. Cloud in 1961, they tried several churches. The kids liked it at First Church, and Ruth felt comfortable here as well. She was too overwhelmed with work at the time to do anything but come to Sunday services. She did, however, sing in the choir.

Serving the church became a priority after Ruth got her feet on the ground. She has served in many capacities, but never teaching Sunday school. The closest she got was serving as co-superintendent with Dixie Purdom. Other committees she served on were Memorials and Fine Arts, Worship, and Adult Education, where she was chair for several years. She also headed up the "Flower Committee," working with Karel Helgeson and Jim Hendershot. She served one year on the Stewardship Committee.

In addition, Ruth has helped get ready for Annual Conference at SCSU. Dorothy Stueve made both red and yellow vests to identify the helpers, and Ruth located the company that sewed the Methodist emblems on each vest. Then she took charge of finding and organizing the helpers for Conference registration for two or three years.

A recent project was getting the church library back into shape after a number of years of neglect.

~Richard and Mary Beth Megarry~

The Megarry name has been on the church rosters since 1945 - the year Richard's father moved the family from Aitkin, Minnesota, to St. Cloud and the year his sister, Pat (now Pat Petraborg), graduated from high school. Another sister, Jean (Eckberg), was also a member of First Church.

Dick was a sophomore at Tech High School that fall and remembers an active Methodist Youth Fellowship (MYF) at the church: "all four of us." There were three active young men and one young woman, whom he described as "very quiet." The young woman was Arlene Mittlestadt (later Helgeson). He reminisces that the MYF met in the granite-walled basement of the old church. There was a small basketball court down there, so the boys would play basketball until Rev. Logan and his wife arrived to lead MYF.

Dick remembers that the old church had a large room separated from the sanctuary by a huge, noisy, roll-down, wooden wall. When the wall was down during a church service, it hid the view, but the congregation could hear everything going on in that room. He remembers that the ladies always wore hats to services. There were many young families, and Sunday school classes were held all over the church, even in the kitchen, with the boys separated from the girls. At that time, the boys were expected to be the ushers for church services. If Dick tried to skip church - and ushering - his mother wouldn't let him have the keys to her car; his attendance, therefore, was quite commendable.

In 1957 Richard married Mary Beth, and she joined the congregation. They were the Junior High MYF leaders until the early 1960's when their own children required their time and energy. Their oldest son, Dirk Richard, was confirmed in 1976 and now resides in Prior Lake, MN; Brent Hugh, confirmed in 1979, resides in New Mexico; and Ross Charles, confirmed in 1983, presently lives in Lakeville, MN.

Memorials, including the artwork displayed in our church, are especially meaningful to both Megarrys. They include the wood carving in the sanctuary, the artwork on the walls of the library, and the stained glass windows. Dick points out the beauty and inspiration those windows bring to the sanctuary when the sun streams through them and floods the church with color. He was very involved with the creation and implementation of our present Memorial Garden.

Now retired, the Megarrys enjoy spending time with their family. Both continue to be active at First United Methodist Church.

~Tony and Fern Michalski~

Tony and Fern Michalski are longtime, active members at First Church. Fern says they came to St. Cloud around 1950 for Tony's teaching job at Tech High School. Although they originally belonged to another Methodist church, Fern began attending a circle at First Methodist, and eventually they transferred their membership.

They were committed participants. Fern commented that she worked at church "a lot" and that she spent a great deal of time in the kitchen. She was very active with United Methodist Women (UMW) and guesses that she worked at thirty annual rummage sales. She also estimates she taught Sunday school classes for more than 25 years, mostly fourth graders. Everything was a pleasurable experience for her, she said, and she was glad to be part of it. She feels that the people she met and knew over the years were wonderful parts of her life - among them, Ruth Haverland, Helen Bensen, and Ruth Skewes.

Tony, an art teacher, was very active, too, and served on many committees. He designed and built the wooden coat 'hooks' near the sanctuary in the office/library hallway.

Fern feels they best served our church when she and Tony took young people from our church to the church in Pine Bend, Minnesota, for one or two weeks in the summer. They conducted a Bible school on the White Earth Indian Reservation for three summers. The entire Michalski family (six children) went along. The first year there were only nine participants, but by the last year, when Fern was the only one of her family to accompany the youth, there were many more. They literally lived in the church - sleeping (Fern remembers lots of bats), eating, and providing activities. She recalled that it wasn't so much about teaching Christianity as it was about just being there with the White Earth young people. Fern served as cook and "the mom in charge of the kids."

Tony eventually taught art at South Junior High for 15 years, and Fern, who was one of the first nontraditional students at St. Cloud State, earned her degree in elementary education in 1969. She was a substitute teacher for five years before retiring when Tony did in 1983. Tony and Fern presently reside at Talahi Care Center.

~Peter and Monica Nayenga~

Peter and Monica Nayenga and their four children left Uganda in 1977 after Idi Amin came to power. Dr. Nayenga taught for one year in Florida and then moved to St. Cloud State University, where he has taught since then. He is presently finishing up his second term as chair of the History Department. His specialty is East African history, with a particular emphasis on Uganda. Monica works for the Faculty Association office at St. Cloud State.

Their family is different from most U.S. families, in that the Nayengas are called "father" and "mother" by more than just their own biological children. This is due to how Africans define what constitutes a family. Peter and Monica adopted a niece and a nephew and brought them to the U.S. They also have been instrumental in the education of three older children of the same family, who became orphans when Monica's sister died. In addition, they have sponsored five relatives, who for years lived with them, finished school, and become gainfully employed in the U.S.

When the Nayengas came to St. Cloud, they needed to find a family church. Although both were Episcopalian, and Peter is the son of an Episcopalian minister, they were looking for a church that fit their family, more than for a particular denomination. Rev. Ken Beck's world view, social activism, and general friendliness pleased them, as did the church's program for the children and its attitude toward people of different races and backgrounds.

Dr. Dale Peterson and Pat Jensen were a special couple to them when they came to St. Cloud, as were Jim and Carolyn Garven. Monica says these two couples "came in and filled the void we had." Both couples were very warm to the children as well. In addition, the Nayengas found that a good number of people whom they met through the University also belonged to the church, and this helped make them feel connected.

They believe that all the ministers of the church have confirmed their decision to join First United Methodist Church. Of Rev. Toby Horst, Peter says, "He was special to us… he practiced what he preached." His concern for racial equality impressed them, as did his concern for those who were having difficult times in life.

Pastor Katie, too, was a favorite. She startled them mightily when the first Christmas she was pastor of the church, she cast their son Peter Mudima and his wife Vivienne as Joseph and Mary in the Christmas pageant, with their baby son as the newborn Jesus. Monica says, "It was very touching."

They look forward to the Rev. Bill Meier years as a continuation of First Church's traditions.

~Chauncey and Carol Oleson ~

Carol and Chauncey Oleson's caring nature is evident in all aspects of their lives. They have always enjoyed working with kids and had five children already (Christopher, Craig, Jennifer, Joni, and Eric) when they adopted Robb. They then decided to serve as foster parents and received their license in the early 70's. During this time they were living in Belgrade, Minnesota, where Chauncey was teaching vocational agriculture.

Their first foster child, a newborn, was a heartbreaker. They had her for seven and one-half months, and it was so difficult for both the child and the Olesons when she was taken away. The welfare rules did not allow foster families to adopt at the time, and all the red tape hindered a quick placement of babies into permanent homes. Their second foster child was Steve, a boy of 13 living at a boarding school, who needed a place to go for holidays. He is now 46 and very much a member of the family, still coming for all the holidays.

In 1980, the Oleson's moved to St. Cloud to establish an emergency shelter for foster kids. Police would bring babies sometimes and teenagers picked up on the streets other times. The Oleson's were on call 24 hours a day for a week at a time. In one year, they had over 100 children stay with them from one day to several weeks. During this time, Chauncey also worked as an agricultural inspector for Benton County. The first Sunday they visited First Church, their beeper went off during a time that Rev. Toby Horst's son Mark was preaching. Carol remembers being so embarrassed, although not too many people noticed.

From 1981 to 1985, Carol served First Church as a parish worker. She would visit newcomers, shut-ins, and those in the hospital, often bringing taped sermons. She also worked as the staff person with several committees, including Outreach and Worship

While their kids were at home, both Carol and Chauncey were active with the church youth activities. Chauncey served on the Missions Committee and often helped as dishwasher for the Pancake Supper. For many years, he served as a volunteer weekend custodian.

Carol has sung in the choir since they first arrived in 1980, and has never missed a Christmas Eve service. She has served as soloist both for Sunday services and also at funerals. It was hard to do the funerals, as she knew many of the people very well after visiting them as parish worker. The hardest one to do was the funeral for Sue Ezell, as she and Carol were friends and the same age. She told Wayland that she didn't know if she could get through it, but he assured her that it would be ok.

Soon after they arrived, Carol joined the UMW Esther Circle, a social and support group. Ellen Deane Schwieger invited her and took her to the meeting at Deb Danneman's. Carol has a sharp memory of little Krista, not yet 2 years old, coming downstairs in her p.j.'s to see what was going on. So, it was pretty special when Carol was the wedding coordinator for Krista's wedding a year ago. Carol served as Wedding Coordinator for our church for ten years.

In 1990, Carol and Chauncey started the first Bed and Breakfast in St. Cloud, Edelbrock House. This has been a labor of love and a way to share the amazing antique collection they have. Guests feel as if they are stepping back in time with the surroundings and the "down home" breakfasts.

Carol and Chauncey Oleson are "salt-of-the-earth" people who are among the first in line whenever someone needs help.

~Betty Partch~

A lot of old memories have been stirred up with this writing. Those six years I worked at the church office were good years. Our girls were of college age, and a little more income came in handy. I worked during the nine-month school schedule, and usually Martha Beck worked the summer hours.

Ken Beck and I worked well together. He respected my religious questioning, and I admired his constant giving of himself. He was available to anyone at any time, and certainly worked more than forty hours a week.

He frequently met other ministers for breakfast. I recall one time when he was at such a meeting and our student minister came rushing into my office with his baby, left her on the floor with a bottle, and hurried off, saying he had a telephone call that his wife was at the hospital, having been injured in a car accident on her way to school where she was a teacher. I located Ken and he went to the hospital, I fed the baby and changed her, I typed a letter, answered phone calls, sorted the mail, changed the baby, and only relaxed when word came that the wife would make a good recovery.

The work week had its own routine. Mondays were quiet days, with time to catch up on some neglected work, or to do some cleaning and straightening up. Tuesdays began to pick up speed. Wednesdays and Thursdays kept me busy, and Friday was hoping the ministers had already given me their material so that I could type up the pages of the bulletin for Sunday. Sometimes they were late, yet my work had to be at the printers by noon! And it was!

I look back on those days, and remember them with gratitude.

~Dale Peterson and Patricia Jensen ~

When we moved to St. Cloud from the Twin Cities in 1966, Florence and Ernest Stennes became our next-door neighbors. They welcomed us warmly, and helped us adjust to our new home. Knowing that we were looking for a church home, they suggested to Ken Beck that he call upon us. In our first conversation with Ken, we realized that we shared goals of equality and social justice. We also learned that a friend from our days in student housing at the University of Minnesota, Ruth Knutson, was a member.

All four of our children, Toni, Jeffrey, Traci, and Jim, were confirmed in First Church. The younger two attended Sunday school. In the summer of 1967 the Vacation Bible School included a study of environmental issues for the older children. During one of the field trips, Jeffrey stepped on a bee's nest and was stung. Ken Beck drove him to the office of Dr. Byron John for treatment, and so we became acquainted with another member of the church, and later with his wife, Joanne.

Music is an important part of our lives, and we soon joined the church choir. We very much appreciated the work of Dick and Joan Clampitt in working toward the purchase of a pipe organ, rather than an electronic one, for our sanctuary. We appreciated the stained glass windows, the marvelous wood sculpture on the sanctuary wall, and the wall hangings that have been woven and sewn by church members through the years. We learned about religion and art from the classes held by Catherine Beck.

As a professor at St. Cloud State University, Dale was asked to serve on the board for the Wesley Foundation, which later became the Ministry of Higher Education.

During the late 1970's Patricia helped to organize a women's Bible study group that met early Wednesday mornings at different downtown restaurants. It continued to meet for several years.

Our children benefitted greatly from the youth program, particularly the work of Carolyn and Jim Garven. Canoe trips, a trip to New York, and spaghetti suppers were some of their experiences. Through the Minnesota Conference our children attended summer camps in the wilderness and music camp at Koinonia. Our family went together to several family camps at Decision Hills, where we met outstanding people from other Minnesota Methodist churches.

One of our humorous memories is the wedding of associate minister, the Reverend Richard Collman. During the ceremony the bride and groom recited to one another selected passages from the Song of Solomon.

We have been blessed by having been members of the First United Methodist Church for over 40 years. The Sunday services have changed, the ministers have changed, the membership has changed, but the worship of God with other followers of Jesus Christ continues to be one of the cornerstones of the church.

~Sherwood and Carol Reid~

We moved to St. Cloud in 1965 where Sherwood completed an education degree at St. Cloud State College, and I taught at St. Cloud Tech. Life-long Methodists, we joined First Methodist and soon found ourselves assisting with the Methodist Youth Fellowship. We enjoyed working with the young people who were frequently also my classroom students at Tech and Sherwood's at the Campus Lab School where he student taught during that time.

Rev. Richard Lewis was the youth minister then, and when it came time to plan the annual, MYF-sponsored, all-church spaghetti dinner, he seemed to believe that all female youth counselors came with spaghetti recipes for 200 people naturally embedded in their knowledge banks. This one did not. Somehow we managed; I remembered that we ran out of pasta and were thankful that Coborn's was right across the street. After that, there was always a recipe/shopping list on file for future reference.

Sherwood remembers the IPG (Inter-Personal Groups) of the late sixties and early seventies. They were made up of groups of First Methodist teens that met frequently to talk about their concerns. It was a form of group counseling, and the groups met at our home on weeknight evenings. We were amazed at the number of young people and their friends who showed up at our door. Eventually, Sherwood's job at St. Cloud State and the births of our children, Michael and Rebecca, forced our retirement from MYF.

The early 1970's stand out in my mind. Carolyn Garven and I agreed to teach the 1971-72 eighth-grade confirmation class. We had planned to share responsibilities until we discovered there were 40 eighth graders enrolled. So we split them - each taking 20. Knowing what I do now, I don't know how we did it. Twenty giggly, wiggly adolescents in a Bible study class that met every Wednesday evening was not an ideal situation.

At about the same time, a group of us with pre-schoolers decided to form a morning church circle. While the group met in the church library, a sitter (often one of us) supervised our children in the nursery. We tapped community resources for speakers who covered subjects useful to mothers of young children - from theology to child development to County Extension Service topics. We published and sold a couple recipe books (I still have them!) and sponsored and stocked a Children's Shopping Room at the annual Church Bazaar. Eventually, the circle disbanded because most of us returned to work once our children entered school. We formed some solid friendships that remain to this day - among both moms and kids.

Sherwood re-surfaced amidst First United Methodist youth twice in the 80's when he accompanied them on trips to the BWCA - a place he still frequents.

Retired since 1998, we both now spend much of our time in out-of-door activities. The dirt under my nails is from my own yard as well as from the First Church gardens. I greatly appreciate every person who has donated plants or spent time weeding, watering, composting, and mulching. Appreciated equally are all those who can take the time to enjoy the results of our labors.

~ Phil and Val Rogosheske~

Phil and Val joined the church in 1972, shortly after they were married and came to live in St. Cloud, where Phil grew up. They spent their youth in the Lutheran Church - Phil was Missouri Synod and Val was ELCA - but they liked the social justice emphasis of First Methodist and Ken. They were honored to talk theology with Ken on occasional evenings in their home when he was making his rounds.

Phil and Val have enjoyed singing in the choir for most of their time here, taking a break for a couple of years when Allie and Abby were young. During those years, Val led a sing-a-long for the church school children to start the Sunday school hour. Both of them believe that our church has been very lucky to have topnotch choir directors over the years: Shirley Holzer, Priscilla Woodley, Bruce Wood, Christopher Larsen, and Steve Mick. Val says, "They all did a wonderful job of expecting great things of the choir, while still making it fun." Both praise Tess Kasling, church organist, as being both inspirational and fun.

Val and Phil served on many committees over the years but, with their education backgrounds, usually returned to Adult Education. With a special interest in changing the church's official stance toward homosexuality, they helped start a new committee with an emphasis on welcoming all. This committee coordinated a 5-week Sunday evening study of an inclusive Biblical view of homosexuality. More recently, they and others have presented a major study each January: on Islam (2006), Christianity (2007), and War and Religion (2008).

First Church's involvement in the Great River Interfaith Partnership (GRIP) has been beneficial for Val. She found that individuals from a variety of faith communities can actually make a difference in their areas by working together. "It was amazing to see what was accomplished with affordable housing, housing discrimination, racial profiling, and a (soon-to-be) Regional Human Rights Office in St. Cloud."

Val is very grateful to Marcia Summers, Jessie Harper, and Joanne R. John for beginning a feminist theology book group that evolved into a progressive theology book gathering. The information, role models, and support she found in this weekly group have been powerful influences on the development of her spirituality. Phil taught confirmation for five years with Jim Garven Evelyn Durkee, and Sharon Olson. Phil's theology continues to be transformed by reading the likes of John T. Robinson, John Spong and Michael Morwood. He also often read books from Val's women's group.

~Jerry Sales~

As a 'farm kid,' Jerry Sales attended Sunday school at the Methodist Church in town. Therefore, when he, his wife, Donna, and their family came to St. Cloud in the early 60's, he said it just seemed natural to attend First Methodist Church.

Reverend Metzger was the pastor at the time, and Jerry recalls that everything was more formal. "We'd bring our three kids to church and hope they'd behave through the entire service." Ministers were always called "Reverend" back then - never by their first names. Now children are included in the service, and the congregation calls the minister by his first name. He feels the less formal, first-name approach "is a good thing because it breaks the barrier of title and brings a congregation closer to its spiritual leader."

Jerry, a former junior high social studies teacher, has always appreciated the emphasis the Methodist Church places on social outreach, locally and beyond. He values the Church's flexibility, open mindedness, and social activism. He also appreciates the opportunity for spiritual retreats that the church offers and the manner in which they bring good changes to an individual's life.

In his forty-plus years at First Church, Jerry has been most impressed by the influence of its people on his spiritual growth - generally and specifically. He recalls Rev. Kenneth Beck - a tennis player like himself - as a 'quiet, charismatic, gentle, supportive individual. "We'd play tennis and then talk." Jerry's associations with various First Church programs and committees have brought him in contact with many others whom he considers "spiritual directors" in his life, instrumental in his becoming a more committed Christian. Among them are Jim and Mary Wagner, whom he cites as exemplary "role models of caring and nurturing in this church."

Finally, involvement with the 150th anniversary and the intricate "visioning" program has caused Jerry to hold in highest respect "all of those active members who have kept this church so viable and socially significant over the years." Basic to this, he emphasizes, have been a dedicated staff, past and present.

Retired since 1993, Jerry enjoys coaching a little tennis, traveling with Donna, attending musical events, toiling in the church gardens, and - as another member stated - tirelessly assisting wherever he may be needed at First United Methodist.

~ Brian and Kim Salisbury ~

Kim has the interesting history of knowing Rev. Bill Meier "back in the day." She grew up in Owatonna, and his father was her minister. She graduated from high school with Bill's older twin sisters. Bill and Kim have an agreement not to tell tales on each other!

Kim graduated from Mankato State University, where she studied microbiology. She met Brian at MSU, but they didn't date until several years later. They married in 1983 and lived in Minneapolis, where Brian worked for Donaldson's. They attended Brooklyn Center Methodist.

Brian took a job with Herberger's, which brought them to St. Cloud in December of 1987. They looked at both Lutheran and Methodist churches. Rev. Toby Horst came to see them, and that helped them decide on First Church. Kim was interested in volunteering at the church from the start. She was a full-time mom to Amanda, and Tony was born two years later.

Kim involved their kids in volunteer work at a young age. She regularly did Meals on Wheels deliveries, and Amanda and Tony helped by being "milk kids."

The most amazing memory Kim has of teaching Sunday school was her first year. She had three sets of twins in the fourth grade class! The Sunday school classes were large at the time. Kim remembers about 15 in a group. With a start like that, it's a wonder that she taught for 10 years, until Tony was ready for confirmation class.

Kim has served on the Children's Committee. She also did several terms on the Church and Society Committee, now called Faith in Action. But one of her biggest passions has been for the Community Meals, now called 3rd Saturday Meal. Kim helped with those for over 10 years.

She and Brian continued working with youth when their kids were older. They several times did spring clean-up at Camp Friendship with a group of teens. Kim has a funny memory of driving with John Harper, and within a minute, he had reset every button on her dashboard!

Kim did some informal activities with church as well, one of which led to the resurrection of her cello. On a canoe trip with First Church women, there was talk about playing instruments. Val Rogosheske mentioned that Phil had been taking violin lessons and was looking for a small group. Kim said that she had played the cello years ago, so it ended up that Kim found a cello, and she and Phil recruited another violin and a viola player, and formed a quartet! They stayed together for some time, played in church, and even participated in the church band/orchestra a time or two.

In later years, Kim has been a member of Lydia Circle, a non-traditional, "working" circle. They choose projects, but have no meetings; they just get together to do the activity.

Brian has been a constant presence and help with all of the projects around church, even the circle ones! He calls himself a charter member of Lydia Circle. But his memories center more around ushering and greeting, work on the pancake supper, and doing the river clean-up. He also helped teach confirmation during those years when their kids were involved. Brian has fun memories of the years First Church had a golf league, and would play on the Veteran's Golf Course.

Kim and Brian have been a steady presence in making sure faith is expressed in action at First Church.

~Brad and Ellen Deane Schwieger~

Ellen Deane and Brad both are life-long Methodists, although Ellen Deane attended Quaker Meeting for five years at one point. They have been members at First Church since they came to St. Cloud in 1976, with a short break in the middle when they were members at Salem Lutheran, where Ellen Deane led a children's choir.

Both have been very active members, contributing to the life of First Church in many ways. Since first joining, they have been members of the choir, and Ellen Deane has served as a soloist on numerous occasions. Ellen Deane directed several youth choirs here, and Brad has worked with the church's finances.

Ellen Deane majored in music and arrived here with children's church choir experience from her time in Tennessee. So her gift to the church was to give First Church youth a quality musical experience. There were two children's choirs, a youth choir and two children's bell choirs. "I didn't do it alone," Ellen Deane protested. She especially remembers the leadership of Karen Sheffield, who worked with the bell choirs. "I remember one evening concert, with all the candelabras lit … the youth walked down the center aisle, ringing as they went, to open the event." That special group of youth, including Scott Halberg, Debbie Peterson, Arthur Schwieger, Sterling Schwieger, Laura Van Nostrand, Cathy Van Nostrand, Lori Wenstrom, and Jim Peterson, really made some beautiful music. Ellen Deane continued her music ministry with her piano studio, The Music Place, in which she instilled a love of music in many of our children.

Bradley has taught accounting at SCSU since coming to St. Cloud. He has shared his financial acumen as a member of the Finance Committee for many years. He also served as Treasurer of First Church. He found it enjoyable, but there was always the worry if we would make it to the end of the year. Brad's take on the church's money issues: "In the 31 years that I have served, we have always had financial difficulties. We are in a situation where we can't afford two ministers and can't get by with one. But every year, the congregation comes through. We have made our conference apportionment payments every year - not every church can say that."

Ellen Deane and Brad have many happy and funny memories of First Church. One spring evening Brad was bringing Arthur home from 7th grade confirmation. Arthur sighed, "Only one more meeting…" Brad replied, "Well, yes, but then there are two more years." He was afraid Arthur was going to open the car door and jump in the river!

They really appreciated Ken Beck's leadership style of trusting a person to get the job done - "he let a person do their thing." One of their favorite stories of Ken's famous evening visits was when they were new to the church and Ken walked in as Ellen Deane was preparing a pizza for supper. "Who threw up on my lefsa?" he exclaimed.

Connecting with people is important to both Ellen Deane and Brad. Whether that is done on an individual basis, or in an organized way, such as potluck groups (which Ellen Deane has led), people are the church. Ellen Deane loves the coffee hour - "The coffee hour is the communion." That is often where the best connections are made.

~Dorothy Stueve~

Dorothy has been a St. Cloud area Methodist her whole life, being baptized in the old church in 1931. Her parents were Lillian and Arthur Bluhm. She remembers the old First Methodist church very well. She used to come to it with her father at 8:30 Sunday morning and help him set up for Sunday school in the basement gymnasium. Then she would go to Sunday school herself, and after that, church, sitting in the pew where the family sat every Sunday. Because services under Rev. Logan were an hour and a half, it was at least 12:30 p.m. before her family headed home for Sunday dinner.

Dorothy has many memories of the old church. When she was high school age, she attended Sunday school in a room off the balcony of the sanctuary, played volley ball, basketball, and shuffle board in the basement gymnasium, and teetered on a narrow ledge to pull Sunday school supplies out of a cupboard by the stairs. She remembers some of her Sunday school teachers: Mrs. Hammond, Mrs. Binnie, Mary Francis Peterson.

Dorothy has served her church well, in the women's society for many years, and then for seven years in the paid position of church hostess. Rev. Beck saw the need for someone to coordinate hospitality for the church - funerals, coffees, and luncheons - as well as to supervise the kitchen. Dorothy seemed the perfect choice because, as Rev. Beck said, "You're down here all the time anyway. You might as well get paid for it." And, Dorothy says, "I enjoyed it." For a while later, she was also responsible for seeing that the church got cleaned, along with some part-time help.

Dorothy continues to serve in UMW, and is presently chair of her circle. She also has worked on the United Methodist Women Conference Team for nominations and is now working on nominations at the District level.

Dorothy married Ernest Stueve, and they had three girls: Kris, Penny, and Jodi Ann. Her husband died in 1992. She has three grandchildren and two great grandchildren.

~Marcia Summers~

Marcia Summers came to St. Cloud in the fall of 1969 to begin her career as a professor of English at St. Cloud State. She and her daughter, Lisa, visited various churches in the community and were drawn to First Methodist Church because of its caring members, its values, and its theology.

Dee and Laurie Halberg were some of the first people to reach out and include them in their own family activities; Marcia credits Dee with helping her to become connected with others in the church. Another was Fern Michalski, whose friendliness and dedication to church school teaching made a deep impression on Marcia. Special relationships developed with elders Anna Johnson and Hazel Rau, who also provided role models for aging gracefully. Especially important for Marcia were long-lasting friendships with Ruth Knutson and Sue Land.

Marcia feels she and Lisa remained with this church because of its "Biblical preaching, its commitment to social justice and action, and the opportunities it offered for serious theological reflection while accepting differing viewpoints." The church's practice of open communion, that all are welcome at the Table of the Lord, is important to her because she grew up in a church where the ritual of communion was for members only. Because her parents were not members of the church, they could not participate in communion, though they attended weekly. That experience of exclusion makes our pastor's welcoming invitation to communion deeply moving for Marcia.

Significant memories include the sermon Talk Backs, held in the church kitchen during the Vietnam era, when Ken Beck welcomed congregational responses to his sermons. Marcia also remembers the fun of family sledding and cross-country ski weekends in the mid-seventies at a Methodist camp in Wisconsin. It was in our church that she gave her one and only sermon, "Jesus and Women," when feminist theology was emerging.

Especially important for spiritual growth, friendship and support over the years have been several women's groups. These began in the 80's, with years of early morning breakfast Bible studies at Perkins before participants went off to work. When they retired, she and Dee Halberg began the Thursday Reading Group, in which women delved into many challenging books of spirituality and contemporary theology as well as shared their lives. More recently, she has been part of the Oasis group and attended several of its retreats led by Pastor Katie.

Missions, Finance, Adult Education, GRIP, and CARE Team are some of the areas in which this active, committed member has been involved over the years.

~Larry and Ruth Sundby~

In 1945, when I [Larry] was four years old, my parents moved to St. Cloud and became members of our Methodist church. Soon after I began attending Sunday school. At that time we were in the church building that preceded our current facility. I recall that we had a good recreation area in the basement that included a short basketball court.

I remember we had a Cub Scout pack and later a Boy Scout troop. It met at the church and was led by Max Partch and was a lot of fun. As a teenager I was active in MYF and had the chance to be the MYF President one year.

Later, since I attended St. Cloud State, I was involved with Wesley Foundation, which was located in a house near the campus. We were an active group, and I recall we often sang as a choir at First Methodist. By that time, the old church was gone, and we were in our current church. Reverend Richard Lewis") was the campus minister, and we became good friends - a friendship no doubt enhanced because we both enjoyed playing tennis. Richard married my wife, Ruth, and me in 1963. It was his first marriage ceremony, and he misspoke and said, "in Holy headlock." We still joke about it.

One of the differences between the 1950 - 1970 years and today is that in the former years, the college-age students were very involved in our church. Now they appear to have no active role in its activities. One good thing about today's youth, however, is the mission trips and social work that they participate in. We did not have the chance to do things of that nature when I was a youth.

Our daughters, Kristin and Julie, grew up at First Church and are still members. They had their weddings in our church. Reverend Lewis") was in St. Cloud for a visit at the time of Kristin's wedding and had a part in the ceremony, which made it especially nice for Ruth and me.

We now have a fourth generation involved in First Church activities. Our grandchildren enjoy Sunday school and actually have been in the church facility quite often because they all attended Montessori School here. Ruth and I cannot imagine not being members at First United Methodist. This church has been a part of our lives for such a long time. Throughout the years we have both served on a variety of committees and have been involved with many activities. We hope to be active members for many years to come.

~Jo Tennison ~

Jo Tennison was Director of Children's Education at First Methodist Church during most of the 1970's. She says that although she had grown up in the Lutheran Church, she and her family were drawn to our church for many reasons - the first being Rev. Kenneth Beck's thought-provoking sermons, which "always took me further in my spiritual growth." Eventually, when she joined the church staff, she was further impressed by his leadership, consistency, and honesty.

She related that the church staff at that time included Jim Garven and Carol Oleson and met each week, with staff members taking turns opening the meetings with devotions. Jo felt it was a meaningful way to gain a deeper understanding of each other and develop collegiality.

Over all, Jo remembers the people in the church being "very giving, giving unselfishly, putting into real life God's love flowing through us." She remembers Dorothy Stueve sewing all new robes for the children's choir. Jo also remembers Betty Partch inviting her and young daughters, Juli and Dana, to her home for a tea party because she felt that all little girls should have a tea party experience. Dee and Laurie Halberg also stand out in her memory for their leadership in many areas and the time and service they devoted to our church.

One story Jo tells was triggered by Michael Barone - the organist at that time. Michael wore his hair in a pony tail and sandals on his feet all year round. One time she overheard some Sunday school children talking in the hall as they saw Michael enter the sanctuary. One of them exclaimed, "That's Jesus!" Jo realized that the children were never in church during a service and had no idea what really occurred. She brought it up at a staff meeting, and it was decided the children should spend ten minutes in the service each Sunday before heading to their classes. Although Ken Beck didn't do children's sermons, this was the beginning of having the youngsters join the congregation in church.

Jo has always been connected to education in some form - earning her Doctorate in Education in 1993 followed by college-level teaching and administration. Retired since 2002, she has researched, written and published stories of the ancestral history of her father's family. She presently enjoys volunteering at a hospital and the Guthrie Theater, as well as spending time with her family and grandchildren.

~Pat Tonnell~

How does a woman who went to Catholic boarding school when she was young and signed up to become a Marine after high school end up at the First United Methodist Church with 30 years of Sunday school teaching on her resume? Pat Tonnell has lead an interesting life. When she was ten and her adoptive mother died, she was sent to boarding school in the South. Because at first she did not have too many friends, she ended up going to mass every day and listening to the service. In addition, a nun whom she very much admired, would lead religious instruction for the Catholic children, and Pat sat back at her desk and listened, probably harder than many of the children being instructed.

This was the first Pat had heard about God, and those new ideas were welcome ones. A loving God was a comfort to a young girl who had lost two mothers and was away from home. Pat never joined the Catholic Church, even though her husband, Wilfred, was a non-practicing Catholic. Instead, when she moved to St. Cloud to take a job at the hospital, she started attending the Methodist church, at a time when it was still the old church and Rev. Huffman was the minister.

Before she even joined the church, she was teaching Sunday school and heading a church circle. As Pat says, "It was a friendly church." In the end, she taught Sunday school for 30 years and taught almost all the grades. She liked the children, and they liked her.

One of her teaching stories happened when she was leading second grade and was having trouble adapting the official curriculum to her children. Rev. Beck was the minister then, and he said that he would come up to the classroom for a few minutes at a time in the church service when he was not leading things. He came, got into conversations with the children, and everyone was having a good time. Soon Pat heard the organ music from downstairs getting louder and louder. She puzzled aloud as to why this was so. Rev. Beck realized that it was his cue to come back to the sanctuary and give his sermon.

Pat's three children, Mary, Harland, and Roberta, were brought up in the church, and Pat worked for many years in the office at Big Bear and then at Jennings Insurance. Her husband died in 1990.

~Annette DeCourcy Towler~

Being an active, involved church worker is nothing new for this busy person. Annette was born into a parsonage family, played for weddings at 16, taught music, raised a family, trained church school teachers, created a niche job for herself at Sherco, and later directed her love of history into heading up the writing team for the 150th Anniversary history of First Church.

Annette's parents were the Rev. Frank and Genevieve Pack DeCourcy. During Annette's high school days, the family lived in Sherburn, Minnesota, close to the Iowa state line. Iowa couples wanting to get married faced a required blood test and a waiting period, so they would come to Minnesota to get married. "Same day" weddings could be performed in Minnesota, which many clergy did. Her father, Annette recalls, did "next-day" weddings and only after visiting with the couples and urging them to "think it over." A phone call to the local high school would get her excused from classes to provide music, playing the organ and running the phonograph so "The Lord's Prayer" was sung from a 33 rpm record for those informal ceremonies, she added. Her Dad would not marry them in the parsonage but at the church. No money was given for playing, just a hankie for each wedding.

After high school graduation, Annette enrolled at Hamline University, from which she graduated with a major in Music, training as an organist, and a minor in Religious Studies (specializing in Christian Education). That training would serve her well through the next period of her life.

It was during visits to her parents in Redwood where she met her future husband, a young man with similar interests in music. Life together after marriage took them to Minneapolis and to Willow River, where they both taught music. For four years, 1972-1976, Annette was a Minnesota Methodist Conference Field Worker, offering training to Sunday school and vacation Bible school teachers in all Conference training workshops in Minnesota Methodist churches. They moved to the St. Cloud area in 1974.

Before attending First Church, the Towlers were associated with one of our neighboring churches, where her husband was choir director, Annette was children's choir director, Sunday school teacher, and organist. Two of the three children, John, and Cheryl, were confirmed there, while the eldest, Nanette, had been confirmed earlier "up north." Music and youth activities at First Church attracted the family - children's choirs, handbells, Methodist Youth Fellowship. The handbell choir also attracted Annette. All three kids and Annette's grandson, Andrew, whom she also raised, were at First Church.

In 1986 Annette took a temporary job at the Sherburne County Generating Plant, Northern States Power Company (NSP), better known as Sherco, auditing drawing changes from the projects of building the three generating units, which led her to help create a unique database. That database made her "indispensable." She was hired full time, eventually becoming the webmaster and IT Business Representative for the Becker plant before her October 2005 retirement.

First Church became "home" for Annette in 2003. Why First Church? "I'm comfortable with the theology and the worship setting and I'm back home in a Methodist Church," Annette quickly responded.

First Church's History Book project, she adds, "is my biggest challenge ever!" One major side-benefit is that the project reconnects her to a fellow Hamline college friend, Nancy Gundersen.

Sunday afternoons might well find Annette playing for Protestant services at St. Benedict's, a volunteer job which she finds fulfilling. In addition to music, Ms. Towler had a continuing passion for genealogy - her own and others. She is an active member of the St. Cloud Area Genealogy (SCAG) organization and National Genealogical Society, and she finds time for classes and further training in the field.

First Church is the beneficiary of Annette DeCourcy Towler's gifts, presence and service.

~Jim and Mary Wagner~

Mary and Jim Wagner arrived at First Methodist Church in 1954 as 21-year old newlyweds. The vote to build a new sanctuary had occurred, and they were just in time for the fund-raising! Since then, the two of them have never stopped giving to the church in numerous ways.

Mary was an active member of the Women's Society of Christian Service, the precursor of the UMW. As often as once per month, they would serve chicken dinners to various groups as fund raisers. This was such a regular occurrence that the WSCS was often referred to as "Women Serving Chicken Suppers." They used the funds from these dinners, along with the proceeds from the Cherry Pie Festival and the Fall Festival, for missions and youth camperships.

Mary does not hesitate to jump in when she sees a need. She was on the original committee to organize Home Delivered Meals in St. Cloud. More recently, someone asked if she would start a prayer-shawl ministry at First Church. Mary does not even knit, but she connected with about 20 people who wanted to help, and now there are two groups going. Mary is also an active member of the Care Team.

Jim has been a stalwart member of the Men's Club for over 50 years. "The Pancake Supper had been started before I arrived - but not too much earlier!" He remembers Dan Chamberlin had the original pancake griddles made at the Vo Tech School and the Men's Pancake Supper becoming an annual event after the new kitchen was fully equipped by the UMW of the church. He always felt good about the local benefits the Men's Club provided: the Bibles for the children, maintenance project money for the church and youth camperships. More recently, they have funded Nets for the World campaign to stop malaria.

Jim has been on the Building Management Committee for about 25 years, and has regularly served as a weekend custodian. First Church can always count on him for help with the building.

Mary remembers that there were only men ushers in the early days, and only about six to eight men involved at a time: Clint Hill, Carl Peterson, Hillis Myers, Harvey Hannahs, Ron Weaver, and Fred Rau were some they remember. These men, always dressed in dark suits and ties, greeted people before each service.

Mary and Jim strongly feel that all our pastors have in their own way been a positive influence on First Church, making our church an open and accepting place of worship.

The Wagners had a special link with Ken Beck. Ken married Jim and Mary in Raymond, Minnesota, Ken's second charge. Catherine Beck still laughs when she remembers Mary coming to the parsonage door and saying, "I want to get married!" Catherine wondered if Mary had anyone in mind when she made her announcement! Jim was stationed in the Army in Indiana, so Mary had to make plans alone.

It was a pleasant surprise when Ken followed them to St. Cloud, and ended up being the marriage celebrant at First Church for both of the Wagners' children, Deb and Tim. Ken and Catherine also were able to attend the Wagners' 50th wedding anniversary.

Jim and Mary conclude, "We are thankful we have had First Church as our place of worship for the past 53 years as we have expanded our Christian faith." And First Church is lucky to have such vital church members!

~Sam Wenstrom~

Sam has lived in the St. Cloud area most of his life. He was born in Waite Park and later lived on a farm in Haven Township. Sam's family was very involved in the Waite Park Methodist Church.

After high school, Sam worked his way through St. Cloud State College as a late night disc jockey at KFAM. He became WJON's first news director in 1955 and assistant manager of the St. Cloud Chamber of Commerce in 1963. His last job was working for 19 years at the St. Cloud Hospital, the final 14 years as the Director for Human Resources and Communication.

Sam's wife, Maxine, was a delightful member of the Church, sunny and friendly. She served as secretary to four St. Cloud mayors and became the first City of St. Cloud Human Resources Director. Maxine died in May 2001. Sam and Maxine had three daughters: Lisa, Lori, and Lynn. Through the years, Sam has been involved in the work of the Church. He laments that the church did not buy nearby houses to give it a parking lot. He says the church could have acquired adequate parking for about $175,000 at one time. Later, when he was chair of the Church Board of Trustees, he decided to lead a campaign to acquire a large, old house across the alley from the church and turn its lot into parking.

Not everyone was enthusiastic about his plans. Money had to be secured to buy the house, and this meant taking on some debt. A campaign was mounted. Church members were informed about the need, and enough were willing to go along with the plan. In addition, the Church had to acquire a conditional use permit to do the lot, as it could not meet the City zoning code. A parking lot was designed similar to the City Hall's parking lot (which also did not meet code), and members of the Church lobbied Council members. In the end the plan received unanimous approval from the Council.

Earlier Rev. Horst asked Sam to head an effort to get an elevator for the church, as well as better handicapped facilities. Sam and a committee accomplished that task as well, completing it in 1987.

Sam speaks of some of the people he has known through the Church: "Glenn Carlson - a prince of a fellow… an honest Christian, hard-working, happy sort of guy." "Ken Beck was one of my favorites… he was a good man." Woody Wilson, Jim Wagner, Bob Kugler, Shirley Echols, Lois Barron, Glenna

Cheney, Jewell Paulson, Dorothy Stueve - "they really kind of lived right and gave so much to our church."

~Dale and Edythe Williams~

Dale and Edythe came to St. Cloud from Tulsa, Oklahoma, in 1987, the same year their oldest daughter, Eileen, went away to college. Their three younger children, Ryan, Leanna, and Priscilla, moved with them.

Before being part of the Chancel Choir at First Church, Dale and Edythe had a long involvement with choirs, starting with them both being in choir as undergraduates at Taylor University. Dale says that they always sang in a church choir wherever they lived.

Edythe has directed a number of children's choirs, including one at Boston Avenue United Methodist Church in Tulsa. That was a big church with about 7,000 members. She also directed the children's choir at First Church in the late 1980's. Her daughters Leanna and Priscilla helped her with this activity, as they too had considerable interest in music. All the the younger Williams are musical, and all have played musical instruments for the congregation at one time or another. Ryan, along with his father, played in the bell choir for some years.

Dale has chaired the Adult Council, chaired the Administrative Council, and was on both the Staff Parish Committee and the Finance Committee, serving as chairman on the later. He is now on the Board of Trustees. Edythe served on the Worship Committee and chaired the Adult Council.

One of Dale's good memories of church work involves supporting Sam Wenstrom in his efforts to get the church's most recent parking lot. Dale felt strongly that the church needed this lot and was pleased when it became a reality.

Dale retired as Associate Dean of the College of Science and Engineering at St. Cloud State University in June 2007. Edythe retired from the Central Minnesota Music School at the same time. She continues to teach piano to a few students in her neighborhood area.

Dale and Edythe plan to keep active in two community chorales: Minnesota Center Chorale and Great River Chorale. Traveling to some new places is also on their schedule of things to do. That includes visiting their children: Eileen and husband, Craig, and granddaughter, Celia, in Evanston, Illinois: Ryan and Nicki and grandson, Wyatt, in Edina, Minnesota; Leanna in Rochester, Minnesota; and Priscilla in Albuquerque, New Mexico.

Eileen is vice president of an arts management firm, Ryan uses his mathematical expertise for investment house work, Leanna is a nurse specialist in oncology and hematology at Methodist Hospital in Rochester, and Priscilla is a civilian architect and interior designer for the air force.

~Harold Zosel~

Harold was born in Wadena and brought up in the Methodist Church. As a young man he went to Anchorage, Alaska, to work for the Bank of Alaska. In 1962 he returned to the Lower Forty-eight, and came to St. Cloud to work in the Murphy Finance office. Here he was an assistant to Woody Wilson, a member of First Church. Harold has been in the insurance and financial services business for the past 42 years.

While new to St. Cloud, he met Mary Hall, daughter of the *St. Cloud Daily Time's* photographer, Myron Hall. She was working as a lifeguard at the swimming pool. Harold says that at that time in St. Cloud, "If you weren't Catholic and if you weren't born here, you were in trouble." Mary, who was a Catholic, must have made allowances for him, however, for they were married soon after. They have two children, Katie and Sam.

In the 1970's, during the time Rev. Beck was here, Harold transferred his church membership from Wadena. Harold says fondly of Ken Beck, "Whether you agreed with him or disagreed with him, you liked him."

Harold has been on church committees for "about everything" over the years, but one assignment he has held for many years is the Men's Club presidency. He explains that this came about during a big meeting. He was nominated for president, and Warren Hutchens was nominated as secretary/treasurer. Both were elected. They remained in charge until Hutchens died, and then Glenn Wischmann became treasurer.

Because the Club is not extremely active but needs someone to keep it running, Harold has remained president since and claims that he was "nominated by John Wesley and seconded by Charles." He signs his local conference reports "President in Perpetuity." The two big events of the club are the summer fishing trip and the fall pancake supper.

Harold mentions with justifiable pride the donations the club is able to make to the church from their pancake meals: Bibles for the third grade students, financial support for the former Boy Scout Troop I, and a variety of other things that normally aren't covered in the church budget.

One other thing: Harold is a deltiologist, a collector of old postcards. Several of his cards were copied for this history. He enjoys researching the cards and being a historical detective.

Growing our Legacy in Christ

150 years
1857-2007

Through the Years

First United Methodist Church

St. Cloud, Minnesota

Above: Grand Hotel 5th Ave South
Left: Drug Store on 5th Ave South
Right: Jane Grey Swisshelm
Bottom Left: Parade of cars, St. Germain Street
Right Bottom: Mississippi River Scene. Postcard

HISTORIAN - GERTRUDE GOVE

Gertrude Gove wrote two histories for First Church, one for the 90th anniversary in 1947 and again for the 100th in 1957. In the process of writing these books, she had the original church records put together and bound in large blue and black books. In these books are pencilled-in page numbers, which some of her former students have identified as her handwriting. We have put Miss Gove's two histories in this book, then added pictures. Some of her sources were found in the Church archives, in St. Cloud newspapers, and Minnesota Methodist Conference journals. The April 1969 *Courier* featured a profile of Gertrude Gove:

"*BE YE DOERS OF THE WORD AND NOT HEARERS ONLY*" James 1:22

This admonition, faithfully followed by Gertrude Gove in her life in various communities as teacher and citizen has made her a long-time "social action" person.

Born in Lakefield, Jackson County, Minnesota, [on 30 Jan 1895 to Charles Wallace Gove and Marcia Helen Bartholomew[1]]. Miss Gove was educated in the Windom public schools, Hamline University and University of Wisconsin.[2] She taught history in the Annandale, Litchfield, Winnebago and St. Cloud public schools,[3] and she has had short-term teaching experiences (St. Cloud History) at State College and Cathedral High School. At St. Cloud Tech she sponsored Gopher Historians.

Writing by Miss Gove include History of St. Cloud Public Schools, 1858-1958; History of St. Cloud, 1856-1956 *(Centennial Album); articles for the local press; and three histories of this church (the last in 1956).[4] She is currently [1969] serving on the Minnesota Methodist Historical Commission.*

Miss Gove has a place in the 1958 Who's Who in Minnesota *and in 1957 received the St. Cloud J. C.'s Award for Distinguished Service.*

---

[1] She had two brothers, Russell Dewey Gove and George Wallace Gove, Hamline, 1921.
[2] In our archives is a handwritten manuscript for Methodism in Illinois, which she had apparently written for her Masters Degree. adt
[3] For many current and past Church members, she was their history teacher at Tech High School.
[4] *History of St. Cloud 1853-1970; A History of St. Cloud in the Civil War 1858-1865; A History of the First Methodist Church, St. Cloud, Minnesota 1857- 1947; A Century of Service, A History of the First Methodist Church, St. Cloud, Minnesota 1858-1958;* and *Blue Cross Society.*

She has always been a Methodist: a Sunday School student, an Epworth League member and advisor, a member of the Blue Cross Society – Wesleyan Service Guild, a Methodist history teacher for confirmation classes, and a member of the church's Official Board.

Retiring from public school teaching in 1963, she entered whole heartedly into such groups as League of Women Voters, Twentieth Century Club, Church Women United, W.S.C.S. and renewed her interest in her old hobbies of button collecting, puzzles, and travel.

Gertrude Gove later co-authored a book on St. Cloud houses with Catherine Beck. Gertrude Gove died on July 26, 1978, in Sartell, Stearns County, Minnesota.

A History of Past Civic Involvement[5]

Beulah Rose Hutchens

Members of the First United Methodist church always had a reputation of involvement in the community. While being active in the life of the church, they still had time to be active in the community and schools. Harry B. Gough served as Superintendent of Schools in St. Cloud for many years, with Methodist principals, instructors, clerical food service and custodial staff for kindergarten through 12th grade. St. Cloud also had classes for special needs children, and the Area Vocational School (which began as a part of the District but has since become a part of the university system). The schools are now known as District 742 rather than St. Cloud School System. Many Methodists served the St. Cloud Normal School, which grew into the St. Cloud Teachers College and later became St. Cloud State University. Dr. Charles Graham, a member of the church, served as President, and many other members were employed there as well. [editor's note: Graham was president of Hamline University, St. Paul, Minnesota, also.]

Lloyd Lillestrand, a long-time, active member of the church, organized Boy Scout Troop #1 in the city. They met in the church basement and included boys of many faiths. Paul Anderson (Walgreen manager), John Peck (SCSU instructor), and Judge Willard Lorette are some of the men who worked with the scouts. Milford Johnson was Executive Director of Boy Scouts in St. Cloud for 20 years. Many Troop #1 members earned their Eagle Scout Award.

---

[5] Editor's note: Beulah Rose Hutchens was the first woman on the St. Cloud Planning Commission. Carolyn Garven and Dave Masters at present serve on the St. Cloud City Council.

Mrs. Viola Topp, also a church member, served as Executive Director of Camp Fire Girls in the St. Cloud Area. Each summer, groups of girls would go for a week's camping experience at Camp SUIMA, and since the local council of Camp Fire owned the camp, men and women from the church would gather to ready the grounds and buildings for camp. Many women from the church were Camp Fire Girl leaders. In addition, there was a Girl Scout troop for young girls, and mothers were leaders. Another opportunity for young girls was the Candy Stripers at the hospital, organized by City Nurse, Rosemary Timmers.

Rev. Kenneth Beck was always tuned to the needs of the community, and he recognized several areas of need. He called all of the ministers and invited them and one member of each congregation to a meeting. They began to assess the needs and how those needs could be addressed. From those meetings came a number of groups. Among those were the First Call for Help, a hot line manned 24 hours a day to help people in crisis; the Opportunity Training Center (OTC), for mentally- and physically-challenged persons; and the Retired & Senior Volunteer Program (RSVP). The OTC started in the basement of First Church.

The Methodist Church is an active participant in the Home Delivered Meals program and for two weeks, twice a year, we provide volunteers to deliver meals from the St. Cloud Hospital. Martha Broker, a church member, was involved early on in the service. She cooked meals at Key Row, a Catholic assisted-housing development for older people. The meals were primarily for those who were able to come to eat, but a few people had meals delivered to them. The program expanded and the St. Cloud Hospital became the provider for Meals on Wheels.

Seeing a need for an apartment building where seniors could live when they no longer could or wanted to maintain a home, Rev. Kenneth Beck was instrumental, along with Father Leisen, in helping to organize the United Christian Development Corporation. In 1974, this corporation, along with the help of HUD (Housing and Urban Development), was responsible for the construction of an 85-unit building, known as Riverside Apartments, at 101 Riverside Drive SE. Several Methodists were residents on the list of first-time tenants.

We are proud to serve the community that has provided us with a progressive, positive place to live and grow.

++++++++++++

150TH ANNIVERSARY COMMITTEE

The 150th Anniversary Committee, which worked for four years prior to the 2007 celebration, was composed of these persons: Dick Megarry, Beulah Rose Hutchens, Lois Barron, Mick Benson, Brian Bensen, Karel Helgeson, Jean Lovelace, Harold Zosel, Jerry Sales, Dan Schneider-Bryan, and Annette DeCourcy Towler. This group was responsible for planning and executing the year's events, with much help from many ministry teams within the Administrative Council.

The committee also sponsored or co-sponsored a number of activities. There was a Church picnic on August 24, 2007, with Catherine Beck and Dr. Russell Huffman, Jr., both from the church's past, attending. A history of the church was also planned (this book) under the direction of Annette DeCourcy Towler. The committee spent many hours identifying pictures and helping make decisions as to how the book would look. Pictures and slides taken by Earle Thompson, a chairman of the Board of Trustees in the 1950's, were in our archives and tell a vital part of the history of this church. Annette was responsible for much of the hunting in the church vault to find the material.

Annette, along with Beulah Rose Hutchens and Lois Barron, also created a temporary church museum, using the old church office as a place to display documents, pictures, old church furniture, scrapbooks, and other accumulations of the church's and Methodism's history. Some of the items Annette had inherited from her father, the Rev. Frank DeCourcy.

Various items were produced for the anniversary celebration: stationery designed by Mick Benson; a banner by Karel Helgeson, as well as a coffee mug, both with the design of the Methodist Cross and Flame on them; a pin with the picture of the church on it; Christmas ornaments, onto which Joyce Moses had painted the anniversary date; wooden table centerpieces of the Cross and Flame, designed and produced by Dr. John, and a poster showing a timeline of the First United Methodist Church, done by Annette DeCourcy Towler.

150th Pin

Cross and Flame centerpieces designed and created by Dr. Byron John, used at the 150th dinner and during 2008 coffee hours

Mug and program cover picture for 150th dinner April 22, 2007, design by Karel Helgeson, also used as divider page in this book.

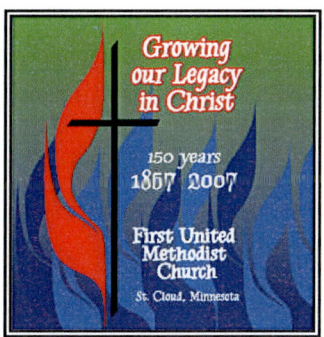

Mugs sold by the Outreach Team

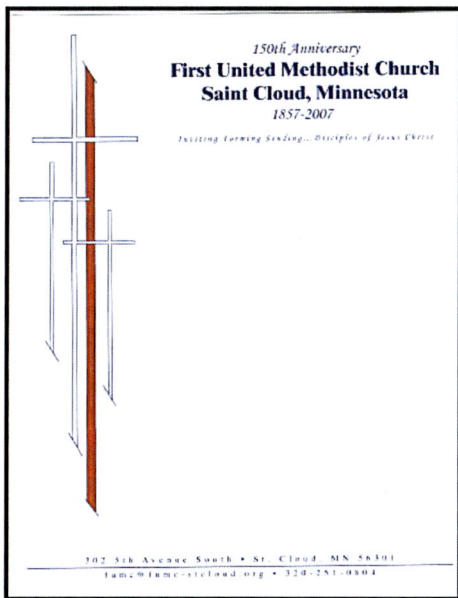

Stationery designed by Mick Benson and used for the 150th celebration

Banner (picture on page iii) created and designed by Karel Helgeson and Barb Kelter, drafter-designer at Golden Plump.

A contest was held to find a theme for the 150th anniversary. The winning statement, "Growing our Legacy in Christ," was a combination of the ideas of two members of the congregation, Ellen Deane Schwieger and Bob Fulton.

Three music performances were held in connection with the celebration. Soul Café performed in February 2007, featuring jazz pianist Laura Caviani, who grew up in the church. In March, Steve Mick, First Church's choir director, directed a performance of the Faure *Requiem* in the sanctuary, with the Apollo Concert Choir and Orchestra, members of First Church choir, and soloists from the Minnesota Center Chorale and St. Cloud State University. Finally, in October 2007 an organ concert was held with organists Charles Echols, Michael Barone, and Tess Kasling performing.

The big day of the anniversary celebration was April 22, 2007, with Bishop Sally Dyck preaching at both services. The congregation then went to the nearby Kelly Inn for a dinner and program. The program was from a script written by Rev. Dr. Bob Kendall. A commentator, Rather Dan, was played by Jim Davis; the radio announcer was Jennifer Galovich; Paula Tompkins portrayed Laura Marlatt; Julia Holscher read Augusta Lunemann's part; and Dorothy Stueve played herself. The sound taping was done by Drew Sevcik, and the director of the play was Annette DeCourcy Towler.

+ + + + + + + + + + + + +

Early Church Records

The following information has been abstracted exactly as found in original First Church records. These records were in three books, which at present are kept in the church vault. The dates are done with a "/60," meaning "1860." Page numbers in the original records are in pencil and were probably added many years later by Gertrude Gove, Church Historian, when she wrote a booklet on the church, printed in 1946. These books contain early church marriages, baptisms, memberships and quarterly conference records.

Some of the practices and terms of the 1980's may be unfamiliar to modern congregations. Early Methodist churches required that when a member transferred from one church (called a class) to another, a "letter for removal" was necessary. In present time, this same notification is called a "transfer of membership." A class leader (leader of church) could be a local preacher, a licensed person, or an ordained deacon/elder. Ambrose Frecman, a Civil War soldier, was a local preacher. Some terms need translating. "Prob" means "probation" (one who attends but is not a member) and "dismemberment," a strange term to modern ears, means "removal by the official board of the local church." A steward is a locally elected leader of the local church.

Early First Church records were microfilmed by the Minnesota Historical Society in 1964. A copy of this microfilm can be viewed at the Minnesota Historical Society Library in St. Paul, in the Archives of SCSU's Miller Learning Center, at the Stearns County History Museum in St. Cloud, or in First Church's archives.

The following records, memberships, baptisms, and marriages were in large, beautiful handwriting/script/printing on two or more lines, but they sometimes did not follow the rules of writing. Records are abstracted here in this book as found, with sometimes irregular punctuation and spellings. You will find Fair Haven spelled on the same page as "Havin" and "Haven" or Central Hotel as "Centersl Hotel." In those days, words were often written as they sounded and not as they were spelled. Even Jane Swisshelm in her writings called her newspaper "Visiter" and "Visitor."

++++++++++++

Early Membership

Name; Residence; Time and Mode of Joining; Class Leader; Remarks

A (page 48-49)

Berlin. T. N., St. Cloud, Joined Oct 2/59 by prob, by Class Leader, Ambrose Freeman, He was removed by letter Oct 18th 1861 [different hand writing] [A. Freeman handwriting] licensed to exhort [?] Oct 3/59 licensed to preach June 9/60.

Berlin. Jane, St. Cloud, Joined Oct 2/59 by prob, by Class Leader, Ambrose Freeman, She was removed by letter Oct 18th 1861

Ball. Eliza A, St. Cloud, Joined June 10/60 by Class Leader, Ambrose Freeman,

Blood. Emilene F, St. Cloud, Joined June 19/61 letter, by Class Leader, Ambrose Freeman

Blain. Mary St. Cloud, Joined Oct 7th 1861 letter, by Class Leader, Ambrose Freeman. [Rev. Bartley Blain's wife]

Emma E Blain, St. Cloud, Joined June 1st 1862 letter, by Class Leader, Ambrose Freeman, removed by letter Sep 1st 1862

C (page 50-51)

Clark Luellen, St. Cloud, joined March / 59, by Class Leader, Ambrose Freeman, Discharged by letter Sept 24.1860.
Crawford Julia, Sauk Rapids, joined March / 59, by Class Leader, Ambrose Freeman

D (page 52 - 53)
Ekiman Mary C, Saint Cloud, Sept 3.1861. by letter, by Class Leader, Ambrose Freeman, Removed by letter May 15th 1862
Freeman. Ambrose Saint Cloud, /58 by letter, by Class Leader, Ambrose Freeman,, Steward. made. Mar 10 / 60
Freeman. Jane E, Saint Cloud, /58 by letter, by Class Leader, Ambrose Freeman " ",
Freeman. Thos St. Cloud, Joined, Saint Cloud, /58 by letter, by Class Leader, Ambrose Freeman, Discharged by letter
Freeman. Maria, St. Cloud, Saint Cloud, /58 by letter, by Class Leader, Ambrose Freeman
Fossett. John, Saint Cloud, /58 by letter, by Class Leader, Ambrose Freeman
Freeman. Elizabeth F, St. Cloud, Joined Apr 15 / 60. by prob., Saint Cloud, /58 by letter, by Class Leader, Ambrose Freeman ",
Freeman. Virginia S., Saint Cloud Joined Apr 15 / 60. by prob, by Class Leader, Ambrose Freeman

G (page 54 – 55)
Garlington. Ann, St Cloud, /58 by letter, by Class Leader, Ambrose Freeman
Garlington. Mary, St. Cloud, Joined Oct 2 / 59 by prob, by Class Leader, Ambrose Freeman " ",
Garlington. Margaret, St. Cloud, Joined Oct 2 / 59 by prob, by Class Leader, Ambrose Freeman ",
Garlington. Edwin, St. Cloud, Joined June 10 /60 by prob by Class Leader, Ambrose Freeman ", , In the Army
Gager. Mary. E, St. Cloud, Joined by Jun 10/60 letter, by Class Leader, Ambrose Freeman , Gone without a letter near Alexandria
Hooper. Wm, St. Cloud, Joined /58 by letter, " by Class Leader, Ambrose Freeman ", Steward. made. Jul 22 / 57 not selected in 1861-----
Hooper. Elisa Ann, St. Cloud, Joined June 18 1861 by letter, by Class Leader, Ambrose Freeman , , Removed to near St. Francis [in pencil]

I (page 56-57)
Jones. John, St. Cloud, Joined, /58 by letter, by Class Leader, Ambrose Freeman
Jains [Jasins?] David, St. Cloud, Joined Oct. 20. 1860., by Class Leader, Ambrose Freeman , Enlisted in the USA army Apr 1862 ~~March~~

(page 58 - 59)
Kotch John, St. Cloud, Joined, Oct 2 / 59 by prob, by Class Leader, Ambrose Freeman ,
Kotch. Eliza, St. Cloud, Joined, Oct 2 / 59 by prob, by Class Leader, Ambrose Freeman
Kidd Martha, St. Cloud, Joined Apr 8 / 60 by letter, by Class Leader, Ambrose Freeman , Discharge by letter, May 7th 1860

Kidd. Kudgson, St. Cloud, Joined Apr 22 / 60 by letter, by Class Leader, Ambrose Freeman Discharge by letter, Aug 13th 1860

Kidd. Elizabeth St. Cloud, Joined Apr 22 / 60 by letter, by Class Leader, Ambrose Freeman, Discharge by letter Aug 13th 1860

~~**Cooper Eliza Anne**~~, near St. Cloud, June 18. 1861, , [in name column with name crossed out & in different handwritten 'wrong place'] should be Hooper/Kooper

King Eli B., Neenah, St. Cloud, Joined Aug 20th 1860 by dismemberment are out Clear Water Ch, by Class leader Eli B. King,

King. Adelia B., Neenah, St. Cloud, Joined Aug 20th 1860 by dismemberment are out Clear Water Ch, by Class leader Eli B. King

King. Amasa D. [?], Neenah, St. Cloud, Joined Aug 20th 1860 by dismemberment are out Clear Water Ch, by Class leader Eli B. King.

King. Harriet., Neenah, St. Cloud, Joined Aug 20th 1860 by dismemberment are out Clear Water Ch, by Class leader Eli B. King.,L (page 60-61)

Marlett. Silas, St. Cloud, Joined, /58 by letter, by Class Leader, Ambrose Freeman Steward . Made 1858

Mann Thos., St. Cloud, Joined June 59 by letter, by Class Leader, Ambrose Freeman, Discharge by letter Feb 13 1860

Mann. Mary A, St. Cloud, Joined June 59 by letter, by Class Leader, Ambrose Freeman, Discharge by letter Feb 13 1860

Morrison Elizabeth, St. Cloud, Joined Nov 24 1861 by Class Leader, Ambrose Freeman

Mitchell Mary, St. Cloud, Joined, Nov 24 1861, by Class Leader, Ambrose Freeman

Nelson D [?] Adelia, St. Cloud, Joined, Oct. 20. 1860, by Class Leader, Ambrose Freeman , Removed by letter Aug 21st 1862 [an assumption that she is the wife of Rev. Andrew J. Nelson]

Norris. S. [Rev. ? Samuel H/N] H., St. Cloud, Joined Aug 24th 1862 by letter, in class leader column "dead [pencil, same handwriting as 'wrong place']", Local Preacher

Norris. J. Ella St. Cloud, Joined Aug 24th 1862 by letter,, by Class Leader, Ambrose Freeman

(page 62-63)
Owen Julia W., St. Cloud, Joined, Aug / 59 by letter, by Class Leader, Ambrose Freeman

Pierpont Mary. J., St. Cloud, Joined, /59 by letter, by Class Leader, Ambrose Freeman, Discharged by letter Sept 11.1860

Q (page 64-65)
Remmel Margaret., St. Cloud, Joined, Feb 12/60 by prob, by Class Leader, Ambrose Freeman, Gone without a letter.

Reily Mary A, St. Cloud, Joined June 10 /60 by Class Leader, Ambrose Freeman

Spaulding Alonzo, St. Cloud, Joined, Dec 15th 1861 by letter Clear Water Ch, by Class Leader, Ambrose Freeman , enlisted in the USA Apr 1862

(page 66 - 67) [bottom right hand corner of page torn]

Thompson. John L., Sauk City, Joined Jun / 59 by letter, Ambrose Freeman, Local Preacher. Not renewed.
Tracy. James. R. St. Cloud, Joined, June 10 /60 by prob, by Class Leader, Ambrose Freeman
Thompson. Ellen Kassen, St. Cloud, Joined, Sept. 12. /61, by Class Leader, Ambrose Freeman
U
V
page 66a - 67a)
Williams. Jas. M., St. Cloud, Joined, /58 by letter, by Class Leader, Ambrose Freeman , Steward. made. Mar 10/ 60 Discharged by letter Sept. 22. 1860
Wilson James C, St. Cloud, Joined, /58 by letter. made. Jul 22 / 57 by Class Leader, Ambrose Freeman
Wilson. Mary A., St. Cloud, Joined, /58 by letter, by Class Leader, Ambrose Freeman ,
West. Caleb. W, St. Cloud, Joined, Apr 15/ 60 by prob, " by Class Leader, Ambrose Freeman, Discharged by letter Apr. 18 / 60.
Webb. Roanna., St. Cloud, Joined, Apr 15/ 60 by Class Leader, Ambrose Freeman ,Discharged By letter.

Following the above record, in red ink and very faded condition, is the following statement by Rev. David Tice, an ordained pastor and a presiding elder in the Minnesota Conference of the Methodist Episcopal Church:

I find it impossible to get any thing like a correct idea of the membership ... As they [the records] have been kept so very miserably. and indexed during the past year. <u>NO</u> Records. Whatever have been kept (A.D. 1862. & 3.) – under the pastoral care of the Rev. S. [Samuel] T. Sterritt. Consequently, I turn over a new leaf and shall for "bounty Sake" and "Book Saving" bill enter in the classes in the Records as they Stand in the "Class Book."

David Tice Pastor St. Cloud, Minn. Dec. 14 / 6.3 [1863]

Early Baptisms

Blue Church Records Book, pages 6-11
Date, Name, Date of Birth, Residence, Minister, Witness

31 Jul 1859, **Margaret Remmel,**, St. Cloud, Rev. David Brooks, C. G. Bowdish & A. Freeman
15 Apr 1860, **Caldo West**, 10 Sep 1837, St. Cloud, Bowdish, T. N. Berlin, J. C. Wilson
15 Apr 1860, **Elizabeth F. Freeman**, 22 Feb 1844, St. Cloud, Bowdish, T. N. Berlin, J. C. Wilson

15 Apr 1860, **Virginia S. Freeman**, 10 Sep 1846, St. Cloud, Bowdish, T. N. Berlin, J. C. Wilson

10 Jun 1860, **Edwin A. Garlington**, 2 Sep 1836, St. Cloud, Rev. David Brooks, Bowdish & Alfred Welch

10 Jun 1860, **Trevanan W. Berlin, Jr**, 14 Nov 1855, St. Cloud, Rev. David Brooks, Bowdish & Alfred Welch

10 Jun 1860, **Julia S. Berlin**, 9 Jun 1858, St. Cloud, Rev. David Brooks, Bowdish & Alfred Welch

3 Feb 1861, **Allen E. Cassey**, 12 Jan 1861, St. Cloud, Rev. Andrew J. Nelson, Congregation

3 Feb 1861, **Martha A Cooper**, 12 Jan 1861, St. Cloud, Rev. Andrew J. Nelson, Congregation

3 Feb 1861, **Barbara Kotz**, 16 Feb 1861,, Rev. Andrew J. Nelson, Freeman & M. A. Nelson

7 Jul 1861, **Elmer Ellsworth Brown**, 10 Aug 1861, St. Cloud, Chessman, Gould & M. A. Nelson

7 Jul 1861, **Chessman Loren Brown**, 10 Aug 1861, St. Cloud, Chessman, Gould & M. A. Nelson

7 Jul 1861, **George Owen**, 18 Jul 1861, St. Cloud, Rev. David Brooks, A. J. Nelson & M. Adelia Nelson

++++++++++++

Early Marriages

Blue Church Records Book, pages 1

Date; Name of Parties; Residence; Place of Marriage; Officiating, Minister; Witnesses

Dec 4, 1859; **William A. Gates Lydia M. Moore**; St Cloud Minn same; house of the brides father, St. Cloud; C. G. Bowdish; Caleb W. West, Elisabeth F. Freeman.

May 11, 1861; **Christopher Hansen Rachel Gunderson**; St. Cloud, Minn; The Parsonage, S^t. Cloud; A. J. Nelson; M. Adelia Nelson, Samuel Gunderson.

July 2nd 1861; **George Johnston, Hannah Johnston**; St. Cloud; At Parsonage; A. J. Nelson; David Jarvis, Irene L. Carrick, Rosanna Jorden ~.

Aug 17 1862; **Charles H Hopper Sarah E. Blain**; Crystal Lake Minn St. Cloud Minn; Parsonage St Cloud; B. Blain; Mary Blain, Emma E. Blain.

February 1st 1864; **Henry B. Johnson Lydia M. Stannard**; St. Cloud, Minn, same; St. Cloud; David Tice; Miss L. M. Johnson. Miss Julia Johnson.

February 28 1864; **Harman Becker, and Hellen M. Ayers**; St. Cloud, Minn, same; Brides father; David Tice; R. C. Burdie and Stitman Ayers.

April 3rd 1864; **Lucius Conger and Anna Shepherd**; Brockway. St. Cloud; "Centersl House"; David Tice; Albert B. Curry & J. E. Hayward.

June 15 1864; **Ambrose W. Tucker Emily J. Norris**; Fair Havin St. Cloud; At the Parsonage; David Tice; Prof. S. H. Norris & J. R. Clark.

July 4th 1864; **Alonzo Spaulding, Christina Langdon**; Main Prairie St Cloud; "Parsonage"; David Tice; Rev. John Scott & E. B. King Esq.

July 4 1864; **John W. Gatchell and Celistia P. Gillett**; Winnebago, St. Cloud; "Parsonage"; David Tice; Otis Gatchell & wife.

April 19 1865; **Andrew F. Perkins, and Mary E. Chamberlain**; Fair Haven, Minn Enfield, Minn; "Parsonage"; David Tice; Mrs. Tice, and Rev. W. Carn.

Oct 6 1861; **Chas W. Stimpson Oliva L. Hubburd**, Sauk Center same; St Cloud; Chas Griswold; J P Hayward Mary Hayward

Octobr 11th 1861; **Christopher Wilkins Irene A Daomjeords** [?]; Clearwater La Sauk; La Sauk; Chas Griswold; no witnesses

Dec 16 1866; **Aaron Becker Eva Reed**; Stearns Co same; John Morris's St Cloud; Noah Lathrop; J. C. Wilson John Morris

Oct | 31 1866; **Edwin S. Rolls Sarah Ridgway**; Sauk Rapids same; House of Minister St Cloud; Noah Lathrop; Sarah F. Lathrop Charlotte Allison

June 22 1867; **Lester B. Gilber Mary L Wait**; Stearns Co. same; Stearns Co; Noah Lathrop; Mary L. Davison Edna W. Getchell

+ + + + + + + + + + + +

MEMBERSHIP NUMBERS FOR THE LAST 150 YEARS

by Annette DeCourcy Towler

The early Minnesota Annual Conferences were held in late September or early October, and mostly in Southern Minnesota. One of the first ones was at Red Wing, Minnesota, where Hamline University was located at the time. After the merger of the Northern Minnesota Conference and the Minnesota Conference at their annual conferences in 1947, all conferences were held in June of each year. Pastors reported at these annual conferences the memberships, baptisms, education participants, and financial information for the church year ending in June of the previous year.

Each year some of the columns changed in the reports. For example, in recent years all baptisms have been counted together and not separated by children and adults. "Probationary members" were people who attended the church but did not become members. Today we call these people "constituents." Confirmation numbers were sometimes in the same column as probationary.

The complete list of journals are in the section under "Bibliography/Sources." Sauk Rapids information is included in the numbers here, but not Waite Park's. Most of the early journals are in the Conference Archives in

Minneapolis. From 1948 on, copies of the journals are in FUMC archives. Thanks to Dudley and Dolores Keech, and Bill Meier, we were able to complete this list.

Key:
- Year = Year of Journal
- M = Members
- D = Deaths
- P = Probation/Confirmation
- LP = Local Preacher
- BA = Baptized Adults
- BC = Baptized Children
- Blank Row = no stats
- SR = Sauk Rapid

Year	M	D	P	LP	BA	BC
1859	31	1	8	2	4	2
1860	70		12	1	4	8
1861						
1862	50	2	4	1		1
1863						
1864	51		9	2	1	3
1865	41	1	10		1	
1866	48		7		1	1
1867	35		7			
1868	40				1	
1869	70	1	35	2	26	3
1870	92	1	12		7	
1871	75					
1872	37		1		1	
1873	45		5		7	1
1874	44	1	5		1	1
1875	32			1		
1876	32			1	1	
1877	42					
1878	30					
1879						
1880	83	3	1	2		1
1881	46		8	1		1
1881 SR	*42*		*7*			*1*
1882	6		2		2	3
1883	81	1	5			5
1883 SR	*47*		*7*			*1*
1884	71		8		2	2
1885	80	3	10		1	0
1885 SR	*61*		*2*		*3*	*2*

Year	M	D	P	LP	BA	BC
1886	95	1	7		1	5
1887	114	3	18		10	3
1888	65		2		2	4
1889	120	2	12	1	5	8
1890	147	2	15	7	1	10
1891	132	2	6		2	6
1892	140	2	10			2
1893	148	1	2		4	3
1894	150	2	25		12	9
1895	118	2	19		2	3
1896	140	4	21		2	4
1897	108		13		1	2
1898	122		18			5
1899	132	1	10		5	9
1900	119	2	7		1	8
1901	113	1	23		4	
1902	137		2		4	9
1903	133		3		1	10
1904	135		13		7	4
1905	180	3	29		16	2
1906	171	1	34		6	3
1907	178		12		3	
1908	165	1	10			4
1909	235	1	16		17	15
1910	270	0	14		6	9
1911	258	0	26	0	12	21
1912	277	1		2	6	6
1913	361	1		1	15	20
1914	400	4	25	0	30	20
1915	244	2	25	1	12	23
1916	276	3	17	1	8	11
1917	250	5	30	1	4	29
1918	260	2	42	1	3	29

Year	M	D	P	LP	BA	BC
1919	323	2	91	2	7	23
1920	318		15	1	8	14
1921	250	3	32	1	6	12
1922	280		30	11	8	9
1923	358	4	42		18	16
1924	396	1	25		5	17
1925	350	3	12		4	18
1926	393		3		3	18
1927	405	2		3	6	15
1928	458	2	60	1	4	21
1929	435	3	57		10	5
1930	610	1	206		24	12
1931	705	3	71	1	17	7
1932	907	8	70	1	17	8
1933	981	7	67	3	12	10
1934	806	3	7	2	1	20
1935	749	8	6	1	4	13
1936	740	5	4	1	9	19
1937	725	3	11	1	10	15
1938	682	8	7	1	2	17
1939	647	2	17	1	7	15
1940	652	77	13	1	3	17
1941	636	68	26	1	13	21
1942	614	47	9	0	10	15
1943	570	28	17	1		10
1944	541	3	14	1	10	24
1945	575	6	42	1	11	30
1946	660	3	4	1	1	13
1947	631	2	20		6	15
1948	715	9	11	1	12	21
1949	757	8	15	2	18	14
1950	807	10	21	4	7	31
1951	957	5	38	4	5	23
1952	883	10	15	4	5	22
1953	889	9	12	1	6	21
1954	902	5	28	1	20	28
1955	875	7	24	NA		16
1956	895			NA	13	
1957	959	5	15	NA	10	28
1958	963	6		NA	12	19
1959	984	6	43	NA		24
1960	1014	8	39	NA	13	25
1961	1050	10	28	NA		
1962	988	2	21	NA	6	19
1963	980	5	24	NA	2	11
1964	983	7	26	NA	5	3
1965	994	6	0	NA	1	12
1966	1012	9	26	NA	6	13
1967				NA		
1968	1095			NA		27
1970	1083	12	44	NA		26
1971	1108	4	48	NA		21
1972	1100	5	48	NA		6
1973	1104	7	24	NA		19
1974	1102			NA		
1975	1122	9	26	NA		17
1976	1155	5	43	NA		14
1977	1147	9	87	NA	2	2
1978	1072	16	79	NA	2	9
1979	1014	15	47	NA	1	2
1980	1048	11	47	NA	2	8
1981	1027	9	47	NA	2	2
1982	1007	9	41	NA	2	3
1983	1005	11	38	NA	2	4
1984	952	11	41	NA	2	20
1985	945	9	35	NA		2
1986	908	10	38	NA	1	7
1987	880	14	37	NA	22	
1988	873	8	19	NA	19	
1989	877	9	31	NA	17	
1990	891	5	21	NA	14	
1991	873	11	20	NA	19	

Year	M	D	P	LP	BA	BC
1992	888		29	NA	1	
1993	908	9		NA	13	
1994				NA	1	
1995				NA	1	
1996	803	0	58	NA	1	3
1997	752	8		NA	18	
1998	754	12	20	NA	1	
1999	746	9	14	NA	4	
2000	741	12		NA	19	
2001	702	14	13	NA	12	
2002	699	3	14	NA	6	
2003				NA		
2004	669	7	9	NA	7	
2005	687	11	12	NA	8	
2006	654	8	14	NA		
2007	687	8	14		8	

Dear Ann Landers:
Please, oh please – lead us out of the wilderness of ignorance. What is a Methodist handshake? Several Methodists in Windom, Minn., who need to know. – Two Swedes and a Norwegian

Dear Friends: A Methodist handshake is a churchy, strictly-business, parting gesture. And please don't accuse me of being anti-Methodist. I learned the expression from the Methodists at Morningside College.[6] adt

---

[6] Newspaper clipping not dated found in FUMC archives.

++++++++++++
Seminary

In January of 1861 a seminary (school) was dedicated. It had been built on the block that is now Barden Park, and the building was probably financed by the people of St. Cloud. The school was run by St. Cloud Methodist Church personnel and was used as an early church. Mrs. Jane Swisshelm, an assertive reformer and editor of her own newspaper, the *St. Cloud Democrat*, published an article describing the new building on January 3, 1861, entitled "The Seminary Dedication." Part of it is reprinted here:

> *This new building was crowded on the occasion of its dedication, with an audience of citizens and strangers. The house is a monument to the personal courage, architectural taste and industry of Rev. Mr. Nelson, the projector and principal of the school. The room is 30 X 50 feet, with half hectagon wings at each end. One for the vestibule, the other for the teacher's desk - over the vestibule is a gallery for a choir and a hectagon belfry. The bell rang for the first time to assemble the audience. - The inside finish is in good taste. The house was beautifully lighted and tastefully decorated.*
>
> *The exercises were opened by the choir singing an anthem; when J. C. Wilson read the history of the Institution - we shall if possible publish next week.*
>
> *It was then proposed, by Mr. Rogers of St. Paul, to raise the money, on the spot, to pay off the debt ($67) on the building. This was done, Mr. R. giving $10, a small subscription compared to his great wealth and the property interest he has here.*

++++++++++++

The Saint Cloud Institute And Pioneer Seminary

by Gertrude Gove

The men returned to find Saint Cloud educationally poor. The Saint Cloud Institute and Pioneer Seminary, which had given so much promise of being a great school when the war began, had declined. In the later part of 1862, this institution lost its dominating spirit, the Reverend A. J. Nelson, who joined the faculty of Hamline University, then at Red Wing, Minnesota. At the same time, hard feelings were developing because the seminary seemed to be so much under the control of the Methodist Episcopal Church, the annual conference having furnished the principal, the Reverend S. H. Morris, and his local congregation worshipping in the school building. Mrs.

Swisshelm, voicing this dissatisfaction, wrote in July, 1862, "An effort is being made to turn the school house over to the conference of the Methodist Episcopal Church. This is a swindle. The land is a public park. No title can be had. The building was put up by the people of Saint Cloud for a school."

In December she wrote: "The Seminary was built by the people of Saint Cloud on the Public Park to be under the control, as they supposed, of a Board of Trustees of prominent citizens. It was to be suited to school purposes but was to be used for lectures and preaching and such other meetings as would not interfere with its chief purposes. By a barefaced swindle, the property has been turned over to the Methodist Episcopal Church, the house converted into a church and left without the first simple requirements of a school house, desks, so that it may better suit church purposes. Against this swindle we have protested and will continue to protest. We have notified the authorities that we shall contest the church title."

Another criticism that the editor made of the seminary was that it was not a proper schoolroom. Her chief objection was that this school was without desks. In August, 1862, she wrote. "The floor is closely packed with little fixed wooden seats and not a desk to support book or slate so that the pupils have to have their feet upon the bench before them and sup their knees as best they can, doubling themselves up and being themselves down as to keep lungs crushed and the spine crooked all the time of study."

Mrs. Swisshelm went still further. She criticized the instructors, In July, 1862, she said, "We do desire to trouble the Conference send us a teacher. We have had enough of experimenting." In August, she wrote, "Some feel aggrieved at our notice of last week; they feel that we should have waited; given Mr. Norris a fair trial. The people of Saint Cloud have spent seven years in giving teachers fair trials and up to this time have had no school. True, we have had true and earnest teachers who have done their best, but the system which has left all to the chances of trial has left them without the means of accomplishing much. We judge of Mr. Norris' fitness by the evidence before us. We took our own daughter from the school and privately made every remonstrance but to no avail. The school ran out as people ceased to send their children."

from Gove's book *St. Cloud in the Civil War* p 38

+ + + + + + + + + + + + +

M. P. SATTERLEE'S STORY

Son of Pioneer Pastor Tells of Early Events in St. Cloud

One of the inevitable laws of nature is constant change, and before her court there are no lawyers, pardon boards or legislatures to interfere with the administration. As I was pondering on the past of St. Cloud, the thought that some others might enjoy a reminiscence prompted this skit. In 1869, my father W. W. Satterlee was appointed to the St. Cloud charge by the Methodist conference.

We were living at Waseca then, and I well remember looking at the map to find St. Cloud. Between the "saint" and "cloud," it seemed a 'heavenly" place, and from the map it sure was far enough "up." It must have been a jolt to father who had to move his family of wife and five healthy kids 150 miles and not even a democrat wagon say nothing of a horse to work with. Raising the fare price may have been hard but it came from somewhere. We arrived about Oct. 25, 1869 and landed with great relief at the St. Paul & Pacific Station on the east side of the river, and by the courtesy of Joe Hayward of the Central House and John Rogers, bus driver (both of whom came to church occasionally) we were landed at the beautiful and kindly home of John Hayward (now 9th avenue at the ravine) where we rested over night, then to our new home on the brow of the hill overlooking the river and lower town.

St. Cloud was divided into sections at that time, known as upper town, lower town and the town proper being Main Street and Washington avenue, which comprised most of the business section, and the east side never claimed any name till christened as East St. Cloud. About the best and one of the oldest buildings was the Broker Block, a brick building of size in which the settlers prepared to fight the Indians during the outbreak of 1862. I can recall only three other brick buildings, the Catholic and Congregational churches and the new Union School house. The Normal school was the old Stearns hotel on the lower end of the present grounds, and might have had 100 attendants, with Prof. Ira Moore as superintendent.

The Methodist church was located directly west of the Normal on what is now Fifth avenue. Being the handiest to the students who roomed as near the school as possible, it became more or less headquarters for the attendance and devotions. An instructor, Miss Walker, was the leader in the musical exercises of the Sunday school, and made them famous. The other churches held their schools following morning service and ours was at 3 p.m. and many there were who attended two regularly. Mollie McIntyre, the organist was something of a wonder to me, for she could play in all different keys and even, with her hands crossed. Among the prominent young ladies were Louisa and Laura Freeman, "Lou" Hayward, Emma Jones, Jennie Bentley, Minnie and Mollie McIntyre, Sarah Kelly, Emma Kimball, Nettie and Mattie Sutton, Lillie and Etta Wilson and the gentlemen Charles Lancaster, Will Lamb, Thomas Gray, Dan Freeman, Leander and Frank Green. Among the prominent men of the church were J. C. Wilson, W. B. McIntryre, Dr. Talbert, Frank Hanscome, and John Hayward. Across the road was a small cemetery in which two soldiers who were murdered by one McManus were buried. Through this I had to pass on my way home but went so fast I never saw their ghosts though it was said they had halted passersby on the road. Below the church was an old building known as William Nelson Seminary, but whose history seemed lost at that time.

A very interesting event was the opening of the new Union school building under Prof. D. W. Sprague. As many of us had been used to sitting on benches with no back and putting our books on the floor underneath. It was some elation to have a seat and desk including an ink well with a cover. The box stove was not in evidence and there was no "burning one side while the other froze." The desks were double; being a preacher's son of doubtful disposition I had to be seated with a girl partner. Minnie Bennett and Julia Noyes (Mrs. C. A. Birch) participated with me in the two years I spent at the school. Among the girl students I recall Mary Noyes, Cora Parson, Mary Lynch, Clara Weary, Maggie Biggerstaff, Anna Edelbrock, Nellie Gilman and Lillie Wilson. Of the boys, Will Metzer, Same Gilman, Bert Wilson, James Bennett, Arthur Hussey, Charles Jones, John Edelbrock, Freeman Wilson, Eugene Hill, George Farwell, Theodore Wing, Frank and Henry Tilmon.

Among the business houses of 1870 that I recall were Clark & Waite flour and feed; C. Brigham, Lumber; Edelbrock, clothing; Stevens, meat market; Talbert, drugs; N. P. Bennett, gunsmith;

Doughty, gunsmith; Rosenberger, bookstore; Hill, photographer; Dam, sash and doors; Weary, wagon maker; St. Cloud Journal, Wm Mitchell, editor; and The Times, J. J. Green, editor; Raymond & Owens planing mill; Thomas Jones, farrier; Powell, hardware.

One of the most exciting events was a Fourth of July celebration when a stand was erected on the avenue and the fireworks assembled on the stand with the committees in charge. About the third rocket set off the whole bunch of combustibles. Those who had a safe place to watch from said it was grand, but most of us got home before the shooting was over.

In memory I live again those happy days, go down to the river bank to see the ice go out in a moving mass of gigantic proportions, or see the log drives pass with the drivers who risked all to keep it moving. I see the faces of those friends of old, some here some far off, some beyond the eternal gates. I hear again the 6 o'clock whistles on the saw mills; as they die out there comes the low sweet chimes from the Augustine Mission down the river. You have a great and beautiful city, but to us that lived there in the long ago comes a picture so pleasing that no wealth or beauty can compare. Such a pleasure is memory.

St. Cloud Daily Times, October 5, 1931

+ + + + + + + + + + + +

SCRAPBOOK

Annette DeCourcy Towler

A scrapbook, which is falling apart and may not last for another 50 years, was found in the archives. It was kept by George R. Crosby, a Church member and owner of a furniture store in downtown Saint Cloud from 1893 to 1900. Here are copies of some pages. The scrapbook is brown, and nine and 3/4 inches in height and seven inches wide. The dates are 1890 to 1900. Pages which are still in the scrapbook have a blue stamped number in upper right or left corner. Odd number pages are on the right. Dark parts on the pages, as on page

39, are printed newspaper bled into the page from the preceding page. There must have been good glue in those days, as the newspaper articles are well attached to the pages. Pages are hand sewed together, and it also looks as if part of the scrapbook was bound. Each sheet has light blue [faded] lines and a 1 1/2 inch indented red line. On pages recopied here, the memorial and dates are in the margin. Between page 32 and 33 is a small brochure of four pages, four by six and a half inches in size, apparently glued[7] or bound to the center part. This brochure is called the "Official Directory and Financial Statement 1898-1899."

The rest of the scrapbook has newspaper articles glued to pages, including pictures and articles on all the other denominations that were in St. Cloud at that time. No dates are on any of the articles that were cut from the newspaper, and they are probably all *St. Cloud Daily Journal*. Rev. Heman F. Parshall, St. John's Episcopal; Rev. Isaac B. Tracy, First Congregational; and other pastors are on each page. Pencil sketches of some of our pastors were found in this scrapbook, along with the Epworth League, 1910, a large, heavy paper poster. Beulah Rose Hutchens every so often will show this book in the church display windows. The following pages are from this book and a valuable resource for our history.

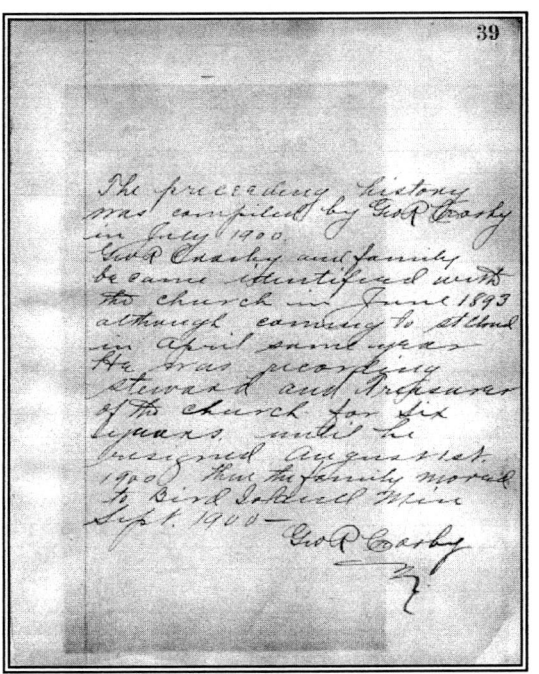

---

[7] Glue was invented in Britain in 1750.

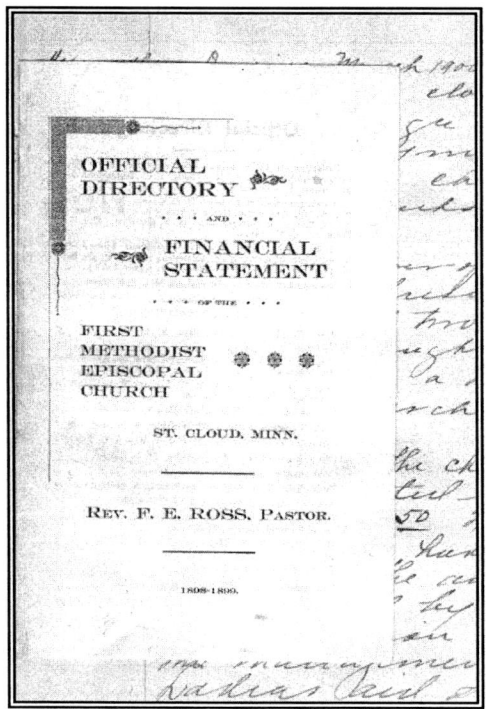
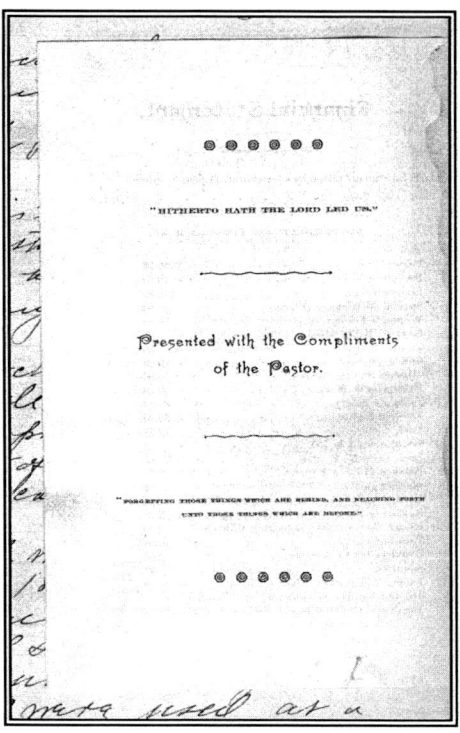

Official Directory.

TRUSTEES—D. H. Freeman, John Schaefer, Geo. C. Hubbard, John Cooper, Geo. R. Crosby, E. D. Hammond, J. F. Stevenson, E. W. Young.

STEWARDS—Geo. R. Crosby, M. L. Glazer, Dr. A. D. Whiting, E. W. Young, N. R. Bell, Mrs. Chas. Hull, Mrs. M. Akers, Mrs. L. A. Marlatt, Mrs. W. S. Hamilton, Mrs. S. C. Hubbard, O. L. Davis.

CHRISTIAN ENDEAVOR SOCIETY—President, Flora Joslin; Vice-President, May Davis; Recording Sec'y, Blanche Bethel; Cor. Sec'y, May Davis; Treasurer, Agnes Ashley.

JUNIOR LEAGUE—Superintendent, Mrs. F. E. Ross.

STANDING COMMITTEES.

MISSIONS—Mrs. M. Akers, Mrs. E. Ingalls, Mrs. F. K. Whitney.

TEMPERANCE—Mrs. Kate Kercher, Mrs. M. Akers, Mrs. Flora Johnson.

SALARY—Geo. R. Crosby, E. W. Young, M. L. Glazer, J. F. Stevenson, Mrs. L. A. Marlatt.

TRACTS—Miss Maud Campbell, Miss Agnes Ashley.

SUNDAY SCHOOLS—Dr. A. D. Whiting, John Isely.

CHURCH EXTENSION—Mrs. M. Coller, Miss A. C. Tyler.

CHURCH RECORDS—John Schaefer, M. L. Glazer.

CONFERENCE CLAIMANTS—John Schaefer.

FREEDMEN—E. A. Garlington, Mrs L. A. Marlatt.

EDUCATION—M. L. Glazer, G. C. Hubbard.

PARSONAGE—E. W. Young, Dr. Whiting, Geo. R. Crosby, E. D. Hammond, Geo. C. Hubbard.

MUSIC—Miss M. L. Hull, Mrs. A. D. Whiting, M. L. Glazer.

DISTRICT STEWARD—The Pastor.

Recording Steward and Treasurer—
GEO. R. CROSBY.

Financial Statement.

Total amount raised by Church during past Conference Year, - - - - - $1,707.20

DISBURSEMENTS AND FUNDS ON HAND.

Pastor,	$900.00
Presiding Elder,	72.00
Benevolences,	142.00
Special Missionary Offering,	20.00
Women's Foreign Missionary Society,	20.00
General Baily, Mission Cause,	15.00
Junior League,	5.00
Sunday School raised	70.00
Mission Sunday School,	25.00
Evangelistic Work,	36.00
Janitor's Salary,	84.60
Electric Lights,	39.36
Fuel,	36.70
Insurance on $1,700,	8.64
Loan from N. R. Bell,	10.12
Balance Moving Expense,	5.50
Singing Books,	6.92
Repairing Furnace and Purchase of Stove,	26.25
Repairing Broken Windows,	5.10
Ladies' Aid Society, Repairing Church,	4.80
Painting Church,	65.00
Booklets for Collections,	3.50
Sundries,	1.58
Ladies' Aid Society, Cash on hand,	28.00
Mission Sunday School, Building Fund,	55.00
Incidental Cash on hand,	1.73
	—$1,707.20

Growing our Legacy in Christ

150 years
1857-2007

The Appointed Ones
Annette DeCourcy Towler

First United Methodist Church

St. Cloud, Minnesota

United Methodist Circuit Rider Symbol, put on all Methodist ministers' grave stones in Minnesota Conference, redrawn by Karel Helgeson from photo of original brass symbol, which is owned and copyrighted by Cokesbury.

STRUCTURE OF THE UNITED METHODIST CHURCH[1]

The Methodist Church in America adopted the "rule of bishops" in 1789. This meant that, just as in the Anglican Church in England, the Methodist denomination was to be governed and unified by a system of bishops. These bishops were elected by delegates to the Methodist Annual Conference and were assigned to serve one or more state or regional conferences. Often in the early years they did not stay in a place more than one year.

Minnesota has always had a bishop. The first bishop of Minnesota was responsible for Minnesota and Wisconsin. Then Minnesota split into two conferences, the Northern and the Minnesota conferences. At one time both the Dakota conferences were with Minnesota.

Today the Minnesota Conference includes only the state of Minnesota, and is divided into six districts. The bishop, who at present is Sally Dyck, has district superintendents (in earlier times called presiding elders) to assist her. Pastor Katie left First Church in 2007 to become the northeast district superintendent (the district St. Cloud is placed in). She is responsible for over forty charges, as are the other district superintendents.

The bishop appoints pastors to a charge, which can be one church or several. Pastors are appointed annually, even if they return to the same charge. While the bishop ultimately appoints pastors, a congregation's need and a pastor's skills play a part in the process. Associate pastors are appointed the same way. Traditionally, appointments are announced at the Minnesota Annual Conference unless there are special circumstances such as death or illness.

HISTORY OF METHODIST PASTORS AND THEIR SPOUSES
by Rev. Dr. James G. Towler

The role of the pastor has remained very similar over the life of the church and our own congregation for 150 years. In the 1940's, women became pastors in many congregations, but without full voting rights at Annual Conference. In 1955, the full rights and official acceptance of women clergy began.

---

[1] *Thanks to Rev. Dr. Jim Towler for help in compiling this information.*

In very early American Methodism, most ministers were single until they became too worn out to be "circuit riders"[2] (if they didn't die first). They would travel between 15 or 20 small scattered churches on the American Frontier. After they left this life, it was then possible for pastors to marry, and bishops were known to encourage single clergy to do so.

The important role of the pastor's spouse, almost always the wife until recently, has been an important strength of the church. The pastor's wife generally had a passion for the work of the Gospel and the Church, and found ways to become a part of a congregation's work. Often her education and skills benefitted the work: pianist, teacher, organizer, advocate for missions, listener, leader in the women's work, part-time secretary, negotiator between the pastor and the congregation, a women's advocate, etc. Some of this was expected of the clergy wife. As to the rest, she had to sort through and negotiate her role in the church. And of course she was to keep the parsonage immaculate, remembering that this was where many meetings of the congregation were held, and the place of reception for visits of the district superintendent, the bishop, and visiting missionaries.

Changes in these expectations came about as churches became larger, as spouses sought regular employment and professions. Some spouses did not have this kind of passion for the work of the church. However, many still do and find ways to exercise church leadership.

First United Methodist Church Pastors

Annette DeCourcy Towler

Early church worship and other activities were accomplished in St. Cloud in a number of ways. Often the appointed pastor served several congregations, sometimes a fair distance from one another. When the pastor was not in attendance, a class leader or a local preacher might lead the worship and activities.

However, all the men and women in the following listing are elders (ordained preachers). Information on these people has been obtained largely from volumes of the Minnesota Conference Journals (1856-present). My thanks go to Kathy Spencer Johnson, Archivist, at the Minnesota United Methodist

---

[2] Usually had a horse and Bible as his companions.

Church Archive Library, for her research of the General Conference databases. Additional information was gathered from census records. Official biographies have been enlarged to include names of wives and children.

In Minnesota's early years, the Minnesota conferences met in October; after 1939, they met in June. However, records show some May appointments. Even then, pastors were assigned outside of conference meetings. Many of the early pastors stayed in a charge for one or two years. The first minister to stay in the St. Cloud area longer was Wiltsie Mayes Martin (1884 -1887) who stayed for three.

The first ministers coming to St. Cloud went through a number of steps to become certified. They often had not attended a seminary, but instead were admitted to a conference as probationers and trained using the guidelines as written in the *Book of Discipline*, a two-year (or longer) course of study. Then they were ordained as deacons by their conference and perhaps a year or two later were fully certified as elders.

There were some seminaries in the East by the time Methodist congregations were being formed in Minnesota. New York City saw the start of United Theological Seminary in 1836; Boston University School of Theology began in 1839; Garrett Bible Institute in Evanston, Illinois, opened in 1853; and Drew Seminary at Madison, New Jersey, began in 1867. These four seminaries and nine other Methodist seminaries operate today.

Today, persons wishing to become pastors must first be recommended to the conference by their local church. If accepted by the conference, they are "on trial" (OT). Seminary training follows after completion of a regular college degree. After seminary, candidates may enter the conference on probation and be eligible for ordination as a deacon. Ordination as an elder, after proven service in local churches, earns "full connection" in the conference. Only then do they have all the privileges of an ordained minister.

Many of the ministers in the Minnesota Conference went to Garrett Bible/Biblical Institute in Evanston, Illinois. After the merger of the Methodist and the Evangelical United Brethren Churches in 1968, Garrett joined with the Evangelical Theological Seminary of Naperville, Illinois. It is now known as Garrett-Evangelical Seminary and is on the campus of Northwestern University in Evanston, Illinois.

Because of changes in the Minnesota Annual Conference's pastor requirements, some Methodist ministers have attended United Theological Seminary in New Brighton, Minnesota. It is a United Church of Christ Seminary. Our current pastor, Bill Meier, is a graduate of the Iliff School of Theology, a Methodist seminary in Denver.

First United Methodist has had many pastors since its beginning. A short, individual biography on each is found in the following pages. The key to abbreviations found in this next section is on page 371.

ASSIGNED PASTORS

John Pugh, **1857**. From the list of assigned pastors, the first one was in 1856. He was admitted a Missionary from Canada 1852. He was ordained a Deacon and an Elder, 1857. In the 1856 journal, he was appointed 7 Aug 1856 to St. Cloud Mission. According to writings of Gertrude Gove, he was only here about 4 weeks. According to Hobart's *History of Minnesota Methodism,* Pugh, Gleason, Griswold were all at Clear Water (Clearwater) during this time. Rev. Pugh continued on in the Minnesota Conference for several years as records were found of him serving other churches and as a Presiding Elder/District Superintendent. In 1860, he transferred to the Detroit Conference and stayed until 1881. He was born in 1801, Oxford, England, of Methodist parents who were trained under the personal ministry of John Wesley. Rev. Pugh was a traveling preacher in Minnesota and Michigan, and died on 20 Feb 1881 at the residence of Mr. Phip, near Verona, Huron County, Michigan.[3] No records were found of a family in this country.

Levi Gleason, **1858.** Clear Water. Admitted in 1858; Deacon 1859; Elder - 1860; Appointed in 1858 to Clear Water, Maine Prairie and Winnebago Prairie. Levi is quoted as saying, "I was the first traveling Methodist preacher at St. Cloud: this was May 7, 1858. I was later at Clearwater for two years. The grasshoppers had consumed nearly everything raised. The people became very destitute. None perished, but many suffered. For my labors upon this field until Conference met, I received a coat, pants and vest, worth perhaps $15.00, and my board. This summer there was a Camp

---

[3] From a letter, the research of Everett Rassmussen, FUMC Archives

Meeting held at Neenah (St. Augusta). It was a glorious one. I think nearly a score was converted."[4] Levi Gleason was born 13 Jun 1833 in New York. In the 8 Jun 1860[5] census, he is listed as a Methodist minister living in St. Cloud, Minnesota, with wife, Martha (Pratt),[6] born in Ohio, age 19, and daughter Cora, born in Minnesota, age 5 months. He was a Mason and served as a Chaplain in the Civil War. He died at Chatfield, Minnesota.

Charles Giles Bowdish, 1858-1859, Sauk River and Clear Water, St. Cloud May **1859 - 1860.** He was admitted on trial 1858 as a Minnesotan Full Connection - 1859; Readmitted - 1861; Ordained Deacon - 1859; Elder - 1862. Supernumerary - 1869-1870. He transferred to New York East Conference in 1870-1873. He was still listed in the Minnesota Conference Journals until 1890. Descendants of this family live in Minnesota, a great granddaughter, Bernice, married Rev. Manning Van Nostrand of First Methodist  Church, St. Cloud, Minnesota. Her brother, Charles Bowdish lives in Brainerd, Minnesota, area. Beatrice said her brother resembles Rev. Charles Bowdish. He is found in the 1860 Stearns County Census, age 26, born about 1834 in New York and listed as a Methodist Clergy. Also living at this address were Ambrose and Elizabeth Freeman. He was born 12 May 1834, Potsdam, NY, and died 5 July 1873, Astoria, NY.

Andrew J. Nelson, 1860-1861. He was appointed to St. Cloud and  Winnebago. He was admitted in 1855 from Wisconsin. He is listed as a visitor (teacher) at Hamline University from 1863-1866. Early First Church records list a Mary Nelson, who was probably his wife. He served only a few months and then became the principal of the St. Cloud Seminary.

Bartley Blain, 1861-1862. He was admitted in 1857, a Minnesotan. He was ordained a Deacon 1858 and an Elder 1860. (Our church records had his name as Bantley Blain). In 1887, he transferred to the Northern Minnesota Conference. In 1886 Journal he is listed as living in Middle Branch, Holt

---

[4] Our Father's Built, p 11
[5] 1860 Minnesota Stearns County Federal Census, NARA Microfilm M653 roll 574 page 865 or 23. Living next door to Reuben Gray.
[6] Research of Gertrude Gove says, daughter of Joseph Pratt of Clearwater vicinity. They lived with Eli King.

County, Nebraska. He was a member of the 1st Minnesota Calvary Regiment with Ambrose Freeman. He married Mary Burriett about 1856 or 1857. In the 1870 census,[7] Bartley and Mary were in St. Charles, Winona county, Minnesota. The census lists Mary and 4 children: Charles age 12, Nellie age 8, Willie E. age 4 and Ada E. age 4 months. He died 19 Nov 1918 in Page, Holt County, Nebraska.

Samuel Thomas Sterrett, 1862-1863. He was admitted to Minnesota - Wisconsin Conference in 1855 from Illinois Conference. According to the General Conference Journal, he was in the St. Cloud area from 1857 to 1863, serving as a Presiding Elder then serving Monticello, Clearwater, Maine Prairie, St. Cloud and Winnebago for one year each. In the 1875 Minnesota State Census, they were in Shakopee with his wife, Mary, born in New York and age 39. Children are Eddie C. (Ida C.), Emma, Samuel O., Sarah Bell, and Augustus. He transferred to East Oregon Washington Conference in 1875.[8] In 1878, he transferred to California Conference. He married Charlotte Smith on 5 Mar 1846 in Gallatin, Illinois. He later married Mary M. Hauer while in St. Cloud, then in California married Mrs. Bell Burroughs, M.D. He was born in Illinois April 16, 1825 and died 1 Dec 1898 probably California.[9]

David Tice, 1863-1865. He was admitted in 1859, a Minnesotan. He was ordained a Deacon in 1860 and an Elder 1861. He married Lizzie/Melissa Howell (1838-1925). While living in St. Cloud, a child, Wesley R. H., was born. David Tice was born in 1829 in Canada and died 25 Feb 1905 and was buried at Lakewood Cemetery, Minneapolis, Minnesota, Sep 15, 1865.

David Tice

---

[7] 1870 City of St. Charles, Winona County, Minnesota, US Federal Population Census. NARA microfilm M593 roll 719 p 14

[8] 1875 Minnesota Annual Conference Journal p 8, but does not match the General Conference Journal information.

[9] 1899 General Conference Journal, Obit

Charles Griswold, 1865-1866. He was admitted on trial in 1860 and then in Full Connection in 1862. He was ordained a Deacon in 1862; an Elder in 1864 in the Minnesota Conference; a Presiding Elder for St. Cloud District - 1866-1869; and a Presiding Elder for Winona District - 1869-1873. He married June and they had the following children: Charles H., Alice B., and Frank H. He was born 7 Oct 1832, Manchester, Connecticut, and died 25 Dec 1906, North St. Paul, Minnesota.

Noah Lathrop, 1866-1867. He was in 1854 on probation in the North Central Indiana Conference. He was admitted in 1856 and was present at the organizational meeting of the Minnesota Conference at Red Wing. He was ordained a Deacon in 1854. Became an Elder in 1857. He was born in Indiana in 1828, graduated from DePauw University, and began his ministry in the Hoosier State. He died 11 May 1914 in California and was buried at Northfield, Minnesota, on 20 May 1914.

John R. Creighton, 1867-1869. He was admitted from Canada in 1865 on probation, became a Minnesotan, Elder in 1867. In the 1870 US Federal Census,[10] he is age 32 in Superior, Wisconsin, with two others, no relationship identified, Maggie age 21 and George K. Creighton age 21. He was born in 1838 in Canada and died 15 Oct 1879.

William Wilson Satterlee, 1869-1871. Joined the Minnesota Conference in 1867. In 1915, he transferred to the North Dakota Conference. In 1887, he was appointed Professor of Scientific Temperance and Hygienic Philosophy in US Grant University, Athens, Tennessee. He spent his summers in Minnesota at his Minnetonka Fruit Farm. He married Sarah Stout and had the following children, Carrie Almeda, William Eugene, Elmvira, Phoebe Adair and Marion Pease. He was born on 11 Apr 1837 at La Porte, Indiana, and died in Minneapolis, Minnesota, 27 May 1893. See his son's (Marion P.) story in "Through the Years" section.

---

[10] 1870 Superior, Douglas County, Wisconsin US population census. NARA microfilm M593 roll 1712 page 76 (ancestry.com) p 6.

Harvey Webb, 1871-1872.  He was admitted in 1863 and ordained an Elder 1867. He transferred to Austin, Texas, Conference in 1879. In 1860, he was in Red Wing living in the home of another Methodist Minister, Rev. G. W. Wright. He resigned from First Methodist Episcopal Church, St. Cloud, 27 Jun 1872. He is listed in the 1880 Federal Census in Texas with wife, Jemima, and daughter, Nellie, born in Minnesota in 1864.

F. A. Rigum, Supply April 1872 – Oct 1872. No information is known about him. This barely readable information was found on page 70, typed by George Crosby in *History of the Methodist Church St. Cloud* scrapbook.[11] This history is typed in the book dated Feb, 1914. (See "Through the Years" section.)

James. T. Lewton, 1872-1874. He was admitted in 1870 on trial and ordained a Deacon and an Elder 1872. In 1875, he transferred to the Florida Conference. In the 1880 Federal Census he is listed in Orange City, Florida, along with these children: James E., Theodore E., May A., Annette, Edmund and his wife, May.

Horatio Southard Hilton, 1874-1875. He was admitted in 1870, was ordained an Elder in 1873. He and his wife, Lucelia, came to St. Cloud from Homer, Winona County, Minnesota, where he was serving a Methodist church. He transferred to Colorado conference in 1878 and then transferred to Indiana Conference, where he was listed in the 1900 Federal Census in Indiana.

John Wesley Klepper 1875-1876. He was admitted on trial in 1858 in Michigan. He was ordained a Deacon in 1860 and an Elder 1862. A member of the Michigan Conference - 1858-1859, the Minnesota Conference - 1859-1886, the Puget Sound Conference from 1886-1887, the Oregon Conference from 1887-1888 and the Northwest Iowa Conference from 1888-1895. He was born 2 Jul 1834, Coles County, Illinois, and died 29 Sep 1895, Hull, Iowa.

---

[11] In FUMC Archives

Isaac Hancock Riddick, 1876-1877. He was admitted to Minnesota Conference in 1870. He was ordained a Deacon 1873, an Elder 1875. He transferred in 1877 to the Detroit Conference in Michigan. He was born 15 Jun 1846 in Ohio and died 12 May 1932 in Michigan.[12] He married Martha in 1870. The 1900 Federal Census listed four children: Mary, Mattie, Foster and Paul. He later married Leena and had a son, Parker.

Isaac M. Marsh, 1877-1879. Admitted On Trial - 1870; Full Connection – 1872. He was ordained a Deacon in 1872 and an Elder in 1874. Minnesota Conference - 1870-1881; St. Cloud and Sauk Rapids - 1877-1878; St. Cloud - 1878-1879; Richfield - 1879-1881. He married Sarah J. Rogers, daughter of Rev. J. M. Rogers. He was born 16 July 1848, Nova Scotia, and died 30 Jan 1881, while serving Richfield Methodist Episcopal Church. Buried Oak Hill Cemetery, Minneapolis.

1879-1880. Conference Journal does not show an appointee assigned to either St. Cloud or Sauk Rapids.

Michael O. McNiff, 1880-1881. He was ordained a Deacon in 1872 and an Elder 1875. Admitted to Minnesota Conference 1872, served 11 years. He was a Civil War Veteran with the 44th New York Regiment. Wounded in 2nd Battle of Bull Run. He was married to Margaret/Susan, as stated in the 1880 Federal Minnesota census and Minnesota State Census 1875. He was born in New York in 1840 and died March 25, 1905, Santa Paula, California.

Joseph B. Starkey, 1881-1882. Admitted to North West Iowa and to Minnesota Conference in 1878. He was born 1844 in New York and died 8 Mar 1917 while a member of the Pittsburgh Conference.

Henry Frank, 1882-1883. Admitted in 1880 from Kansas Conference. Ordained an Elder in 1882. Found with his wife Mary of 19 years (married 1881) in the Hartford, Hartford County, Connecticut, 1900 Federal Census, as a clergyman, but was listed as an insurance man by the 1910 census in New York.

---

[12] General Conference Roll of the Dead on-line index, accessed by Kathy Spencer Johnson.

Edward S. Ferry, 1883-1884. Admitted to and transferred from Newark Conference 1883. In 1885, he transferred to New York Central Conference, lived at Pine St (street, New York City?)[13] New York.

Wiltsie Mayes Martin 1884-1887. Admitted to Minnesota Conference in 1881, ordained a Deacon in 1885 and an Elder 1885. In 1887, transferred to Hammond, Indiana. He was born in Pennsylvania in 1850.

John Wilson Briggs 1887-1889. Admitted in 1876 to Bay of Quinte Conference, Ontario. Transferred to Minnesota 1884, ordained a Deacon in 1884 and an Elder. He lived during 1888-1889 at 421 4th Avenue South, St. Cloud, Minn. He resigned in Jan 1889 from FUMC, went to Syracuse, NY. He was born in Canada in 1853. He died 15 Jan. 1921, while serving Central New York Conference.

Charles H. Brace, 7 Oct 1889 He was an Illinois Conference supernumerary (retired pastor) filling in. Our conference journal listed him as a supply Oct 7 1889, but could find no trace of this person in our written church records. He died 8 Nov 1892. His memorial, or obituary, is in the 1893 Central Illinois Journal, which stated that he retired here in St. Cloud.

Robert R. Atchison, 1889-1891 He was admitted to Minnesota in 1886 on probation, He was born in New Jersey in 1844 and died 30 Sep 1918, Michigan Conference. No other records found.

---

[13] as found in Church Record Book

James H. Dewart, **1891-1896.** Admitted in 1872 on probation at Erie Conference (New York). Transferred to Minnesota Conference in 1882 as an Elder. He was born in Canada 1838 and he died 18 March 1923 after 37 years of service and is buried in Roselawn Cemetery, St. Paul, Minnesota. His picture sketch from the St. Cloud paper was found in Crosby's Scrapbook,[14]. He and his wife Harriet lived at 401 8th Avenue South,[15] while in St. Cloud.

In 1895, The Minnesota Conference became too large, so it was split into the Northern and Southern Minnesota Conferences of the Methodist Episcopal Church. St. Cloud and Minneapolis were part of the Northern Conference; St. Paul was in the Southern Conference.

Lyman W. Ray, **1896-Mar 1898.** Admitted in 1893 from South Dakota. He was ordained a Deacon and an Elder. He left the conference and was living in Minneapolis, Minnesota, in 1898. He came Oct 7, 1896, and resigned 11 Mar 1898. The family lived at 405 9th Avenue South[16] while in St. Cloud. Rev. Lyman used a red stamp in our Church records book instead of signing his name.

Frederick E. Ross, **1898 Mar -Fall 1901.** Admitted on probation in 1893 and was an Elder 1894. In the Crosby scrapbook is the statement "Rev. F. E. Ross of Moorhead, Minnesota was sent to St Cloud to fill out the conference year - he came here May 1st 1898." He was pastor here at the time of the re-opening of First M.E. Church on 22 July 1900. He was born in 1869 in Canada. The family lived at 370 5th Avenue South[17] while in St. Cloud.

Charles William Lawson, **1901-1904.** In 1883 he was on probation in the Minnesota Conference. He was ordained a Deacon in 1885 and an Elder in 1887. He and his wife, Harriett Pullen (married in 1885), came to St. Cloud in October 1901. He was born 21 Jan 1855 in Jamestown, New York. He died 22 April 1914 after 43 years with the Conference and is buried at

---

[14] Scrapbook in FUMC archives
[15] 1984-1895 St. Cloud City Directory p 39
[16] 1898-1899 St. Cloud City Directory p 102
[17] 1898-1899 St. Cloud City Directory p 104

Anoka, Minnesota. He was survived by 4 children. He and his wife, Harriett, lived 354 6th Avenue South[18] while in St. Cloud.

Charles Wilbur Stark 1904-1906. Admitted in 1897 from Kansas. He was ordained an Elder in 1900. He left St. Cloud to work for Anti-Saloon League. In 1894 he married Carrie E. Goodell, who was born in 1866 in Pennsylvania. He was born in 1867 in Washington and died 1926, Minneapolis, Minnesota. They lived at 119 4th Avenue South[19] while in St. Cloud.

Lawrence B. Schei, 1906-1907. Supply, a 1907 graduate of Hamline University. 1966 Hamline Alumni Directory says graduated with a BA degree. Only record in our archives is a letter. He was not on Journal appointment lists.

Thomas Stanley Oadams, 1907-1909. Transferred 1912 out to Congregational Church in Wisconsin. He was born in England and immigrated to the United States in 1881/1882. He married in 1886. In the 1900 census, he and family are in Kane County, Illinois. In 1909, they are at River Forest, Wisconsin. 1910 US population census lists wife, Josie, and 2 daughters, Florence and Hazel, in Two Harbors, Lake County, Minnesota. He participated in the dedication of the new church on 24 May 1914, as he was serving the Monticello Methodist church during this time frame. They lived at 202 3rd Avenue South[20] while in St. Cloud.

Frederick William Hill, 1909-1915. He graduated from Hamline University, 1900, and Boston University School of Theology in 1905. He was admitted on trial in 1899 and became a member in Full Connection in 1904. He was ordained a Deacon in 1901 and an Elder in 1905. A member of the Northern Minnesota Conference from 1899-1904; New England Conference in 1904; Northern Minnesota Conference again from 1904-1948. He

---

[18] 1904-1905 St. Cloud City Directory p 117
[19] 1906-1907 St. Cloud City Directory p 193
[20] 1908-1909 St. Cloud City Directory p 159

was a school teacher prior to being a minister. He was in St. Cloud when the Twentieth Century Methodist church was dedicated on 24 May 1914. On 27 Mar 1900, he married Winona Mues (1872-1946) a graduate of Hamline University from Winona, Minnesota. She died 26 Oct 1946. In 1947 he married Bessie Fasholt of St. Cloud, Minnesota. No children are listed in the obituary. Rev. Hill was born 3 Nov 1873, Toronto, Ontario, Canada, and died 26 Oct 1948, Wadena, Minnesota, and is buried in Minneapolis at Lakewood Cemetery. Family lived at 613 4th Avenue South in 1910[21] and then moved in 1914 to 422 7th Ave South[22] while in St. Cloud.

William Chappell Lee, 1915-1917. He was admitted on trial in 1896 after being in the banking business at Edgerton, Minnesota. He became a member in full connection in 1898 serving the Southern Minnesota Methodist Conference. In 1915, he transferred to St. Cloud in the Northern Minnesota Conference. During the 1917 Conference, he became Litchfield District Superintendent, of which St. Cloud was a part. Rev. Lee was born 30 Jun 1868 at Kingsend near Plymouth, Devonshire, England. He was one of eight children and came to America to join his elder brother, Rev. John Lee, at Sioux City, Iowa. He attended Morningside College and Cornell College, Mount Vernon, Iowa. He was married on 5 May 1896 to Helen Leonia Morris at Detroit, Iowa. They had two children, William Morris Lee, who died in infancy, and Helen Morris Lee. He died 31 Oct 1946, Minneapolis, Minnesota, and is buried at Lakewood Cemetery, Minneapolis, Minnesota. While living in St. Cloud, the family lived at 202 3rd Ave South with the McKelvy family.[23]

William Chappell Lee 1915-1917

---

[21] 1910 St. Cloud City Directory p 109
[22] 1914 St. Cloud City Directory p 114
[23] 1916 St. Cloud city Directory p 163, 304

George E. Tindall, 1917-1923. He was admitted in 1893. He was ordained a

George E. Tindall 1917-1923

Deacon 1891 and an Elder in 1893. He graduated from the Collegiate Institute of Barrie, Ontario, in 1885 and taught school for 4 years. In 1890, he received a letter from a Dr. Joseph B. Hingeley, requesting him "to come over to Minnesota." On 15 Nov 1893, he married Mary A. McAfee of Bradford, Ontario. He was born on 23 Dec 1861 near Bradford, Ontario, Canada. He died 9 May 1933 after 42 years of ministry and a long illness. He was survived by his wife and 6 children: Matthew E., George B., J. Merritt, Frank M., Mae, and Pauline. He is buried at Alexandria, Douglas County, Minnesota. They lived at 310 5th Avenue South[24] while in St. Cloud.

Harry Winstanley Bell, 1923-1925. He was received on trial in the Central

H. W. Bell 1923-1925

Illinois Conference in 1904 and Full Connection in 1906. He was ordained a Deacon in 1905 and an Elder in 1908. He transferred to Northern Minnesota Conference in 1918. He aided in the placement of the Wesley Hospital at Wadena and was appointed its executive secretary for 5 years. He received his B. S. degree from Illinois Wesleyan University in 1910 and the degree of D. D. (Doctorate of Divinity), Oskaloosa College, in 1918. He married Mable Rudell on 31 Dec 1901. They had one child, Elizabeth. The family lived at 310 5th Avenue South[25] while in St. Cloud. He was born on 20 Jun 1873 at Watseka, Illinois, and passed away 28 April 1953 after 54 years in the Methodist ministry.

---

[24] 1919-1920 St. Cloud City Directory p 313, Church address is 302 5th Ave So. No houses between so must be the parsonage.
[25] 1925-1926 St. Cloud City Directory p 70

Andrus Laverne Richardson, **1925-1927.** Admitted on Trial - 1894; Full Connection - 1899 to 1939. He was ordained a Deacon 1898 and an Elder 1907. He graduated from Hamline University in 1898 and was a member of Northern Minnesota Conference and retired in 1951 . He was known as "the PILOT." He married Anne E. Denny at Anoka, Minnesota, on 27 Jan 1898. After retiring they moved to Montana. He was born 6 Mar 1869, Cherry Creek, New York, and died in July 1951, Great Falls, Montana, and is buried at Great Falls Highland Cemetery. Surviving children were R. B. Richardson, William, Philip, James, and Athea Roberts.

J. Arthur Edwards, 1927-1930. Admitted to and was ordained a Deacon and then an Elder in 1901. Transferred into the Northern Minnesota Conference in 1920. Then, in 1930, he transferred to Central Falls, Rhode Island, in the New England South Conference.

Harold E. Mayo, 1930-1937. Admitted to and was ordained a Deacon and an Elder. On 28 April 1930, he transferred from Maine Conference. In 1934, he transferred to Iowa Conference. He was a Navy chaplain in World War II, and in 1957 was executive secretary of the New York Port Society, an organization interested in promoting the gospel among seamen of all nations.

Harland Chester Logan, 1934-1946. Admitted and was ordained a Elder in 1902, then in 1934 transferred to Minnesota from Wisconsin Conference. He married Mabel Gott 16 Aug 1905. She died 7 Oct 1935, right after moving to St. Cloud. He married Alice M. Lewis, a member of Technical High School faculty, in 1937/8 at Simpson Methodist Episcopal Church in Minneapolis, Minnesota. He was born on 2 Sep 1874 at Hortonville, Wisconsin, and died 12 Dec 1961 in Shell Lake, Wisconsin. He was survived by three daughters,

Mrs. J. W. Coatsworth, Mrs. Marshall Hulbert, and Mrs. Loren Gilbert and one son, Gordon Logan.

Merger of the Northern Methodist Conference and the Methodist Conference of the Methodist Church Minnesota. Last separate conference was in 1947.

Russell Allan Huffman, 1946-1955. Admitted on Trial in 1928, a member in Full Connection in 1931. He was ordained a Deacon 1931 and an Elder in 1934. He graduated from Evanston in 1935 and Garrett Seminary in 1938, received an honorary Doctor of Divinity from Hamline University in 1960. He was a member of the Indiana Conference, 1927-1938; Midlothian, Illinois Conference from 1936-1938; Northern Minnesota Conference from 1938-1948. Transferred to North Dakota Conference in 1955. He retired in 1974. He  married Winifred Terry 16 Aug 1930. They had two children, Russell, Jr., and Susan. He was born 26 Nov 1908, Henryville, Indiana, and died 19 Jul 1989 in Paynesville, Minnesota, and is buried at the Paynesville Cemetery.

Russell Luther Hubbard, 1955-1957. Graduated from Michigan in 1936 and  Drew Seminary in 1939. Admitted to Minnesota Conference in 1950. He was ordained a Deacon in 1938 Detroit Conference and an Elder 1940, Detroit Conference. Transferred to Minnesota in 1948 to become the Executive Secretary of the Conference Board of Education, then the District Superintendent of Duluth District in 1951. He retired in 1973. He was born 25 Dec 1909 and died 21 Aug 1993 in Minnesota.

Paul Otto Metzger, 1957-1963. He graduated from University of Minnesota 1947, Garrett Seminary in 1950. He was admitted in 1947 and he was ordained a Deacon in 1949 and an Elder in 1950. He married Phyllis Rhoda. in 1945, and they had three children, Stephen, Cynthia (Woodbury) and Barbara Jean. He was born in Newport, Minnesota 28 Dec 1915 and died 9 Aug 1980 in Walker, Minnesota.

Kenneth Oscar Beck, **1963-1979.** He graduated from Hamline University in 1948 and Garrett Seminary in 1951. He was admitted to the conference in 1948 and became a Deacon in 1950, then an Elder 1951. He served 5 congregations during his 36 years in the Conference. He married Catherine Billings at Lake Harriet Methodist on 20 Aug 1948. They have a son, Peter, daughters Martha Beck and Sarah (Jack) Garrett. He was part of the Selma March in 1963 and very active as a trustee of Hamline University. He was born on 7 Mar 1922 in Des Moines, Iowa. He passed away on 20 Mar 2006 in Minneapolis, Minnesota, and is buried in Fort Snelling National Cemetery.

W. Thoburn (Toby) Horst, 1979-1994. He graduated from Albion College, Michigan, in 1951, and Garrett Theological Seminary in 1955. He was ordained in 1953 in the Ohio Conference and admitted to Minnesota in 1954. He is one of the rare pastors who served only three churches in his 40 years in this conference. He is retired and lives with his wife, Locky, in St. Cloud, Minnesota. They have three grown children, Sara, Scot, and Mark.

Kathryn A. Schneider-Bryan, 1994 -2007. She graduated from Hamline University in 1977 (BA) and from Garrett in 1982 (MDiv). She was admitted to the Minnesota Conference in 1979 and ordained as a Deacon; she became an Elder in 1981. She was UMHE[26] chaplain at St. Cloud State University in 1993 before becoming First Church pastor. She currently is North East District Superintendent. She is married to Daniel Schneider-Bryan. Having a couple serve as pastors

---

[26] United Ministries in Higher Education

was a new experience for First Church. Their children are Greg and Anna.

William (Bill) F. Meier, 2007. He graduated from Dakotan Wesleyan (BA), Mitchell, South Dakota, in 1982 and from Iliff Seminary, Denver, Colorado, in 1984 (MDiv). He was admitted and ordained a Deacon in Minnesota 1983 and an Elder in 1986. He has served Hendricks-Ivanhoe 1984-1989, Dexter – Grand Meadow 1989-1995 and Detroit Lakes 1995-2007. He married Linda Schoenrogge, August 8, 1981. They are parents of 3 children, Nicole Lee (Tyson) Zitzow, Aaron William, and Sarah Elizabeth.

LIST OF ASSOCIATE PASTORS

This list was accumulated from research done in the Conference Journals. Many of these pastors were not appointed by Minnesota Conference to First United Methodist. They were appointed to Waite Park and Sauk Rapids Methodist, then were hired by First Methodist Church as either a youth, education or Wesley Foundation pastor.

John W. Mower, 1899. Youth Preacher. He was admitted to the conference in 1879. He was born in 1846 in Pennsylvania and died 27 Sep 1908, buried at Lakewood Cemetery, Minneapolis, Minnesota.

L. L. Erickson, 1913-1914. Associate with Sauk Rapids.

Albert J. Oliver, 1914-1916. Associate with Sauk Rapids, died in 1915 leaving a wife and son. They lived on Grand Street,[27] Sauk Rapids.

Frederick J. Bryan, 1916-1917. Associate with Sauk Rapids from Michigan Conference to W. Wisconsin in 1906, then to Minnesota in 1909. He retired in 1931. He served Sauk Rapids with his wife, Mary. He was born in England, came through Canada in 1881 and died 24 Aug 1950 and was buried in Clearwater, Minnesota.

---

[27] 1916 St. Cloud City Directory p 361

Leon S. Koch, 1917-1919. Associate with Sauk Rapids. Admitted to the conference in 1892. He was born in 1857 and died 29 May 1934. He was buried at Faribault, Minnesota.

William E. Peterson, 1919-1922. Associate. Admitted on trial 1919. He became a Deacon 1923 and an Elder in 1925. He served in the army 1918-1919. He was born 1892, died 23 Mar 1961 and was buried at Crystal Lake, Minneapolis, Minnesota.

Truman Benton Clark, 1922-1924. Associate Waite Park. Admitted on Trial, 1922. Ordained a Deacon 1923, then an Elder in 1925. He was a 1916 graduate of Hamline University. He was born on 28 Oct 1881 at Emporia, Kansas, and died 15 November 1961 at the St. Cloud Hospital, St. Cloud, Minnesota. He was survived by his wife, Alma, Annandale, Minnesota, and three daughters Alma Jean Connell, Marjorie Olson, Constance Schey, and one son, Dr. Truman Clark. He was buried at Roselawn Cemetery, St. Paul, Minnesota. They lived in Waite Park.[28]

E. B. Service, 1923. Waite Park and Sauk Rapids, not found in Conference lists.

Raymond F. Mattock, 1924 - 1927. Associate one year, served Waite Park. Admitted on Trial 1924, ordained a Deacon in 1924 and an Elder in 1932. He died 17 Jun 1955 and was buried at Estes Brook (near Oak Park), Minnesota. They lived in Waite Park, Minnesota.[29]

Stephen M. Bowles, 1925.

L. W. Bartholow, 1927.

George Tindall, 1928-1932. See pastors list.

---

[28] 1923-1924 St. Cloud City Directory, p 494
[29] 1925-1926 St. Cloud City Directory p 512

Allyn Hans Hanson, **1933 – 1936.** Waite Park. He was ordained and  admitted 1928 and an Elder in 1932. He was a bachelor while serving FUMC and Waite Park. He graduated from Hamline University in 1929, then Garrett Seminary in 1932. He married Enid Shorts on 3 Mar 1938. He was born 24 Sept 1907, Stewart, Minnesota. and died 23 May 2005.

Arthur Kent, **1937-1938.** Accepted Supply by the conference lists. Accepted in 1933, Waite Park 1937-1939, no record of ordination.

Shigeo Tanabe, 1953-1954. The first minister of Japanese ancestry to unite  with the Minnesota Conference, came to St. Cloud as associate pastor and youth director. In 1954 the church at large requested his release so he could serve the Harris Memorial Methodist Church in Honolulu, Hawaii. Currently living in Hawaii. He was born in 1908, Fort Thomas, Washington. He received his MDiv in 1937. On 14 Aug 2008, he celebrated his 100th birthday. He married Haru.

Irving Harrison Palm, 1954-1955. Associate. He was admitted and became a Deacon in 1949 and an Elder in 1951. He graduated from University of Minnesota in 1943 and Garrett Seminary in 1951. He was born 11 Apr 1920 and died 9 March 2002. He married Lois Black on 10 Sept 1947. He served in the Navy during World War II.

Malcolm E. Shattuck, 1956-1957. Waite Park and Associate as Youth Pastor at FUMC. He graduated from Foley High School, Hamline University and Drew University. He served Clinton Methodist and in the New York Conference before coming to St. Cloud. He was married and has one daughter, Carol Lee.

Donald Day, 1961. Associate hired by First Church (not appointed), also 1961 – 1966 was Waite Park Church minister. He graduated from Hamline University in 1956 and from Boston in 1959. He was ordained a Deacon in 1957, then an Elder in 1961. Retired; he and his wife Virginia are living in Park Rapids, Minnesota.

Richard F. Collman, 1961-1971. He graduated from the University of Minnesota, Duluth, in 1965 and Yale in 1969. He also earned a degree from Notre Dame in 1979. He was ordained a Deacon in 1967 and an Elder in 1969. St. Cloud as an associate was his first appointment. He was involved with adding the current Wicks organ to our music program.

Richard Lewis, 1962-1973. Associate and Wesley Foundation. Graduate of Washburn University, Kansas, and Garrett Biblical Seminary, Evanston, IL. Ordained a Deacon in 1961 and an Elder in 1962. He was transferred from Winona Central Methodist and associate director of Wesley Foundation, Winona State College. Lived in Wesley House at 913 Third Ave South in St. Cloud and divided his time between First United Methodist and Wesley Foundation at St. Cloud State University.

Marvin Repinski, 1973-1974. He graduated from North Central Bible College in 1959 and Northwestern Lutheran in 1964. He was admitted and ordained a Deacon in 1964 and became an Elder in 1967. He worked with Wesley Foundation at St. Cloud State University and was Associate with First Church.

Larry A. Hager, 1979-1981. Associate. He graduated from Illinois Wesleyan in 1968 and from Union School of Theology seminary (UTS) in New York City, New York, in 1974. He was admitted and ordained a Deacon in 1970 and an

Elder in 1976. He served Becker and Zimmerman before coming to First UMC. (Annette D. Towler, as lay delegate from Becker UMC, was privileged to stand up for his ordination at St. John's Abbey in 1976.)

Evelyn Durkee, 1975-1979 and **1985-1995**. Associate. She is a member of  Iowa Conference. She graduated from Union Theological Seminary in New York City, NY, in 1966 and became an elder in the Northeast Iowa United Methodist Church Conference in 1975. She was the campus minister at Iowa City Wesley College from 1967-73 and served Wyoming and Oxford Junction in Iowa from 1973-1975.

Kathryn Schneider-Bryan, 1993-1994 see Pastor list.

Shane Allen Burton, 1995 - Jan 1999. He graduated from Concordia, Moorhead, then Garrett Theological Seminary in 1995. He  was admitted and ordained in 1995 and an Elder in 1998. He was the Youth/Education Associate during his time at First Church.

Daniel G. Schneider-Bryan, Jan 1999 – 2007. He graduated from McKendree University, Illinois, in 1977 (BA) and from Garrett Theological Seminary in 1980 (MDiv). He was admitted and ordained a Deacon in 1979 in Southern Illinois Conference and ordained an Elder in 1984, Minnesota Conference. Dan was an Associate at FUMC responsible for youth and confirmation.

Randall L. Johnson, 2007. BA Bethel College 1974; MA U of Minnesota  1977; MDiv Bethel Seminary 1978; Ord: 1979 ABC; Pastor: Grace Chapel, St Paul 1978; Temple Baptist, Mpls, 1986; Second Union Church, San Juan, 1992; LMFT: Caritas, St. Cloud 1998; Center for Family Counseling, St. Cloud, 2003; Hired on the Pastoral Staff: First United Methodist Church 2007.

+ + + + + + + + + + + +

Local Preachers

Licenses need to be renewed by the local Church Conference and now are also approved by the Minnesota Conference Board of Ministry.

Charles Quinn, 1922 -   Clarence Nelson, Jan 1927
Paul Evans, Jan 1927   Dolores Keech, 1956 – 2006

+ + + + + + + + + + + +

Pastors from this Congregation

(Note: Key to abbreviations used in the biographies listed below)

Adm = Admitted   E = Elder
App: = Appointed   ED = Education
AS = At school   FM = full member
A = Associate   Mdiv/MDiv = Masters of Divinity
BA = Bachelor of Arts   Ord: = ordained
BS = Bachelor of Science   OT = on trial
Ct = Circuit or charge   PhD = Doctor of Philosophy
D = Deacon   PM = probationary member
DD = Doctor of Divinity   R = retired
DM = Doctor of Divinity   UTS = United Theological
DS = District Superintendent   Seminary

Wayne Carver. He is the class leader for 15 Sep 1865 of a class of 29. The records say Rev. W. Carver 'Leader' [30] on page 80 of the same book. Members list states "Carver, Rev. W., Elder, Residence: St. Cloud, date: Nov 1st 1865. Joining by transfer. Class leader: Rev. W. Carver. Remarks: Entered pastoral work 1866." He added members from 1858-1867.

W. D. Bennett. The 20 Aug 1865 St. Cloud Quarterly Conference lists this information: "The character of W. D. Bennett was passed – his license renewed - and he was recommended to Garrett Biblical Institute."

---

[30] Church Records Blue Book page 76.

Duane J. Lunemann, Ed: BA St. Cloud 1953; Mdiv Garrett 1956; Adm: OT 1953; FM 1957; Ord: D 1954; E 1957; App: AS 1953 (Des Plaines, IL (A), (1955-1957); Newport 1957; Mpls Hennepin Ave (A) 1965; Crystal 1969; DS MW 1986; Roseville 1991; R 1994

Russell A. Huffman, Jr., ED: BA St. Cloud 1952, STB Iliff Methodist School of Theology, Adm: OT 1953, FM 1957, Ord: D 1954, E 1957; App. AS 1953-1956; Luverne 1958-1958, Northfield 1958-1961. He left the conference in 1961 to pursue a medical degree. U of Minnesota 1965, PhD Dartmouth Medical Center, New Hampshire. US Navy Flight Surgeon, Alaska. Currently residing in Nashville, TN, with his own psychology clinic. [Picture in FUMC archives from St. Cloud State University Alumni Newspaper.]

Manning Van Nostrand. Ed: BA St. Cloud 1952, STB Boston 1955, MA Minn 1958, PhD Boston U. 1970; Adm: OT 1953 FM 1955 App: AS 1953 Bethel 1955; Mahtomedi 1956: Mpls Wesley (A) 1957; N Hamp Salisbury, Mass 1958, Hampton 1961 Minn: Owatonna 1967; Golden Valley 1973; Albert Lea 1974; Division of Discipleship; (Australia); St. Paul Central Park 1981. He was born 31 May 1908 and died 18 Jun 1990 in Morrison County, Minnesota.

Marva Jean Hutchens. Ed: BS St. Cloud 1970; MDiv UTS TC 1980; Adm: PM 1979; FM 1981; Ord: D 1979; E 1981; App: Crystal (A) 1980; Bemidji 1984; Metro West DS 1991; Farmington 1997; Grand Rapids 2002.

Rick Carlson. . Graduate of Concordia College and Wartburg Theological Seminary. Ph.D, Union Theological Seminary of Virginia, Easter 1983. Clergy in the American Lutheran Church in 1983. Ordained a Lutheran pastor in First Church sanctuary.

Retired Pastors Attached
to First Church Quarterly Conference

Ministers are not members of the current church they are serving/attending, but are members of the Quarterly Conference of that church. Wives of ministers can be members of the churches they are attending.

Wolfram Fliegel, Moravian Pastor. Moravian College, Bethlehem, PA, VA 1953; Moravian Theological Seminary, BD 1956; Princeton Theological Seminary M Theology, 1978; Interim pastorates, as student, 1st Moravian Church, New York City, 1955. Pastor: Dominican Republic – Moravian Church, 1956-1960. Virgin Islands: St. John, 1960-1962; Nicaragua: Bluefields, Managua 1962-1973; MN: Northfield Yoked Parish (1 Moravian and 2 UMC) 1973-1979. WI Ephraim 1973-1990; Lake Mills 1990-1995; R 1995 with his wife Faith.

Wolfram & Faith Fliegel

Dudley A. Keech, Minnesota Conference ED: BA Hamline 1939; STB Boston, 1942; Adm: OT 1940; FM 1944; Ord: D 1941; E. 1944, App: West St. Paul 1937-1938; AS 1940 Blooming Prairie-Lansing 1942; Kellogg-Weaver 1945; Gordonsville-Glenvill 1948; Lake Benton-Hendricks-Ivanhoe 1952; Heron Lake-Okabena 1957; Winnebago 1966; Pine River-Pequot Lakes 1972; West Concord-Kenyon 1974; R 1982 in St. Cloud with wife, Dolores. (Currently living in Sioux Falls, SD.)

Rev. Dudley & Dolores Keech

Robert D. Kendall, Minnesota Conference ED: BA Denver 1954; Drew 1957; MA U of Minnesota 1968; PhD U of Minnesota 1973; Adm OT: 1955; FM 1957 Ord: 1955 Eld: 1957; App: N NY Westmoreland-Clark Mills; 1955, N IA Winthrop-Masonville 1958; Minnesota Mpls Lake Harriet (A) 1960; Fridley 1962; AS 1968: Mound (A) 1971; Min to Society 1972; Professor of Speech Communication St. Cloud State University 1976; Retired 1993 in St. Cloud with wife, LuBell.

Robert & LuBell Kendall

Donald A Kinzer, Minnesota Conference Education: AB Central 1956; BD St. Paul 1962; Admitted on Trial 1957, Full Member 1963 Ordained a Deacon 1960; Elder 1963; App: MO Fayette CT 1950; Bolkow CT 1952; Mokan CT 1953; Columbia Community 1957; Hardin 1959; MN: Annandale-Kimball 1961; Monticello 1964; Howard Lake-Montrose 1968; Racine-Grand Meadow 1970; Olivia Faith-Bird Island 1975; So. St. Paul's 1982 (name change to Mendota Heights, St. Paul's 1986); Hutchinson Vineyard, 1989; Motley 1992; R 1993 moved to St. Cloud in 2007 with wife, Joanne.

Donald and JoAnn Kinzer

James G. Towler, Dakota Conference (North and South) was born 26 Apr 1929, Clarkfield, Minnesota. Education: BS 1951 Mankato State Teachers College, 1955 MDiv Drew Theological Seminary, Doctor of Ministry(DM) 1980 McCormick Theological. Admitted on Trial, Ordained Minnesota as a Deacon 1951, Full Membership 1955; 51 MN: -- 1955 Pine River-Emily; 1959 Jeffers-Amo; 1961 Eveleth-Meadowlands; Transferred to North Dakota -- 1964 Fargo 1st; 1968 Bowbells-Coteau-Kenmare; 1971; Arthur-Hunter-Erie; 1976; Langdon-Hannah; Transferred to South Dakota -- 1982 Miller-Greenleaf; 1987; Timber Lake-Timber Lake ELCA-Timber Lake ABC-Isabel UCC; 1992; Presho-Kennebec-Reliance; 1994; Retired; 1989 in St. Cloud with wife, Arlene.

Jim & Arlene Towler

Growing our Legacy in Christ

150 years
1857–2007

First Families

Mary Beth Wheeler

First United Methodist Church

St. Cloud, Minnesota

Hayward Family

From *Stearns History*, Mitchell p 85, 74

Josiah Eaton Hayward

son-in-law, John S. Coates

Mary Stinson Gray Hayward

FIRST FAMILIES
THE FREEMANS, GRAYS, HAYWARDS & McCLURES

Mary Beth Wheeler of California, an avid family history researcher, has given First Church permission to include her research of the early families that were members in the early years of this congregation. Gertrude Gove, in the first two chapters of this book, talks about many of these people. Relationships were not always stated so you could follow the family lines. Two St. Cloud residents also have connections to this family: Jan Panger and Janet Gray's children. Benjamin Asbury Gray settled in the Elk River area, and was great grandfather of the Janet's children. Hayward family were the owners of the Grand Hotel, which stood where the Radisson Hotel is today. The majority of these families are buried in the North Star Cemetery, St. Cloud, Minnesota. You will find multi listings for members of the Gray, Freeman and Hayward families as there was several intermarriages. For further information on the resources for this family, please contact Mary Beth Wheeler at the website listed below.

Descendant List of Ambrose (Lt.) FREEMAN, GRAY, Hayward, & McClure
compiled by Mary Beth Wheeler, www.wheeler.org

FREEMAN DESCENDANTS

1-Lt. Ambrose FREEMAN
b: 25 Feb 1823 in Culpeper Courthouse, Culpeper Co., Virginia
d: 24 Jul 1863 in Sibley, Richland Co., North Dakota
 +Jane Elizabeth COLE
b: 11 May 1817 in Culpeper Courthouse, Culpeper Co., Virginia
m: 9 Feb 1843 in Chesterfield Co., Virginia
d: 8 Jul 1895 in St. Cloud, Stearns Co., Minnesota
.....**2-Elizabeth "Betty" FREEMAN**
    b: 22 Feb 1844 in Culpeper Co., Virginia
    d: aft Jul 1895 in Jamestown, North Dakota?
..... +A. T. (Lt.) DEARBORN
.....**2-Virginia S. FREEMAN**
    b: 10 Sep 1847 in Culpeper Co., Virginia
    d: 27 Nov 1910 in St. Cloud, Stearns Co., Minnesota
..... +George Burdette MARVIN
    b: 25 Jun 1839 in Homer, Cortland Co., New York
    m: 16 Sep 1863 in St. Cloud, Stearns Co., Minnesota
    d: in of St. Cloud, Stearns Co., Minnesota
.....**2-Daniel Harris FREEMAN**

b: 16 Jun 1849 in Logan, Edgar Co., Illinois
d: 7 Nov 1931 in St. Cloud, Stearns Co., Minnesota
..... +Clara Hortense HAYWARD
b: 1851 in Wesley, Washington Co., Maine
m: 17 Jul 1870 in St. Cloud, Stearns Co., Minnesota
d: 12 Dec 1936 in buried St. Cloud, Stearns Co., Minnesota
.... 3-Minnetta FREEMAN
b: 10 Mar 1871 in St. Cloud, Stearns Co., Minnesota
d: 16 Feb 1873 in St. Cloud, Stearns Co., Minnesota
.... 3-Ambrose FREEMAN
b: 12 Dec 1872 in St. Cloud, Stearns Co., Minnesota
d: 15 Oct 1874 in St. Cloud, Stearns Co., Minnesota
.... 3-Warren H. FREEMAN
b: 14 Oct 1874 in St. Cloud, Stearns Co., Minnesota
d: 24 Dec 1970 in Minneapolis, Hennepin Co., Minnesota
.... +Caroline "Mary" MCCLURE
b: 8 Sep 1876 in St. Cloud, Stearns Co., Minnesota
m: in St. Cloud, Stearns Co., Minnesota
d: 13 Aug 1950 in Moose Lake, Carlton Co., Minnesota
.... 3-Willard S. FREEMAN
b: 23 Apr 1879 in St. Cloud, Stearns Co., Minnesota
d: 27 May 1950 in St. Cloud, Stearns Co., Minnesota
.... +Grace E. GARDNER
b: abt 1872 in Unknown
m: 20 Apr 1904 in St. Cloud, Stearns Co., Minnesota
d: 19 Dec 1949 in St. Cloud, Stearns Co., Minnesota
.... 3-Son FREEMAN
b: 27 May 1883 in St. Cloud, Stearns Co., Minnesota
d: bef 1900 in St. Cloud, Stearns Co., Minnesota
.... 3-Zelah M. FREEMAN
b: 30 Jun 1889 in St. Cloud, Stearns Co., Minnesota
d: 25 Sep 1977 in Tallahassee, Leon Co., Florida
.... +Warren H. STEWART
b: 23 Jun 1889 in St. Cloud, Stearns Co., Minnesota
m: 1916 in St. Cloud, Stearns Co., Minnesota
d: 20 Jun 1959 in Sauk Rapids, Stearns Co., Minnesota
.............4-Mary Hortense STEWART
b: abt 1916 in St. Cloud, Stearns Co., Minnesota
d: 1998 in of Tallahassee, Leon Co., Florida
.............4-Elora Jean STEWART
b: abt 1918 in St. Cloud, Stearns Co., Minnesota
d: Sep 1995 in Tallahassee, Leon Co., Florida
.............4-Marjorie "Peg" STEWART
b: abt Mar 1920 in St. Cloud, Stearns Co., Minnesota
d: in of Jacksonville, Duval Co., Florida
.............4-Dr. Daniel Freeman STEWART , D.D.S.
b: 23 Jan 1922 in St. Cloud, Stearns Co., Minnesota
d: 4 Dec 1990 in Woodland, Yolo Co., California
.... 3-Don A. FREEMAN
b: abt 1900 in St. Cloud, Stearns Co., Minnesota
d: 26 Sep 1957 in Hennepin Co., Minnesota?
.... +Grayce S. SIMONS
b: abt 1876 in Rosemount, Dakota Co., Minnesota
m: 18 Nov 1903 in Chicago, Cook Co., Illinois
d: 25 Nov 1956 in Brainerd, Crow Wing Co., Minnesota
.............4-Mary Hortense FREEMAN

```
              b: bef 1931 in Minnesota
. . . . . . . . . . . . . .4-Elora Jean FREEMAN
              b: bef 1931 in Minnesota
. . . . .2-Lovisa Catherine FREEMAN
      b: 31 Jul 1850 in Paqris, . Edgar Co., Illinois
      d: aft Jul 1895 in St. Cloud, Stearns Co., Minnesota
. . . . . +J. F. STEVENSON
      b: 1824
      m: Feb 1876 in St. Cloud, Stearns Co., Minnesota
      d: 1915 in St. Cloud, Stearns Co., Minnesota
. . . . .2-Laura A. FREEMAN
      b: 1855 in Illinois
      d: 1888 in St. Cloud, Stearns Co., Minnesota
. . . . . +Thomas Jefferson GRAY
      b: abt 1852
      m: Dec 1872 in St. Cloud, Stearns Co., Minnesota
      d: May 1907 in St. Cloud, Stearns Co., Minnesota
```

+ + + + + + + + + + +

GRAY DESCENDANTS

1-John GRAY , Jr
b: bef 19 Sep 1773 in Marblehead, Essex Co., Massachusetts
d: 17 May 1832 in Wesley, Washington Co., Maine
 +Mary BURTON
b: 5 Mar 1776 in Winslow, Kennebec Co., Maine
m: 12 Mar 1793 in Winslow, Kennebec Co., Maine
d: abt Oct 1854 in Enroute to Minnesota from Maine
. . . . .**2-Sheldon GRAY**
        b: 25 Apr 1794 in Hancock Plantation, Clinton, Kennebec Co., Maine
        d: aft 1860 in of Pleasant Valley, LaCroix Co., Wisconsin
. . . . . **+Patience COBB**
        b: bet 1800 and 1807 in Waterville, Kennebec Co., Maine
        d: aft 1860 in of Pleasant Valley, LaCroix Co., Wisconsin
. . . . **3-Joel GRAY**
              b: abt 1816 in Cathance Lake, Washington Co., Maine?
              d: 1890 in of Twp. 14, Washington Co., Maine
. . . . **+Persis P.**
              b: abt 1817 in New Brunswick, Canada
              m: bef 1841
              d: aft 1880 in of Twp. 14, Washington Co., Maine
. . . .**4-Drusilla GRAY**
                    b: abt 1841 in Twp. 14, Washington Co., Maine
. . . .**4-Elisha GRAY**
                    b: abt 1844 in Twp. 14, Washington Co., Maine
                    d: aft 1880 in of Twp. #14, Washington Co., Maine
. . . .**4-Horace GRAY**
                    b: abt 1848 in Twp. 14, Washington Co., Maine
. . . .**4-Seth E. GRAY**
                    b: abt 1854 in of Twp. #14, Washington Co., Maine
                    d: aft 1880 in of Twp. #14, Washington Co., Maine
. . . . **3-Sheldon GRAY , Jr**
              b: 18 Aug 1818 in Cathance Lake, Washington Co., Maine
              d: 9 Jul 1902 in Chico, Butte Co., California

.... +Juletta "Julia" DAY
.... b: 15 May 1830 in Wesley, Washington Co., Maine
.... m: 18 Aug 1847 in Cooper, Washington Co., Maine
.... d: 1 Aug 1908 in Chico, Butte Co., California
.... 4-Frank Austin GRAY
.... b: 8 Jan 1849 in Wesley, Washington Co., Maine
.... d: 26 Feb 1857 in Menomonee, Waukesha Co., Wisconsin
.... 4-Charles Henry GRAY
.... b: 18 Nov 1851 in Menomonee, Waukesha Co., Wisconsin
.... d: 18 Dec 1867 in Boone, Boone Co., Iowa
.... 4-Laura Frances GRAY
.... b: 11 Apr 1855 in Lakeland, Washington Co., Minnesota
.... d: 18 Nov 1922 in Washington, D.C.
.... 4-Mary Cecelia "Minnie" GRAY
.... b: 28 Sep 1858 in Lakeland, Washington Co., Minnesota
.... d: aft 1914
.... 3-Lena GRAY
.... d: in Alberta, Canada?
.... +John STEVENS
.... 3-Kate GRAY
.... b: UNKNOWN
.... 3-Reuben GRAY
.... 3-Irving GRAY
.... b: abt Jan 1824 in Ogalley, Plantation #14, Washington Co., Maine
.... d: aft 1880 in of Menominie, Dunn Co., WI &, perhaps, San Francisco Co., CA
.... +Olive BLAKE
.... b: in Maine
.... d: bet 1873 and 1880
.... 4-Louis GRAY
.... b: abt 1873 in Minnesota
.... 3-Frank GRAY
.... 3-Sarah GRAY
.... 3-Seeneeth GRAY
.... 3-Eli GRAY
.... 3-John GRAY
.... 3-James Burton "Burt" GRAY
.... b: 1 Nov 1838 in Machias, Washington Co., Maine
.... d: 29 Jan 1920 in Guess Ranch, near Vulcan, Alaberta, Canada
.... +Margaret Maria DUNCAN
.... b: 12 Jan 1851 in Maine
.... m: 4 Jul 1869 in Sauk Center, Stearns Co., Minnesota
.... d: 1933 in Guess Ranch, near Vulcan, Alaberta, Canada
.... 4-Rheuben GRAY
.... b: bef 1876 in Texas
.... d: May 1876 in Texas
.... 4-Fred GRAY
.... b: abt 1876 in Texas
.... d: May 1876 in Texas
.... 4-Lena GRAY
.... b: bef 1876 in Texas
.... d: May 1876 in Texas
.... 4-Lillie Cora GRAY
.... b: 3 Dec 1880 in Osakis, Douglas Co., Minnesota
.... d: Jan 1975 in Clareholm Hospital, near Champion, Alberta, Canada
.... 4-Violet Dell GRAY
.... b: Jan 1882 in Osakis, Douglas Co., Minnesota

............4-Irving Ellsworth GRAY
            b: 2 Feb 1887 in Osakis, Douglas Co., Minnesota
            d: 28 Jun 1948 in Los Angeles Co., California
............4-Jesse Leroy GRAY
            b: 20 Sep 1883 in Osakis, Douglas Co., Minnesota
........3-Benjamin GRAY
.....2-Priscilla\Peace GRAY
        b: 27 Sep 1795 in Clinton, Kennebec Co., Maine
        d: bef 1835 in Athens, Somerset Co., Maine?
..... +Samuel JONES
        b: bet 1778 and 1781 in Wells, York Co., Maine
        m: abt 1815 in Maine
        d: 1876 in Cooper, Washington Co., Maine
........3-John JONES
            b: 12 Mar 1816 in Athens, Somerset Co., Maine
........3-Eleanor JONES
            b: abt Mar 1818 in Athens, Somerset Co., Maine
            d: 14 Oct 1899 in Wesley, Washington Co., Maine
.... +James HAYWARD
            b: 24 Sep 1817 in Shepody, Hopewell Parish, Albert Co., New Brunswick, Canada
            m: 10 Aug 1837 in Wesley, Washington Co., Maine
            d: abt 1 Dec 1885 in Wesley, Washington Co., Maine
............4-Vianna HAYWARD
                b: abt May 1837 in Wesley, Washington Co., Maine
                d: 21 Jan 1839 in Wesley, Washington Co., Maine
............4-Constantina HAYWARD
                b: abt 1840 in Wesley, Washington Co., Maine
                d: aft 1850
............4-Margaret Elvira HAYWARD
                b: 12 Jun 1840 in Wesley, Washington Co., Maine
                d: 18 Mar 1879 in Cooper, Washington Co., Maine
............4-Vianna A. HAYWARD
                b: abt 1845 in Wesley, Washington Co., Maine
                d: 1886 in Alexander, Washington Co. Maine
............4-Amanda F. HAYWARD
                b: abt 1847 in Wesley, Washington Co., Maine
                d: 1 Nov 1895 in East Machias, Washington Co., Maine
............4-Inza E. HAYWARD
                b: 1850 in Wesley, Washington Co., Maine
                d: aft 1880 in of Wesley, Washington Co., Maine
............4-Adeline E. "Addie" HAYWARD
                b: 25 Apr 1853 in Wesley, Washington Co., Maine
                d: 13 Oct 1926 in Bar Harbor, Hancock Co., Maine
............4-Leona H. HAYWARD
                b: May 1857 in Wesley, Washington Co., Maine
                d: 1935 in Machias, Washington Co., Maine
............4-Lenora E. HAYWARD
                b: abt Jul 1859 in Wesley, Washington Co., Maine
                d: 11 Sep 1864 in Wesley, Washington Co., Maine
........3-Elizabeth Eleanor "Betsy" JONES
            b: 2 Feb 1820 in Athens, Somerset Co., Maine
            d: 21 Sep 1842 in Wesley, Washington Co., Maine
.... +Joel DAY
            b: 11 Dec 1808 in Leeds, Androscoggin Co., Maine
            m: 2 Mar 1836 in Wesley, Washington Co., Maine

             d: 25 Jan 1884 in Wesley, Washington Co., Maine
.... 3-Sylvester\Samuel S. JONES
             b: 4 Mar 1822 in Athens, Somerset Co., Maine
             d: 1889 in perhaps Machias, Washington Co., Maine
.... +Clementine PARKER
             b: bet 1825 and 1827 in Kennebec Co., Maine
             d: 1906 in Machias, Washington Co., Maine
.............4-Lydia Clementine JONES
                 b: Jul 1845 in Wesley, Washington Co., Maine
                 d: 23 Apr 1913 in Mechanic Falls, Androscoggin Co., Maine
.............4-Charles C. JONES
                 b: abt Feb 1850 in Wesley, Washington Co., Maine
.............4-Albert JONES
                 b: aft 1850 in Wesley, Washington Co., Maine
.... 3-Learnard\Leonard JONES
             b: 5 Sep 1824 in Athens, Somerset Co., Maine
.... 3-William D. JONES
             b: 2 Dec 1825 in Athens, Somerset Co., Maine
             d: aft 1905 in possibly Wisconsin
.... 3-Calvin Herman JONES
             b: 23 Aug 1830 in Athens, Somerset Co., Maine
             d: 3 Jul 1909 in Augusta, Kennebec Co., Maine
.... +Mary HARDING
             m: 26 Nov 1892
.....2-James GRAY
         b: abt Dec 1797 in Fairfield, Somerset Co., Maine
         d: 21 May 1859 in Wesley, Washington Co., Maine
..... +Hannah JONES
         b: abt 1795 in Wells or Shapleigh, York Co., Maine
         m: abt Oct 1818 in Harmony, Somerset Co., Maine
         d: abt 17 Dec 1842 in Wesley, Washington Co., Maine
.... 3-Belinda GRAY
             b: 21 Nov 1819 in Warren's Town, now Hartland, Somerset Co., Maine
             d: bet 1850 and 1870 in perhaps Maine
.... +Abraham HUNTLEY
             b: abt 1810 in Machias or Wesley, Washington Co., Maine
             m: 2 May 1839 in Wesley, Washington Co., Maine
             d: 2 May 1840 in Wesley, Washington Co., Maine
.... +Perrin GETCHELL
             b: abt 1810 in Maine
             m: abt 1841
             d: aft 1870 in of St. Anthony, Hennepin Co., Minnesota
.... 3-Clarinda GRAY
             b: 15 May 1822 in North Hill, now Brighton, Somerset Co., Maine
             d: 31 Oct 1913 in of Wesley, Washington Co., Maine
.... +Davis Washington ROLLINS
             b: 25 Nov 1819 in Marion, Washington Co., Maine
             m: 17 Oct 1842 in St. Davids, Charlotte, New Brunswick, Canada
             d: 14 Nov 1908 in of Wesley, Washington Co., Maine
.............4-Cyrus Chase ROLLINS
                 b: 13 Feb 1844 in Wesley, Washington Co., Maine
                 d: 1923 in of Wesley, Washington Co., Maine
.............4-Elizabeth Hannah "Lizzie" ROLLINS
                 b: 30 Dec 1845 in Wesley, Washington Co., Maine
                 d: in of Middletown, Penobscot Co., Maine
.............4-Davis Washington ROLLINS , Jr

b: 4 Jan 1848 in Wesley, Washington Co., Maine
d: 25 Apr 1849 in Wesley, Washington Co., Maine
............4-Davis Washington ROLLINS , Jr
b: 7 May 1850 in Wesley, Washington Co., Maine
d: 3 May 1896
............4-Daniel W. ROLLINS
b: 25 Mar 1852 in Wesley, Washington Co., Maine
............4-Mary B. ROLLINS
b: 16 Mar 1854 in Wesley, Washington Co., Maine
d: 10 May 1861 in buried Wesley, Washington Co., Maine
............4-John W. ROLLINS
b: 1856 in Wesley, Washington Co., Maine
d: 14 Nov 1885 in buried Wesley, Washington Co., Maine
............4-Josephine "Josie" F. ROLLINS
b: abt 1858
............4-Loring Abram ROLLINS
b: abt 1860
............4-Viola Annie ROLLINS
b: 1864 in Wesley, Washington Co., Maine
d: 1945 in Wesley, Washington Co., Maine
........3-Elizabeth GRAY
b: 15 Sep 1824 in North Hill, now Brighton, Somerset Co., Maine
d: 24 Jul 1884 in buried Wesley, Washington Co., Maine
.... +Daniel CHASE
b: 17 Jul 1822 in Frankfort, Waldo Co., Maine
m: 20 Nov 1846 in Wesley, Washington Co., Maine
d: 10 Mar 1885 in of Cutler, Washington Co., Maine
........3-James GRAY , Jr
b: 26 Aug 1826 in North Hill, now Brighton, Maine
d: 3 Apr 1886 in Wesley, Washington Co., Maine
.... +Ann Eliza POLLARD
b: 31 Jul 1828 in St. David's, New Brunswick, Canada
m: 10 Apr 1851 in Wesley, Washington Co., Maine
d: 12 May 1902 in Cooper, Washington Co., Maine
............4-James W. GRAY
b: abt 1852 in of Wesley, Washington Co., Maine
............4-Henry H. GRAY
b: 22 Dec 1853 in Wesley, Washington Co., Maine
d: 4 Mar 1935 in Milbridge, Maine
............4-Austin Leander GRAY
b: 20 Mar 1859 in of Wesley, Washington Co., Maine
d: 31 Jul 1944 in Wesley, Washington Co., Maine
............4-Ernest GRAY
b: abt 1862 in of Wesley, Washington Co., Maine
............4-Lena\Linna GRAY
b: abt 1865 in of Wesley, Washington Co., Maine
........3-John Harrison GRAY
b: 2 Jun 1831 in Brighton, Somerset Co., Maine
d: 5 May 1914 in Baring, Washington Co., Maine
.... +Hannah R. BIRD
b: 22 Mar 1834 in Maine
m: 1854 in Maine
d: 18 Aug 1897 in Baring, Washington Co., Maine
............4-John GRAY
b: abt 1854 in of Wesley, Washington Co., Maine
............4-James Harrison GRAY

                b: 1856 in Wesley, Washington Co., Maine
.............4-Mary GRAY
                b: abt 1858 in of Wesley, Washington Co., Maine
.............4-Lyman E. GRAY
                b: abt 1864 in Maine
                d: 15 Sep 1883 in buried Wesley, Washington Co., Maine
........3-Granville Clifford GRAY
            b: abt 14 Jun 1834 in Brighton, Somerset Co., Maine
            d: 4 Jul 1890 in of Wesley, Washington Co., Maine
.... +Harriet Mann POLLARD
            b: 1836 in New Brunswick
            m: BET. 1854 - 1855
            d: 1911 in of Wesley, Washington Co., Maine
.............4-Serena Mariam Getchell GRAY
                b: 21 Apr 1856 in Wesley, Washington Co., Maine
.............4-Mary Elizabeth "Lizzie" GRAY
                b: abt 1857 in of Wesley, Washington Co., Maine
.............4-Victor Clifton GRAY
                b: abt Sep 1860 in of Wesley, Washington Co., Maine
                d: 28 Jul 1893 in buried Wesley, Washington Co., Maine
.............4-Annie C. GRAY
                b: abt Jun 1862 in Maine
                d: 1 Apr 1866 in buried Wesley, Washington Co., Maine
.............4-Addie A. GRAY
                b: abt 1866 in of Wesley, Washington Co., Maine
.............4-Lois E. GRAY
                b: abt 1874 in Wesley, Washington Co., Maine
.....+Louisa E. SWEET
        b: 5 Feb 1809 in of Machias, Washington Co., Maine
        m: abt Apr 1847 in Wesley, Washington Co., Maine
        d: 13 Nov 1890 in Buchanan Co., Iowa
........3-Roxannah Shephard GRAY
            b: 16 Mar 1849 in Wesley, Washington Co., Maine
            d: 9 Sep 1911 in Buchanan Co., Iowa
.... +William Henry KINT
            b: 10 Sep 1841
            m: 3 Oct 1866 in Independence, Buchanan Co., Iowa
            d: 22 Sep 1916 in Buchanan Co., Iowa
.....2-Gideon GRAY
        b: abt 1800 in Clinton, Kennebec Co., or Fairfield, Somerset Co., Maine
        d: bet 1880 and 1885 in of Orange Twp., Douglas Co., Minnesota
.....+Abigail DOW
        b: abt 1800
        d: BET. 22 - 29 JAN 1835 in Wesley, Washington Co., Maine
........3-David GRAY
            b: abt 1814
........3-3 other children GRAY
            b: in Wesley, Washington Co., Maine
........3-John A. GRAY
            b: abt 1831 in Maine
            d: aft 1870 in of Orange, Douglas Co., Minnesota
.... +MARTHA
            b: abt 1842 in Illinois
            d: aft 1870 in of Orange, Douglas Co., Minnesota
.............4-Eddie GRAY
                b: abt 1859 in Wisconsin

............4-Charles GRAY
            b: abt 1861 in Wisconsin
............4-Sarah GRAY
            b: abt 1866 in Wisconsin
............4-Minnie GRAY
            b: abt 1868 in Wisconsin
........3-Reuben GRAY
            b: abt 1833 in Maine
            d: aft 1860 in of Pleasant Valley, LaCroix Co., Wisconsin
........3-Daughter GRAY
            b: bef 29 Jan 1835 in Wesley, Washington Co., Maine
            d: abt 1835 in Wesley, Washington Co., Maine
.....+Sarah FIEGLEY
        b: 15 Apr 1803 in Hagerstown, Washington Co., Maryland
        m: 14 Sep 1845 in probably Minnesota
        d: abt Nov 1888 in Lawrence, Douglas Co., Kansas
.....2-John GRAY III
        b: aft 1799 in Harmony, Somerset Co., Maine?
.....2-Phoebe GRAY
        b: aft 1799 in Maine
.....+David DAVIS
.....2-Mary "Polly" GRAY
        b: BET. 1801 - 1802 in Maine
        d: aft 1860 in of East Machias, Washington Co., Maine
.....+Joseph "Joe" ANDREWS
        b: 6 Mar 1787 in Machias, Washington Co., Maine
        d: 17 Jun 1858 in East Machias, Washington Co., Maine
........3-Thankful Anne ANDREWS
            b: 11 Feb 1826 in Maine
            d: 13 Oct 1868 in East Machias, Washington Co., Maine
.... +John Wilber HASTY
            b: abt 1816 in Maine
            m: 4 Dec 1845 in East Machias, Washington Co., Maine
            d: aft 1860 in of East Machias, Washington Co., Maine
........3-Phebe ANDREWS
            b: bet 1827 and 1829 in of East Machias, Washington Co., Maine
........3-Winslow Benjamin ANDREWS
            b: abt 1835 in of East Machias, Washington Co., Maine
            d: aft 1880 in of Portland, Cumberland Co., Maine
.... +GEORGIE
            b: abt 1846 in Maine
            d: abt 1879 in of Portland, Cumberland Co., Maine
........3-William H. ANDREWS
            b: abt 1837 in of East Machias, Washington Co., Maine
........3-Mary E. ANDREWS
            b: abt 1840 in of East Machias, Washington Co., Maine
            d: in Lawrence, Essex Co., Massachusetts?
.... +? BLOOD
........3-Mira F. ANDREWS
            b: abt 1842 in of East Machias, Washington Co., Maine
........3-Roswell Nelson ANDREWS
            b: abt 1844 in of East Machias, Washington Co., Maine
.....2-Benjamin GRAY
        b: 1803 in Harmony, Somerset Co., Maine?
        d: 4 Oct 1881 in St. Cloud, Stearns Co., Minnesota
.....+Mary Stinson LOVEJOY

        b: 16 Jul 1806 in Albion, Kennebec Co., Maine
        m: 1849 in Wesley, Washington Co., Maine
        d: 29 Mar 1884 in Minneapolis, Hennepin Co., Minnesota
.... 3-Mary Stinson GRAY
            b: 22 Jan 1830 in Wesley, Washington Co., Maine
            d: 1 Sep 1912 in St. Cloud, Stearns Co., Minnesota
.... +Josiah Eaton HAYWARD
            b: 2 Feb 1826 in Maine, Washington Co. or Mechanics Falls, Androscoggan Co.
            m: 28 Apr 1848 in Wesley, Washington Co., Maine
            d: 13 Mar 1895 in St. Cloud, Stearns Co., Minnesota
.............4-Mary Orinda HAYWARD
                b: 26 Oct 1849 in Wesley, Washington Co., Maine
                d: 12 Feb 1917 in St. Cloud, Stearns Co., Minnesota
.............4-Clara Hortense HAYWARD
                b: 1851 in Wesley, Washington Co., Maine
                d: 12 Dec 1936 in buried St. Cloud, Stearns Co., Minnesota
.............4-Elora H. HAYWARD
                b: 2 Feb 1852 in Wesley, Washington Co., Maine
                d: 2 Sep 1926 in Big Fish Lake, Cold Spring, buried St. Cloud, Stearns Co., MN
.............4-Daniel Sheck HAYWARD
                b: Feb 1854 in Baring, Washington Co., Maine
                d: 25 Mar 1929 in Riverside, Riverside Co., California
.............4-Samuel L. HAYWARD
                b: Aug 1856 in Wesley, Washington Co., Maine?
                d: 21 Feb 1936 in St. Cloud, Stearns Co., Minnesota
.............4-William H. HAYWARD
                b: 3 Apr 1859 in Brockway, Stearns Co., Minnesota
                d: 10 Jan 1890 in Chicago, Cook Co., Illinois
.............4-Jean Odell "Jennie" HAYWARD
                b: Oct 1867 in St. Cloud, Stearns Co., Minnesota
                d: 7 Sep 1937 in Orange Co., California
.............4-John A. HAYWARD
                b: 25 Mar 1871 in St. Cloud, Stearns Co., Minnesota
                d: 1 May 1876 in St. Cloud, Stearns Co., Minnesota
.... 3-Melinda J. GRAY
            b: 15 Feb 1831 in Wesley, Washington Co., Maine
            d: 14 Sep 1916 in Riverside, Riverside Co., California
.... +John HAYWARD , Jr
            b: 19 May 1828 in probably Washington Co., Maine
            m: 25 Apr 1850 in Wesley, Washington Co., Maine
            d: 28 Aug 1870 in St. Cloud, Stearns Co., Minnesota
.............4-Ellen HAYWARD
                b: abt 1854 in Stearns Co., Minnesota
                d: bef 1870 in probably St. Cloud, Stearns Co., Minnesota
.... +John C. COOPER
            b: 1 Jan 1836 in Canton, Bradford Co., Pennsylvania
            m: 1873 in St. Cloud, Stearns Co., Minnesota
            d: 8 Jan 1907 in Riverside, Riverside Co., California
.............4-Arthur C. COOPER
                b: 1866 in Brooklyn, New York
                d: Feb 1928 in Minneapolis, Hennepin Co., Minnesota
.............4-Charles A. COOPER
                b: in Brooklyn, New York
                d: aft 1920 in Plummer, Benewah Co., Idaho?
.... 3-Lavinia "Vina" GRAY
            b: 22 May 1832 in Wesley, Washington Co., Maine

.... d: 26 Apr 1922 in Riverside, Riverside Co., California
.... +John Wesley DAY
.... b: 24 Oct 1832 in Wesley, Washington Co., Maine
.... m: 3 Nov 1854 in Minneapolis, Hennepin Co., Minnesota
.... d: 27 Jul 1910 in Riverside, Riverside Co., California
.... .4-Cora DAY
.... b: 3 Apr 1856 in Minneapolis, Hennepin Co., Minnesota
.... d: aft 1916 in Riverside, Riverside Co., California
.... .4-Ida Florence DAY
.... b: 6 Nov 1859 in Richfield, Hennepin Co., Minnesota
.... d: 17 May 1912 in London, England
.... .4-Eugene Wesley DAY
.... b: 24 May 1865 in Minneapolis, Hennepin Co., Minnesota
.... d: 24 Aug 1866 in Minneapolis, Hennepin Co., Minnesota
.... .4-Eugene Harry "Gene" DAY
.... b: 26 May 1867 in Minneapolis, Hennepin Co., Minnesota
.... d: 6 Dec 1943 in Los Angeles Co., California
.... .4-C. Benjamin DAY
.... b: 1 Apr 1875 in Minneapolis, Hennepin Co., Minnesota
.... d: in Minneapolis, Hennepin Co., Minnesota
.... .4-Charles DAY
.... b: abt 1877 in Minnesota
.... d: aft 1880
.... 3-Henrietta "Etta" Elizabeth GRAY
.... b: 12 Feb 1835 in Wesley, Washington Co., Maine
.... d: aft 1915 in of Riverside, Riverside Co., California
.... +Lorenzo Dow DAY
.... b: 28 Jan 1835 in Wesley, Washington Co., Maine
.... m: 2 Oct 1854 in Wesley, Washington Co., Maine
.... d: 25 Mar 1905 in Riverside, Riverside Co., California
.... .4-Leonora Beatrice "Lo" DAY
.... b: 6 Apr 1856 in Richfield, Hennepin Co., Minnesota
.... d: 22 Aug 1952 in Napa Co., California
.... .4-Leonard Austin DAY
.... b: 16 Nov 1861 in Richfield, Hennepin Co., Minnesota
.... d: aft 1892 in of Minneapolis, Hennepin Co., Minnesota
.... .4-Mary Lois "Mamie" DAY
.... b: 30 Apr 1866 in Minneapolis, Hennepin Co., Minnesota
.... .4-Florence Elizabeth DAY
.... b: 3 Apr 1872 in Minneapolis, Hennepin Co., Minnesota
.... d: in of Minnesota
.... 3-Josephine GRAY
.... b: 23 Mar 1837 in Wesley, Washington Co., Maine
.... d: 28 Jun 1923 in Orange Co., California
.... +Joseph S. CARRICK
.... b: abt 1838 in Maine
.... d: bet 1874 and 1880 in Minnesota
.... .4-Minnie E. CARRICK
.... b: abt 1862 in Maine
.... .4-Leola\Lenora CARRICK
.... b: abt 1865 in Minnesota
.... .4-Jessie M. CARRICK
.... b: abt 1874 in Minnesota
.... 3-Helena GRAY
.... b: abt 1840 in Wesley, Washington Co., Maine
.... d: bef 1915 in Minnesota?

........3-Benjamin Franklin "Frank" GRAY
        b: 28 Apr 1841 in Wesley, Washington Co., Maine
        d: abt Sep 1904 in New Paynesville, now Paynesville, Stearns Co., Minnesota
.........+LOUISA
        b: Dec 1847 in Maine
        m: in St. Cloud, Stearns Co., Minnesota?
        d: bef Sep 1904 in probably Stearns Co., Minnesota
.............4-Harrison GRAY
        b: abt 1869 in St. Cloud, Stearns Co., Minnesota
.............4-Benjamin A. GRAY
        b: Aug 1878 in St. Cloud, Stearns Co., Minnesota
        d: aft 1900
........3-Samuel A. "Asa\Asbury" GRAY
        b: Aug 1844 in Wesley, Washington Co., Maine
        d: 24 Jul 1903 in Hudson, St. Croix Co., Wisconsin
.........+Mary Elizabeth COOPER
        b: Oct 1844 in Maine
        d: 8 Oct 1916 in North Yakima, Yakima Co., Washington
.............4-Burton "Bertie" GRAY
        b: abt 1864 in St. Cloud, Stearns Co., Minnesota
        d: bef 25 Jul 1903 in perhaps Minnesota
.............4-Blanche L. GRAY
        b: Aug 1873 in St. Cloud, Stearns Co., Minnesota
        d: in perhaps North Yakima, Yakima Co., Washington
........3-Laura A. "Lauretta" GRAY
        b: 1845 in Wesley, Washington Co., Maine
        d: 18 Nov 1929 in Riverside, Riverside Co., California
.........+Dr. Silas MARLATT
        b: 8 Jul 1826 in Yates, Orleans Co., New York
        m: 15 May 1862 in St. Cloud, Stearns Co., Minnesota
        d: 13 Sep 1903 in Minneapolis, Hennepin Co., Minnesota
.............4-Albert SMITH
        b: abt 1861 in perhaps New York
.............4-Alberta Helena MARLATT
        b: 24 Aug 1864 in St. Cloud, Stearns Co., Minnesota
        d: 6 Jan 1866 in St. Cloud, Stearns Co., Minnesota
.............4-Willie Edgar MARLATT
        b: abt Jul 1867 in St. Cloud, Stearns Co., Minnesota
        d: 12 Feb 1871 in St. Cloud, Stearns Co., Minnesota
.............4-John C. MARLATT
        b: abt 1872 in St. Cloud, Stearns Co., Minnesota
        d: 19 Jul 1886 in St. Cloud, Stearns Co., Minnesota
.............4-Mary J. "May" MARLATT
        b: abt 1877 in St. Cloud, Stearns Co., Minnesota
        d: aft 1945 in of Riverside, Riverside Co., California
........3-Isadora I.\G. GRAY
        b: abt 1847 in Wesley, Washington Co., Maine
        d: aft 1930 in of San Antonio, Bexar Co., Texas
.........+Alfred G. SNOW
        b: abt 1840 in Maine
        m: bef 1870
        d: bet 1880 and 1919 in of Otsego, Wright Co., Minnesota
.............4-Ada C. SNOW
        b: Aug 1870 in perhaps Otsego Twp., Wright Co., Minnesota
        d: abt 1931 in of San Antonio, Bexar Co., Texas
.............4-Mary SNOW

............b: abt 1871 in perhaps Otsego Twp., Wright Co., Minnesota
............4-Arthur SNOW
............b: 17 Jul 1872 in perhaps Otsego Twp., Wright Co., Minnesota
............d: Feb 1964 in North Dakota
.....2-Joseph GRAY
....b: abt 1806 in Harmony, Somerset Co., Maine?
....d: abt 1875 in Minnesota?
.....+Abigail JONES
....b: 20 Mar 1808 in Bridgton, Cumberland Co., Maine
....m: abt Jan 1830 in Maine
....d: 5 Apr 1845 in Wesley, Washington Co., Maine
.........3-Samuel Wesley GRAY
........b: 26 Feb 1831 in Wesley, Washington Co., Maine
........d: 1919 in Minnesota
.... +Lucetta A. GETCHELL
........b: BET. 1845 - 1846 in Maine
........m: 26 Feb 1865 in Stearns Co., Minnesota
........d: 22 Nov 1875 in Minnesota
............4-Son GRAY
.........3-Harriett Jane GRAY
........b: 1 Feb 1833 in Wesley, Washington Co., Maine
........d: bef 1865 in Canada
.... +Jesse HUFF
........b: 1827 in Maine
........m: 6 Sep 1854 in Wesley, Washington Co., Maine
........d: bef 1865 in Canada
.........3-Eliza A. GRAY
........b: 12 Jan 1835 in Wesley, Washington Co., Maine
.... +John F. RAMSDELL
........b: in probably Washington Co., Maine
........m: 20 Feb 1866 in Wesley, Washington Co., Maine
.........3-William S. GRAY
........b: 3 Feb 1837 in Wesley, Washington Co., Maine
........d: 1922
.... +Frances "Elvina\Elzina" HANSCOM
........b: abt 1842 in Washington Co., Maine
........m: 23 Aug 1859 in Wesley, Washington Co., Maine
.........3-Martha E. GRAY
........b: abt 1839 in Wesley, Washington Co., Maine
........d: 28 Jul 1863 in Machias, Washington Co., Maine
.........3-Lovina\Sylvina A. GRAY
........b: abt 1840 in Wesley, Washington Co., Maine
.... +Ellsworth Melvin HANSCOM
........m: 13 Oct 1861 in Wesley, Washington Co., Maine
.........3-Clarinda GRAY
........b: abt Feb 1843 in Wesley, Washington Co., Maine
........d: 23 Aug 1843 in buried Wesley, Washington Co., Maine
.....+Theresa\Thirza H. "Clarissa" HUNTLEY
....b: abt 1820 in Wesley, Washington Co., Maine
....m: 13 Feb 1852 in Wesley, Washington Co., Maine
....d: in Minnesota?
.........3-Abigail "Abbie" GRAY
........b: 23 Nov 1853 in Wesley, Washington Co., Maine
........d: 5 Aug 1864 in Wesley, Washington Co., Maine
.........3-Eugene GRAY
........b: abt 1855 in Wesley, Washington Co., Maine

.... 3-Arthur GRAY
            b: abt 1858 in Wesley, Washington Co., Maine
..... 2-Hannah GRAY
        b: abt 1807 in Harmony, Somerset Co., Maine?
        d: 7 Dec 1888 in Brockway Twp., Stearns Co., Minnesota
..... +Winslow GETCHELL
        b: 10 Oct 1801 in Anson, Somerset Co., Maine
        m: 24 Apr 1825 in perhaps Wesley, Washington Co., Maine
        d: 13 Dec 1887 in Brockway Twp., Stearns Co., Minnesota
.... 3-John Winslow GETCHELL
            b: 11 Nov 1827 in Wesley, Washington Co., Maine
            d: 24 Oct 1870 in Brockway Twp., Stearns Co., Minnesota
.... +Celestia P. GILLETT
            b: in of St. Cloud, Stearns Co., Minnesota
            m: 4 Jul 1864 in "The Parsonage," Stearns Co., Minnesota
.... 3-Nathaniel GETCHELL
            b: 9 Nov 1828 in Wesley, Washington Co., Maine
            d: 30 Sep 1910 in Southside Twp., Wright Co., Minnesota
.... +Alma Maria WING
            b: 8 Jul 1849 in Vassalborough, Kennebec, Co., Maine
            m: 21 May 1864 in Stearns Co., Minnesota
            d: 11 Mar 1883 in Brockway, Stearns Co., Minnesota
.... 4-Anna M. "Annie" GETCHELL
                b: abt 1866 in Brockway, Stearns Co., Minnesota
                d: aft 1915 in of Southside Twp., Wright Co., Minnesota
.... 4-Carrie A. GETCHELL
                b: abt 1868 in Brockway, Stearns Co., Minnesota
.... 4-Ernest A. GETCHELL
                b: 1873 in Brockway, Stearns Co., Minnesota
                d: 13 May 1952 in St. Cloud, Stearns Co., Minnesota
.... 4-Herbert W. GETCHELL
                b: abt 1880 in Brockway, Stearns Co., Minnesota
.... 4-Alma M. GETCHELL
                b: Jan 1883 in St. Cloud, Stearns Co., Minnesota
                d: 11 Jul 1883 in Red Wing, Goodhue Co., Minnesota
.... 3-Orinda GETCHELL
            b: 9 Feb 1831 in Wesley, Washington Co., Maine
            d: 10 Nov 1895 in Brockway Twp., Stearns Co., Minnesota
.... +Mark Harris FENLASON
            b: abt 1825 in Maine, probably Washington Co.
            m: 29 Nov 1849 in Wesley, Washington Co., Maine
            d: in of Brockway Twp., Stearns Co., Minnesota
.... 3-Sarah A. "Sally" GETCHELL
            b: 8 Jun 1833 in Wesley, Washington Co., Maine
            d: 14 Oct 1872 in St. Cloud, Stearns Co., Minnesota
.... +S. A. HANSCOM
.... 3-Phebe E. GETCHELL
            b: 25 Apr 1835 in Wesley, Washington Co., Maine
            d: 1 Jan 1878 in Brockway Twp. Cemetery, Stearns Co., Minnesota
.... +William GORDON
            m: Jan 1854 in Bangor, Penobscot Co., Maine
.... 3-Otis GETCHELL
            b: 3 Mar 1837 in Wesley, Washington Co., Maine
            d: bef 1886
.... +Amelia M. GLIDDEN
            m: 4 Jan 1864 in Stearns Co., Minnesota

.... **3-Mary Elizabeth GETCHELL**
> b: 4 Apr 1840 in Maine
> d: 21 Mar 1913 in Brockway, Stearns Co., Minnesota

.... **+John Nelson PERRY**
> b: 29 Mar 1836 in Penobscot Co., Maine
> m: 7 Aug 1859 in Stearns Co., Minnesota
> d: 26 Feb 1910 in Brockway, Stearns Co., Minnesota

.... **.4-Everett O. PERRY**
> b: 12 Nov 1868 in Brockway, Stearns Co., Minnesota
> d: aft 1915 in Brockway, Stearns Co., Minnesota?

.... **.4-Fannie PERRY**
> b: in Brockway, Stearns Co., Minnesota
> d: aft 1915 in Benton Co., MN?

.... **.4-Albert O. PERRY**
> b: in Brockway, Stearns Co., Minnesota
> d: aft 1915 in North Dakota?

.... **.4-Melvin N. PERRY**
> b: 7 Mar 1878 in Brockway, Stearns Co., Minnesota
> d: aft 1915

.... **.4-Ralph W. PERRY**
> b: in Brockway, Stearns Co., Minnesota
> d: aft 1915

.... **.4-Laura Etta PERRY**
> b: in Brockway, Stearns Co., Minnesota
> d: bef 1915

.... **.4-Nettie PERRY**
> b: in Brockway, Stearns Co., Minnesota
> d: bef 1915

.... **.4-Infant PERRY**
> b: in Brockway, Stearns Co., Minnesota
> d: bef 1915 in Brockway, Stearns Co., Minnesota

.... **3-Van Rensselaer GETCHELL**
> b: abt 1844 in of Wesley, Washington Co., Maine
> d: 5 Oct 1908 in Minneapolis, Hennepin Co., Minnesota

.... **+Mary Jane HICKS**
> b: 21 Jul 1836
> m: 2 Oct 1863 in Stearns Co., Minnesota
> d: 12 Dec 1882 in Sauk Rapids, Benton Co., Minnesota

.... **+Alice E. HYKE**
> m: 1 Aug 1883 in St. Cloud, tearns Co., Minnesota

.... **3-Lucetta A. GETCHELL**
> b: BET. 1845 - 1846 in Maine
> d: 22 Nov 1875 in Minnesota

.... **+Samuel Wesley GRAY**
> b: 26 Feb 1831 in Wesley, Washington Co., Maine
> m: 26 Feb 1865 in Stearns Co., Minnesota
> d: 1919 in Minnesota

.... **.4-Son GRAY**

.... **3-Everett Oscar GETCHELL**
> b: abt 1849 in Maine
> d: 6 Jul 1875 in Minnesota

.... **3-Frank L. GETCHELL**
> b: abt 1851 in Maine
> d: aft 1887 in of Brockway Twp. Cemetery, Stearns Co., Minnesota

.... **+Ida B. FOOT**
> m: Nov 1878 in St. Cloud, Stearns Co., Minnesota

........3-2 other children GETCHELL
        b: UNKNOWN
.....2-Elizabeth\Eliza GRAY
      b: abt 1813 in Massachusetts
      d: aft 1850 in of Wesley, Washington Co., Maine
.....+John DAY
      b: Apr 1801 in Leeds, Androscoggin Co., Maine
      m: 25 Sep 1829 in Crawford, Washington Co., Maine
      d: 23 Mar 1841 in Wesley, Washington Co., Maine
........3-John Alvin DAY
        b: 22 May 1831 in Wesley, Washington Co., Maine
        d: 9 Mar 1841 in Wesley, Washington Co., Maine
........3-Abiah D. DAY
        b: 24 Mar 1833 in Wesley, Washington Co., Maine
        d: 30 Mar 1888 in Cooper, Washington Co., Maine
........+Margaret Elvira HAYWARD
        b: 12 Jun 1840 in Wesley, Washington Co., Maine
        m: 30 Sep 1855 in Wesley, Washington Co., Maine
        d: 18 Mar 1879 in Cooper, Washington Co., Maine
............4-Vianna A. "Anna" DAY
            b: 29 Aug 1856 in Wesley, Washington Co., Maine
            d: 8 Nov 1920 in buried East Poland, Androscoggin Co., Maine
............4-Ella May Hayward DAY
            b: 26 Jun 1860 in Cooper, Washington Co., Maine
            d: 12 Jul 1895 in Lowell, Middlesex Co., Massachusetts
............4-Willis Gilbert DAY
            b: 28 Jan 1865 in Wesley, Washington Co., Maine
            d: aft 25 Sep 1939
............4-Vernanus Onslow "Vern" DAY
            b: 20 Nov 1867 in Cooper, Washington Co., Maine
            d: 1938 in Cooper, Washington Co., Maine
............4-Alice M. DAY
            b: 29 Dec 1871 in Wesley, Washington Co., Maine
............4-Burton "Bert" DAY
            b: 30 May 1874 in Cooper, Washington Co., Maine
............4-Elsie DAY
            b: 14 Dec 1876 in Cooper, Washington Co., Maine
            d: 19 Feb 1893 in Cooper, Washington Co., Maine
............4-Alphonso "Torn" DAY
            b: 5 Jul 1879 in Cooper, Washington Co., Maine
            d: in California?
........+Mary "May" MCCARLIE
        b: in St. David, New Brunswick, Canada
        m: 8 Dec 1885 in "The Ledge, " Cooper, Washington Co., Maine
        d: 13 Jun 1896
........3-Samuel DAY
        b: 30 Jun 1836 in Wesley, Washington Co., Maine
        d: 2 Mar 1903 in Wesley, Washington Co., Maine
........+Adelia Clark ELSEMORE
        b: 9 Mar 1842 in Wesley, Washington Co., Maine
        m: 4 Oct 1860 in Wesley, Washington Co., Maine
        d: 12 Jun 1900 in Wesley, Washington Co., Maine
............4-Arlington Jordan DAY
            b: 7 Oct 1861 in Wesley, Washington Co., Maine
            d: 1921 in of Wesley, Washington Co., Maine
............4-Emma Etta DAY

............b: 1 Mar 1863 in Wesley, Washington Co., Maine
..............4-John Wilbur DAY
............b: 23 Dec 1864 in Wesley, Washington Co., Maine
............d: aft 1916 in Wesley, Washington Co., Maine?
..............4-Annella Gelana DAY
............b: 15 Dec 1866 in Wesley, Washington Co., Maine
............d: 2 Nov 1906 in Northfield, Washington Co., Maine
..............4-Justin Ulysses DAY
............b: 3 Dec 1868 in Wesley, Washington Co., Maine
............d: 25 Nov 1941 in Carroll, Penobscot Co., Maine
..............4-Julia Ann DAY
............b: 7 Dec 1870 in Wesley, Washington Co., Maine
............d: 20 Apr 1908 in Limerick, York Co., Maine
..............4-Roy Eldridge DAY
............b: 13 Oct 1874 in Wesley, Washington Co., Maine
..............4-Ralph Elbridge DAY
............b: 9 Aug 1875 in Wesley, Washington Co., Maine
............d: 24 Jan 1961 in Northfield, Washington Co., Maine
..............4-Nellie Gertrude DAY
............b: 12 Nov 1877 in Wesley, Washington Co., Maine
..............4-Lorenzo Sabine DAY
............b: 20 May 1879 in Wesley, Washington Co., Maine
............d: 1936
..............4-Charles Whitney DAY
............b: 20 Dec 1880 in Wesley, Washington Co., Maine
............d: 28 Aug 1913 in Pine Bluff, Jefferson Co., Arkansas
..............4-Mary Rich DAY
............b: 25 Feb 1882 in Wesley, Washington Co., Maine
............d: 27 Jul 1883 in Wesley, Washington Co., Maine
..............4-Ivory Milburn DAY
............b: 3 Apr 1883 in Wesley, Washington Co., Maine
............d: 13 Jan 1895 in Wesley, Washington Co., Maine
..............4-Jennie Florence DAY
............b: 23 Jul 1884 in Wesley, Washington Co., Maine
............d: 28 Jul 1897 in Wesley, Washington Co., Maine
..........3-Hannah DAY
........b: 20 May 1838 in Wesley, Washington Co., Maine
.... +Jordan Willey (Capt.) HALL
........b: 9 Nov 1827 in Harrington, Washington Co., Maine
........m: 23 Jul 1856 in Harrington, Washington Co., Maine
........d: Oct 1889 in at sea
..........3-John Wilbur DAY
........b: Jul 1841 in Wesley, Washington Co., Maine
........d: 24 Feb 1863 in New Orleans, Jefferson Parish, Louisiana
.....+William DAVIS
....b: abt 1822 in Maine
....m: BET. 1841 - 1842 in Maine
....d: aft 1850 in of Wesley, Washington Co., Maine
..........3-Lucretia A. DAVIS
........b: abt 1842 in Wesley, Washington Co., Maine
..........3-Willis G. DAVIS
........b: abt 1845 in Wesley, Washington Co., Maine
..........3-Christiania DAVIS
........b: abt 1847 in Wesley, Washington Co., Maine
.....2-Reuben GRAY
....b: abt 1815 in Calais, Washington Co., or Harmony, Somerset Co., Maine

d: 30 May 1905 in Brainerd, Crow Wing Co., Minnesota
..... +Adeline AVERILL
    b: 23 Nov 1816 in East Machias, Washington Co., Maine
    m: 27 Mar 1836 in Wesley, Washington Co., Maine
    d: abt 1858 in Brockway Twp., Stearns Co., Minnesota
.... 3-Henry Washington GRAY
    b: 11 Jan 1837 in Wesley, Washington Co., Maine
    d: aft 1880 in of Machiasport, Washington Co., Maine
.... +Lydia A.
    b: abt 1846 in Maine
    d: aft 1880 in of Machiasport, Washington Co., Maine
.... 4-Mary E. GRAY
    b: abt 1867 in of Machiasport, Washington Co., Maine
.... 3-Cynthia E. GRAY
    b: abt 1838 in Wesley, Washington Co., Maine
    d: abt 1893 in buried Duluth, St. Louis Co., Minnesota
.... +Edward B. GLASS
    b: abt 1834 in Maine
    m: 1858 in Brockway Twp., Stearns Co., Minnesota
    d: aft 1880 in Fond du Lac, St. Louis Co., Minnesota
.... 3-Andrew GRAY
    b: abt 1840 in Wesley, Washington Co., Maine
    d: 1870 in buried Old Minneapolis Cemetery, Minneapolis, Hennepin, MN
.... 3-Jefferson G. "Jeff" GRAY
    b: abt 1842 in Wesley, Washington Co., Maine
    d: 1913 in Otsego, Wright Co., Minnesota
.... +Mary Ann HULBERT
    b: bet 1842 and 1850 in Westmoreland Co., Pennsylvania
    m: 2 Apr 1869 in Minnesota
    d: 23 Mar 1918 in St. Paul, Ramsey Co., Minnesota
.... 4-Mildred GRAY
    b: abt 1877 in Otsego, Wright Co., Minnesota
    d: aft Mar 1918 in of Minneapolis, Hennepin Co., Minnesota
.... 4-Florence GRAY
    b: abt 1879 in Otsego, Wright Co., Minnesota
    d: aft Mar 1918 in of Minneapolis, Hennepin Co., Minnesota
.... 4-Raymond Hulbert "Ray" GRAY
    b: 13 Dec 1883 in Otsego, Wright Co., Minnesota
    d: 20 Mar 1937 in Minneapolis, Hennepin Co., Minnesota
.... 3-Justus M. GRAY
    b: abt 1844 in Wesley, Washington Co., Maine
    d: aft 2 Jun 1905 in of Brainerd, Crow Wing Co., Minnesota
.... +Mary "MOLLIE"
    d: aft 2 Jun 1905 in of Brainerd, Crow Wing Co., Minnesota
.... 3-Lydia GRAY
    b: abt 1846 in Wesley, Washington Co., Maine
.... 3-Edwin GRAY
    b: abt 1847 in Wesley, Washington Co., Maine
    d: 1872 in buried Old Minneapolis Cemetery, Minneapolis, Hennepin, MN
.... 3-Francis "Frank" GRAY
    b: BET. 1849 - 1850 in Wesley, Washington Co., Maine
    d: abt 1890 in St. Peter State Hospital, perhaps Brainerd, Crow Wing Co., MN
.... +UNKNOWN
.... 4-Mary GRAY
.... 3-Charles "Walter" GRAY
    b: abt 1851 in Wesley, Washington Co., Maine

    d: Nov 1898 in Mille Lacs, buried Garrison, Crow Wing Co., Minnesota
.... +AMILIE
    b: abt 1857 in Minnesota
    d: aft 1880 in of Lake Henry, Stearns Co., Minnesota
.............4-Frederick "Fred" GRAY
     b: abt 1876 in of Lake Henry, Stearns Co., Minnesota
     d: Jul 1898 in Lake Edward, Crow Wing Co., Minnesota, drowned
.............4-Artha GRAY
     b: abt 1878 in of Lake Henry, Stearns Co., Minnesota
.............4-Edward GRAY
     b: BET. 1879 - 1880 in of Lake Henry, Stearns Co., Minnesota
.........3 Daniel GRAY
    b: BET. 1853 - 1854 in Wesley, Washington Co., Maine
    d: bef 1870 in Brockway Twp., Stearns Co., Minnesota
.........3-Adeline A. GRAY
    b: abt 1858 in Brockway Twp., Stearns Co., Minnesota
.....+Ann Eliza SAUNDERS
  b: abt 1822 in Vermont
  m: aft 1860 in probably Cass Co., Minnesota
  d: 19 Feb 1901 in Lake Edward, buried Brainerd, Crow Wing Co., Minnesota

+ + + + + + + + +

HAYWARD DESCENDANTS

1-John HAYWARD
b: 9 May 1787 in probably Windsor Township, Hants Co., Nova Scotia, Canada
d: 1 May 1875 in St. Cloud, Stearns Co., Minnesota
 +Margaret SHECK
b: abt 1786 in Sussex Corner, Kings Co., New Brunswick, Canada
m: 1808 in Kingston, Kings Co., New Brunswick, Canada
d: 25 Dec 1872 in Baring, Washington Co., Maine
.....2-Allen C. HAYWARD
  b: 22 Mar 1810 in Sussex, Kings Co., New Brunswick, Canada
  d: 11 Apr 1889 in Wesley, Washington Co., Maine
.....+Thankful SMITH
  b: 26 May 1812 in Tower Hill, St. David, Charlotte Co., New Brunswick, Canada
  m: abt 1833 in Moores Mills, Charlotte Co., New Brunswick
  d: 6 May 1890 in Wesley, Washington Co., Maine
.........3-John (Sgt.) Wesley HAYWARD
   b: 26 Apr 1835 in St. David, Charlotte Co., New Brunswick, Canada
   d: 27 Nov 1893 in Glenwood, Mills Co., Iowa
.... +Mary Louise LOWELL
   b: 15 Dec 1836 in Whitneyville, Washington Co., Maine
   m: 23 Feb 1856 in Wesley, Washington Co., Maine
   d: 11 Aug 1894 in Glenwood, Mills Co., Iowa
.............4-Frank (Rev.) Leslie HAYWARD
    b: 27 Apr 1857 in Wesley, Washington Co., Maine
    d: 24 Jan 1925 in Harpswell, Cumberland Co., Maine
.............4-Fred L. HAYWARD
    b: 28 May 1859 in Wesley, Washington Co., Maine
    d: 7 Feb 1883 in Wesley, Washington Co., Maine
.............4-Allen Berry "Allie" HAYWARD
    b: 22 Sep 1861 in Wesley, Washington Co., Maine
    d: 1937 in Wesley, Washington Co., Maine
.............4-Charlotte Helen "Lottie" HAYWARD

............4-May Louise HAYWARD
        b: 24 May 1866 in Wesley, Washington Co., Maine
        d: 15 Mar 1944 in Mystic, New London Co., Connecticut
............4-May Louise HAYWARD
        b: 23 Dec 1868 in Wesley, Washington Co., Maine
        d: aft 1952 in of Otsego Township, Wright Co., Minnesota
............4-Melvina "Mell" M. HAYWARD
        b: 5 Jan 1872 in Wesley, Washington Co., Maine
        d: aft 1952 in Anoka, Anoka Co., Minnesota?
............4-George C. HAYWARD
        b: 23 Dec 1874 in Wesley, Washington Co., Maine
        d: 1918 in Mildred, Prairie Co., Montana?
............4-John Perlie HAYWARD
        b: 13 Mar 1878 in Wesley, Washington Co., Maine
        d: 20 May 1963 in Machias, Washington Co., Maine
........3-Thankful H. HAYWARD
    b: 25 Feb 1837 in Wesley, Washington Co., Maine
    d: bef Jun 1900
........3-Helen T. HAYWARD
    b: abt Mar 1839 in Wesley, Washington Co., Maine
    d: 15 Dec 1864 in Wesley, Washington Co., Maine
........3-Ebenezer Smith "Eben" HAYWARD
    b: abt Aug 1843 in Wesley, Washington Co., Maine
    d: 16 Jan 1898 in Wesley, Washington Co., Maine
........+Mary Amanda "Mandy" PORTER
    b: 8 Jun 1843 in Princeton, Washington Co., Maine
    m: 1 Oct 1864 in Wesley, Washington Co., Maine
    d: 1911 in Wesley, Washington Co., Maine
............4-Lynn H. HAYWARD
        b: in Wesley, Washington Co., Maine
........3-Christopher A. HAYWARD
    b: abt May 1843 in Wesley, Washington Co., Maine
    d: 6 Mar 1844 in Wesley, Washington Co., Maine
........3-Louisa J. HAYWARD
    b: bet 1839 and 1846 in Wesley, Washington Co., Maine
    d: 2 Feb 1867 in Wesley, Washington Co., Maine
........+Ellis Smith COFFRON
    b: 25 May 1839 in Moores Mills, St. David's Parish, New Brunswick, Canada
    m: 16 Apr 1863 in Wesley, Washington Co., Maine
    d: 6 Aug 1906 in Ferndale, Humboldt Co., California
............4-Eva A. COFFRON
        b: abt May 1863 in Wesley, Washington Co., Maine
        d: 27 Jan 1865 in Wesley, Washington Co., Maine
............4-Andrew J. COFFRON
        b: Jan 1864 in Wesley, Washington Co., Maine
        d: 6 Oct 1944 in Bangor, Penobscot Co., Maine
............4-Jennie COFFRON
        b: abt 1866 in Wesley, Washington Co., Maine
........3-Andrew J. HAYWARD
    b: abt Jun 1847 in Wesley, Washington Co., Maine
    d: 1 Dec 1864 in Wesley, Washington Co., Maine
........+never MARRIED
........3-Charlotte S. HAYWARD
    b: abt Jun 1852 in Wesley, Washington Co., Maine
    d: 10 Dec 1864 in Wesley, Washington Co., Maine
........+never MARRIED
........3-Mary Jane HAYWARD

b: 1853 in Wesley, Washington Co., Maine
..... 2-Henry HAYWARD
    b: 29 May 1812 in Shepody, Hopewell Parish, Albert Co., New Brunswick, Canada
    d: 24 Jun 1900 in Calais, Washington Co., Maine
..... +Asuba "Nellie" K. HIGGINS
    b: 23 Jun 1818 in Eden (now Bar Harbor), Hancock Co., Maine
    m: 18 Sep 1834 in West River/Wesley, Washington Co., Maine
    d: 28 Oct 1885 in Cooper, Washington Co., Maine
.... 3-John "Freeman" HAYWARD
    b: 26 Apr 1835 in Wesley, Washington Co., Maine
    d: 19 Jul 1911 in Milltown, Washington Co., Maine
.... +Mary Ann (AYERS?)
    b: abt 1840 in Maine
    m: 18 Aug 1861 in Cooper, Washington Co., Maine
    d: bef 4 Jan 1899 in probably Washington Co., Maine
.... 4-Elora H. HAYWARD
    b: abt 1863 in Cooper, Washington Co., Maine
.... 4-Charles H. HAYWARD
    b: abt 1865 in Cooper, Washington Co., Maine
.... 4-Mina HAYWARD
    b: abt 1877 in Clay Co., Dakota Territory
.... +Marion LEEMAN
    b: abt 1847 in Eastport, Washington Co., Maine
    m: 4 Jan 1899 in Calais, Washington Co., Maine
    d: aft 19 Jul 1911
.... 3-Isabelle HAYWARD
    b: abt 1837 in Washington Co., Maine
    d: bef 1864 in perhaps Maine
.... +Aaron J. HAYNES
    b: 7 Jul 1838 in Edinburg, Passadumkeag, Penobscot Co., Maine
    m: 12 Sep 1861 in Portland, Cumberland Co., Maine
    d: aft 1880 in of Santa Clara, Santa Clara Co., California
.... 3-Eben\Edwin L. HAYWARD
    b: abt 1839 in Washington Co., Maine
    d: bef 1860 in of Cooper, Washington Co., Maine
.... +never MARRIED
.... 3-William H. HAYWARD
    b: abt 1841 in Cooper, Washington Co., Maine
    d: bef Jun 1900
.... 3-Annie Dolly HAYWARD
    b: 13 Jan 1843 in Cooper, Washington Co., Maine
    d: 24 Feb 1916 in Calais, Washington Co., Maine
.... +Charles N. YEATON
    b: 12 Jul 1840 in Cooper, Washington Co., Maine
    m: 28 Dec 1863 in Alexander, Washington Co., Maine
    d: 4 Apr 1921 in Calais, Washington Co., Maine
.... 4-Edward Lincoln YEATON
    b: BET. 1864 - 1865 in Cooper, Washington Co., Maine
    d: aft Feb 1916 in perhaps Bridgeport, Fairfield Co., Connecticut
.... 4-Frank Percy YEATON
    b: 13 May 1870 in Cooper, Washington Co., Maine
    d: 26 Jul 1958 in Ellsworth, Hancock Co., Maine
.... 4-Alice Flora YEATON
    b: abt 1872 in Cooper, Washington Co., Maine
    d: 3 Apr 1897 in Calais, Washington Co., Maine
.... 4-John Robert YEATON

b: 15 Apr 1873 in Cooper, Washington Co., Maine
d: 26 Jun 1940 in Waterville, Kennebec Co., Maine
.... 3-Charles Ethan HAYWARD
b: abt 1845 in Cooper, Washington Co., Maine
d: 2 Jul 1863 in Civil War
.... 3-Richard Thaddeus HAYWARD
b: abt 1847 in Cooper, Washington Co., Maine
d: bef Jun 1900
.... 3-Harriet E. HAYWARD
b: abt 1849 in Cooper, Washington Co., Maine
d: aft Jun 1900 in of Dennysville, Washington Co., Maine
.... +Samuel A. CONNICK
b: abt 1850 in Meddybemps, Washington Co., Maine
m: in Washington Co., Maine
d: aft 1880 in of Cooper, Washington Co., Maine
.............4-Florence CONNICK
b: abt 1874 in Cooper, Washington Co., Maine
d: bef 1930 in of Meddybemps, Washington Co., Maine
.............4-Mabel CONNICK
b: abt 1877 in Cooper, Washington Co., Maine
.............4-Grace E. CONNICK
b: abt 1879 in Cooper, Washington Co., Maine
d: aft 1920 in of Robbinston, Washington Co., Maine
.... 3-Flora E. HAYWARD
b: abt 1851 in Cooper, Washington Co., Maine
d: aft Jun 1900 in of Arcata, Humboldt Co., California
.... +Francis D. "Frank" CANBARRUS
b: Aug 1853 in Missouri
d: aft 1900 in of Arcata, Humboldt Co., California
.... 3-Spencer M. HAYWARD
b: abt 1853 in Cooper, Washington Co., Maine
d: bet 1860 and 1870
.... 3-Manley M. HAYWARD
b: abt 1856 in Cooper, Washington Co., Maine
d: aft Feb 1916 in of Cambridge, Middlesex, MA & California
.... +Sarah Elizabeth "Lizzie" MORRISEY
b: abt 1855 in Maine
m: 22 Mar 1875 in Alexander, Washington Co., Maine
d: aft 1880
.............4-(Perlin\Perley?) HAYWARD
b: 16 Apr 1878 in Maine
d: 31 Jan 1965
.... 3-Howard "Leslie" HAYWARD
b: 22 Feb 1858 in Cooper, Washington Co., Maine
d: 17 Mar 1925 in buried East Poland, Androscoggin Co., Maine
.... +Vianna A. "Anna" DAY
b: 29 Aug 1856 in Wesley, Washington Co., Maine
m: 19 Aug 1882 in Milltown, Washington Co., Maine
d: 8 Nov 1920 in buried East Poland, Androscoggin Co., Maine
.............4-Edythe Flora HAYWARD
b: 20 Aug 1887 in Cooper or Wesley, Washington Co., Maine
d: 5 Apr 1963 in Rockville, Tolland Co., Connecticut
.............4-Goldie Alice HAYWARD
b: 28 Oct 1889 in Cooper, Washington Co., Maine
d: 28 Oct 1977 in Lewiston, Androscoggin, buried East Poland, ME
.............4-Ruth Blanche HAYWARD

      b: 10 Mar 1898 in Lewiston, Androscoggin Co., Maine
      d: 1 Apr 1899 in Lewiston, Androscoggin Co., Maine
.... 3-Samuel "Arthur" (Rev.) HAYWARD
    b: 5 May 1862 in Cooper, Washington Co., Maine
    d: 5 Jul 1939 in Freeport, Cumberland Co., Maine
.... +Jennie Temperance LANE
    b: 4 Aug 1867 in Cooper, Washington Co., Maine
    m: 18 Sep 1885 in Cooper, Washington Co., Maine
    d: in Princeton, Washington Co., Maine
.... 4-Ethel Hazel HAYWARD
      b: 22 Feb 1887 in Cooper, Washington Co., Maine
      d: 22 Nov 1953 in West Princeton, Washington Co., Maine
.... 4-Marcia Belle HAYWARD
      b: 21 Jan 1891 in Washington Co., Maine
      d: 31 Mar 1972 in Springvale, York Co., Maine
.... 4-Georgia E. "Georgie" HAYWARD
      b: 30 Mar 1896 in Cooper, Washington Co., Maine
      d: 19 Mar 1920 in Washington Co., Maine?
.... 4-Earle Clifton HAYWARD
      b: 9 Sep 1902 in Cooper, Washington Co., Maine
      d: 16 Sep 1962 in of Rhode Island
.... +Lucy DRUMMOND\DAY
    b: abt 1872 in Maine
    m: 2 Aug 1928 in Maine
    d: aft 5 Jul 1939 in of Freeport, Cumberland Co., Maine
..... 2-Daughter HAYWARD
  b: bef 1815 in probably Hopewell Parish, Albert Co., New Brunswick, Canada
..... 2-James HAYWARD
  b: 24 Sep 1817 in Shepody, Hopewell Parish, Albert Co., New Brunswick, Canada
  d: abt 1 Dec 1885 in Wesley, Washington Co., Maine
..... +Eleanor JONES
  b: abt Mar 1818 in Athens, Somerset Co., Maine
  m: 10 Aug 1837 in Wesley, Washington Co., Maine
  d: 14 Oct 1899 in Wesley, Washington Co., Maine
.... 3-Vianna HAYWARD
    b: abt May 1837 in Wesley, Washington Co., Maine
    d: 21 Jan 1839 in Wesley, Washington Co., Maine
.... 3-Constantina HAYWARD
    b: abt 1840 in Wesley, Washington Co., Maine
    d: aft 1850
.... 3-Margaret Elvira HAYWARD
    b: 12 Jun 1840 in Wesley, Washington Co., Maine
    d: 18 Mar 1879 in Cooper, Washington Co., Maine
.... +Abiah D. DAY
    b: 24 Mar 1833 in Wesley, Washington Co., Maine
    m: 30 Sep 1855 in Wesley, Washington Co., Maine
    d: 30 Mar 1888 in Cooper, Washington Co., Maine
.... 4-Vianna A. "Anna" DAY
      b: 29 Aug 1856 in Wesley, Washington Co., Maine
      d: 8 Nov 1920 in buried East Poland, Androscoggin Co., Maine
.... 4-Ella May Hayward DAY
      b: 26 Jun 1860 in Cooper, Washington Co., Maine
      d: 12 Jul 1895 in Lowell, Middlesex Co., Massachusetts
.... 4-Willis Gilbert DAY
      b: 28 Jan 1865 in Wesley, Washington Co., Maine
      d: aft 25 Sep 1939

............4-Vernanus Onslow "Vern" DAY
   b: 20 Nov 1867 in Cooper, Washington Co., Maine
   d: 1938 in Cooper, Washington Co., Maine
............4-Alice M. DAY
   b: 29 Dec 1871 in Wesley, Washington Co., Maine
............4-Burton "Bert" DAY
   b: 30 May 1874 in Cooper, Washington Co., Maine
............4-Elsie DAY
   b: 14 Dec 1876 in Cooper, Washington Co., Maine
   d: 19 Feb 1893 in Cooper, Washington Co., Maine
............4-Alphonso "Torn" DAY
   b: 5 Jul 1879 in Cooper, Washington Co., Maine
   d: in California?
........3-Vianna A. HAYWARD
   b: abt 1845 in Wesley, Washington Co., Maine
   d: 1886 in Alexander, Washington Co. Maine
.... +Charles Sumner HAYWARD
   b: 29 Jan 1860 in Wesley, Washington Co., Maine
   m: in probably Washington Co., Maine
   d: 27 Jul 1901 in Bangor, Penobscot Co., Maine
........3-Amanda F. HAYWARD
   b: abt 1847 in Wesley, Washington Co., Maine
   d: 1 Nov 1895 in East Machias, Washington Co., Maine
.... +John "Wellington" ELSEMORE
   b: abt 1840 in Wesley, Washington Co., Maine
   m: 20 May 1865 in Wesley, Washington Co., Maine
   d: aft 1883 in Calais, Washington Co., Maine?
........3-Inza E. HAYWARD
   b: 1850 in Wesley, Washington Co., Maine
   d: aft 1880 in of Wesley, Washington Co., Maine
.... +Merrill ALLEN
   b: 25 May 1843 in Deblois, Washington Co., Maine
   m: 3 Jul 1867 in Wesley, Washington Co., Maine
   d: aft 1880 in of Wesley, Washington Co., Maine
............4-Lillian Marita ALLEN
   b: 1869 in Wesley, Washington Co., Maine
............4-Elwood M. ALLEN
   b: 1872 in Wesley, Washington Co., Maine
   d: bef 27 Jun 1908
............4-Eleanor M. ALLEN
   b: 1875 in Wesley, Washington Co., Maine
............4-Glenora A. ALLEN
   b: 1878 in Wesley, Washington Co., Maine
............4-John W. ALLEN
   b: 18 Apr 1880 in Wesley, Washington Co., Maine
   d: 7 Oct 1891 in Wesley, Washington Co., Maine
........3-Adeline E. "Addie" HAYWARD
   b: 25 Apr 1853 in Wesley, Washington Co., Maine
   d: 13 Oct 1926 in Bar Harbor, Hancock Co., Maine
.... +Ebenezer Smith COFFRON
   b: 14 Oct 1849 in Moores Mills, St. David's Parish, New Brunswick, Canada
   m: 8 Nov 1872 in Wesley, Washington Co., Maine
   d: 26 Jan 1930 in Bar Harbor, Hancock Co., Maine
............4-Roger E. "Royce" COFFRON
   b: 1875 in Wesley, Washington Co., Maine
   d: 1944 in Bar Harbor, Hancock Co., Maine

............4-Nellie L. "Nan" COFFRON
    b: 1879 in Wesley, Washington Co., Maine
    d: 1960 in Boston, Suffolk Co., Massachusetts
............4-Maude Lillian COFFRON
    b: 6 Jul 1882 in Grand Lake Stream, Washington Co., Maine
    d: 10 Apr 1942 in Bar Harbor, Hancock Co., Maine
............4-Thomas H. COFFRON
    b: 31 Jan 1884 in Wesley, Washington Co., Maine
    d: 10 Sep 1970 in East Orland, Hancock Co., Maine
............4-Forest Hollis COFFRON
    b: 8 Nov 1889 in Wesley, Washington Co., Maine
    d: 13 Jun 1971 in Scarborough, Cumberland Co., Maine
............4-Daisy COFFRON
    b: 1897 in Bar Harbor, Hancock Co., Maine
    d: 1938
........3-Leona H. HAYWARD
    b: May 1857 in Wesley, Washington Co., Maine
    d: 1935 in Machias, Washington Co., Maine
.... +James Alfred HATT
    b: Jul 1859 in St. George, New Brunswick, Canada
    m: 24 Aug 1879 in Wesley, Washington Co., Maine
    d: 5 Oct 1931 in Machias, Washington Co., Maine
............4-Edith E. HATT
    b: 10 Dec 1879 in Wesley, Washington Co., Maine
    d: abt 1954
............4-Percy L. HATT
    b: 10 Jul 1882 in Wesley, Washington Co., Maine
    d: 5 Jul 1967 in Bowdoin, Sagadahoc Co., Maine
............4-Susie E. HATT
    b: 29 Jul 1886 in Wesley, Washington Co., Maine
    d: Mar 1977 in Augusta, Kennebec Co., Maine
............4-Everett E. HATT
    b: 14 Feb 1889 in Wesley, Washington Co., Maine
    d: Aug 1891 in Wesley, Washington Co., Maine
............4-Mildred M. HATT
    b: 9 Jul 1891 in Wesley, Washington Co., Maine
............4-Mabel M. HATT
    b: Nov 1894 in Wesley, Washington Co., Maine
............4-Elsie A. HATT
    b: 21 Jan 1897 in Wesley, Washington Co., Maine
    d: 7 Jan 1986 in Biddeford, York Co., Maine
........3-Lenora E. HAYWARD
    b: abt Jul 1859 in Wesley, Washington Co., Maine
    d: 11 Sep 1864 in Wesley, Washington Co., Maine
.....2-Samuel Freeze HAYWARD
    b: 13 Jun 1819 in Shepody, Hopewell Parish, Albert Co., New Brunswick, Canada
    d: 26 Aug 1902 in Baring, Washington Co., Maine
..... +Sarah "Sally" Graves AVERILL
    b: 6 Oct 1824 in Wesley, Washington Co., Maine
    m: 29 Apr 1849 in Wesley, Washington Co., Maine
    d: 21 Apr 1892 in Baring, Washington Co., Maine
........3-Georgiana Fales Wesley HAYWARD
    b: abt Mar 1850 in Wesley, Washington Co., Maine
    d: 13 Oct 1851 in Wesley, Washington Co., Maine
........3-George Napoleon HAYWARD
    b: 19 Aug 1851 in Wesley, Washington Co., Maine

....   d: 23 Oct 1872 in Newburyport, Essex Co., Massachusetts
....   +never MARRIED
.... 3-Georgiana "Georgie" F. HAYWARD
            b: 3 Apr 1853 in Wesley, Washington Co., Maine
            d: aft 11 Nov 1902 in New Hampshire?
....   +Unknown MCLELLAN
....   .4-Marion MCLELLAN
.... 3-Samuel Weare HAYWARD
            b: 18 Feb 1855 in Wesley, Washington Co., Maine
            d: 1920 in Alexander, Washington Co., Maine
....   +Vienna "Annie" COLSON
            b: 1857 in Washington Co., Maine
            m: in Washington Co., Maine?
            d: 1886 in Alexander, Washington Co., Maine
....   .4-Minetta HAYWARD
                b: 4 Oct 1878 in of Calais, Washington Co., Maine at her marriage
                d: 1925 in Maine
....   .4-Vesta M. HAYWARD
                b: Jun 1880 in Washington Co., Maine
                d: 23 Aug 1889 in Alexander, Washington Co., Maine
....   .4-Clinton S. HAYWARD
                b: Apr 1876 in Maine
....   .4-Zora H. HAYWARD
....   +Harriet "Hattie" M. COLSON
            b: abt Jun 1869 in Machias, Washington Co., Maine
            m: 1887 in perhaps Charlotte Co., NB, Canada
            d: 9 Dec 1893 in Baring, Washington Co., Maine
....   .4-Henry Clay HAYWARD
                b: 29 Mar 1891 in Baring, Washington Co., Maine
                d: aft 1920 in of Baring, Washington Co., Maine
....   .4-Nellie M. HAYWARD
                b: in Washington Co., Maine
....   .4-Harris H. HAYWARD
                b: 8 Mar 1893 in Wesley, Washington Co., Maine
.... 3-Arabella S. A. HAYWARD
            b: 24 Feb 1856 in Wesley, Washington Co., Maine
            d: 5 Mar 1857 in Wesley, Washington Co., Maine
.... 3-Josiah E. HAYWARD
            b: 13 Mar 1858 in Wesley, Washington Co., Maine
            d: 18 Sep 1925 in Baring, Washington Co., Maine
....   +Amanda J. JAENSON
            b: 30 Oct 1862 in Sweden
            m: in St. Cloud, Stearns Co., Minnesota
            d: 30 Oct 1925 in Baring, Washington Co., Maine
.... 3-Charles Sumner HAYWARD
            b: 29 Jan 1860 in Wesley, Washington Co., Maine
            d: 27 Jul 1901 in Bangor, Penobscot Co., Maine
....   +Vianna A. HAYWARD
            b: abt 1845 in Wesley, Washington Co., Maine
            m: in probably Washington Co., Maine
            d: 1886 in Alexander, Washington Co. Maine
.... 3-Winfield HAYWARD
            b: 26 Jul 1861 in Wesley, Washington Co., Maine
            d: 21 Sep 1861 in Wesley, Washington Co., Maine
.... 3-Henrietta M. HAYWARD
            b: 3 Mar 1863 in Wesley, Washington Co., Maine

.... d: 1956 in Milltown, Washington Co., Maine
.... +Benjamin W. (Rev.) CORLISS
.... b: 1868 in Milltown, Washington Co., Maine?
.... m: 4 Mar 1894 in Baring, Washington Co., Maine
.... d: 1956 in Baring, Washington Co., Maine
.... 4-Leon R. CORLISS
.... b: 6 Jul 1898 in Washington Co., Maine
.... d: 9 Dec 1981 in Portland, Cumberland Co., Maine
..... 2-Maryan Elizabeth HAYWARD
.... b: 15 Sep 1822 in Shepody, Hopewell, Albert Co., New Brunswick, Canada
.... d: 30 Mar 1865 in Wesley, Washington Co., Maine
..... +William MILLER
.... b: 1815 in Nova Scotia, Canada
.... m: 11 Feb 1841 in Wesley, Washington Co., Maine
.... d: 18 Jul 1878 in Wesley, Washington Co., Maine
.... 3-Rachel MILLER
.... b: abt 1840 in Wesley, Washington Co., Maine
.... d: 25 Apr 1852 in Wesley, Washington Co., Maine
.... 3-Margaret J. MILLER
.... b: abt Oct 1843 in Wesley, Washington Co., Maine
.... d: 13 Nov 1870 in Wesley, Washington Co., Maine
.... 3-George H. MILLER
.... b: abt 1844 in Wesley, Washington Co., Maine
.... 3-Samuel H. MILLER
.... b: abt 1847 in Wesley, Washington Co., Maine
.... 3-Mary E. MILLER
.... b: 1850 in Wesley, Washington Co., Maine
.... 3-Azubah H. "Lula" MILLER
.... b: 1851 in Wesley, Washington Co., Maine
.... d: 27 Mar 1865 in Wesley, Washington Co., Maine
.... 3-Adrianna A. "Adra" MILLER
.... b: abt 1853 in Wesley, Washington Co., Maine
.... d: 4 Mar 1865 in Wesley, Washington Co., Maine
.... 3-Josiah MILLER
.... b: 1856 in Wesley, Washington Co., Maine
.... 3-Sarah MILLER
.... b: 1857 in Wesley, Washington Co., Maine
.... 3-William "Willie" MILLER , Jr
.... b: abt 1859 in Wesley, Washington Co., Maine
.... d: 16 Mar 1865 in Wesley, Washington Co., Maine
.... 3-Elizabeth "Lizzie" MILLER
.... b: 1861 in Wesley, Washington Co., Maine
.... 3-Clara M. MILLER
.... b: 1863 in Wesley, Washington Co., Maine
..... 2-Josiah Eaton HAYWARD
.... b: 2 Feb 1826 in Maine, Washington Co. or Mechanics Falls, Androscoggan Co.
.... d: 13 Mar 1895 in St. Cloud, Stearns Co., Minnesota
..... +Mary Stinson GRAY
.... b: 22 Jan 1830 in Wesley, Washington Co., Maine
.... m: 28 Apr 1848 in Wesley, Washington Co., Maine
.... d: 1 Sep 1912 in St. Cloud, Stearns Co., Minnesota
.... 3-Mary Orinda HAYWARD
.... b: 26 Oct 1849 in Wesley, Washington Co., Maine
.... d: 12 Feb 1917 in St. Cloud, Stearns Co., Minnesota
.... +John S. COATES
.... b: 9 Dec 1844 in Lincolnshire, England

m: abt Sep 1870 in St. Cloud, Stearns Co., Minnesota
d: 8 Jan 1924 in St. Cloud, Stearns Co., Minnesota
............4-Charles Ambrose COATES
b: 28 Feb 1872 in St. Cloud, Stearns Co., Minnesota
d: 2 Aug 1956 in Los Angeles Co., California
............4-Harry Sheck COATES
b: 8 Aug 1878 in St. Cloud, Stearns Co., Minnesota
d: 8 Apr 1945 in Los Angeles, Los Angeles Co., California
............4-Frank Hayward COATES
b: 17 Aug 1879 in St. Cloud, Stearns Co., Minnesota
d: 8 Nov 1935 in Kalispell, Flathead Co., Montana
............4-Arthur John COATES
b: 28 Sep 1882 in St. Cloud, Stearns Co., Minnesota
d: 9 Jun 1916 in of Miles City, Custer Co., Montana; buried Stearns Co., MN
............4-Florence M. COATES
b: Feb 1886 in St. Cloud, Stearns Co., Minnesota
d: 9 Sep 1946 in Wayzata, Hennepin Co., Minnesota
............4-Daughter COATES
b: UNKNOWN
............4-Lucille COATES
b: Mar 1887 in St. Cloud, Stearns Co., Minnesota
d: 20 Mar 1969 in Wayzata, Hennepin Co., Minnesota
........3-Clara Hortense HAYWARD
b: 1851 in Wesley, Washington Co., Maine
d: 12 Dec 1936 in buried St. Cloud, Stearns Co., Minnesota
.... +Daniel Harris FREEMAN
b: 16 Jun 1849 in Logan, Edgar Co., Illinois
m: 17 Jul 1870 in St. Cloud, Stearns Co., Minnesota
d: 7 Nov 1931 in St. Cloud, Stearns Co., Minnesota
............4-Minnetta FREEMAN
b: 10 Mar 1871 in St. Cloud, Stearns Co., Minnesota
d: 16 Feb 1873 in St. Cloud, Stearns Co., Minnesota
............4-Ambrose FREEMAN
b: 12 Dec 1872 in St. Cloud, Stearns Co., Minnesota
d: 15 Oct 1874 in St. Cloud, Stearns Co., Minnesota
............4-Warren H. FREEMAN
b: 14 Oct 1874 in St. Cloud, Stearns Co., Minnesota
d: 24 Dec 1970 in Minneapolis, Hennepin Co., Minnesota
............4-Willard S. FREEMAN
b: 23 Apr 1879 in St. Cloud, Stearns Co., Minnesota
d: 27 May 1950 in St. Cloud, Stearns Co., Minnesota
............4-Son FREEMAN
b: 27 May 1883 in St. Cloud, Stearns Co., Minnesota
d: bef 1900 in St. Cloud, Stearns Co., Minnesota
............4-Zelah M. FREEMAN
b: 30 Jun 1889 in St. Cloud, Stearns Co., Minnesota
d: 25 Sep 1977 in Tallahassee, Leon Co., Florida
............4-Don A. FREEMAN
b: abt 1900 in St. Cloud, Stearns Co., Minnesota
d: 26 Sep 1957 in Hennepin Co., Minnesota?
........3-Elora H. HAYWARD
b: 2 Feb 1852 in Wesley, Washington Co., Maine
d: 2 Sep 1926 in Big Fish Lake, Cold Spring, buried St. Cloud, Stearns Co., MN
.... +Emmet Clark HOLDEN , D.D.S.
b: 25 Aug 1851 in Rutland, Rutland Co., Vermont
m: Nov 1882 in St. Cloud, Stearns Co., Minnesota

............4-Genevieve H. HOLDEN
        b: 22 Feb 1884 in St. Cloud, Stearns Co., Minnesota
        d: 4 Nov 1897 in St. Cloud, Stearns Co., Minnesota

        d: 8 Aug 1908 in St. Paul, Ramsey Co., Minnesota
............4-Genevieve H. HOLDEN
        b: 22 Feb 1884 in St. Cloud, Stearns Co., Minnesota
        d: 4 Nov 1897 in St. Cloud, Stearns Co., Minnesota
............4-Paul Martin Truzinski HOLDEN
        b: Jan 1894 in St. Cloud, Stearns Co., Minnesota
        d: Apr 1938 in Seattle, King Co., Washington
........3-Daniel Sheck HAYWARD
        b: Feb 1854 in Baring, Washington Co., Maine
        d: 25 Mar 1929 in Riverside, Riverside Co., California
.... +Virginia "Jennie" K. MOORE
        b: abt 1857 in Illinois or Missouri
        m: Aug 1874 in St. Cloud, Stearns Co., Minnesota
        d: aft 23 Sep 1904 in perhaps San Francisco, San Francisco Co., California
............4-Mary "Vernie" HAYWARD
        b: abt 1876 in St. Cloud, Stearns Co., Minnesota
        d: 23 Sep 1904 in San Francisco, San Francisco Co., California
.... +Martha A. PATOCK
        b: 19 Jan 1861 in probably Darslub, Neustadt Co., West Prussia
        m: 1 Oct 1888 in St. Cloud, Stearns Co., Minnesota
        d: 22 Sep 1938 in St. Cloud, Stearns Co., Minnesota
............4-Josiah Eaton "Joe" HAYWARD
        b: Feb 1890 in St. Cloud, Stearns Co., Minnesota
        d: 25 Dec 1949 in Veterans Hospital, Fort Snelling, Hennepin Co., Minnesota
............4-Laura E. HAYWARD
        b: Dec 1891 in St. Cloud, Stearns Co., Minnesota
        d: 5 Apr 1969 in of Norwood, Norfolk Co., Massachusetts
............4-Daniel Sheck HAYWARD , Jr
        b: 31 Jan 1895 in St. Cloud, Stearns Co., Minnesota
        d: 11 Nov 1935 in Veterans Hospital, Minneapolis, Hennepin Co., Minnesota
............4-Mary Martha HAYWARD
        b: May 1897 in St. Cloud, Stearns Co., Minnesota
        d: 1970 in Riverside, Riverside Co., California
........3-Samuel L. HAYWARD
        b: Aug 1856 in Wesley, Washington Co., Maine?
        d: 21 Feb 1936 in St. Cloud, Stearns Co., Minnesota
.... +Mary A. LOCKE
        b: Dec 1854 in Ohio
        m: 20 Aug 1879 in St. Cloud, Stearns Co., Minnesota
        d: aft 1909 in Kent, King Co., Washington?
............4-John E. HAYWARD
        b: Aug 1883 in St. Cloud, Stearns Co., Minnesota
        d: aft 1936 in of Enumclaw, King Co., Washington
............4-Leonard E. HAYWARD
        b: Jan 1884 in St. Cloud, Stearns Co., Minnesota
        d: aft 1936 in of Los Angeles, Los Angeles Co., California
............4-Mary E. HAYWARD
        b: Jul 1886 in St. Cloud, Stearns Co., Minnesota
        d: bef 1936
............4-Mildred L. HAYWARD
        b: Apr 1887 in St. Cloud, Stearns Co., Minnesota
        d: aft 1936 in of Los Angeles, Los Angeles Co., California
............4-Corinne Loretta HAYWARD
        b: May 1888 in St. Cloud, Stearns Co., Minnesota
        d: 24 Feb 1909 in Kent, King Co., Washington
........3-William H. HAYWARD

                b: 3 Apr 1859 in Brockway, Stearns Co., Minnesota
                d: 10 Jan 1890 in Chicago, Cook Co., Illinois
.... +**Hattie M. RUSSELL**
                b: in New York?
                m: 26 Nov 1882 in St. Cloud, Stearns Co., Minnesota
                d: May 1929 in Kewanee, Henry Co., Illinois
.............4-NONE
.... 3-**Jean Odell "Jennie" HAYWARD**
                b: Oct 1867 in St. Cloud, Stearns Co., Minnesota
                d: 7 Sep 1937 in Orange Co., California
.... +**Clarendon Parker MCCLURE**
                b: 28 Dec 1862 in St. Cloud, Stearns Co., Minnesota
                m: 16 Jan 1889 in St. Cloud, Stearns Co., Minnesota
                d: 20 Mar 1907 in Ocean Park Beach, Venice, Los Angeles Co., California
.............4-**Clara Louise MCCLURE**
                    b: 20 May 1890 in St. Cloud, Stearns Co., Minnesota
                    d: 21 May 1905 in St. Cloud, Stearns Co., Minnesota
.............4-**Delphine Jean MCCLURE**
                    b: 25 Oct 1892 in St. Cloud, Stearns Co., Minnesota
                    d: 30 Jan 1974 in Santa Barbara Co., California
.... 3-**John A. HAYWARD**
                b: 25 Mar 1871 in St. Cloud, Stearns Co., Minnesota
                d: 1 May 1876 in St. Cloud, Stearns Co., Minnesota
.....2-**John HAYWARD , Jr**
        b: 19 May 1828 in probably Washington Co., Maine
        d: 28 Aug 1870 in St. Cloud, Stearns Co., Minnesota
..... +**Melinda J. GRAY**
        b: 15 Feb 1831 in Wesley, Washington Co., Maine
        m: 25 Apr 1850 in Wesley, Washington Co., Maine
        d: 14 Sep 1916 in Riverside, Riverside Co., California
.... 3-**Ellen HAYWARD**
                b: abt 1854 in Stearns Co., Minnesota
                d: bef 1870 in probably St. Cloud, Stearns Co., Minnesota

+ + + + + + + + + + +

MCCLURE DESCENDANTS

1-**Thomas Archibald MCCLURE**
b: 14 Aug 1790 in Acworth, Cheshire Co., New Hampshire
d: 15 Sep 1866 in Brooks, Waldo Co., Maine
 +**Betsey ARMOUR**
b: 1796 in New Hampshire
m: 30 Nov 1823 in Belfast, Waldo Co., Maine
d: 1889 in buried Brooks, Waldo Co., Maine
.....2-**Mary Elizabeth MCCLURE**
        b: 4 Jan 1825 in of Waldo, Waldo Co., Maine
        d: aft 1850 in of Boston, Suffolk Co., Massachusetts
..... +**Austin LEVANSALAER**
        b: abt 1823 in Maine
        m: 1 Dec 1847 in Roxbury, Suffolk Co., Massachusetts
        d: aft 1850 in of Boston, Suffolk Co., Massachusetts
.... 3-**Frank E. LEVANSALAER**
                b: abt Apr 1850 in Boston, Suffolk Co., Massachusetts
.....2-**Thomas Clarendon MCCLURE**

b: 17 Mar 1827 in Waldo, Waldo Co., Maine
d: 12 Aug 1881 in St. Cloud, Stearns Co., Minnesota
..... +**Clara Swan CLARKE**
b: 27 Jan 1839 in Hubbardston, Worcester Co., Massachusetts
m: 4 Dec 1859 in St. Cloud, Stearns Co., Minnesota
d: 10 Feb 1899 in St. Cloud, Stearns Co., Minnesota
.... 3-**Clara Louise MCCLURE**
b: 11 Oct 1861 in St. Cloud, Stearns Co., Minnesota
d: 7 Sep 1869 in St. Cloud, Stearns Co., Minnesota
.... 3-**Clarendon Parker MCCLURE**
b: 28 Dec 1862 in St. Cloud, Stearns Co., Minnesota
d: 20 Mar 1907 in Ocean Park Beach, Venice, Los Angeles Co., California
.... +**Jean Odell "Jennie" HAYWARD**
b: Oct 1867 in St. Cloud, Stearns Co., Minnesota
m: 16 Jan 1889 in St. Cloud, Stearns Co., Minnesota
d: 7 Sep 1937 in Orange Co., California
.... .4-**Clara Louise MCCLURE**
b: 20 May 1890 in St. Cloud, Stearns Co., Minnesota
d: 21 May 1905 in St. Cloud, Stearns Co., Minnesota
.... .4-**Delphine Jean MCCLURE**
b: 25 Oct 1892 in St. Cloud, Stearns Co., Minnesota
d: 30 Jan 1974 in Santa Barbara Co., California
.... 3-**Thomas Shepard "Shep" MCCLURE**
b: Mar 1871 in St. Cloud, Stearns Co., Minnesota
d: Jun 1932 in San Antonio, Bexar Co., Texas
.... +**Ada C. SNOW**
b: Aug 1870 in perhaps Otsego Twp., Wright Co., Minnesota
m: abt 1905 in St. Cloud, Stearns Co., Minnesota
d: abt 1931 in of San Antonio, Bexar Co., Texas
.... 3-**Caroline "Mary" MCCLURE**
b: 8 Sep 1876 in St. Cloud, Stearns Co., Minnesota
d: 13 Aug 1950 in Moose Lake, Carlton Co., Minnesota
.... +**Warren H. FREEMAN**
b: 14 Oct 1874 in St. Cloud, Stearns Co., Minnesota
m: in St. Cloud, Stearns Co., Minnesota
d: 24 Dec 1970 in Minneapolis, Hennepin Co., Minnesota
.... 3-**Alice Clarke MCCLURE**
b: 4 Mar 1877 in St. Cloud, Stearns Co., Minnesota
d: 12 Jan 1943 in Seattle, Kings Co., Washington
.... +**Delroy GETCHELL**
b: 27 Oct 1861 in Galion, Crawford Co., Ohio
m: 30 Jun 1908 in Paynesville, Stearns Co., Minnesota
d: 18 Nov 1939 in Medford, Jackson Co., Oregon
.... .4-**Bayard McClure GETCHELL**
b: 24 Mar 1909 in Medford, Jackson Co., Oregon
d: 15 Apr 1986 in Medford, Jackson Co., Oregon
.... .4-**Gloria Valerie GETCHELL**
b: 1915 in Medford, Jackson Co., Oregon
.... 3-**John Otis MCCLURE**
b: 1 Sep 1878 in St. Cloud, Stearns Co., Minnesota
d: 24 Jan 1910 in Medford, Jackson Co., Oregon
..... .2-**Edwin Mitchell MCCLURE**
b: 31 Jan 1830 in probably Waldo, Waldo Co., Maine
d: bef 1884 in of Bangor, Penobscot Co., Maine
..... +**Anne M. "Annie" HARRIS**
b: 10 Dec 1832 in Massachusetts

        m: aft 1850
        d: aft 1884 in of Bangor, Penobscot Co., Maine
.... **3-Harry Thomas MCCLURE**
        b: 31 Dec 1875 in Massachusetts, probably Peabody, Essex Co.
        d: 1958 in of East Greenwich, Kent Co., Rhode Island
.... **+Jennie M. AYER**
        b: 1880 in Maine
        d: 1956 in of East Greenwich, Kent Co., Rhode Island
.............**4-Robert A. MCCLURE**
          b: 28 May 1916 in Massachusetts
          d: Oct 1986 in of Manville, Providence Co., Rhode Island
.....**2-Margaret Armour MCCLURE**
    b: 15 Mar 1832 in probably Waldo, Waldo Co., Maine
    d: 6 Sep 1833 in Brooks, Waldo Co., Maine

* * * * * * * * *

Family Index

"MOLLIE"
   Mary, 394
(AYERS?)
   Mary Ann (b. 1840), 397
A.
   Lydia (b. 1846), 394
ALLEN
   Eleanor M. (b. 1875), 400
   Elwood M. (b. 1872), 400
   Glenora A. (b. 1878), 400
   John W. (b. 1880), 400
   Lillian Marita (b. 1869), 400
   Merrill (b. 1843), 400
AMILIE
   (b. 1857), 395
ANDREWS
   Joseph "Joe" (b. 1787), 385
   Mary E. (b. 1840), 385
   Mira F. (b. 1842), 385
   Phebe (b. 1827), 385
   Roswell Nelson (b. 1844), 385
   Thankful Anne (b. 1826), 385
   William H. (b. 1837), 385
   Winslow Benjamin (b. 1835), 385
ARMOUR
   Betsey (b. 1796), 407
AVERILL
   Adeline (b. 1816), 394
   Sarah "Sally" Graves (b. 1824), 402
AYER
   Jennie M. (b. 1880), 408
BIRD
   Hannah R. (b. 1834), 383
BLAKE
   Olive, 380
BLOOD
   ?, 385
BURTON
   Mary (b. 1776), 379
CANBARRUS
   Francis D. "Frank" (b. 1853), 398
CARRICK
   Jessie M. (b. 1874), 388
   Joseph S. (b. 1838), 387

Leola (b. 1865), 387
Minnie E. (b. 1862), 387
CHASE
   Daniel (b. 1822), 383
CLARKE
   Clara Swan (b. 1839), 407
COATES
   Arthur John (b. 1882), 404
   Charles Ambrose (b. 1872), 404
   Daughter, 404
   Florence M. (b. 1886), 404
   Frank Hayward (b. 1879), 404
   Harry Sheck (b. 1878), 404
   John S.* (b. 1844), 404
   Lucille (b. 1887), 404
COBB
   Patience (b. 1800), 379
COFFRON
   Andrew J. (b. 1864), 396
   Daisy (b. 1897), 401
   Ebenezer Smith (b. 1849), 401
   Ellis Smith (b. 1839), 396
   Eva A. (b. 1863), 396
   Forest Hollis (b. 1889), 401
   Jennie (b. 1866), 396
   Maude Lillian (b. 1882), 401
   Nellie L. "Nan" (b. 1879), 401
   Roger E. "Royce" (b. 1875), 401
   Thomas H. (b. 1884), 401
COLE
   Jane Elizabeth* (b. 1817), 377
COLSON
   Harriet "Hattie" M. (b. 1869), 402
   Vienna "Annie" (b. 1857), 402
CONNICK
   Florence (b. 1874), 398
   Grace E. (b. 1879), 398
   Mabel (b. 1877), 398
   Samuel A. (b. 1850), 398
COOPER
   Arthur C. (b. 1866), 386

Charles A., 387
John C. (b. 1836), 386
Mary Elizabeth (b. 1844), 388
CORLISS
   Benjamin W. (Rev.) (b. 1868), 403
   Leon R. (b. 1898), 403
DAVIS
   Christiania (b. 1847), 394
   David, 385
   Lucretia A. (b. 1842), 394
   William (b. 1822), 393
   Willis G. (b. 1845), 394
DAY
   Abiah D. (b. 1833), 392, 399
   Alice M. (b. 1871), 392, 400
   Alphonso "Torn" (b. 1879), 392, 400
   Annella Gelana (b. 1866), 393
   Arlington Jordan (b. 1861), 393
   Burton "Bert" (b. 1874), 392, 400
   C. Benjamin (b. 1875), 387
   Charles (b. 1877), 387
   Charles Whitney (b. 1880), 393
   Cora (b. 1856), 387
   Ella May Hayward (b. 1860), 392, 400
   Elsie (b. 1876), 392, 400
   Emma Etta (b. 1863), 393
   Eugene Harry "Gene" (b. 1867), 387
   Eugene Wesley (b. 1865), 387
   Florence Elizabeth (b. 1872), 387
   Hannah (b. 1838), 393
   Ida Florence (b. 1859), 387
   Ivory Milburn (b. 1883), 393
   Jennie Florence (b. 1884), 393
   Joel (b. 1808), 381
   John (b. 1801), 392
   John Alvin (b. 1831), 392

John Wesley (b. 1832), 387
John Wilbur (b. 1841), 393
John Wilbur (b. 1864), 393
Juletta "Julia" (b. 1830), 380
Julia Ann (b. 1870), 393
Justin Ulysses (b. 1868), 393
Leonard Austin (b. 1861), 387
Leonora Beatrice "Lo" (b. 1856), 387
Lorenzo Dow (b. 1835), 387
Lorenzo Sabine (b. 1879), 393
Mary Lois "Mamie" (b. 1866), 387
Mary Rich (b. 1882), 393
Nellie Gertrude (b. 1877), 393
Ralph Elbridge (b. 1875), 393
Roy Eldridge (b. 1874), 393
Samuel (b. 1836), 392
Vernanus Onslow "Vern" (b. 1867), 392, 400
Vianna A. "Anna" (b. 1856), 392, 399, 400
Willis Gilbert (b. 1865), 392, 400

DEARBORN
A. T. (Lt.), 377

DOW
Abigail (b. 1800), 384

DRUMMOND
Lucy (b. 1872), 399

DUNCAN
Margaret Maria (b. 1851), 380

ELSEMORE
Adelia Clark (b. 1842), 393
John "Wellington" (b. 1840), 400

FENLASON
Mark Harris (b. 1825), 390

FIEGLEY
Sarah (b. 1803), 385

FOOT
Ida B., 392

FREEMAN

Ambrose (b. 1872), 378, 404
Ambrose* (Lt.) (b. 1823), 377
Daniel Harris* (b. 1849), 377, 404
Don A. (b. 1900), 378, 405
Elizabeth "Betty"* (b. 1844), 377
Elora Jean (b. 1931), 379
Laura A.* (b. 1855), 379
Lovisa Catherine* (b. 1850), 379
Mary Hortense (b. 1931), 379
Minnetta (b. 1871), 378, 404
Son (b. 1883), 378, 404
Virginia S.* (b. 1847), 377
Warren H. (b. 1874), 378, 404, 407
Willard S. (b. 1879), 378, 404
Zelah M. (b. 1889), 378, 405

GARDNER
Grace E. (b. 1872), 378

GEORGIE
(b. 1846), 385

GETCHELL
2 other children, 392
Alma M. (b. 1883), 390
Anna M. "Annie" (b. 1866), 390
Bayard McClure (b. 1909), 408
Carrie A. (b. 1868), 390
Delroy (b. 1861), 407
Ernest A. (b. 1873), 390
Everett Oscar (b. 1849), 391
Frank L. (b. 1851), 392
Gloria Valerie (b. 1915), 408
Herbert W. (b. 1880), 390
John Winslow (b. 1827), 390
Lucetta A., 389
Lucetta A.*, 391
Mary Elizabeth (b. 1840), 391
Nathaniel (b. 1828), 390
Orinda (b. 1831), 390
Otis (b. 1837), 391
Perrin (b. 1810), 382

Phebe E. (b. 1835), 390
Sarah A. "Sally" (b. 1833), 390
Van Rensselaer* (b. 1844), 391
Winslow** (b. 1801), 390

GILLETT
Celestia P., 390

GLASS
Edward B. (b. 1834), 394

GLIDDEN
Amelia M., 391

GORDON
William, 391

GRAY
3 other children, 384
Abigail "Abbie" (b. 1853), 390
Addie A. (b. 1866), 384
Adeline A. (b. 1858), 395
Andrew (b. 1840), 394
Annie C. (b. 1862), 384
Artha (b. 1878), 395
Arthur (b. 1858), 390
Austin Leander (b. 1859), 383
Belinda (b. 1819), 382
Benjamin, 381
Benjamin (b. 1803), 386
Benjamin A. (b. 1878), 388
Benjamin Franklin "Frank" (b. 1841), 388
Blanche L. (b. 1873), 388
Burton "Bertie" (b. 1864), 388
Charles "Walter" (b. 1851), 395
Charles (b. 1861), 385
Charles Henry (b. 1851), 380
Clarinda (b. 1822), 382
Clarinda (b. 1843), 389
Cynthia E. (b. 1838), 394
Daniel, 395
Daughter (b. 1835), 385
David (b. 1814), 384
Drusilla (b. 1841), 379
Eddie (b. 1859), 385
Edward, 395
Edwin (b. 1847), 394
Eli, 380
Elisha (b. 1844), 379
Eliza A. (b. 1835), 389
Elizabeth (b. 1824), 383
Elizabeth(b. 1813), 392

Ernest (b. 1862), 383
Eugene (b. 1855), 390
Florence (b. 1879), 394
Francis "Frank", 395
Frank, 380
Frank Austin (b. 1849), 380
Fred (b. 1876), 380
Frederick "Fred" (b. 1876), 395
Gideon (b. 1800), 384
Granville Clifford (b. 1834), 384
Hannah* (b. 1807), 390
Harriett Jane (b. 1833), 389
Harrison (b. 1869), 388
Helena (b. 1840), 388
Henrietta "Etta" Elizabeth (b. 1835), 387
Henry H. (b. 1853), 383
Henry Washington (b. 1837), 394
Horace (b. 1848), 379
Irving (b. 1824), 380
Irving Ellsworth (b. 1887), 381
Isadora I.. (b. 1847), 388
James (b. 1797), 382
James (b. 1826), 383
James Burton "Burt" (b. 1838), 380
James Harrison (b. 1856), 384
James W. (b. 1852), 383
Jefferson G. "Jeff" (b. 1842), 394
Jesse Leroy (b. 1883), 381
Joel (b. 1816), 379
John, 380
John (b. 1773), 379
John (b. 1799), 385
John (b. 1854), 384
John A. (b. 1831), 384
John Harrison (b. 1831), 383
Joseph (b. 1806), 389
Josephine (b. 1837), 387
Justus M. (b. 1844), 394
Kate, 380
Laura A. "Lauretta"* (b. 1845), 388
Laura Frances (b. 1855), 380
Lavinia "Vina" (b. 1832), 387

Lena, 380
Lena (b. 1876), 380
Lena(b. 1865), 383
Lillie Cora (b. 1880), 380
Lois E. (b. 1874), 384
Louis (b. 1873), 380
LovinaA. (b. 1840), 389
Lydia (b. 1846), 394
Lyman E. (b. 1864), 384
Martha E. (b. 1839), 389
Mary, 395
Mary "Polly", 385
Mary (b. 1858), 384
Mary Cecelia "Minnie" (b. 1858), 380
Mary E. (b. 1867), 394
Mary Elizabeth "Lizzie" (b. 1857), 384
Mary Stinson (b. 1830), 386
Mary Stinson* (b. 1830), 404
Melinda J. (b. 1831), 386, 406
Mildred (b. 1877), 394
Minnie (b. 1868), 385
Phoebe (b. 1799), 385
Priscilla(b. 1795), 381
Raymond Hulbert "Ray" (b. 1883), 394
Reuben, 380
Reuben (b. 1815), 394
Reuben (b. 1833), 385
Rheuben (b. 1876), 380
Roxannah Shephard (b. 1849), 384
Samuel A. "Asa" (b. 1844), 388
Samuel Wesley (b. 1831), 389, 391
Sarah, 380
Sarah (b. 1866), 385
Seeneeth, 380
Serena Mariam Getchell (b. 1856), 384
Seth E. (b. 1854), 379
Sheldon (b. 1794), 379
Sheldon (b. 1818), 379
Son, 389, 391
Thomas Jefferson (b. 1852), 379
Victor Clifton (b. 1860), 384
Violet Dell (b. 1882), 381
William S. (b. 1837), 389
HALL

Jordan Willey (Capt.) (b. 1827), 393
HANSCOM
Ellsworth Melvin, 389
Frances "Elvina" (b. 1842), 389
S. A., 390
HARDING
Mary, 382
HARRIS
Anne M. "Annie" (b. 1832), 408
HASTY
John Wilber (b. 1816), 385
HATT
Edith E. (b. 1879), 401
Elsie A. (b. 1897), 401
Everett E. (b. 1889), 401
James Alfred (b. 1859), 401
Mabel M. (b. 1894), 401
Mildred M. (b. 1891), 401
Percy L. (b. 1882), 401
Susie E. (b. 1886), 401
HAYNES
Aaron J. (b. 1838), 397
HAYWARD
(Perlin?) (b. 1878), 398
Adeline E. "Addie" (b. 1853), 381, 401
Allen Berry "Allie" (b. 1861), 396
Allen C. (b. 1810), 395
Amanda F. (b. 1847), 381, 400
Andrew J. (b. 1847), 397
Annie Dolly (b. 1843), 397
Arabella S. A. (b. 1856), 402
Charles Ethan (b. 1845), 398
Charles H. (b. 1865), 397
Charles Sumner (b. 1860), 400, 403
Charlotte Helen "Lottie" (b. 1866), 396
Charlotte S. (b. 1852), 397
Christopher A. (b. 1843), 396
Clara Hortense* (b. 1851), 378, 386, 404
Clinton S. (b. 1876), 402
Constantina (b. 1840), 381, 399

Corinne Loretta (b. 1888), 406
Daniel Sheck (b. 1854), 386, 405
Daniel Sheck (b. 1895), 405
Daughter (b. 1815), 399
Earle Clifton (b. 1902), 399
Ebenezer Smith "Eben" (b. 1843), 396
EbenL. (b. 1839), 397
Edythe Flora (b. 1887), 399
Ellen (b. 1854), 386, 406
Elora H. (b. 1852), 386, 405
Elora H. (b. 1863), 397
Ethel Hazel (b. 1887), 399
Flora E. (b. 1851), 398
Frank (Rev.) Leslie (b. 1857), 395
Fred L. (b. 1859), 396
George C. (b. 1874), 396
George Napoleon (b. 1851), 402
Georgia E. "Georgie" (b. 1896), 399
Georgiana "Georgie" F. (b. 1853), 402
Georgiana Fales Wesley (b. 1850), 402
Goldie Alice (b. 1889), 399
Harriet E. (b. 1849), 398
Harris H. (b. 1893), 402
Helen T. (b. 1839), 396
Henrietta M. (b. 1863), 403
Henry (b. 1812), 397
Henry Clay (b. 1891), 402
Howard "Leslie" (b. 1858), 398
Inza E. (b. 1850), 381, 400
Isabelle (b. 1837), 397
James (b. 1817), 381, 399
Jean Odell "Jennie" (b. 1867), 386, 406, 407
John "Freeman" (b. 1835), 397
John (b. 1828), 386, 406
John (Sgt.) Wesley** (b. 1835), 395
John *(b. 1787), 395
John A. (b. 1871), 386, 406
John E. (b. 1883), 405
John Perlie (b. 1878), 396
Josiah E. (b. 1858), 402
Josiah Eaton "Joe" (b. 1890), 405
Josiah Eaton (b. 1826), 386
Josiah Eaton* (b. 1826), 404
Laura E. (b. 1891), 405
Lenora E. (b. 1859), 381, 401
Leona H. (b. 1857), 381, 401
Leonard E. (b. 1884), 406
Louisa J. (b. 1839), 396
Lynn H., 396
Manley M. (b. 1856), 398
Marcia Belle (b. 1891), 399
Margaret Elvira (b. 1840), 381, 392, 399
Mary "Vernie" (b. 1876), 405
Mary E. (b. 1886), 406
Mary Jane (b. 1853), 397
Mary Martha (b. 1897), 405
Mary Orinda (b. 1849), 386
Mary Orinda* (b. 1849), 404
Maryan Elizabeth (b. 1822), 403
May Louise (b. 1868), 396
Melvina "Mell" M. (b. 1872), 396
Mildred L. (b. 1887), 406
Mina (b. 1877), 397
Minetta (b. 1878), 402
Nellie M., 402
Richard Thaddeus (b. 1847), 398
Ruth Blanche (b. 1898), 399
Samuel "Arthur" (Rev.) (b. 1862), 399
Samuel Freeze (b. 1819), 402
Samuel L. (b. 1856), 386, 405
Samuel Weare (b. 1855), 402
Spencer M. (b. 1853), 398
Thankful H. (b. 1837), 396
Vesta M. (b. 1880), 402
Vianna (b. 1837), 381, 399
Vianna A. (b. 1845), 381, 400, 403
William H. (b. 1841), 397
William H. (b. 1859), 386, 406
Winfield (b. 1861), 403
Zora H., 402

HICKS
Mary Jane (b. 1836), 391
HIGGINS
Asuba "Nellie" K. (b. 1818), 397
HOLDEN
Emmet Clark (b. 1851), 405
Genevieve H. (b. 1884), 405
Paul Martin Truzinski (b. 1894), 405
HUFF
Jesse (b. 1827), 389
HULBERT
Mary Ann (b. 1842), 394
HUNTLEY
Abraham (b. 1810), 382
TheresaH. "Clarissa" (b. 1820), 389
HYKE
Alice E., 391
JAENSON
Amanda J. (b. 1862), 402
JONES
Abigail (b. 1808), 389
Albert (b. 1850), 382
Calvin Herman (b. 1830), 382
Charles C. (b. 1850), 382
Eleanor (b. 1818), 381, 399
Elizabeth Eleanor "Betsy" (b. 1820), 381
Hannah (b. 1795), 382
John (b. 1816), 381
Learnard(b. 1824), 382
Lydia Clementine (b. 1845), 382
Samuel (b. 1778), 381
SylvesterS. (b. 1822), 382
William D. (b. 1825), 382
KINT
William Henry (b. 1841), 384
LANE
Jennie Temperance (b. 1867), 399
LEEMAN

LEVANSALAER
- Marion (b. 1847), 397

LEVANSALAER
- Austin (b. 1823), 407
- Frank E. (b. 1850), 407

LOCKE
- Mary A. (b. 1854), 405

LOUISA
- (b. 1847), 388

LOVEJOY
- Mary Stinson (b. 1806), 386

LOWELL
- Mary Louise (b. 1836), 395

MARLATT
- Alberta Helena (b. 1864), 388
- Dr. Silas* (b. 1826), 388
- John C. (b. 1872), 388
- Mary J. "May" (b. 1877), 388
- Willie Edgar (b. 1867), 388

MARRIED
- never, 397, 402

MARTHA
- (b. 1842), 384

MARVIN
- George Burdette* (b. 1839), 377

MCCARLIE
- Mary "May", 392

MCCLURE
- Alice Clarke (b. 1877), 407
- Caroline "Mary" (b. 1876), 378, 407
- Clara Louise (b. 1861), 407
- Clara Louise (b. 1890), 406, 407
- Clarendon Parker (b. 1862), 406, 407
- Delphine Jean (b. 1892), 406, 407
- Edwin Mitchell (b. 1830), 408
- Harry Thomas (b. 1875), 408
- John Otis (b. 1878), 408
- Margaret Armour (b. 1832), 408
- Mary Elizabeth (b. 1825), 407
- Robert A. (b. 1916), 408
- Thomas Archibald (b. 1790), 406
- Thomas Clarendon (b. 1827), 407
- Thomas Shepard "Shep" (b. 1871), 407

MCLELLAN
- Marion, 402
- Unknown, 402

MILLER
- Adrianna A. "Adra" (b. 1853), 403
- Azubah H. "Lula" (b. 1851), 403
- Clara M. (b. 1863), 403
- Elizabeth "Lizzie" (b. 1861), 403
- George H. (b. 1844), 403
- Josiah (b. 1856), 403
- Margaret J. (b. 1843), 403
- Mary E. (b. 1850), 403
- Rachel (b. 1840), 403
- Samuel H. (b. 1847), 403
- Sarah (b. 1857), 403
- William "Willie" (b. 1859), 403
- William (b. 1815), 403

MOORE
- Virginia "Jennie" K. (b. 1857), 405

MORRISEY
- Sarah Elizabeth "Lizzie" (b. 1855), 398

NONE:, 406

P.
- Persis (b. 1817), 379

PARKER
- Clementine (b. 1825), 382

PATOCK
- Martha A. (b. 1861), 405

PERRY
- Albert O., 391
- Everett O. (b. 1868), 391
- Fannie, 391
- Infant, 391
- John Nelson (b. 1836), 391
- Laura Etta, 391
- Melvin N. (b. 1878), 391
- Nettie, 391
- Ralph W., 391

POLLARD
- Ann Eliza (b. 1828), 383
- Harriet Mann (b. 1836), 384

PORTER
- Mary Amanda "Mandy" (b. 1843), 396

RAMSDELL
- John F., 389

ROLLINS
- Cyrus Chase (b. 1844), 382
- Daniel W. (b. 1852), 383
- Davis Washington (b. 1819), 382
- Davis Washington (b. 1848), 383
- Davis Washington (b. 1850), 383
- Elizabeth Hannah "Lizzie" (b. 1845), 382
- John W. (b. 1856), 383
- Josephine "Josie" F. (b. 1858), 383
- Loring Abram (b. 1860), 383
- Mary B. (b. 1854), 383
- Viola Annie (b. 1864), 383

RUSSELL
- Hattie M., 406

SAUNDERS
- Ann Eliza (b. 1822), 395

SHECK
- Margaret (b. 1786), 395

SIMONS
- Grayce S. (b. 1876), 378

SMITH
- Albert (b. 1861), 388
- Thankful (b. 1812), 395

SNOW
- Ada C. (b. 1870), 389, 407
- Alfred G. (b. 1840), 388
- Arthur (b. 1872), 389
- Mary (b. 1871), 389

STEVENS
- John, 380

STEVENSON
- J. F.* (b. 1824), 379

STEWART
- Daniel Freeman (b. 1922), 378
- Elora Jean (b. 1918), 378
- Marjorie "Peg" (b. 1920), 378
- Mary Hortense (b. 1916), 378
- Warren H. (b. 1889), 378

SWEET

Louisa E. (b. 1809), 384
UNKNOWN:, 395
WING
Alma Maria (b. 1849), 390

YEATON
Alice Flora (b. 1872), 398
Charles N. (b. 1840), 397
Edward Lincoln, 398

Frank Percy (b. 1870), 398
John Robert (b. 1873), 398

BIBLIOGRAPHY

Editor Notes:
> All conference journals have a list of appointments each year. Only Journals with page numbers are listed, which have obituaries, transfers to another Conference or Service records are recorded.

+ + + + + + + + + + +

Computer Software used:
- *Microsoft Office Word*, 2003. SP2 (11.8106.8221)
- *Scansoft PDF Professional.* V. 4.2
- *Adobe Photoshop Elements.* V.5.0 (20060914.r.77)
- *Roots Magic.* [Section, First Families only] copyright © 2001-2008, RootsMagic, Inc. V. 3.2.6.

First United Methodist Church Records Books. Archives First United Methodist Church, St. Cloud, Minnesota
- Church Membership Books
- Scrapbooks
- Picture/photos
- 1949 - 2007 Minnesota Methodist Conference Journals

Gove, Gertrude Belle. *A History of the First Methodist Church St. Cloud, Minnesota 1857 – 194.*

Gove, Gertrude Belle. *A Century of Service A History of the First Methodist Church St. Cloud, Minnesota 1857 – 1957.*

Gove, Gertrude Belle. *A History of St. Cloud in the Civil War 1858 - 1865.* Stearns County Historical Society. 1976.
- Seminary. page 38 – 39, 64 which she took from: *St. Cloud Democrat* December 12, 1861, October 31, 1865, Sept 26, 1861, July 31, 1962, April 26, 1860, *Journal,* November 19, 1868, December 10, 1868.

Stearns History Museum Archives, St. Cloud, Minnesota.
- Bob Lommel
- John Decker
- Surname Files
- *North Star Lodge 50th Anniversary Book,* 1907, St. Cloud Chapter, St. Cloud, Minnesota.
- Map 1869 Bird's Eye
- Stearns County Information

St. Cloud Democrat.
- 9 April 1873.
- 4 September 1873.
- January and September, 1864

St. Cloud Times and Daily Journal Press.
   October 5, 1931

St. Cloud Daily Times. St. Cloud, MN
- October 6, 1920.
- 11 Mar 1898, "First Methodist"
- Oct. 22, 1873
- 11 Mar 1898, "First Methodist"
- 21 Jul 1908, "Re-Opening of M. E. Church"
- 16 May 1914 p 1,3,4, "St. Cloud Methodist Episcopal Church"
- 23 May 1914 p 2, "New Methodist Church…"
- 20 May 1914 Obituary
- 28 Nov 1919, Waite Park
- 20 May 1920 Minnesota Annual Conference
- 27 Apr 1929, Sauk Rapids Methodist

St. Cloud Daily Times/Times Media. St. Cloud, MN gave permission to use the following articles. [federal law says need permission to publish any articles within the last 75 years.]
- 31 May 1943, "Mortgage Burning" p 3 Col 2
- 8 Jun 1955 p 4, "Ordination of St. Cloud Man…"
- 29 Mar 1965 p 1, "March in Snow Warms Rally"
- 14 Nov 1969, "1st Methodist Plans Pipe Organ Dedication" p

12 Col 1
- 11 May 1997, Family Page, Dan and Katie Schneider-Bryan, p 5b

St. Paul Pioneer Press, St. Paul, MN gave permission to use the following article.
- 14 Jun 1953, "Three Sons are..." p 13 Col 2.

U.S. Federal Population Census, National Archives, Washington, DC on microfilm on http://www.ancestry.com
- 1860 Census Minnesota Stearns County, NARA Microfilm M653_ 574; Image 288,
- 1870. St. Charles, Winona County, Minnesota, NARA Microfilm Roll M593_719 p 326
- 1900, Hartford, Hartford Connecticut; NARA Microfilm, T623_137 p 11A Enumeration Dist 174 Edward S. Ferry
- 1930, Minnesota, Lester Prairie NARA Microfilm, T626_1105 p 5A Frederick J. Bryan

Nall, Bishop T. Otto. *Minnesota Methodism: Forever Beginning 1969.*

Detroit Conference Methodist Episcopal Church, obit from the 26th journal. Research by Everett Rasmussen, 5 Nov 1982

Dr. Chauncey Hobart. *History of Minnesota Methodism, 1887.* p 31

Pace, Charles Nelson, *Our Fathers Built, A Century of Minnesota Methodism.* Historical Society of the Minnesota Methodist Conference 1956 p 11, 18

Conference Memorials Index. A database index to the memorials which appear in all nationwide conference journals of the United Methodist tradition prior to 1968. Includes: the Methodist Episcopal Church, the Methodist Protestant Church, the Methodist Episcopal Church, South, The Methodist Church, the Church of the United Brethren in Christ, the Evangelical Association, the United Evangelical Church, the Evangelical Church and the Evangelical United Brethren. Created by the General Commission on Archives and History at Drew University, Madison, New Jersey.

Minnesota Methodist Conference Archives,
- Thelma Boeder, 1964 - 2006 archivist.
- Kathy Spencer Johnson, archivist, 2006 to

Minnesota Conference of the Methodist Episcopal Church Journal; 1856 – 1898
- *First Session 1*856, p 6 21 Red Wing
- *1*858 p 21 no stats
- *1*862 no stats
- *1*863, p 16 Sabbath School to Sunday School
- *1*865 p 26 Seminary
- *1*867 p 6 - Local Preacher T. N. Berlin
- *1*872*1*873 p 13 p 8 Wayne Carver transfer Rocky Mt. conference.
- 1875 p 8 Sterrett & Lewton transfer
- *1*876 p 8
- *1*877 p 8 p 6 Riddick transfer
- *1*879 p 7 Harvey Webb transfer no appointment
- *1*881 p 49 Obit I. M. Marsh
- *1*884 p 7 on Conf Roll
- *1*885 ; p12-15 Roll of Members....
- *1*887 p 28 Blaine to N. Nebraska conference.
- *1*888 p 13 -22; Service Records
- *1*890 p 33-38 Roll of members...
- *1*893 p 80-81 Obit William

BIBLIOGRAPHY

William Satterlee; p 19; Service Record

Northern Minnesota Episcopal Church Conference Journal, 1895-1947
- 1900 p 89 obit Noah Lathrop.
- 1901 p Ross transferred to Barbos WI.
- 1905 p3 Obit, David Tice
- 1907 p297 Schei, L. B.
- 1908 p16 Transferred T. Stanley Oadhams
- 1909 p 146 E. H. Nicholson DS
- 1914 p 235/236 Obit, Charles William Lawson p 234-235 Noah Lathrop
- 1915 p 277 W. W. Satterlee Transfer North Dakota Conference
- 1923 p 310 Obit, James Harley Dewart
- 1926 p 233 obit, Charles Wilbur Stark
- 1930 p 235, J. A. Edwards transferred to New England South Conference C. W. Stark transferred to Pacific NW Conference
- 1934 p 220-221, obit, George Edward Tindall
- 1936 p101-102, Obit, Mrs. Mary Logan

Northern Minnesota Church Conference Journal, 1940-1947
- 1944, p 154 -155, "Roll Dead" James H. Dewart, Charles William Lawson
- 947, p 700, obituary Mrs. Fred W. Hill

The Uniting Session of the Minnesota and Northern Minnesota Conferences, 1948,
  1948 p 264-289 Rolls of Members

Official Journal and Year Book Minnesota Annual Conference of the Methodist Church 1949-1968
- 1949 p 166 Obit, Frederick William Hill
- 1962 p 243 Obit, Harland C. Logan

Minnesota Annual Conference of the United Methodist Church, "Official Journal and Year Book 1968 - 2007
- 1977, p 321, 329 Service Record
- 1981, p 252, Obit, Paul Otto Metzger; p 339 Service Record, Manning E. Van Nostrand
- 2002, p 245, Obit, Irving Harrison Palm; p 248, Russell Luther Hubbard; "Roll of the Dead", p 312-330 Service Records
- 2005, p 268, Obit, Allyn Hans Hanson; p 339, 370, Service Records
- 2006, p 264, Obit, Kenneth O Beck; p 370, p 359 Service Records

Minnesota Death Records online at Minnesota Historical Society Web Site

Mitchell, William B; *History of Stearns County*, Vol. 1 & 2,
- p 1102. p 1101-2. p 1107 Vol. 1 p 701, 702 Cole Freeman; p 1078,
- Vol. 2 p 1453 . 525 S 4th Ave, Block 33, Lot 6 Curtis Survey, Parcel Number 82.52028.000

http://www.rootsweb.com, World Connect files. Research 17 Sept 2007, obit, Rev. Samuel Thompson Sterrett.

INDEX

Editor's Note: "First Families" has its own index.

A

Abbott, Dr. Tom 126
Ackerman, Dr. Edgar 91
Aigner, Bob 163
Akers, Millie (Ellis) 38, 41, 45, 56
Akers, Nannie 38
Akers, Rev. J. M. 38
Allen, Donald 113
Allen, Ruth 55
Anderson, Dr. and Mrs. E. M. 87
Anderson, Lynn 205
Anderson, Mary Theresa .. 124
Anderson, Mrs. Roland 78
Anderson, Paul 326
Anderson, Roland 260
Anderson, Winness 281
Andrus, H. H. 59, 63, 68
Andrus, Mrs. H. H. 69
Arendt, Dale 174
Asbury, Bishop 79
Ashley, Agnes 41
Atchison, Rev. Robert R. .. 38, 39, 358
Atkins, Blanche 77, 81
Atwood, Allen A. .. 68, 74, 81, 85
Atwood, C. L. 57
Ayer, Mr. and Mrs. 20

B

Bak, Bronislaw "Bruno" .. 110, 113, 178, 182, 183, 184, 186
Ball, Eliza A 23, 331
Ball, John 19
Barnum, P. T. 206
Barone, Michael 98, 120, 126, 127, 132, 134, 135, 177, 204, 251, 314, 330
Barr, Charles 59
Barr, J. E. 52, 59
Barrett, Darlene 111
Barrett, Dr. Roger 111
Barron, John 157, 206, 238, 270
Barron, Laura 271
Barron, Linda 271
Barron, Lois ...... i, x, 270, 271, 319, 328

Barron, Mary 271
Barron, Paul 271
Bartholow, L. W. 367
Bastien, Herbert 80
Baumhofer, Rev. Earl 74
Beck, Catherine (Billings) . 78, 110, 132, 186, 194, 242, 251, 253, 286, 303, 318, 326, 328, 365
Beck, Martha ... 110, 242, 302, 365
Beck, Peter 110, 242, 289, 365
Beck, Rev. Kenneth Oscar 98, 110, 111, 112, 114, 117, 118, 119, 120, 121, 122, 123, 125, 127, 130, 131, 132, 135, 137, 140, 152, 182, 197, 208, 221, 242, 243, 244, 245, 246, 249, 251, 253, 254, 255, 257, 258, 270, 273, 275, 279, 282, 284, 285, 286, 287, 288, 289, 290, 293, 294, 299, 302, 303, 305, 307, 310, 311, 312, 313, 314, 315, 318, 319, 321, 327, 365
Beck, Sarah 110, 132, 242, 354, 365
Bell, Mabel (Rudell) 362
Bell, Rev. Harry Winstanley 63, 362
Bemis, Cecyl 148, 157
Bennett, James 343
Bennett, Minnie 343
Bennett, Rev. W. D. 371
Bensen, Brian 328
Bensen, Helen .. 135, 238, 242, 298
Bensen, Helen (Cater) .. 69, 84
Bensen, Jack 133, 242, 286
Bensen, Jan 227, 228
Bensen, John 56, 60, 81
Benson, Mick .. 170, 189, 271, 272, 328
Bentley, Jennie 343
Berglund, A. R. 63
Bergquist, N. T. 69, 74
Berlin, Jane 17, 331
Berlin, Julia S. 335
Berlin, Trevanan N. 16, 17, 18, 20, 331, 334

Berlin, Trevanan W. Jr 335
Bethel, Blanche 41
Bethel, Mrs. W. N. 45
Bethel, W. H. 68
Bethel, W. N. 52, 53, 63
Bies-Jaede, Kathy 169
Biggerstaff, Maggie 343
Binney, Mrs. 260
Binnie, Doug 289
Binnie, Ernest J 45, 59
Binnie, James 45, 59
Binnie, Mrs. Ernest J. ... 68, 81
Binnie, Zela (Harland) 45, 310
Black, Lois 368
Blain, Ada E 354
Blain, Charles 354
Blain, Emma E 331
Blain, Mary 331
Blain, Mary (Burriett) 354
Blain, Nellie 354
Blain, Rev. Bartley 21, 353
Blain, Willie E. 354
Block, Mrs. 63
Blood, Emilene F 331
Bluhm, Arthur F. ... 63, 68, 81, 105, 257, 258, 260, 293, 310
Bluhm, Lillian 310
Bordewick, Mark 165
Borsheim, Arnold 284
Borsheim, Ruby 284
Bowdish, Rev. Charles Giles 16, 20, 353
Bowers, L. L. 60
Bowing, Bert 52
Bowing, Mr. J. E. 31
Bowing, Mrs. J. E. (Ellis) .. 31, 38
Bowles, Stephen M. 367
Boy Scout Troop #1 .. 106, 121
Brace, Rev. Charles H. 358
Brace, Rev. H. S. 38
Bridgeman, Dr. George H. 41, 53
Bridges, Bill 272, 273
Bridges, Craig 273, 274
Bridges, Jo Ann 155, 231, 272, 273
Bridges, Risa 272, 273, 274
Bridges, William 115, 119
Briggs, Rev. John Wilson .. 38, 358

419

INDEX

Brink, Allen 126
Brinkman, Jan 229
Broker, Martha 327
Brooks, Rev. David 16, 23
Brooks, Rev. Jabez 24
Brossoit, Maggie......155, 195, 196, 238
Brossoit, Mark .155, 195, 196, 238
Brown, Barbara................ 274
Brown, Chessman Loren . 335
Brown, Elmer Ellsworth .. 335
Brown, John..................... 274
Brown, L. C. 52
Brown, Robert 274
Brown, Virginia............... 274
Brown, W. E. 63, 66
Bryan, Mrs. Frederick J. 81
Bryan, Rev. F. J. 274
Bryan, Rev. Frederick J. ... 58, 62, 72, 77, 81, 366
Bublitz, Carl 222, 275, 276
Bublitz, Diane ...217, 275, 276
Burlingame, Mrs. 64, 66
Burmeister, Margaret......... 64
Burroughts, Bell 354
Burton, Karen 153
Burton, Patrick................. 153
Burton, Rev. Shane Allen 153, 155, 158, 159, 160, 162, 210, 234, 370
Burton, Tucker................. 158

C

Campbell, Harold............... 81
Campbell, J. W.52, 57, 59, 60, 63, 68, 69, 83
Campbell, Rev. E. V. 29, 61
Carlson, Blanche............... 147
Carlson, Glenn .105, 226, 238, 319
Carlson, Rev. Rick....138, 372
Carpenter, Mrs. James 70
Carroll, Mrs. Gladys Hasty 70
Carver, Rev. Wayne.....17, 25, 371
Cassey, Allen E. 20, 335
Cater, Charles W....59, 63, 65, 66, 68, 69, 74, 80, 81, 83, 85
Cater, Donald................... 225
Cater, Doreene E.......224, 225
Caviani, Laura (Van Nostrand) 177, 208, 330
Chamberlin, Daniel.....82, 317
Chan Sakhon................... 130

Cheney, Glenna 173, 236, 320
Christensen, Tasha ... 166, 210
Christie, Ken 205
Chute, Winifred 70
Clampitt, Joan . 139, 205, 206, 228, 303
Clampitt, Richard.... 121, 134, 204, 238, 303
Clark, Addie................ 45, 56
Clark, Alma 367
Clark, George W. 59
Clark, Heather.................. 276
Clark, Jill 276
Clark, Jonathan 276
Clark, Luellen 17, 332
Clark, Rev. Thurman B..... 62, 367
Clark, Sharyn 276, 277
Clark, William 105
Cleveland, M. J..... 52, 59, 63, 65, 68
Cleveland, Mrs. M. J... 56, 65, 68, 69, 83
Clokey, Constance 70
Coatsworth, Mrs. J. W. 364
Colaw, Bishop Emerson .. 138
Cole, Ruth 78
Colgan, Kim..................... 205
Colgan, Teresa 205
Collignon, Mayor Phil 69
Collman, Katherine (Kennedy) 254
Collman, Rev. Richard F. 119, 120, 121, 122, 123, 204, 209, 254, 303, 369
Cook, Deanie 231
Cook, Dr. E. A. 53
Cook, Marge 231
Cooney, Rev. E. B............. 74
Cooper, Agnes 57
Cooper, Arthur C. . 52, 53, 56, 57, 59
Cooper, Eliza Anne.......... 333
Cooper, John 34, 41
Cooper, Martha A 335
Cooper, Mary J. (Marlatt).. 38
Cooper, Mrs. A. C............. 59
Coors, Bishop D. Stanley. 91
Copp, Rev. 29
Corliss, Dick ... 117, 126, 139, 141
Corliss, Mary .. 117, 130, 141, 231
Coughtry, Erma................ 227
Crawford, Julia 17, 332
Creighton, George K........ 355

Creighton, Maggie 355
Creighton, Rev. John R..... 25, 355
Crosby, Amos 81, 82
Crosby, George R. 41, 344, 359

D

Daggett, Clair....... 78, 81, 135
Daggett, Doris.................. 135
Dallmann, Otto G. 91, 92, 178, 180, 189
Dam, F. H. 52
Daniels, H. A. 39, 52
Daniels, Julie (Echols) 164, 279, 280
Danneman, Deb 301
Danneman, Krista 301
Danneman, Scott.............. 166
Danzl, Cathy 290
Davis, Jan......................... 277
Davis, Jim 236, 277, 278, 330
Davis, May........................ 41
Davis, Todd..................... 277
Day, Annette 256
Day, Elizabeth................. 256
Day, Rev. Donald.... 110, 113, 255, 274, 369
Day, Virginia .. 248, 255, 274, 369
Dean, Deborah 127
Dean, Don 257
Dean, Priscilla 231, 273
Dean, Susan 223
Decker, John ix
DeCourcy, Genevieve Pack 315
DeCourcy, Rev. Frank 315, 328
DeHaan, Bob.................... 227
Dewart, Rev. Dr. James H. 28, 39, 40, 41, 359
Diekmann, Father Godfrey 244
Dingman, H. E. 68
Dobson, James Martin . 68, 92
Dobson, Mrs. J. M. 69, 81, 83, 85
Dobson, Mrs. James........... 80
Dobson, Mrs. Joseph R. 72
Dobson, Mrs. Norma M. ... 68, 69
Drews, Edward A. 81, 205
Drews, Mary J.................... 85
Drews, May J. 205, 209
Drews, Mrs. E. A. 75, 81

INDEX

Dryfas, Mr. 60
Dunlop, Julie 136
Dunlop, Ken 136
Durkee, Chris 249
Durkee, Rachel 249
Durkee, Rev. Dr. Phillip..128, 249
Durkee, Rev. Evelyn128, 129, 131, 139, 140, 142, 148, 150, 152, 238, 249, 306, 370
Dyck, Bishop Sally.. 175, 176, 220, 330, 349

E

Eakin, Ruth Skewes 226
Eastman, Kermit 296
Echols, Charles 177, 204, 278, 279, 280, 330
Echols, Shirley 102, 139, 140, 151, 205, 238, 278, 279, 319
Eckberg, Carlton 91, 110, 125, 245, 246, 286
Eckberg, Jean (Megarry) .226, 245, 297
Eckberg, John 238
Edeburn, AnnElise ... 174, 235
Edelbrock, Anna 343
Edelbrock, John 343
Edelheit, Dr. Joseph 172
Edwards, Rev. J. Arthur 37, 65, 67, 363
Ekiman, Mary C 332
Ellens, Bruce 281
Ellens, Dave 171, 280
Ellens, Diane (DeeDee)....281
Ellens, Joan 171, 280, 281
Ellens, Melissa 281
Ellens, Michael 281
Ellis, Beatrice 81
Ellis, Mary A. 56, 57, 59
Ellis, Mechtild (Tilde) 197, 245, 246, 254
Ellis, Mollie 33, 38, 41
Embury, Philip 79
Emery, Charles 110
Emery, Mrs. Charles 81
Emery, Ursula 231, 292
Erickson, L. L.. 52, 53, 55, 56, 366
Evans, Paul 65
Ezell, Sue 205, 301
Ezell, Wayland 139, 301

F

Farnham, Dr. J. M. ..52, 59, 68
Farnham, Mrs. J. M. 69
Farwell, George 343
Fasholt, Bessie. 55, 57, 61, 63, 66, 361
Fasholt, Maud 57
Fasholt, Mrs. Wm 45
Fasholt, William 52
Ferrario, JoAnn 289
Ferry, Rev. Edward S. 37, 358
Fliegel, Faith 373
Fliegel, Rev. Wolfram 373
Fossett, John 17
Frank, Mary 357
Frank, Rev. Henry 37, 357
Frechette, Alice 227
Fredrickson, Lois..... 226, 231, 281, 282
Fredrickson, Ray 281, 282
Fredrickson, Richard 282
Fredrickson, Susan 282
Freeman Family 21
Freeman, Ambrose 16, 17, 18, 19, 20, 34, 37, 331, 332, 333, 354
Freeman, Clara H. (Hayward) 18, 23
Freeman, Daniel H.18, 25, 34, 41, 343
Freeman, Elizabeth F 334
Freeman, Hortense (Hayward) 34
Freeman, Jane Cole 332
Freeman, Jane Cole (Gray) 17, 18, 23, 34
Freeman, Laura 343
Freeman, Lavisa 25
Freeman, Louisa 343
Freeman, Maria 17, 332
Freeman, Thomas 17
Freeman, Thos 332
Freeman, Virginia S. 335
Friedrich, Mrs. Geo 76
Fueman, Elizabeth F 332
Fueman, Virginia S 332
Fulton, Bob 330

G

Gager, Mary. E 332
Galovich, Jennifer 330
Galuzzo, Greg 158
Garlington, Ann 17, 332
Garlington, Conway 18

Garlington, Edwin A. ..18, 41, 332, 335
Garlington, Margaret ...17, 18, 332
Garlington, Mary 17, 332
Garlington, Mrs. Colin. 16
Garlington, Mrs. Conway ...18
Garrett, Jack 365
Garven, Carolyn 167, 282, 283, 299, 303, 304, 326
Garven, Cindy 283
Garven, James (Jim) 124, 125, 135, 147, 152, 155, 159, 160, 208, 238, 249, 251, 279, 282, 283, 286, 299, 303, 306, 313
Garven, Stephanie 283
Gauerke, Paul 227
Gaylord, ___ 39
Geer, Rev. James 55
Gilbert, Mrs. Loren 364
Gilleland, Mrs. S. M. 56
Gilman, Nellie 343
Gilman, Same 343
Glaser, M. L. 41
Gleason, Cora 353
Gleason, Martha 353
Gleason, Rev. Levi 16, 20, 352, 353
Goodrich, Flo 151
Gosswiller, Elsie 72, 81
Gott, Mabel 363
Gough, H. B. 259
Gough, Harry B. 68, 73, 74, 81, 84, 85, 326
Gove, Charles Wallace 325
Gove, George Wallace 325
Gove, Gertrude B.i, ix, 15, 64, 79, 81, 84, 86, 98, 117, 133, 189, 245, 325, 326, 330, 340
Gove, Marcia Helen (Bartholomew) 325
Gove, Russell Dewey 325
Graham, David 136
Graham, Dr. Charles 326
Graner, Ardell 147, 149
Graner, Gordon 147, 149, 163, 238
Graner, Ardell 238
Grannis, Armenia Jane 224
Grannis, Edith 81, 224
Grannis, Samuel Higbee ...224
Gratz, Rev. W. E. J. 61
Gray Family 21
Gray, Blanche 38

421

INDEX

Gray, Janet .... i, x, 284
Gray, Laura (Marlatt) ..18, 23, 31, 32, 36, 38, 46
Gray, Rev. David 284
Gray, Thomas 343
Gray, Thomas J. 27, 34
Green, Frank 343
Green, Leander 343
Greenstreet, Aural 228, 272
Griswold, Alice B. 355
Griswold, Charles H. 355
Griswold, Frank H. 355
Griswold, June 355
Griswold, Rev. Charles 25, 352, 355
Gross, Jerome 80
Gundersen, Lee 285
Gundersen, Mark 285
Gundersen, Nancy ... i, x, 102, 250, 270, 285, 317
Gundersen, Ralph 285, 286
Gustafson, Eric 190
Gustafson, T. A. 74, 81, 83

H

Haak, Jill ...170, 193, 194, 236
Haeg, Richard ..133, 136, 178, 181, 184, 185, 186, 246
Hafferman, O. M. 81
Hager, Rev. Larry A. 132, 134, 251, 369
Halberg, Dee 245, 286, 287, 311, 312, 314
Halberg, Irene 78
Halberg, Laurie 129, 186, 187, 193, 245, 246, 286, 311, 314
Halberg, Scott 309
Halenbeck, Dr. 182
Halenbeck, Grace (Weiss) 182
Hall, Charles 63, 64
Hall, Evelyn 66
Hall, Larry 274
Hall, Myron 321
Hamilton, Mrs. W. S. 41
Hammond, Blair 70
Hammond, Della 259, 310
Hammond, Ed. D. ...41, 52, 59, 63, 68
Hammond, Jean 70
Hammond, Mrs. E. D. ...45, 68, 69, 81, 83
Hammond, Shirley 70
Hannahs, Harvey 318
Hanscome, Frank 27, 343
Hanson, Dora 135

Hanson, Earl 135
Hanson, Enid Shorts 368
Hanson, Mrs. H. E. 59
Hanson, Rev. Allyn Hans . 68, 69, 368
Hansen, Ted 144
Harland, E. D. 41
Harland, Ed. 52
Harland, Mr. 45
Harland, Mrs. Ed. 45
Harper, Jessie ...... x, 102, 228, 231, 270, 271, 306
Harper, Jim 271, 272
Harper, John 308
Harper, Steve 271, 289
Hartman, Anton 68
Hauer, Mary M. 354
Hauser, Dr. and Mrs. 62
Haverland, Fred 123, 207, 242, 245, 253
Haverland, Rev. Mark 137
Haverland, Ruth 207, 231, 245, 298
Hayes, Mr. A. C. 70
Hayward Family 21
Hayward, "Lou" 343
Hayward, J. E. 34
Hayward, Joe 342
Hayward, John ... 27, 342, 343
Hayward, Josiah 23
Hayward, Mrs. J. E. 31
Hayward, Mrs. Melinda (Gray) 31, 34
Hebei, Elizabeth 69, 78
Heck, Barbara 79
Hedgren, Michelle 205
Heiser, Rod 144
Helgeson, Arlene (Mittlestadt) 129, 132, 287, 289, 294, 297
Helgeson, Don 147, 227, 287, 289
Helgeson, Glen 288
Helgeson, Karel 170, 193, 197, 228, 289, 290, 296, 328
Helgeson, Mike 135, 288, 289, 290
Helgeson, Scott 288
Helgeson, Stefan (Steve) . 166, 254, 288
Hendershot, Jim 148, 191, 238, 296
Henningsgaard, Charlotte 131, 231
Hill, Clinton F. 81, 135, 318

Hill, Eugene 343
Hill, Margaret 135
Hill, Miss M. L. 41
Hill, Mrs. Frederick William 56
Hill, Rev. Frederick William 51, 56, 57, 61, 360
Hill, Winona (Mues) 361
Hilton, Lucelia 356
Hilton, Rev. Horatio Southard 31, 32, 356
Hines, Ardis 231
Hines, Phillip 205
Hingeley, Dr. Joseph B. ... 362
Hobart, Dr. Chauncey ... ix, 16
Hoerber, Fred 181
Hoerber, Nan 181
Hoffman 190
Hoffman, Earl 81
Holes Brothers 52
Holscher, Bob 215, 276
Holscher, Julia 155, 330
Holzer, Shirley . 139, 142, 305
Hooper, Elisa Ann 23, 332
Hooper, William ... 16, 17, 19, 332
Hoover, Irving B. 59
Hopkins, Harold 285
Hopkins, Pauline 117
Horst, Elizabeth 133
Horst, Locky ... 133, 134, 141, 149, 151, 238, 240, 241, 285, 365
Horst, Mark 365
Horst, Martha 240
Horst, Rev. Mark 240, 269, 300
Horst, Rev. W. Thoburn (Toby) 133, 134, 135, 137, 138, 139, 140, 141, 142, 144, 145, 146, 147, 148, 150, 151, 152, 187, 188, 191, 196, 197, 238, 249, 273, 279, 280, 283, 285, 286, 299, 300, 307, 319, 365
Horst, Sara 240, 365
Horst, Scot 240, 365
Houg, Sharon 170
Hoyt, Mr. 59
Htke, Mr. 33
Hubbard, George C. 41
Hubbard, Kevin 291
Hubbard, Mert. 129, 227, 290, 291, 292
Hubbard, Nancy 290

INDEX

Hubbard, Neil 291
Hubbard, Rev. Russell Luther 89, 92, 94, 102, 182, 364
Hubbard, Todd 291
Huffman, Rev. Dr. Russell Arthur ... 88, 255, 264, 268, 328, 364, 372
Huffman, Rev. Russell Allen 15, 84, 87, 89, 91, 102, 111, 137, 206, 255, 259, 260, 264, 288, 315, 364
Huffman, Susan (Pederson) 84, 364
Huffman, Winifred Terry . 265
Hulbert, Marshall 80
Hulbert, Mrs. Marshall 364
Huls, Mrs. Helen Steen 70
Huser, Bea 231
Huser, Norm 150
Hussey, Allen E 23
Hussey, Arthur 52, 343
Hutchens, Beulah Rose . x, 87, 144, 167, 176, 189, 292, 326, 328, 345
Hutchens, Marlin 293
Hutchens, Marlowe 293
Hutchens, Marvin 292
Hutchens, Rev. Marva Jean 106, 138, 257, 292, 293, 372
Hutchens, Warren 189, 292, 321

I

Inveiss, Liz 157, 161, 211
Isely, John 41

J

Jaede, Mark 216
Jains, [Jasins?] David 332
James, B. B. 41
Jenkins, Dr. J. P. 62
Jensen, Boysen 80
Jensen, Larry 80
Jensen, Patricia . 299, 302, 303
Jensen, Theodore 68
Jenson, John 53
John, Carl 293
John, Dr. Byron 157, 177, 194, 293, 294, 303, 328, 329
John, Elizabeth 293
John, Joanne R. 121, 122, 155, 293, 294, 303, 306
John, Keith 293
Johnson, Anna 311

Johnson, Arthur L. W. 68
Johnson, Betty 238
Johnson, Bonnie x
Johnson, Cliff 238
Johnson, Irene 70
Johnson, Kathy Spencer .. 350, 357
Johnson, Leah C. 74, 80
Johnson, Merrill 74, 205
Johnson, Milford 326
Johnson, Miss 81
Johnson, Mrs. Merrill 205
Johnson, Rev. Randy L. ... 165, 216, 370
Johnson, Scott 226
Jones, B. M. 61
Jones, Carol 230
Jones, Charles 343
Jones, Dr. R. N. 68, 81, 83, 85
Jones, Ellen 70
Jones, Emma 343
Jones, John 332
Jones, Katherine (Mrs. R. N.) 15, 81
Jordan, Rev. Dr. W. H. 55, 56, 61, 62
Joslin, Flora 41
Joyce, Bishop Isaac 42

K

Kagawa, Dr. 86, 89
Kasling, Tess ... 134, 169, 177, 187, 204, 205, 236, 305, 330
Keech, Dolores 154, 231, 337, 373
Keech, Rev. Dudley A. 337, 373
Kelly, Doris 162, 227
Kelly, Sarah 343
Kendall, Dean 295
Kendall, Janelle . 98, 160, 166, 210, 295
Kendall, John 98, 160, 166, 210, 295
Kendall, LuBell 150, 294, 295, 373
Kendall, Rev. Dr. Robert D. 125, 127, 140, 150, 294, 295, 330, 373
Kennedy, Katherine 123
Kent, Arthur 368
Kidd, Elizabeth 333
Kidd, Kudgson 333
Kidd, Martha 332
Kimball, Emma 343

King, Adelia B. 333
King, Amasa D. 333
King, Dr. Martin Luther ... 109
King, Eli B. 16, 19, 333
King, Harriet 333
King, Rev. Dr. Martin Luther Jr 266
Kingsley, Bishop 24
Kinzer, Joanne 374
Kinzer, Rev. Donald A 374
Kirt, Karen 142, 144
Klein, Barb 289
Kleinschmidt, Karen 227
Klepper, Rev. John Wesley 32, 356
Kline, Margaret 141
Knudson, Charlotte 78
Knutson, Katherine 296
Knutson, Martha (Imani) .. 296
Knutson, Russell 296
Knutson, Ruth (Carlson) .. 150, 155, 295, 296, 302, 311
Koch, Rev. L. S. 62, 367
Koep, A. L. 68
Kohlstead, Dr. E. D. 60
Kotch, Eliza 17, 332
Kotch, John 17, 332
Kothman, Marie 55
Kotz, Barbara 335
Krichbaum, Cheryl (Towler) .... x, 316
Krueger, David 155
Krueger, Patricia 155, 238
Kugler, Bob 319
Kummer, Kristin 277

L

Lafler, Larry 226
Lamb, Will 343
Lancaster, Charles 343
Land, Sue 205, 311
Larsen, Christopher . 170, 205, 305
Lathrop, Rev. Noah 25, 355
Lawson, Harriet (Pullen) .. 359
Lawson, Rev. Charles William 44, 359
Leah, Miss 81
Lease, Charles 52
Lee, Helen Morris 361
Lee, Rev. John 361
Lee, Rev. William Chappell 57, 58, 60, 63, 69, 361
Lee, William Morris 361
Leeseberg, Anna Mary 231
Lehman, Yolanda 173

423

INDEX

Leigh, James J. 15
Leisen, Father 327
Lemon, J. T. 29
Lenger, Jim 141
Leopard, Bertha Binnie 45
Leopard, Brant 45
Leopard, Howard 45
Leopard, Mr. 45
Leopard, Mrs. 45
Leopard, W. H. 53
Lewis, Alice 71, 363
Lewis, Rev. Richard ("Revy Eddy") .107, 110, 111, 112, 242, 243, 289, 304, 312, 313, 369
Lewton, Annette 356
Lewton, Edmund 356
Lewton, James E. 356
Lewton, May A. 356
Lewton, Rev. James T. 29, 31, 356
Lewton, Theodore E. 356
Lichtenberger, Francis 59
Lillestrand, Lloyd 74, 85, 326
Lillestrand, Mabel (Mrs. Lloyd) 15
Lillestrand, N. L. 81
Lillico, Rev. J. W. 74
Lilliquist, Mr. 52
Lindquist, Julie 204
Lindsay, Mrs. 56
Logan, Alice (Lewis) ... 71, 76, 78
Logan, Gordon 364
Logan, Mabel 71
Logan, Mrs. Harland Chester 79
Logan, Rev. Dr. Harland Chester ..70, 71, 72, 73, 78, 79, 80, 83, 85, 91, 259, 274, 288, 297, 310, 363
Logan, Ruth 71, 79, 80
Lommell, Bob ix
Lorenz, Don 195
Lorenz, Evelyn 193, 194, 195, 236
Lorette, Willard (Bill) 326
Lovelace, Jean 328
Lowry, Rev David 24
Lund, Florence .. 103, 106, 107
Lund, Mrs. P. S. 70
Lund, P. S. 74
Lund, Paul 68
Lunemann, Augusta 63, 74, 75, 77, 81, 260

Lunemann, J. Miller 259
Lunemann, James Miller ... 81, 84
Lunemann, Myrtle 260
Lunemann, Rev. Duane J. 88, 137, 255, 258, 259, 372
Lynch, Mary 343

M

Madeson, Robert 113
Madsen, Jean 227
Magee, Bishop J. Ralph 69
Magnuson, Binnie 45
Magnuson, Ed. 63
Magnuson, J. Ed. 59
Malmborg, Rev. A. F. 69
Mann, A. Z. 62
Mann, Mary A 17, 333
Mann, Thomas 17
Mann, Thos 333
Myers, Marie 245
Marlatt Family 21
Marlatt, Dr. Silas ... 16, 17, 18, 30, 33, 333
Marlatt, Mrs. L. A. 41
Madsen, Russell 226
Marsh, Rev. Issac M. .. 33, 35, 36, 357
Marsh, Sarah J. (Rogers) .. 357
Marshall, Jessie 79
Martin, Mamie 78, 224
Martin, Rev. Wiltsie Mayes 37, 351, 358
Masters, Dave 326
Mathison, Rev. Richard .. 284, 285
Matteson, J. A. 59
Matthias, Howard 129, 135
Matthias, Lorraine 205
Mattock, Rev. Raymond F. 62, 63, 367
Mattseon, John 57
Mattson, Mayor 61
May, Annie 180
Mayo, Mrs. Mary E. 69
Mayo, Rev. Harold E. .. 67, 68, 69, 70, 363
Mc Intire, W. B. 27
McAfee, Mary A. 362
McCalib, Paul 120
McCall, Virginia (Mrs. H. K.) 15
McCutchan, Jean 70
McCutchan, Juanita 292
McCutchan, Julian F. ... 63, 64, 68, 69, 70, 75, 81

McCutchan, Mrs. Julian F. .. 81
McIntyre, Minnie 343
McIntyre, Mollie 343
McIntyre, W. B. 343
McKelvy, Margaret (Garlington) 31, 46
McNiff, Margaret/Susan .. 357
McNiff, Rev. Michael O. ... 36, 357
Mecklenburg, Rev. Dr. George 61
Medin, Polly 231
Megarry, Bill 260
Megarry, Brent Hugh 297
Megarry, Dirk Richard 297
Megarry, Mary 260, 273
Megarry, Mary Beth 162, 221, 224, 227, 257, 297
Megarry, Mrs. Charles 81
Megarry, Mrs. William 81, 85
Megarry, Richard (Dick) . 176, 227, 257, 297, 328
Megarry, Ross Charles 297
Meier, Aaron William 366
Meier, Linda (Schoenrogge) 177, 366
Meier, Rev. William F. (Bill) .... iv, v, 98, 177, 300, 307, 337, 352, 366
Meier, Sarah Elizabeth 366
Merkle, Dr. John 172
Metzer, Will 343
Metzger, Barby 102, 364
Metzger, Cindy 102
Metzger, Paul 98
Metzger, Phyllis (Rhoda) 102, 364
Metzger, Rev. Paul Otto.... 15, 94, 102, 103, 104, 105, 106, 107, 109, 257, 274, 281, 306, 364
Metzger, Steve 102, 364
Meyers, Hillis 81, 109
Michalski, Fern 165, 231, 283, 298, 311
Michalski, Tony 238, 298
Mick, Steven ... 177, 205, 247, 305, 330
Miller, Mrs. Bert 38
Miller, Wally 124, 126
Mitchell, Bishop Charles Bayard 60, 61, 62
Mitchell, H. Z. 18
Mitchell, Margaret 70
Mitchell, Mary 333
Mitchell, William Bell ix

INDEX

Moonier, Denis.................81
Moonier, Mrs. Denis..........81
Moore, Prof. Ira................342
Morey, Mike....................161
Morgan, Arthur E. 57
Morris, Helen Leonia 361
Morris, Mrs. 56
Morris, Mrs. William 55
Morris, Rev. S. H. 340
Morris, Robert 161
Morris, William.....59, 63, 64, 68, 69, 72
Morrison, Elizabeth..........333
Morrison, Mrs. Vernon ..75, 82
Morrison, Vernon...81, 83, 85
Moses, Joyce 328
Mower, J. W....................366
Murphy, W. J. 52
Murray, Shirley Erena 176
Musser, Howard 61
Myers, Hillis......15, 113, 245, 286, 318

N

Nall, Bishop T. Otto............ix
Nash, Leona 205, 206, 207, 257
Nayenga, Dr. Peter 299
Nayenga, Monica 299
Nayenga, Mudima 300
Nayenga, Vivienne...........300
Nelson, Clarence 65
Nelson, D. Adelia.............333
Nelson, Mary....................353
Nelson, Mrs. Andrew J.......23
Nelson, Rev. Andrew J......19, 20, 21, 23, 25, 340, 353
Nelson, Rev. Loren ..152, 153
Newton, Mrs. J. J...............56
Nicholson, Rev. E. H....51, 53
Nielsen, Carl.....................144
Nielsen, Dave 289
Nielsen, Jim......................205
Norris, J. Ella 333
Norris, Mrs. W. K. 75
Norris, Rev. Samuel N.17, 21, 23, 25, 333
Noyes, Julia 343
Noyes, Mary.....................343

O

O'Connell, Joseph ...144, 178, 187, 189, 238, 246, 286
O'Keefe, Police Chief Dennis......................219

Oadams, Florence.............360
Oadams, Hazel 360
Oadams, Josie..................360
Oadams, Mrs. 45
Oadams, Rev. Thomas Stanley............45, 55, 360
Oatman, Theresa................69
Ohs, Lloyd........................82
Ohs, Mrs. Lloyd....74, 79, 81
Oleson, Carol...134, 137, 148, 300, 301, 313
Oleson, Chauncey.....300, 301
Oleson, Christopher..........300
Oleson, Craig...................300
Oleson, Eric.....................300
Oleson, Jennifer................300
Oleson, Joni.....................300
Oleson, Robb...................300
Oliver, Rev. A. J.........56, 366
Olson, Deanie 231
Olson, Heidi 147
Olson, Jennifer 205
Olson, Leanne..................227
Olson, Marjorie Clark,......367
Olson, Mike.....................205
Olson, Sharon 306
Opitz, Adella 227
Opitz, E. G..................81, 85
Orr, Dr. E. H.....................68
Orth, Wanda 113
Orton, A............................37
Orton, Charles 63
Orton, Irwin J....................57
Owen, George..................335
Owen, Julia...........17, 23, 333
Owen, Mrs. Charles............16

P

Pace, Rev. Charles Nelson ..ix
Palm, Rev. Irving Harrison 89, 284, 368
Paradise, Victor 180
Park, Thomas...................129
Parson, Cora 343
Partch, Betty 117, 119, 127, 129, 205, 208, 231, 302, 314
Partch, Max 312
Patridge, Liz 231
Patridge, Mark..................289
Paulson, Jewell................320
Payne, Mrs. Frank 82
Pearson, Bonive................15
Peck, John 120, 121, 286, 326
Peck, Linda......................120
Pederson, Dr. P. O..............68

Perconti, Bill.....141, 142, 280
Peterson, Carl 135, 318
Peterson, Dale...299, 302, 303
Peterson, Debbie..............309
Peterson, Jeffrey 303
Peterson, Jim 303, 309
Peterson, Mary Francis.....310
Peterson, Minnie.......135, 231
Peterson, Rev. William E. .60, 62, 367
Peterson, Toni..................303
Peterson, Traci.................303
Petraborg, Pat (Megarry)..297
Phillips, Ellen 127
Phip, Mr...........................352
Pierpoint, Mary..................17
Pierpont, Mary J 333
Pilger, Clarence L....74, 81, 85
Pilger, Mrs. Clarence L. 81
Pope John XXIII...............244
Porter, Mrs........................57
Porter, Mrs. J. A. 54
Poulter, D. D.....................68
Pramann, J. W. 63
Pramann, John E....59, 68, 74, 81
Pramann, Mrs. John E. 81
Pugh, Rev. John..........16, 352
Purdom, Dixie 296

Q

Quayle, Bishop 54
Quickstad, Nathaniel 55
Quinn, Charles.59, 60, 63, 64, 66, 69, 77, 79, 81, 261
Quinn, Evelyn..................149

R

Rasmussen, Everett......ix, 135, 137, 238
Rau, Fred 318
Rau, Hazel 311
Rawhouser, Ruth 142
Ray, Rev. Lyman W...41, 359
Reid, Carol...........x, 270, 304
Reid, Michael 304
Reid, Rebecca..................304
Reid, Sherwood (Woody) 120, 304, 305
Reily, Mary A..................333
Reinke, Rev. E. C. 62
Remmel, Margaret......20, 333, 334
Repinski, Rev. Marvin.....118, 253, 254, 369

INDEX

Retherford, Mabel............ 205
Retherford, Randy 205
Richardson, Anne E (Denny)
.... 363
Richardson, Athea (Roberts)
.... 363
Richardson, James 363
Richardson, Philip 363
Richardson, R. B............. 363
Richardson, Rev. Andrus
Laverne 63, 69, 363
Richardson, William........ 363
Riddick, Rev. Isaac H..32, 33, 34, 357
Riggin, Rev. F. A............... 28
Rigum, F. A 356
Robinson, Deborah..141, 146, 249
Rogers, John 342
Rogers, Rev. J. M. 357
Rogosheske, Abby........... 305
Rogosheske, Allie............ 305
Rogosheske, Phil 171, 305, 306, 308
Rogosheske, Val..x, 143, 163, 170, 171, 217, 270, 305, 306, 308
Rorer, John 60
Ross, Rev. Dr. Frederick E. .41, 42, 43, 44, 59, 60, 359

S

Sacher, Dorothy 88
Sales, Donna............306, 307
Sales, Jerry........306, 307, 328
Salisbury, Amanda....307, 308
Salisbury, Brian 307, 308
Salisbury, Kim..........307, 308
Salisbury, Tony........307, 308
Sanborn, Jack 80
Satterlee, Carrie Almeda.. 355
Satterlee, Elmvira 355
Satterlee, Marion Pease 26, 342, 355
Satterlee, Phoebe Adair ... 355
Satterlee, Rev. William
Wilson.....26, 27, 342, 355
Satterlee, Sarah (Stout) 355
Satterlee, William Eugene 355
Scheel, John 103, 119, 124
Schei, L. B. 44
Schelske, Al..................... 242
Schelske, Alvin................ 111
Schelske, Phyllis......111, 128, 137
Scherfenberg, Wallace 82

Scheel, John 242
Schey, Constance Clark ... 367
Schneider, Rev. James 137
Schneider-Bryan, Anna... 152, 235, 366
Schneider-Bryan, Greg ... 152, 235, 366
Schneider-Bryan, Rev. Daniel G. ..98, 151, 163, 164, 168, 171, 174, 176, 177, 235, 247, 276, 328, 365, 370
Schneider-Bryan, Rev. Katie 98, 151, 152, 155, 156, 158, 160, 163, 164, 167, 170, 171, 176, 177, 192, 216, 227, 234, 236, 247, 271, 277, 290, 291, 300, 312, 349, 365, 370
Schoenheider, Rev. Nor ... 243
Scholz, David... 163, 205, 247
Schwartz, Joy.. 134, 135, 136, 141
Schwieger, Arthur.... 309, 310
Schwieger, Brad170, 309, 310
Schwieger, Ellen Deane.. 134, 136, 205, 231, 301, 309, 310, 330
Schwieger, Sterling.......... 309
Scott, Rev. John 24
Scruby, Dr......................... 37
Scruby, Dr. and Mrs.......... 38
Seamans, Dottie 162, 227
Seberger, Mayor P. J.......... 53
Seeley, Kay..................... 118
Seibert, Mrs. E. A. 82
Selke, George.................... 69
Service, E. B. 62, 367
Seutter, Nancy.. 161, 204, 205
Sevcik, Drew 210, 330
Shaefer, John 41
Shaefer, Mrs...................... 46
Shannon, Rev. William...... 61
Shattuck, Rev. Malcolm E. 94, 103, 368
Sheffield, Karen............... 309
Shei, Lawrence B............. 360
Shepard., Sue 289
Sherk, Raymond 68
Siddens, Virgil E.......... 85, 91
Silianoff, Milcho 92, 182
Skewes, George 78, 81, 85, 226, 255
Skewes, Richard 120, 281
Skewes, Ruth ... 94, 103, 106, 108, 111, 114, 119, 120,

125, 128, 134, 137, 226, 251, 255, 298
Skalbeck, Cheryl............. 147
Slack, Natalie... 124, 205, 209
Slack, Sam 209
Slobetz, Mrs. Wilma 103
Smart, G. S....................... 57
Smart, H. G. 45, 52, 54, 59
Smart, Harry..................... 63
Smart, Mrs. H. G............... 59
Smith, A. L 68
Smith, Charlotte 354
Smith, Howard 217
Smith, Rev. Roy L. 62
Smith, W. E....................... 81
Snyder, Gordon................ 217
So Yang 130
Soder, Gertrude.................. 69
Soltman, Dr. John Henry ... 85
Sorenson, Ralph 112, 207
Sovereign, Mrs. Robert...... 81
Spater, Samuel 16
Spaulding, Alonzo 333
Spenser Johnson, Kathy...... ix
Sprague, Prof. D. W......... 343
Sprague, Rolla........ 59, 63, 69
Stai, Anna Holmberg 55
Stai, Anne 81
Stai, Mrs. Kurt 15, 64, 69, 70, 79, 83
Stai, Robert 80
Staples, Mrs. L. D. 69
Stark, Carrie E. (Goodell) 360
Stark, Charles..... 82, 135, 207
Stark, Mary 135
Stark, Rev. Charles Wilbur 44, 55, 360
Starkey, Mrs. Joseph B. 37
Starkey, Rev. Joseph B. 36, 357
Steckling, Henry P. 52
Stenger, John................... 205
Stennes, Ernest......... 108, 302
Stennes, Florence 108, 302
Sterrett, Augustus............. 354
Sterrett, Eddie C. 354
Sterrett, Emma 354
Sterrett, Rev. Samuel
Thomas/Thompson. 16, 23, 334, 354
Sterrett, Samuel O. 354
Sterrett, Sarah Bell........... 354
Stevenson, Adelide (Dunn)
.... 225
Stevenson, Emma (Ellis).... 31

INDEX

Stevenson, James F. 28, 31, 41, 56, 57
Stevenson, Lavisa Freeman 25
Stevenson, Lovica Ellis [Mrs. J. M.] 56
Stevenson, Robert F. 225
Steward, Darius 55
Steward, Dorothy 55
Stigaard, Nancy 205, 206
Stiles, Mr. 39
Stiles, Mrs. _____ (Daniels) 39
Strand, Rudy....................260
Stueve, Dorothy (Bluhm) 102, 105, 128, 133, 157, 231, 271, 296, 310, 314, 320, 330
Stueve, Ernest..................311
Stueve, Jodi Ann 311
Stueve, Kris 311
Stueve, Penny 311
Suffield, Rev. Walter........138
Summers, Lisa 139, 311
Summers, Marcia 163, 217, 226, 227, 228, 306, 311
Sundby, Julie 313
Sundby, Kristin 313
Sundby, Larry..................312
Sundby, Ruth....141, 312, 313
Sutton, Mattie..................343
Sutton, Nettie 343
Swanson, Russell..............123
Swanson, Svea 69, 81
Swisshelm, Jane Grey ..ix, 20, 21, 324, 331, 340, 341
Sykora, Merle..193, 194, 195, 245, 246

T

Talbert, Dr.......................343
Talbert, G. E. 59
Talbot, J. E. 68
Talbot, John E. 69, 77, 81, 83, 85
Talcott, Francis..................26
Tanabe, Haru 368
Tanabe, Rev. Shigeo 88, 284, 368
Taylor, D. M......................69
Taylor, D. N. 41
Taylor, Rev. A. W..............39
Tennison, Dana 314
Tennison, Dr. Phil 149
Tennison, Jo 126, 208, 313
Tennison, Juli 314

Thompson, Earle ...15, 69, 81, 82, 84, 89, 328
Thompson, Ellen (Kasson/Kassen) 23, 334
Thompson, John L. 17, 334
Thompson, Shirley..............88
Tice, Melissa (Howell).....354
Tice, Rev. David..24, 25, 334, 354
Tice, Wesley R. H. 354
Tifft, Judge M. C. 59
Tillich, Dr. Paul................144
Tilmon, Frank...................343
Tilmon, Henry 343
Timmers, Rosemary 327
Tindale, George B. 362
Tindall, Frank M. 362
Tindall, J. Merritt 362
Tindall, Mae 362
Tindall, Matthew E...........362
Tindall, Pauline 362
Tindall, Rev. George E......58, 60, 61, 62, 67, 362, 367
Tix, Leslie 205
Tompkins, Paula........171, 330
Tonnell, Harland...............315
Tonnell, Mary...................315
Tonnell, Pat 231, 283, 314
Tonnell, Roberta...............315
Tonnell, Wilfred...............315
Topp, Viola 81, 327
Towler, Andrew 316
Towler, Annette DeCourcy ..i, ix, 176, 204, 205, 211, 315, 328, 330, 334, 336, 344, 350, 370
Towler, Arlene .206, 223, 374
Towler, Cheryl 316
Towler, John....................316
Towler, Nanette 316
Towler, Rev. Dr. James G. 216, 217, 349, 374
Tracy, James R. 334
Trettel, David 238
Trettel, Janet....................238
Trevanan, Julia 20
Trulson, Roni...................205
Trulson-Lindsey, Angela..205
Tufte, Carolyn 205

V

Valentine, Rev. G. G. 61
Van Alstyne, A J. 69
Van Nostrand, Bernice (Bowdish) 262, 353

Van Nostrand, Catharine .125, 128, 205, 206, 208, 209
Van Nostrand, Cathy 309
Van Nostrand, David (Dave) 206, 207, 281
Van Nostrand, Laura 309
Van Nostrand, Rev. Dr. Manning 88, 138, 255, 260, 262, 353, 372
Varner, Helen Johnson 274
Varner, Julia Farrand 274
Varner, Leslie 274
Varner, W. N. 52
Varner, William.....59, 63, 64, 274
Von Levern, Mrs. E. 46

W

Wagner, Deb....................318
Wagner, Jim......119, 150, 235, 307, 317, 319
Wagner, Mary..119, 141, 231, 276, 307, 317
Wagner, Tim....................318
Walker, Miss 26
Walker, Mrs. Walter...........82
Ward, F. A. 56, 59, 63, 69
Ward. C. E. 81
Watt, Jennie 59
Way, Carl.........................135
Way, Edith........135, 257, 293
Weary, Clara....................343
Weaver, Ron....................318
Webb, Jemima 356
Webb, Nellie....................356
Webb, Rev. Harvey 27, 28, 356
Webb, Roanna.,................334
Wegner, Robert 80
Weiss, Mrs. W. A. 182
Weiss, Rev. W. A. 182
Welsh, Mayor Lee E...........60
Welsh, Mrs. Lee 75
Wendt, Edwin...63, 69, 81, 83
Wendt, Mrs. Edwin.......69, 79
Wenstrom, Lisa 319
Wenstrom, Lori 309, 319
Wenstrom, Lynn...............319
Wenstrom, Maxine 319
Wenstrom, Sam 131, 142, 150, 238, 261, 319, 320
Wesley, Charles........202, 321
Wesley, John 200, 261, 321
West, Caldo 334
West, Caleb W,................334
West, Mrs. C. S. 56

427

INDEX

West, Mrs. Charles 59
Westhaver, Mr. 63, 64
Westhoff, Orville 70
Wheeler, Mary Beth ...21, 377
Whiting, Dr. A. D. 41, 52
Whitinger, Julius............... 70
Whitney, F. K. 52
Whitney, Mrs. F. K. 39, 41
Wigstead, Rev. D. S. 39
Williams, Dale..........157, 320
Williams, Edythe 161, 211, 320
Williams, Eileen 320
Williams, James C. 17
Williams, Jas.................... 17
Williams, Jas. M 334
Williams, Leanna......211, 320
Williams, Priscilla 211, 320
Williams, Ryan 320
Wilson, Bert..................... 343
Wilson, Claire 54
Wilson, Eleanor 105, 111, 114, 273
Wilson, Etta 343
Wilson, Freeman.............. 343
Wilson, James C. .. 16, 18, 26, 334, 335, 340, 343
Wilson, John L. 24
Wilson, Lillie 343
Wilson, Mary 17
Wilson, Mary A 334
Wilson, Peary................... 114
Wilson, Woodrow (Woody) 105, 111, 114, 273, 286, 319, 321
Wing, James Edison........... 34
Wing, Theodore 343
Wischmann, Glenn 321
Wischmann, Kelly 231
Wonder, Mrs. . C. . F. 56
Wood, Bruce... 152, 161, 247, 305
Wood, Lori............... 152, 161
Wood, Mrs. Ina 81
Woodley, Priscilla... 142, 152; 305
Wright, Rev. G. W. 356
Wygant, Sister Naomi...... 254

Y

Young, Catherine 78

Z

Zim, Miss.......................... 57
Zitzow, Nicole Lee (Meier) 366
Zosel, Harold ix, 29, 141, 150, 163, 226, 321, 328
Zosel, Katie 321
Zosel, Mary (Hall) 321
Zosel, Sam 321